THE WEB OF
WORLD POLITICS

THE WEB OF WORLD POLITICS

Nonstate Actors
in the Global System

RICHARD W. MANSBACH
Rutgers University, New Brunswick

YALE H. FERGUSON
Rutgers University, Newark

DONALD E. LAMPERT
Arizona State University

PRENTICE-HALL, INC., ENGLEWOOD CLIFFS, NEW JERSEY

Library of Congress Cataloging in Publication Data

Mansbach, Richard W. (date)
   The web of world politics.

   Includes bibliographical references and index.
   1. International relations. 2. World politics—
1945–   3. International relations—Research.
I. Ferguson, Yale H. (date), joint author. II. Lampert,
Donald E. (date), joint author. III. Title.
JX1395.M29   327   75–33215
ISBN 0–13–947952–X

© 1976 by Prentice-Hall, Inc.
Englewood Cliffs, New Jersey

Printed in the United States of America

10 9 8 7 6 5 4 3 2 1

PRENTICE-HALL INTERNATIONAL, INC., LONDON
PRENTICE-HALL OF AUSTRALIA, PTY. LTD., SYDNEY
PRENTICE-HALL OF CANADA, LTD., TORONTO
PRENTICE-HALL OF INDIA PRIVATE LIMITED, NEW DELHI
PRENTICE-HALL OF JAPAN, INC., TOKYO
PRENTICE-HALL OF SOUTHEAST ASIA (PTE.) LTD., SINGAPORE

Contents

CHAPTER THREE

The Emergence and Disappearance of International Actors. International Tasks. The Panoply of Global Actors. The Complex Conglomerate System.

CHAPTER FOUR

The Glorious Revolution. The Birth of Jacobitism. Jacobitism: 1690–1701. The Second Phase: 1701–1715. The Final Phase of Jacobitism.

PART II
Nonstate Actors in
Three Regional Systems

CHAPTER FIVE

The Middle East 1948–1956: Israeli Consolidation and Colonial Conflict. The Middle East 1956–1967: The Nasser Era. The Middle East 1967–1972: Israel Beleaguered. The Middle East as a Complex Conglomerate.

CHAPTER SIX

The Six Day War and the Transformation of the Palestine Issue. Fission and Fusion in the Palestine Movement: The Politics of Disunity. The Palestinian Movement and Regime Stability. The Fruits of Disunity: Civil War in Jordan. Conclusion.

CHAPTER SEVEN

A Decade of Strife and Ideological Competition: 1948–1958. The Long Shadow of the Cuban Revolution: 1959–1967. The Decline of the "Special Relationship": 1967–1972. Latin America as a Complex Conglomerate.

PART III

The Complex Conglomerate Model and
Contemporary Global Politics

Preface

In this book we seek to achieve two basic goals. First, we attempt to point up, assess, and remedy what we see as a major gap in the literature on world politics. The reader of any daily newspaper is aware of the growing importance of nonstate groups and organizations that are not recognized as sovereign governments. Such groups, ranging from terrorist bands to great corporate empires, continually demand our attention, intrude on our consciousness and often offend our sense of propriety. They cannot, however, be wished away in order to regain the simplicity of a past age anymore than world politics can be viewed simply as a stark drama of confrontation between East and West. It seems to us, therefore, that traditional models of international relations, models that do not account for these new phenomena, are perpetuating the gap between the scholar's theory and the reality of the universe with which the scholar should be concerned.

A second purpose of the book is to understand these newly-recognized phenomena in the context of a changing global political system and its processes. To this end, we analyze the relationship between actors and changing issues, alignments, and capabilities. In these tasks, we have combined several well-established quantitative and analytic procedures with other techniques that we believe to be novel (though simple) and have embedded these in the context of a substantive discussion of three regional systems.

The data upon which much of our empirical analysis relies are derived from the Nonstate Actor (NOSTAC) Project which is being conducted at Rutgers University. We must thank the Rutgers University Research Council and the Center for Computer and Information Services for their valuable support. The collection and analysis of the considerable data required the talents and time of many able students, only some of whom we can thank here. Jeffrey Ranney and William Kiley served as most capable research assistants during various phases of the project. Michael Detzky, Jerry Effren, Barry Faden, Steven Kartzman, Robert Laurino, Dennis Levine, and Gary Marks provided willing assistance in collecting and organizing data. Finally, without the aid of more than sixty students in our international relations classes the event data could not have been collected and coded.

In addition, several colleagues at various universities, including James Cocroft, Raymond Hopkins, Willard Keim, Robert Keohane, and James Rosenau provided, wittingly or unwittingly, advice and guidance. We must also mention Carolyn Falkowski and Phyllis Moditz who typed the manuscript with both skill and patience.

Nevertheless, none of this would have been possible without the patience, affection, and cuisine of Kitty Ferguson, Ethel Lampert, and Rhoda Mansbach.

Beyond Conservatism in the Study of Global Politics

PART I

Introduction:
The State-Centric Model
and the Complexity of Global Politics

(T)here is ample evidence to show that the United Nations and its agencies, the European Coal and Steel Community, the Afro-Asian bloc, the Arab League, the Vatican, the Arabian-American Oil Company, and a host of other nonstate entities, are able on occasion to affect the course of international events. When this happens, these entities become actors in the international arena and competitors of the nation-state. Their ability to operate as international or transnational actors may be traced to the fact that men identify themselves and their interests with corporate bodies other than the nation-state.[1]

Paraphrasing Jonathan Swift, we could say that ours is a modest proposal intended to encourage students and scholars to review critically their efforts in the field of international relations. We do not suggest that efforts to account for the behavior of units other than nation-states is novel nor do we deny the paramount position that nation-states still occupy in international politics. Our claim is simply that the behavior of nonstate actors has not been studied systematically and has not been integrated into the dominant model of the global political system—to the detriment of that model.

For several hundred years most discussions of world politics have started from the assumptions that the state or nation-state is the core unit of the global political system and that knowledge of interstate relations is

1. Arnold Wolfers, "The Actors in International Politics," in Wolfers, ed., *Discord and Collaboration* (Baltimore: Johns Hopkins Press, 1962), p. 23.

sufficient to understand and explain behavior in that system. "The ideal type of international politics," Karl Kaiser declares, "stresses two points: First, the field of action of politics lies in the area between the nation-states (*inter* nationes); second, the actors involved are states (inter *nationes*)."[2] The traditional position is succinctly summarized by Robert Keohane and Joseph Nye:

> Students and practitioners of international politics have traditionally concentrated their attention on relationships between states. The state, regarded as an actor with purposes and power, is the basic unit of action: its main agents are the diplomat and soldier. The interplay of governmental policies yields the pattern of behavior that students of international politics attempt to understand and that practitioners attempt to adjust or to control.[3]

Among the implications of the state-centric assumption are the following:

> 1. Global politics is based on the interaction of nation-states, with states as both actors and targets of action.
> 2. Each nation-state is the "sovereign equal" of every other.
> 3. Each nation-state is treated as if it forms a homogeneous political system with a central government controlling a domestic monopoly of the means of coercion.
> 4. Nation-states are independent of one another, are distinguishable from one another, and are subject to no higher earthly authority.
> 5. Nation-states possess exclusive control of an explicit range of territory and number of subjects; the world is divided into neat geographic compartments.
> 6. The foreign policy agents of nation-state governments are the sole participants in world politics; all other groups make their presence felt through the medium of a government.
> 7. Nation-states are the secular repositories of the highest human loyalties.

These seven postulates are the components of the state-centric model of international politics depicted in Fig. 1.

The central problem with this model is the notion that "sovereign states" exhaust the universe of relevant or possible actors in global politics.

An actor in global politics should be defined neither by the ascriptive quality of sovereignty nor by the descriptive characteristic of territoriality;

2. Karl Kaiser, "Transnational Politics: Toward a Theory of Multinational Politics," *International Organization* 25:4 (Autumn 1971), p. 791.
3. Robert O. Keohane and Joseph S. Nye, Jr., "Transnational Relations and World Politics: An Introduction," in Keohane and Nye, eds., "Transnational Relations and World Politics," special edition of *International Organization* 25:3 (Summer 1971), p. 329.

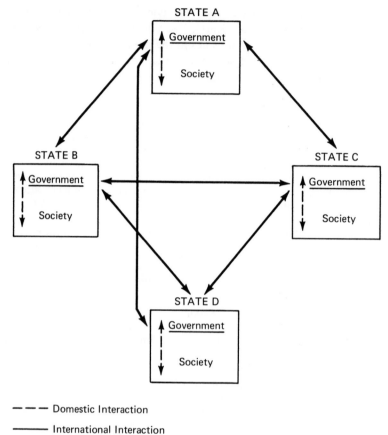

— — — Domestic Interaction

——— International Interaction

Figure 1
The State-Centric Model[4]

instead, it should be defined by the *behavioral* attribute of autonomy. *Autonomy* refers to the ability of leaders of an organized unit to undertake behavior that could not be predicted by reference to other actors or authorities. As Karl Deutsch declares, an actor is autonomous "if its responses are not predictable, even from the most thorough knowledge of the environment" and "if it possesses a stable and coherent decision-making machinery within its boundaries."[5] More simply put, we must ask: Do

4. Adapted from Joseph S. Nye, Jr., and Robert O. Keohane, "Transnational Relations and World Politics: An Introduction," in Keohane and Nye, eds., "Transnational Relations and World Politics," special edition of *International Organization*, 25:3 (Summer 1971), p. 333.
5. Karl W. Deutsch, "External Influences in the Internal Behavior of States," in R. Barry Farrell, ed., *Approaches to Comparative and International Politics* (New York: Free Press, 1966), p. 7.

actors other than nation-states freely exercise influence in world politics?

In order to behave autonomously an actor must have an independent capacity to solicit and receive information, to process and refine it, and finally to respond to it. This sequence constitutes decision-making that in nation-states is largely undertaken by government bureaucrats. Any intrusion into this process by outsiders infringes upon autonomy. Thus the presence of Soviet "experts" advising the leaders of the countries of Eastern Europe after World War II reduced these states to the status of Soviet "satellites" even though the states remained legally "sovereign."

In reaching decisions the autonomous actor combines past and present information and charts a course that its decision-makers perceive to be in their interest or that of the collectivity. "As long as it has autonomy," declares Deutsch referring to a decision-making unit, "the (decision) net wills what it is."[6]

Political scientists have long recognized that the central process in world politics is the exercise of influence. Hans Morgenthau, for example, in a famous definition of the discipline suggested that "international politics, like all politics, is a struggle for power."[7] Without accepting this definition in its entirety, we recognize that what attracts our attention to political units is their ability to make decisions and to adopt policies that influence others. Morgenthau is surely correct when he observes that "international politics cannot be reduced to legal rules and institutions."[8] While all nation-states are "sovereign," many are unable to make decisions independently or to influence people situated outside their political boundaries; whereas nonstate actors lack sovereignty, many are relatively autonomous and influential.[9]

The global political system consists of numerous, more or less autonomous actors interacting in patterned ways to influence one another. Their independent decisions and policies serve as stimuli for one another and induce or constrain the behavior of others. The high level of transactions among actors and the high degree of interdependence in contemporary political, social, and economic life mean that no actor is fully autonomous. Its behavior is affected by the choices and perceived prospective choices of other actors, and its policies are structured by their decisions. The relationship between the level of interdependence in a system and the degree of autonomy enjoyed by actors was observed by Jean-Jacques Rousseau in the eighteenth century when he wrote that the states of Europe "touch each other at so many points that no one of them can move without giving a jar to all the rest; their variances are all the more deadly, as their ties are more

6. Deutsch, *The Nerves of Government* (New York: Free Press, 1963), p. 108.
7. Hans J. Morgenthau, *Politics Among Nations,* 5th ed. (New York: Alfred A. Knopf, 1973), p. 27.
8. *Ibid,* p. 17.
9. For more on this subject, see *infra* Chap. 2, pp. 22–31.

closely woven."[10] Rousseau's observation is especially important today in light of greatly improved communication and transportation technologies, mutually destructive weapons systems, and high levels of economic interdependence. Some actors, however, including those other than nation-states, are able to frame policies relatively independently and can "make up their own minds," while others, including certain nation-states, have neither the will nor the ability to make decisions freely.

In the first part of this book we shall suggest the variety of actors whose behavior is important for world politics and seek the reasons that they have tended to be ignored. We shall then put forward our own model of the contemporary global political system and suggest a research framework that may prove profitable to others in this field. The model is used to look systematically at a series of cases that illustrate the growing importance of nonstate actors in global outcomes. A new model is necessary to determine the implications of nonstate units for the foreign policies of the major powers and for planetary crises of world order: war, population pressures, resource shortages, and environmental spoilage. We have used both qualitative and quantitative data to sensitize ourselves and our readers to the role of actors other than nation-states.

10. Cited in Kenneth N. Waltz, *Man, the State and War* (New York: Columbia University Press, 1959), p. 183.

The Genesis
of the
State-Centric Model

ONE

Over the bulk of recorded history, man has organized himself for political purposes on bases other than those now subsumed under the concepts 'state' and 'nation-state.'[1]

The sovereign state arrived at the center of world relations theory through a chain of historical circumstance. The term "international" was used first by the political philosopher Jeremy Bentham in 1780 at a time when national states were becoming both the principal actors in world affairs and the major secular objects of popular loyalties. The widespread currency of the term owed much to the fact that the doctrine of sovereignty acquired a lofty status in the European political lexicon and became the theoretical underpinning of studies of the European state system. Our purpose is to investigate whether it has become necessary to revise our thinking about global politics so as to take account of units other than nation-states.

The Peace of Westphalia

The state-centric model of international politics is generally dated from the Peace of Westphalia of 1648. "The system of states," argues one scholar, "is supposed to have been . . . legislated into existence . . . by the Peace of Westphalia."[2] The Peace, actually consisting of two separate

1. Oran R. Young, "The Actors in World Politics," in James N. Rosenau, Vincent Davis, and Maurice A. East, eds., *The Analysis of International Politics* (New York: Free Press, 1972), p. 127.
2. Clive Parry, "The Function of Law in the International Community," in Max Sørensen, ed., *Manual of Public International Law* (New York: St. Martin's Press, 1968), p. 14.

7

treaties,[3] brought an end to the Thirty Years' War of religion that had ravished European society and had demolished the remnants of the medieval political organization. Among the major consequences of the Peace of Westphalia was the redrawing of the map of Europe, the reduction of the number of political units from 900 to 355 in the German Empire,[4] and the regularization of a system of permanent diplomatic missions and of a system of rules governing diplomatic etiquette.[5]

The most significant aspect of the Peace, however, was in the political ideas that it confirmed. Westphalia marked the end of the view of the world as an organized system based on a hierarchical Christian commonwealth governed by Pope and Holy Roman Emperor. Imperial pretensions had been defeated on the battlefield; Papal objections to the terms of Westphalia were simply disregarded. Thereafter the international system would be viewed as a society of legally equal states, each exercising sovereignty within well-defined frontiers and subject to no higher secular authority. The concept of state is, after all, antithetical to the concept of empire. It implies local, as opposed to universal, dominion. As long as the imperial idea dominated European thinking, there could not, in theory, exist any state other than the universal one. The universal state was supposed to be governed by a single law, loosely based on an amalgam of Church law and the *jus gentium* of ancient Rome.[6]

It is from the decisive year of 1648 that historians and political scientists see the shift to a view of international law *among* states from a view of law *above* states, as well as the emergence of balance of power principles that were to become so central to international relations theory in the eighteenth and nineteenth centuries.

> The Peace of Westphalia, for better or worse, marks the end of an epoch and the opening of another. It represents the majestic portal which leads from the old into the new world.[7]

The Roman-Medieval Imperium

The Peace of Westphalia did not result in some magical and sudden transformation of Europe from an imperial form of organization into the modern state system. The transformation occurred over a period of cen-

3. The two treaties were the Treaty of Onasbrück between the Empire and Sweden and the Treaty of Munster between the Empire and France.
4. Hans J. Morgenthau, *Politics Among Nations,* 5th ed. (New York: Alfred A. Knopf, 1973), p. 340.
5. It has been argued that it took eight years to settle the Thirty Years' War primarily because of the lack of such rules. Gerhard von Glahn, *Law Among Nations,* 2d. ed. (Toronto: Macmillan, 1970), p. 383.
6. The *jus gentium,* different than the *jus civile* of the city of Rome, was the product of the customs of the different peoples of the Roman Empire.
7. Leo Gross, "The Peace of Westphalia, 1648–1948," in Robert S. Wood, ed., *The Process of International Organization* (New York: Random House, 1971), p. 42.

turies, and the state-centric model that the Peace legitimized evolved in the same time frame.

The imperial model arose from the Roman Empire. Although the Roman Empire was dominated by a single law, it was not totally centralized. The universal law existed side by side with local jurisdictions. The Empire was divided into territorial provinces, grounded in geographical reality, that exercised local jurisdiction. When Rome was destroyed, its conquerors, themselves Roman citizens, were familiar with and fond of Roman institutions. They brought with them, however, the notion that law was "personal"; that is, that each tribe had inherited its own set of laws. Thus,

> as the barbarians abandoned their nomadic ways and settled down among the conquered populations, what began as a principle of personality became a principle of territoriality. Laws and systems of law became local. And the lines of division between them came to correspond roughly with the Roman Provincial frontiers. . . . Such was the pattern of legal organization which was established when the Dark Ages began.[8]

The imperial model survived the death of Rome and continued to dominate the political thought of the Middle Ages. Indeed, it was gradually reinforced by the triumph of Christianity which fostered the principle of the divine origin of a universal order with the Pope as God's earthly representative. In time, the Church became a pillar of the imperial model.

The second major pillar of the imperial model was the Holy Roman Empire, which was ruled by a monarchy and which at its height dominated much of Germany and Italy. The title of Holy Roman Emperor was adopted by Otto the Great in 962, and, although neither he nor his successors were able to exercise practical authority over much of Western Europe, the Empire claimed to be the direct successor to the ancient Roman state.[9] Many theorists supported these imperial pretensions, including Dante Alighieri, perhaps the greatest of all Italian poets and the author of *The Divine Comedy*. In his *De Monarchia* (*On Monarchy*), written in 1310, Dante began with the initial premise that it was "the intention of God that all created things should represent the likeness of God, so far as their proper nature will admit." Since God was universal and one, the human race would resemble Him most closely "when it is united wholly in one body, and it is evident that this cannot be except when it is subject to one prince."[10]

The existence of two institutions with imperial pretensions inevitably led to conflict between them, conflict that dominated the international rela-

---

8. Parry, "The Function of Law," p. 11.
9. Even within Germany and Italy political power was shared with the feudal lords, some of whom, like the Archbishop of Cologne, exercised temporal authority by virtue of their ecclesiastical office.
10. Dante Alighieri, "De Monarchia" in William Ebenstein, ed., *Great Political Thinkers,* 4th ed. (New York: Holt, Rinehart and Winston, 1969), p. 252.

tions of Europe between the eleventh and fourteenth centuries. Both Pope and Emperor sought to dominate the other and to exercise sole authority over Europe. For a time the German Emperor succeeded in wresting control of papal selection from the hands of the Roman families that had previously exercised it. When Gregory VII became Pope in 1073, however, papal resistance to imperial influence began in earnest. Gregory claimed that only his representatives could invest authority in bishops. But, since Catholic bishops were feudal lords as well as church figures, Gregory's claim involved a challenge to the secular authority of the Empire in Germany and elsewhere. The Holy Roman Emperor, Henry IV, his realm divided by civil war, finally capitulated to Gregory at Canossa. The quarrel was rekindled some years later when Henry invaded Rome and forced Gregory to flee, and the papal-imperial conflict continued after the death of both. A crude bipolarity thus came to characterize Europe.

With the death of Emperor Henry V in 1125, the Franconian dynasty ended. Shortly after began a struggle for the succession to the imperial throne. The great feudal nobles of Germany supported the claims of the Hohenstaufen family to the throne, and thus the Hohenstaufen dynasty was born in 1138. Ultimately, the succession controversy became part of the general conflict between Pope and Emperor with the partisans of the former known as "Guelphs" and the supporters of the Hohenstaufen emperors known as "Ghibellines."

Succeeding emperors, notably Frederick Barbarossa and Frederick II, sought to limit the temporal influence of the Papacy while strong popes such as Innocent III sought to subdue the Hohenstaufens. The Papacy emerged triumphant with the death of the last Hohenstaufen in 1254. For a period of almost twenty years known as the *Great Interregnum* there was no Holy Roman Emperor at all. In 1273 the obscure Rudolf of Hapsburg was chosen Emperor, and the Hapsburgs held the position almost continuously until Napoleon "officially" decreed an end to the Empire in 1806. In practice, however, the imperial authority had long before receded to such a level that the French philosopher Voltaire exclaimed, "This agglomeration which was called and which still calls itself the Holy Roman Empire was neither holy, nor Roman, nor an Empire."

Medieval politics was the product of feudalism, an agrarian economic system based on landed wealth in which most people were subject to a few powerful lords. Theoretically, these lords were themselves subject to Emperor and Pope, but, in fact, the feudal system was in important respects decentralized and parochial. Politically, "feudalism coincided with a profound weakening of the State (the impaired unit), particularly in its protective capacity."[11] Each "layer" of the hierarchy was under the protection of the "layer" above it, to which it owed military and economic obligations. Land and authority went hand in hand. Those who were lords

11. Marc Bloch, *Feudal Society*, trans. by L. A. Manyon (Chicago: University of Chicago Press, 1961), p. 443.

were also warriors whose military power was based on the horse and heavy armor. Nevertheless, the authority of even the greatest lords was often more illusory than real. The extremely restricted range of local authority and the overarching framework provided by the imperial model made any distinction between domestic and foreign affairs a tenuous one.

Hence, the principles of order and unity embodied in the imperial model were not challenged until the emergence of both larger autonomous political units under local monarchs in Western Europe and self-sufficient city-states in Italy. It was necessary for statesmen to be able to distinguish between an harmonious domestic society ruled by a single power with a monopoly of the means of violence in its hands and an anarchic society of local powers over which no single power had authority for there to develop a view of international politics based on autonomous states. This could not occur until the economic, social, and political bases of feudalism had begun to erode. Marc Bloch accurately depicts the feudal order:

> European feudalism should . . . be seen as the outcome of the violent dissolution of older societies. It would in fact be unintelligible without the great upheaval of the Germanic invasions which, by forcibly uniting two societies originally at very different stages of development, disrupted both of them and brought to the surface a great many modes of thought and social practices of an extremely primitive character. . . . It involved a far-reaching restriction of social intercourse, a circulation of money too sluggish to admit of a salaried officialdom, and a mentality attached to things tangible and local. When these conditions began to change, feudalism began to wane.[12]

The Challenge of the Renaissance

One of the major features accompanying the collapse of Rome and the triumph of feudalism was the decay of urban civilization in Europe and its replacement by an agrarian economy attached to the self-sufficient feudal manor. Land became the criterion of wealth and station and the source of political power. From the eleventh century on, however, there grew up, particularly in the city-states of Italy such as Florence and Milan, a new bourgeois elite whose economic power rested on money, manufacturing, and trade. The Papacy, one of the greatest of Europe's landholders, and the higher aristocracy of the Empire viewed this economic transformation and the cities in which it took place with extreme mistrust. Their hostility grew out of the refusal of the new bourgeoisie to accept the static social system and the privileges of the landed aristocracy that were the bases of feudalism. In addition, the new class resisted the political hegemony of both Church and Empire.

Within the rising Italian urban centers, classical Greek and Roman philosophy and literature were revived, culminating in the intellectual and

12. *Ibid.,* p. 443.

artistic flowering we know as the Renaissance. These cities gradually assumed the intellectual leadership of Europe as well as becoming commercial, technological, and financial centers. As part of the process, political thought was secularized, and the city-states gradually threw off Papal-Imperial control.[13] Not only did the city-states resist the authority of the great feudal institutions, but they began to compete for political power among themselves. While they were too small to be regarded as modern nation-states on the European model, they nevertheless were independent sources of political power and status. Imperial and Papal authority had begun to wane as early as the division of Charlemagne's empire, and the process had been hastened during the Great Interregnum (1254–1273) and the Great Schism in the Catholic Church (1387–1417). The rise of the Italian city-states, of the independent kingdoms of Western Europe, and of the ideas generated by the Renaissance and, later, by the Reformation finally transformed the imperial model of international relations, a stateless model, into a practical irrelevancy.

The discovery of gunpowder and the use of artillery undermined the military foundation of the feudal system. Fortified localities and armored knights were rendered obsolete, and these changes had inevitable effects on the nature of people's loyalties. "The relative protection which the sway of certain moral standards and the absence of destructive weapons had afforded groups and individuals in the earlier Middle Ages," declares John Herz, "gave way to total insecurity under the dual impact of the breakdown of common standards and the invention of gunpowder."[14] Moreover, the social and economic changes ushered in by the city-states made new forms of military organization practicable and desirable. In the feudal system the knight was bound to fight for his overlord in return for the rights to land. The knight was also obligated to protect the vassals and serfs who occupied his land in return for their economic services.

This intricate system of economic and military interdependence was shattered by the creation of a manufacturing economy. The secularization of political ideas undermined the medieval concept of war as a religious struggle in which knights, guided by a code of chivalry, protected the Church and rendered justice. City-states could secure soldiers with money, and vassals were no longer necessary for military security. The Italian city-states came to depend on mercenary armies. In addition, only the very wealthy could afford the new tools of warfare such as artillery, and military recruitment could no longer be restricted to an aristocratic class.

13. An awareness of classical history revived European interest in the Greek interstate system. For more on the Greek system, see Alfred Zimmern, *The Greek Commonwealth,* 5th ed. (New York: Oxford University Press, 1931), pp. 314–445.
14. John H. Herz, *International Politics in the Atomic Age* (New York: Columbia University Press, 1959), p. 45.

Towards the end of the Hohenstaufen period of the Holy Roman Empire, the many minor political units that had characterized the Italian peninsula began to merge into regionally powerful city-states. One of the reasons that "interstate" politics developed earlier in Italy than elsewhere in Europe was that feudalism had never become as institutionalized there as in Germany. The Holy Roman Emperors had broken up the larger fiefdoms in Italy in order to increase their own direct political control over the area; as "direct rule" from Germany gradually weakened, local elites were able to exercise political autonomy. As commerce and manufacturing began to dominate economic relationships, the urban centers of Italy gradually extended their authority over the surrounding countryside. The desire for trade and the need to protect it contributed to the expansion of the city-states and to the growth of patterned interaction among them.

The pattern of interstate relations that developed in Italy was founded on diplomatic techniques that were first elaborated in Venice, a small republic situated in the Adriatic Sea. Venice had gradually escaped Byzantine hegemony by the astute conduct of commerce and the use of seapower. By the eleventh century it had become the leading commercial power in the Mediterranean, exercising dominion over the trade routes to the East. The Venetian contribution to the evolution of modern international practices and to the triumph of the state-centric model cannot be overemphasized. Venice's commercial position "was due primarily to the continuous and methodical study of foreign affairs,"[15] made possible by the use of a professional corps of diplomats sent abroad. In Venice we see the creation of the first permanent diplomatic service in history. For rather complex historical reasons, Venetians had become "nationalists" at an early date, and Venetian dependence on trade stimulated a lively and continuous interest in foreign affairs.[16] Indeed, the Venetians were the first to keep systematic archives concerning their transactions with foreign states, as well as the first to demand systematic reports from their diplomats concerning conditions abroad. From these archives we know that they acutely perceived certain principles of national interest and were concerned with maintaining a continuous and accurate flow of information about those with whom they had to deal. Adda Bozeman succinctly summarizes the Venetian contribution to the evolution of the state-centric model:

> There was no organized system of diplomacy in medieval Western Europe before the Venetian was transplanted to the Italian and European courts. . . . For diplomacy . . . was organically associated with the

15. Adda B. Bozeman, *Politics and Culture in International History* (Princeton: Princeton University Press, 1960), p. 464.
16. Cf. Jacob Burckhardt, *The Civilization of the Renaissance in Italy* (New York: Random House), pp. 54 ff., and Bozeman, *Politics and Culture,* pp. 457–77.

sovereign state, and the sovereign state was not recognized, either *de jure* or *de facto,* in the medieval European system.[17]

The Venetian diplomatic method was adapted to Italian conditions as the city-states of the peninsula were consolidated. "Since the prototype Western state was developed in Italy, where the decay of the unifying medieval structure became apparent earlier than elswhere," writes Bozeman, "it was also in Italy that the new forms for conducting relations between states were first elaborated and tested."[18] However, the concept of the large territorial state imbued with sovereignty and governed by complex bureaucracies that evolved in France and England remained alien to the smaller states of Italy with their more personal governments. In *The Prince,* published by the Florentine statesman and philosopher Niccolo Machiavelli in 1513, a picture emerges of political conflict among petty rulers seeking to maintain or acquire political power against internal and external rivals. While Machiavelli's attention was riveted on competitive states in a system of anarchy rather than on an imperial world, it is clear that his was a system of conspiracies and domestic factionalism in which the princes of rival city-states jealously protected their political prerogatives against foreign invasion and domestic subversion. The small size of the city-states, the personal and often familial nature of their governments, the perpetual danger of domestic unrest, and the general sense of unrelieved political movement centering on particular personalities made it impossible for there to develop a concept of state sovereignty which marked an abrupt frontier between the internal and external realms of state. Only with this development could the modern state-centric model, with its assumption that international relations are subject to their own principles and laws unlike those of domestic politics, become dominant. Only then could the state be perceived as something organic in which the whole was greater than the sum of its parts.

Between 1100 and 1300 the Italian city-state system was formed. Lacking any imperial authority above them, the city-states sought diplomatic devices that would reduce the effects of unbridled anarchy yet at the same time protect the essential independence of most of the participants. Negotiation and bargaining in order to form and reform coalitions became diplomatic tasks of even greater importance than simply providing information for home governments. By the fourteenth century these tasks had become sufficiently complicated for the Dukes of Mantua and Milan to institute the unprecedented practice of permanent diplomatic missions.[19]

---

17. Bozeman, *Politics and Culture,* pp. 475–76.
18. *Ibid,* p. 457.
19. Garrett Mattingly, *Renaissance Diplomacy* (Boston: Houghton Mifflin, 1955), p. 71.

In addition, an early system of diplomatic rights and immunities developed in the Italian state system as a whole.

After the fourteenth century, a notion of a balance of power began to prevail in which actors saw themselves as obliged to protect themselves and the city-state system itself by using diplomacy, alliances, and, if necessary, war in order to prevent any one of them from attaining political preponderance. In that century a series of conflicts among the leading city-states indicated "the rising level of interregional, as distinguished from intraregional, interaction on the one hand and sharply diminishing interference by non-Italian powers on the other hand."[20] Thereafter until the end of the fifteenth century the major city-states, principally the Papacy, Florence, Milan, Venice, and Naples, each with well-defined regional spheres of interest, interacted in a balance of power system that would be inexplicable in terms of the imperial model. Each unit tried "to prevent the other from extending its territory and from becoming so powerful that it would be a threat to the others. They eagerly observed the slightest move in the political chess board and made a great fuss whenever the smallest castle changed its ruler."[21] In this way by the fifteenth century Italy had abandoned the imperial model of international relations and had substituted for it a rudimentary state-centric model in which "it was clear to all statesmen that Italy was in actuality a society of separate but interdependent states, which could exist only so long as the representatives of the pentarchy employed diplomacy for the maintenance of a continuous, if precarious, balance between their respective governments."[22] Under these conditions the imperial assumptions of order and unity were obsolete.

The Impact of Absolutism and Sovereignty in Western Europe

In 1494 the state system of Italy was abruptly swallowed up by the invasion of a French army under King Charles VIII. Of this calamity Francesco Guicciardini, the greatest Italian historian of the age, wrote:

> (H)is passage into Italy not only gave rise to changes of dominions, subversion of kingdoms, desolation of countries, destruction of cities and the cruelest massacres, but also new fashions, new customs, new and bloody

20. Winfried Franke, "The Italian City-State System as an International System," in Morton A. Kaplan ed., *New Approaches to International Relations* (New York: St. Martin's Press, 1968), p. 436.
21. Felix Gilbert, "Machiavelli: The Rennaissance of the Art of War," in Edward Mead Earle, ed., *Makers of Modern Strategy* (New York: Atheneum, 1967), p. 8.
22. Bozeman, *Politics and Culture,* p. 486. See also Franke, "The Italian City-State System," pp. 426–58.

ways of waging warfare, and diseases which had been unknown up to that time. Furthermore, the incursion introduced so much disorder into Italian ways of governing and maintaining harmony, that we have never been able to reestablish order.[23]

Although the disaster was partly the consequence of Italian military inferiority, particularly in artillery and infantry, it also revealed the growing significance of the centralized territorial states of Western Europe that were larger, wealthier, and more populous than the divided Italian city-states. So struck was Machiavelli by the technological and organizational inferiority of the city-states that in the final chapter of *The Prince* he inveighed against Italian disunity and called for a prince who could unite the peninsula and drive out the invaders.

In the course of his treatise Machiavelli also developed the concept of "reason of state" in which the assumption of a universal harmony and interest was abandoned and princes were exhorted to behave in ways that, while immoral in the context of interpersonal relations, were nevertheless deemed necessary for the survival and prosperity of the state as a whole. This marked a major step in the development of an autonomous theory of international politics in which states, forming a distinctive political system, were seen as subject to different principles and laws than individuals in domestic society. From this point it became possible to conceive of states as having interests different than those of the citizens that constituted them and different even than those of the transient princes who ruled them.

It was the creation of the great monarchical and absolutist states of Western Europe that provided the final proof of the eclipse of the imperial model of international politics. The kings of France and England in particular had long been waging a struggle to escape the tutelage of Pope and Emperor. The process was gradual as kings took advantage of Papal-Imperial conflict to wrest greater local autonomy from both. After many fits and starts the process culminated in the Peace of Westphalia. In France the struggle was particularly acute as the Valois kings sought to weaken Papal control of the kingdom's finances by gaining influence over the vast ecclesiastical properties in that country. Resistance to Papal authority continued to grow after the beginning of the Protestant Reformation in Northern Europe in the sixteenth century.

Finally, in France, in the midst of civil and religious strife that threatened to destroy the monarchy and the kingdom, a theory emerged of the state as greater than the sum of its parts and as representing a timeless institution above any particular government. This theory owed much to Jean Bodin, a French lawyer and a member of a group of French Catholics

23. Francesco Guicciardini, *The History of Italy,* trans. by Sidney Alexander (London: Macmillan, 1969), pp. 48–49.

known as the "Politiques," whose major aims were to secure an end to the civil disunion that saw French Catholics pitted against French Protestants (Huguenots), thereby encouraging foreign intervention, and to restore the power and majesty of the monarchy. In 1576 Bodin published *Six Books on the State* in which he defined sovereignty as "the absolute and perpetual power of the state, that is, the greatest power to command." For Bodin sovereignty existed apart from governments and meant that there could legally be no authority above the state. While the doctrine of sovereignty implied supreme power within the state's territory, particularly in the making and executing of laws, it also implied equality and independence in international relations. Only within its frontiers was a state's power supreme; the existence of a multiplicity of sovereign states implied an international system of shared authority and decentralized power. As each state was deemed to be sovereign within its own realm, so no imperial institution could be permitted to exercise authority over the system as a whole. Moreover, no institution within the state, except the state itself, was legally or physically capable of conducting foreign affairs. This doctrine, coinciding with the growth of bureaucracies to administer the business of state, achieved general acceptance with the end of the religious wars and the emergence of autocratic monarchies in Western Europe. Bodin himself was, perhaps, somewhat premature since political parties and sects continued to conduct "private" foreign relations right into the seventeenth century.[24] Only after domestic turmoil had ceased and monarchs had become masters in their own domains was it possible for the doctrine of sovereignty to become a political reality.

　　It is perhaps in the realm of international law that the abandonment of the imperial model is most clearly seen. Theorists of international law were, after all, confronted by the phenomenon of powerful independent actors for which they had to make provision and whose behavior they felt had to be regulated and moderated. Hugo Grotius, for example, was no longer impressed by myths of imperial-imposed unity and harmony when he declared his reason for having written *The Law of War and Peace* (*De Jure Belli ac Pacis*) which was published in 1625.

> Throughout the Christian World I observed a lack of restraint in relation to war, such as even barbarous races should be ashamed of; I observed that men rush to arms for slight causes, or no cause at all, and that when arms have once been taken up there is no longer any respect for law, divine or human; it is as if, in accordance with a general decree, frenzy had openly been let loose for the committing of all crimes.[25]

24. See Chap. 4.
25. Hugo Grotius, *Prolegomena to the Law of War and Peace,* trans. by Francis W. Kelsey (Indianapolis: Bobbs-Merrill, 1957), p. 21.

International law, as most theorists perceived it, derived from two principal sources: Nature and God, on the one hand, and the customs and agreements of states on the other. Those who emphasized natural and divine law were strongly influenced by imperial assumptions concerning the unity and harmony of the political universe, viewing international law as a set of norms *above,* rather than *between,* states. By the fifteenth century, however, even many of these "naturalists" began to eliminate the "middle man" and rejected the authority of Emperor or Pope over princes. Instead, they began to substitute a model of law as regulator of the relations of independent states interacting in a political system. Typical was the work of Francisco Suárez (1548–1617), a Spanish theologian and lawyer, who wrote:

> (A)lthough a given sovereign state . . . may constitute a perfect community in itself . . . each one . . . is also . . . a member of that universal society; for these states . . . are never so self-sufficient that they do not require some mutual assistance, association, and intercourse. . . .[26]

This passage reveals a view of international relations that is at the core of the state-centric model; namely, an international system consisting of sovereign states, under no earthly authority but their own, which must nevertheless continuously interact with one another and seek ways to adjust their mutual relations. Similar ideas were expressed by Francisco de Vitoria (1480–1546), Albericus Gentilis (1552–1602), Hugo Grotius (1583–1645), and Emmerich de Vattel (1714–1767). Under their guidance, international law was separated from religion and ethics and emerged as an autonomous legal system intended to govern the relations of sovereign states.

The commanding role of states in international relations received further confirmation with the development of the "positivist" school of international law. Positivism declares international law to be the exclusive product of the customs of states and of agreements made among them. Thus, while proclaiming the superiority of natural law, even Gentilis admitted that in determining a "just" war the definition of justice had to be based on the perceptions of states themselves. This process reached its logical conclusion after the Peace of Westphalia with Vattel who "was the father of the doctrine of the equality of states . . . with a consistent and exaggerated emphasis on the sovereign independence of states found throughout (his) work."[27] In Vattel the ideas of international law based on the agreements of states regulating relations among them merges with the notion of a balance of power as a fundamental political *and* legal

26. Cited in Gross, "The Peace of Westphalia," p. 45.
27. Von Glahn, *Law Among Nations,* pp. 44–45.

principle. No longer is there reference to the old imperial order; instead, we see a state-centric model rooted in the notion of sovereignty.

> Europe forms a political system in which the Nations . . . are bound together by their relations and various interests into a single body. . . . The constant attention of sovereigns to all that goes on, the custom of resident ministers, the continual negotiations that take place, make of modern Europe a sort of Republic, whose members—each independent, but all bound together by a common interest—unite for the maintenance of order and the preservation of liberty. This is what has given rise to the well-known principle of the balance of power. . . .[28]

The triumph of the state-centric model coincided with the spread of the idea of "popular sovereignty." The growing belief after the French Revolution that the institutional apparatus of the state derived its legitimacy from the people as a national group tended to blur the distinction between the former and the latter, which was a self-conscious ethnic, linguistic, and cultural collectivity. What had been regarded as the territorial property of a dynasty or monarch came to be viewed as the political expression of distinct national groupings like the French or the Spanish. Consequently, the symbols of state and nation were fused, and it was assumed, at least in Europe, that the frontiers of states also delineated nations. The fusing of the two ideas lent the concept "nation-state" an emotive content that the concepts "nation" and "state" had formerly lacked and made it a secular substitute for the universal politico-religious unions of earlier epochs.

The relatively "soft" boundaries of states were hardened by an increasing "we-they" consciousness among nationalities during and after the Napoleonic Wars of the nineteenth century, and the nation-state became the apex of political loyalties. The merger of state apparatus with national myth endowed both with a legitimacy that neither had before enjoyed. Philosophers like Hegel, Burke, and Treitschke came to regard the nation-state as a corporate body with a life and spirit of its own and as the rightful object of men's highest loyalties. The energizing potential of linking state with nation was revealed with explosive suddenness as revolutionary and then Napoleonic France spread its ideology across Europe and as *la patrie* replaced *l'état*.

---

28. Emmerich de Vattel, "The Law of Nations," in M. G. Forsyth, H. M. S. Keens-Soper, and P. Savigear, eds., *The Theory of International Relations* (New York: Atherton, 1970), p. 118.

The Growing Irrelevance
of the
State-Centric Model

TWO

(I)n developing an apparatus of concepts and theories and in conducting research, political scientists have acted as if the ideal type of international politics were a reality and, in fact, the only reality. As a consequence research and explanation of events inside nation-state units and of events between these units have developed independently of one another. . . . The notion of sovereignty shields the two fields from each other methodologically.[1]

As we have seen, the doctrine of sovereignty triumphed by the seventeenth century. The doctrine owed much to philosophers such as Bodin and Thomas Hobbes who sought to explain and justify the emergence of centralized statist bureaucracies in France and England. As such, the doctrine was largely the product of a search for order and stability after an era of feudal dissolution and religious strife. Although it was essentially a legal "fiction," the doctrine provided a means of identifying international actors that was generally accurate and adequate for the period, even though oversimplified.

Global politics in the eighteenth century, at least in Europe, resembled a game of billiards in which the states appeared as homogeneous actors constantly caroming off one another. In this image "the stage is preempted by a set of states, each in full control of all territory, men, and resources within its boundaries."[2] The major nation-states of the eighteenth and nineteenth centuries were self-sufficient units of relatively equal power. They were hierarchically organized and capable of protecting themselves against internal and external sources of instability and change. Their

1. Karl Kaiser, "Transnational Politics: Toward a Theory of Multinational Politics," *International Organization* 25:4 (Autumn 1971), p. 792.
2. Arnold Wolfers, "The Actors in International Politics," in Wolfers, ed., *Discord and Collaboration* (Baltimore: Johns Hopkins Press, 1962), p. 19.

frontiers were clearly demarcated by international treaties. The Peace of Westphalia, which endorsed the principle of state sovereignty, was signed at a time when "clear-cut, hard-shell, 'closed' units no longer brooking" foreign interference were emerging.[3]

Under these conditions international law and political reality coincided to a considerable extent. The state-centric model with its assumption of "sovereign equality" reflected the essential ability of national governments to control their internal and external environments. These states disposed of sufficient territory and resources to defend themselves against foreign enemies and centralized the means of coercion within their territory. They were indeed subject to no higher secular authority. "Now that power . . . had become centralized, with its 'headquarters' in impermeable units, and measurable in relation to other external power," observes Herz, "it made sense to translate power relations into legal relationships, to distinguish 'rights' and 'duties' of different states in their mutual relations, to speak of treaties 'binding' nations, and so forth."[4]

However, there was always a discernible normative element in the doctrine of sovereignty as propounded by both Bodin and Hobbes. Whether or not a state actually possessed absolute authority over its citizens and could in reality regulate the citizens' relations with foreigners, it remained that the state *should* possess such authority. "Bodin was convinced," declared J. L. Brierly, "that a confusion of uncoordinated independent authorities must be fatal to a state."[5] In time what originally had been regarded as an attribute of a monarch came to be perceived as a quality of the state itself. Rousseau and the German philosophers of the nineteenth century were in part responsible for this shift in emphasis.

> With Rousseau . . . the cult of sovereignty is justified by the rightness of the general will. With Fichte and the German romantics generally . . . the emotional content of frustrated nationalism finds expression in the glorification of the state. . . . With Hegel . . . philosophical absolutism is reflected in . . . the concept that the State as a harmony of the whole society is the absolute power on earth. . . .[6]

But, the facts of political life and the fiction of sovereignty were congruent only during the brief era of monarchical absolutism and, even then, only in Europe. Yet, "so strong had the hold of sovereignty upon the imagination of political scientists become," argues Brierly, "that when it

3. John H. Herz, *International Politics in the Atomic Age* (New York: Columbia University Press, 1959), p. 51.
4. *Ibid,* p. 58.
5. J. L. Brierly, *The Law of Nations,* 6th ed. (New York: Oxford University Press, 1963), p. 8.
6. A. Larson et al., *Sovereignty Within the Law* (Dobbs Ferry, New York: Oceana, 1965), p. 25.

became obvious . . . that the personal monarch no longer fitted the role, they [political scientists] started a hunt for the 'location' of sovereignty, almost as if sovereignty, instead of being a reflection in theory of the political facts of a particular age, were a substance which must surely be found somewhere in every state if only one looked for it carefully enough."[7]

The Relative Irrelevance of Sovereignty

In earlier centuries the doctrine of sovereignty had an empirical basis. Today this doctrine does not have such a basis. All nation-states are subject to diverse internal and external conditioning factors that induce and constrain their behavior. American elections are influenced by events in Saigon and Peking, and American and British petroleum prices are affected by decisions made in Baghdad, Tripoli, or the headquarters of international petroleum corporations. James Rosenau describes this situation well:

> Almost every day incidents are reported that defy the principles of sovereignty. Politics everywhere, it would seem, are related to politics everywhere else. Where the functioning of any political unit was once sustained by structures within its boundaries, now the roots of its political life can be traced to remote corners of the globe.[8]

The confusion between sovereignty as prescription and the practical issue of state power is the main reason why it is so difficult to employ the concept of sovereignity meaningfully. No nation-state disposes of sufficient resources to prevent foreign intrusions upon its freedom of action or to realize and select goals without competing or cooperating with other actors; no nation-state enjoys the unqualified loyalty of its citizens. Dual and multiple loyalties are common today as illustrated by many communists who are at the same time loyal nationalists and ardent believers in a world movement. Although all nation-states enjoy some of the legal privileges of sovereignty (for example, all member states in the United Nations General Assembly have equal voting rights), in practice some states are obviously more "sovereign" than others.

Certain units that manifest the trappings of sovereignty or are recognized by others as being sovereign do not and cannot behave independently. The Ukraine and Belorussia, for instance, are members of the United Nations General Assembly with a vote equal to that of the United States and the Soviet Union, yet they are scarcely independent actors with

7. Brierly, *Law of Nations,* pp. 13–14.
8. James N. Rosenau, "Introduction: Political Science in a Shrinking World," in Rosenau, ed., *Linkage Politics* (New York: Free Press, 1969), p. 2.

their own foreign policies. States such as Nepal, Outer Mongolia, and Bulgaria are, at best, marginally independent, and their behavior in the global arena can usually be predicted by reference to some larger state. "Microsovereignties" such as the Republic of Maldive and the Comoro Islands are scarcely relevant to global politics.

Students of global and comparative politics have begun to recognize that many of the more than fifty nation-states that have acquired formal political independence since World War II and have been admitted as "sovereign equals" to the United Nations are vastly different than those states that constituted the global system of the eighteenth and nineteenth centuries. "There is surely at least a *prima facie* case," argues David Vital, "for asserting that one of the notable characteristics of the modern international scene is the growing disparity in human and material resources to be found where important categories of states are compared—with the result that the only genuine common denominator left is the purely *legal* equality of states that carries with it only such tenuous advantages as membership in the United Nations."[9] Oran Young declares: "If the basic attributes of statehood are taken to be such things as a clearly demarcated territorial base, a relatively stable population, more or less viable central institutions of government, and external sovereignty, the contemporary situation immediately begins to appear unclear and confusing." He continues: "Many of the 'new states,' for example, are of doubtful viability in political terms, poorly integrated as communities, geographically fluid, and sufficiently dependent upon other states and organizations (albeit often on an informal basis) to compromise seriously their external sovereignty."[10]

With few exceptions poor nation-states remain economically and/or politically dependent upon other actors, often the former metropole. For instance, several of the countries of what was formerly French Equatorial Africa continue to rely on France to provide minimal economic and social services, and one of them, the Republic of Chad, was involved in a civil war in which the government depended upon French troops and arms to retain power. Similarly, Israel relies on the United States, and Cuba on the Soviet Union for a semblance of economic stability. Certain states, notably the former Belgian Congo (Zaïre) after 1960, the Dominican Republic in 1965, and Bangladesh (formerly East Pakistan) since 1971, have required the assistance of international organizations, not only for economic and social services, but for administrative guidance as well.

After World War I it became fashionable to assume that most states

9. David Vital, "Back to Machiavelli," in Klaus Knorr and James N. Rosenau, eds., *Contending Approaches to International Politics* (Princeton: Princeton University Press, 1969), pp. 155–56.
10. Oran R. Young, "The Actors in World Politics," in James N. Rosenau, Vincent Davis, and Maurice A. East, eds., *The Analysis of International Politics* (New York: Free Press, 1972), p. 131.

that comprised the global system coincided or should coincide with ethnically or linguistically-defined national groups; hence, actors were commonly referred to as "nation-states." The destruction of the Austro-Hungarian, Ottoman, and Russian empires during the war appeared, to many historians and political scientists, to have brought the evolution of the state system to its close. States whose frontiers did not reflect national boundaries were considered anomalous. What few scholars and statesmen grasped, however, was that the nation-state, like the empire, was the product of a particular historical train of events and was "therefore bound to disappear in the course of history."[11]

Currently throughout Africa and Asia there are self-proclaimed states in which any coincidence between legal and national frontiers is imaginary. "If the entry of the third world onto the stage of modern socioscientific consciousness has had one immediate result (or should have had), it is the snapping of the link between state and nation."[12] Thus Nigeria, held up for a time after its independence in 1960 as a model of political development in Africa, was the scene of one of that continent's bloodiest civil wars. As is the case in many other former colonies in Africa and Asia, Nigerian loyalties remained parochial or tribal. Members of the various Nigerian tribal groups had a greater affinity for fellow tribe members living outside the state than for members of other tribes within the state. In fact "almost every sizeable ethnic group had its own particular fear of domination by someone else, not only nationally, but in each region which a secure majority called its own."[13] Nigeria was further cleaved along linguistic, religious, and economic lines. The existence of such profound cleavages explains in large part the recurrence of civil strife in many of the less developed areas.

Their lack of national identity and cohesion coupled with their weakness and poverty have made many of the newer states vulnerable to governmental instability, military coups d'etat, and civil war. Since 1960 violent civil wars have erupted in countries as diverse as Cyprus, Yemen, Zaïre, Indonesia, Cambodia, Laos, South Vietnam, Chad, the Sudan, Iraq, Jordan, Lebanon, Pakistan, the Dominican Republic, and, of course, Nigeria. Perhaps the most extreme example of a national group that lacks a state is that of the Palestinians who were driven from or left their homes in what is now Israel or who live in the Israeli-occupied territories on the west bank of the Jordan River. Many of them are settled in refugee camps

11. Hans J. Morgenthau, *Politics Among Nations*, 5th ed. (New York: Alfred A. Knopf, 1973), p. 10.
12. J. P. Nettl, "The State as a Conceptual Variable," *World Politics* 20:4 (July 1968), p. 560; see also, Walker Conner, "Self-Determination: The New Phase," *World Politics* 20:1 (October 1967), pp. 30–53.
13. Jean Herskovits, "One Nigeria," *Foreign Affairs* 51:2 (January 1973), p. 392.

scattered in Egypt, Lebanon, Syria, and Jordan. Some 550,000 of Jordan's total population of 1,700,000 are Palestinian refugees.[14] This large and volatile minority represents a major threat to the Hashemite monarchy of King Hussein. Moreover, the inability or unwillingness of the states of the region to respond to the economic and social needs of the Palestinians has made the United Nations virtually responsible for their survival; in addition, it has created the conditions necessary for the growth of potent Palestinian guerrilla groups.

Owing to their lack of political and social stability, their military and economic weakness, and the linkages between domestic groups and foreign interests within their states, many of the Third World states are "externally ill-defined, internally fragile and chaotic (calling) to mind sponges."[15] Often they cannot prevent foreign intervention or externally-supported subversion and insurrection as well as more subtle forms of "penetration."[16] The frustration engendered by this situation has often been behind the claims of "imperialism" and "neocolonialism" made by their leaders.

Nonstate Actors

The far-reaching changes that have taken place in the global system since 1945 challenge not only the concept of sovereignty but also the adequacy of regarding the nation-state as the sole actor in world politics. Activities not accounted for by the traditional interstate model repeatedly direct our attention to more encompassing sets of concerns, requiring us to locate, enumerate, and describe a more complex universe of actors than before. After all, the state has not always been the *primary* actor in global politics and has never been the *sole* actor. And, unless we believe that history is irrelevant, we cannot even assume *a priori* that the nation-state will always remain the *most important* autonomous actor.

Before the emergence of the modern nation-state, global structure lacked the territorial divisions among units that characterize a world of "sovereign equals." A variety of other actors were generally recognized as constituent parts of the global system and its several subsystems. Mercenaries without national loyalties, empires consisting of several nations, bankers, clans, trading companies, tribes, religious groups, and nomadic groups (to name just a few) were all recognized as participants in the system.

14. Data from John Paxton, ed., *The Stateman's Year Book 1972–1973* (London: Macmillan, 1972), p. 1111.
15. Kenneth N. Waltz, "The Politics of Peace," *International Studies Quarterly* 11 (1967), p. 205.
16. See Andrew M. Scott, *The Revolution in Statecraft: Informal Penetration* (New York: Random House, 1965).

Even after the rise of the nation-state system in Europe, other actors continued to exist alongside the state.[17] James Field points out that, paradoxically, it was during the eighteenth and nineteenth century struggles for national self-determination that such "transnational individuals as the Marquis de Lafayette, Tadeusz Kosciuszko, Tom Paine, and the 'titled freebooter' Lord Cochrane and such groups as the Philhellenes, Garibaldians, Fenians, and Zionists" were active.[18] In addition, regions like Africa, Asia, and the Americas were characterized by units other than nation-states, such as empires, colonies, and tribes.

While national governments remain the principal actors in the contemporary global system, the past decade has witnessed an explosive increase in popular participation in "affairs of state." The global political process involves individuals acting as spokesmen, surrogates, or executioners for social and political collectivities. Private individuals usually participate only indirectly as taxpayers, voters, or (conscript) soldiers. Nevertheless, "private" citizens or groups have increasingly intruded in world politics without reference to governments or interstate organizations. On occasion, even a single individual may behave independently and with impact. James Donovan, a New York attorney, negotiated the exchange of prisoners held in Cuba and arranged for the exchange of U-2 pilot Francis Gary Powers for a convicted Soviet spy; Ché Guevara fought for revolution in Bolivia; and H. Ross Perot, a Texas millionaire, flew to Indochina to attempt to arrange the repatriation of American prisoners of war held in North Vietnam. Hijackings, kidnappings, assassinations, and street demonstrations illustrate some of the ways in which private individuals and groups have sought to modify the behavior of national governments. Such groups, often lacking identifiable national affiliations, are "difficult to punish in normal ways even for international crimes."[19] The extralegal activities of James Bond, particularly against "Spectre," illustrate an imaginative solution to the problem. Growing concern with the potential role of private individuals is apparent, for instance, in scenarios that depict the theft of nuclear weapons from American stockpiles.[20]

17. See infra, Chap. 4.
18. James A. Field, Jr., "Transnationalism and the New Tribe," in Robert O. Keohane, and Joseph S. Nye, eds., "Transnational Relations and World Politics," special edition of Internal Organization 25:3 (Summer 1971), p. 355.
19. J. Bowyer Bell, "Contemporary Revolutionary Organizations," in Keohane and Nye, eds., "Transnational Relations," p. 514. Such groups may lack the primary commitment to self-preservation we ascribe to state actors. They might be insensitive to the kinds of retaliatory threats that have been a mainstay of order in a decentralized world system. What this means is that they fall outside the scope of the logic of deterrence—a fact with profoundly destabilizing implications.
20. See, for example, Jack Anderson, "Will Nuclear Weapons Fall into the Hands of Terrorists?" Parade, 29 September 1974, pp. 12–14.

In the contemporary global system, certain units that appear to behave independently and whose behavior has a marked effect on outcomes are not recognized as sovereign. Actors such as Al Fatah, the Viet Cong, the European Common Market, and even the Mafia play a larger role in global transactions than is customarily recognized. The Roman Catholic Church, for instance, "has fashioned a transnational organization that provides it with a visible center from which its moral principles can be communicated and through which it attempts to exercise influence and social control."[21] Similarly, the Ford Foundation "has promoted economic planning in much of the less developed world" and "is the largest financial supporter of social science research in Latin America."[22] Organizations like the United Nations and its agencies, NATO, and even the International Red Cross, while possessing neither the legal nor territorial attributes of sovereignty, are significant actors on the world stage. In certain cases, these organizations have developed large bureaucracies, have disposed of substantial budgets, and have acquired modes of routinized behavior. They have gained the loyalties of civil servants or other functional groups, and many of their activities are perceived as "legitimate" by nation-states.[23]

It is increasingly evident that in the contemporary global system, as in political systems that existed before 1648, nonstate actors, often "transnationally" organized, possess their own military capabilities, economic assets, and sources of information. The Palestinian guerrilla groups, for instance, dispose of organized military forces, negotiate formal agreements with Arab states, and threaten to undermine diplomatic understandings that were painfully achieved by representatives of major powers. Referring to the Palestinian group led by George Habash, J. Bowyer Bell observes: "Whatever Habash may claim, it is apparent that a revolutionary movement actively engaged in undermining (either by subversion or rebellion) a dozen recognized regimes is playing a significant transnational role."[24] Similarly, economic cartels and industrial corporations with productive and marketing facilities in several countries dispose of large-scale economic assets that provide them with substantial direct and indirect political influence. In some respects multinational corporations such as International Business Machines and Shell Oil are more independent than a government

21. Ivan Vallier, "The Roman Catholic Church: A Transnational Actor," in Keohane and Nye, eds., "Transnational Relations," p. 483.
22. Peter D. Bell, "The Ford Foundation as a Transnational Actor," in Keohane and Nye, eds., "Transnational Relations," p. 466.
23. See, for example, Ernst B. Haas, *The Uniting of Europe* (Stanford: Stanford University Press, 1958); Haas, *Beyond the Nation-State* (Stanford: Stanford University Press, 1964); Chadwick F. Alger, "United Nations Participation as a Learning Experience" *Public Opinion Quarterly* 27 (Fall 1963); Johan Galtung, "The Status of Technical Assistance Experts: A Study of U.N. Experts in Latin America," *Journal of Peace Research* 4 (1966).
24. J. Bowyer Bell, "Contemporary Revolutionary Organizations," p. 513.

such as that of Jordan, although the latter represents a "sovereign" state.

The potential impact of new types of international actors is suggested by contrasting the dollar values of sales of multinational corporations with the gross domestic products (GDPs) of several new nation-states as of 1970. For instance, the average GDP of Equatorial Guinea, Rwanda, South Yemen, Malta, Botswana, Dahomey, Gambia, and Lesotho is $134 millions; none have GDPs in excess of $227 millions. In contrast, General Motors, Standard Oil of New Jersey, Ford, General Electric, and Chrysler had average sales in 1973 of just under $22 billions![25] Thus, "one finds that General Motors, Ford, Standard Oil of New Jersey, Royal/Dutch Shell, General Electric, Chrysler, Unilever, and Mobil Oil are eight of the forty largest entities of the world."[26]

Sheer size alone, however, does not reflect the impact that multi-national corporations have on small countries or the threat that they may represent to the political and economic independence of these nation-states. As such corporations penetrate these countries, major economic sectors and large numbers of people may become obligated and responsive to foreigners. "If a similar chain of command existed in public organizations," writes one observer, "the poor country would be deemed a colony."

> Because multinational corporations are private economic organizations, chains of command leading outside the state may multiply without ostensible loss of political sovereignty. Yet, national autonomy, the ability of a nation-state as a collectivity to make decisions which shape its political and economic future, has been diminished.[27]

Conservatism in the Study of Global Politics

Despite the accumulation of conflicting evidence, most present-day students of global politics have been reluctant to abandon the state-centric model to which they have become so accustomed. In this respect, although the "real world" has marched on since the era of Bodin, contemporary students of world politics have lagged behind. Even attempts to pioneer new approaches and methods have remained rooted in traditional concepts like sovereignty. The state-centric model has imposed research blinders and has inhibited an accurate mapping of the increasingly complex global system. As J. David Singer observes, "The national state is—in most theoreti-

25. Data on GDPs from *Yearbook of National Accounts Statistics 1973*, vol. 3 (New York: United Nations, 1975), Table 1A, pp. 3–8. Data on MNC sales from *Fortune* (May 1974), p. 232.
26. Jonathan F. Galloway, "Multi-National Enterprises as Worldwide Interest Groups," paper delivered at the 1970 Meeting of the American Political Science Association, p. 9.
27. Peter B. Evans, "National Autonomy and Economic Development," in Keohane and Nye, eds., "Transnational Relations," p. 676.

cal formulations—assigned too prominent a role, and . . . competing entities must be more heavily emphasized than has been customary."[28] Although it is "mandatory to first describe the population about which one is generalizing,"[29] precious little time or effort have gone into performing this task.[30]

The continuing state-centric bias is no better illustrated than in a recent edition of essays about international relations theory in which the editors conclude that, despite disagreements among the contributors, they all conceive "the subject to consist of the individuals and groups who initiate and sustain the actions and interactions of nation-states."[31] In addition, under contemporary international law only states are sovereign.[32] States and some international organizations have traditionally been regarded as the sole subjects of international law, and William Tung's view is not an uncommon one even today. "International persons," Tung declares, "are primarily states to which rights and duties are generally attributed. . . . (The) position of states in the international community corresponds to that of individuals under municipal law."[33] The more politically minded of international legal theorists do little more than mention in passing that traditional theory does not reflect either the differences in the power and independence of nation-states or rules generated by "supranational" entities like the European Economic Community (EEC).[34]

28. J. David Singer, "The Global System and Its Sub-systems: A Developmental View," in James N. Rosenau, ed., *Linkage Politics* (New York: Free Press, 1969), p. 22.

29. J. David Singer, "The Incompleat Theorist: Insight without Evidence," in Knorr and Rosenau, eds., *Contending Approaches*, p. 69.

30. Recently, several techniques of investigation have been developed that promise to stimulate cumulative research on international behavior. These include analyses of aggregate data and cross-national transactions, the replication of international situations through the use of simulation, and indirect access to real situations by reconstructing decisional processes, coding and interpreting government exchanges, and content analysis of elite attitudes. While these techniques vary methodologically and in the focuses of their interest, they are strikingly similar in one respect; they all seek to explain "the behavior men organized into nations exhibit toward each other." Richard A. Brody, "The Study of International Politics Qua Science; The Emphasis on Methods and Techniques," in Knorr and Rosenau, eds., *Contending Approaches,* p. 115.

31. Klaus Knorr and James N. Rosenau, "Tradition and Science in the Study of International Politics," in Knorr and Rosenau, eds., *Contending Approaches,* p. 4.

32. Only states have territoriality, another commonly cited attribute of international actors.

33. W. L. Tung, *International Law in an Organizing World* (New York: Thomas I. Crowell, 1968), p. 39.

34. Cf. Morton A. Kaplan and Nicholas deB. Katzenbach, *The Political Foundations of International Law* (New York: John Wiley & Sons, 1961), especially Chap. 4. These authors acknowledge their debt to Harold Lasswell and Myles McDougal, pioneers of the so-called "New Haven School" of international legal theory.

There are several reasons for this apparently conservative bias in the study of global politics. In the first place, empirical data concerning nation-states, particularly aggregate data, are practically the only data readily available. While many of the details of specific governmental interactions are denied to scholars for many years, we are confident that they will ultimately be made part of the public record and be available to historians. Moreover, information concerning the leadership, population, economic status, and so forth of nation-states is usually a matter of public record. Similar information about nonstate units is often hard to come by. Furthermore, newspapers, journals, U.N. reports, and government publications all tend to reify nation-states and to present data in tidy national pigeonholes.

Second, there is a natural desire on the part of scholars and practitioners to work with data that are readily comparable. Previously it has been assumed that all nation-states are sufficiently similar so that we can consider them as members of the same class of units. Each in sovereign, has its own GNP, population, territory, army, and so forth. The assumption that similar nation-states can be conveniently distinguished on the basis of geographic criteria facilitates the tasks of aggregation and comparison and eliminates "sloppy" overlap.

Yet some of these simplifying, albeit comforting, assumptions are misleading. "Although many social scientists still insist on 'comparing states' as if they were equivalent units," Ivan Vallier reminds us that "this is unfruitful."[35] Even though comparable data are difficult to obtain and calculate if we include nonstate actors, such data do exist or can be created. Many nonstate actors like corporations have a "population" or membership, a "government," and goals, objectives, and resources. As actors, nation-states and nonstate actors are certainly analogous and perhaps are even homologous.

> The question is whether they are sufficiently similar to permit comparison and combination for the theoretical purposes at hand. To borrow a metaphor . . . , there is absolutely nothing wrong with adding apples and oranges if fruit is the subject at hand![36]

The traditional mark of sovereignty nevertheless remains as a supposedly defining attribute of "international" actors. It seems paradoxical that scholars, especially those who declare their desire to break away from traditional methods, should resort to traditional legal and diplomatic concepts to justify their continued focus on the nation-state. Their eyes are riveted to an artificial construct—an "incomplete global system"—the existence of which is inferred as much from prescriptive norms as from empirical observation.

35. Vallier, "The Roman Catholic Church," p. 501.
36. Singer, "The Incompleat Theorist," p. 77.

A final reason for the intellectual procrastination of many international relations scholars is that the study of international politics did not originate as an autonomous discipline but evolved as an offshoot of the study of the state, as "the untidy fringe of domestic politics." As Martin Wight suggests: "The principle that every individual requires the protection of a state which represents him in the international community, is a juristic expression of the belief in the sovereign state as the consummation of political experience and activity which has marked Western political thought since the Renaissance."[37] But it is precisely because no national government exercises complete control over the individuals and groups for which it is legally responsible that nonstate actors can enter independently into relations with other actors.

The time has come to cast aside what Wight terms "the intellectual prejudice imposed by the sovereign state."[38] The conservative bias of the past, as Oran Young remarks, has too long precluded "the analysis of a wide range of *logically* possible and empirically interesting models of world politics."[39] Since scholars are concerned with investigating global *behavior,* it is reasonable to propose that actors be identified and classified according to *behavioral* rather than legal or normative criteria.

37. Martin Wight, "Why Is There No International Theory?" in Herbert Butterfield and Martin Wight, eds., *Diplomatic Investigations* (Cambridge: Harvard University Press, 1968), p. 21.
38. *Ibid.,* p. 20.
39. Young, "The Actors in International Politics," p. 126.

Towards a New
Conceptualization
of Global Politics

THREE

Although the great breakthroughs in empirical political theory have yet to
occur, the last decade of theoretical efforts has been marked by forward
movement. . . . (M)ore theorizing is needed . . . across-systems-level
theory. . . . The across-systems breakthroughs may still be decades
away, but it is not too early to consider what conceptual and methodological equipment they may require.[1]

All human activity may be analyzed in terms of purposive systems,
each of which involves men intensively interacting with one another around
particular activities. Thus we can identify ethnic systems, economic systems, defense systems, and so forth. Individuals and groups who occupy
roles in such systems are functionally linked.

The Emergence and Disappearance of Actors

Individuals and groups become functionally linked as they discover that
they share common interests and common needs that transcend existing
organizational frontiers. They may then develop common views and even
cooperative approaches to the problems that they confront. The complexity
of contemporary modes of industrial production, for example, may generate a linkage between business firms in different countries that depend upon
each other for raw materials, parts, expertise, or marketing facilities.
Industrialists in several countries may discover that they share problems
with which they can cope more effectively by pooling their resources; they

1. James N. Rosenau, "Theorizing Across Systems: Linkage Politics Re-
visited," paper delivered at the 1971 Meeting of the American Political Science
Association, p. 1.

may seek, for instance, common tax and pricing policies from the governments of the states in which they reside. In the course of collaborating, their common or complementary interests may grow and deepen beyond mere economic expediency. "There is," argues Werner Feld, "an emotive side to such efforts which produces in the staff members concerned with collaboration a distinct feeling of being involved in a 'united or cooperative' endeavor."[2]

When one begins to identify the many functional systems that link men, the world appears "like millions of cobwebs superimposed one upon another, covering the whole globe."[3] Functional systems themselves tend to be interdependent and related to each other in complex ways. Each system requires the existence of others to perform effectively; in this respect systems, too, may be said to be linked. In J. W. Burton's words:

> Linked systems create clusters that tend to be concentrated geographically. . . . Linked systems tend to consolidate into administrative units. . . . Once consolidated . . . linked systems and their administrative controls acquire an identity and a legitimized status within their environment.[4]

From this perspective, governments of nation-states may be seen as functional (administrative) systems whose central function since the seventeenth century has been to regulate and manage clusters of other functional systems. More accurately perhaps, in their function as administrators for many functional systems, states have been essentially multifunctional actors organizing collective efforts toward objectives which could not be realized by individuals in their private capacity. The boundaries of nation-states have tended to coincide with the boundaries of other functional systems, and therefore political frontiers have seemed to represent "marked discontinuities in the frequency of transactions and marked discontinuities in the frequency of responses."[5] States were able to control and limit the transactions which crossed their frontiers as well as those that occurred within their borders. As long as states remained relatively impermeable, they were able, for example, to regulate the economic or cultural relations of their citizens with those living abroad and with foreign nationals.

2. Werner Feld, "Political Aspects of Transnational Business Collaboration in the Common Market," *International Organization* 24:2 (Spring 1970), p. 210. For an elaboration of the thesis that transnationalism promotes complementary views among elites, see Robert C. Angell, *Peace on the March* (New York: Van Nostrand, 1969).
3. J. W. Burton, *Systems, States, Diplomacy and Rules* (New York: Cambridge University Press, 1968), pp. 8–9.
4. *Ibid*, p. 8.
5. Karl W. Deutsch, "External Influences on the Internal Behavior of States," in R. Barry Farrell, ed., *Approaches to Comparative and International Politics* (Evanston, Ill.: Northwestern University Press, 1966), p. 15.

In theory, however, it is *not necessary* that the governments of nation-states be the umbrella administrative systems through which all other systems are regulated. The boundaries of such systems coincide with nation-state frontiers only insofar as national governments can control them and can independently open or close their state borders to transnational influences. Consider the situation of many states whose political or historical frontiers do *not* coincide with the national boundaries of groups residing within them. Ties may develop across borders, and loyalties may shift away from governments. There are many historical cases of such phenomena; the Austro-Hungarian Empire, for example, consisted of a patchwork of different national groups, and Serbian, Italian, and Croatian nationals tended to reserve their highest loyalties for fellow-nationals living outside the Empire and for the idea of "their nation." In recent years violence in areas as diverse as Cyprus, the Congo (Zaïre), Nigeria, Canada, and Ireland suggest the way in which the loyalties of national groups may transcend the borders of states and lead to conflict.

The question of human loyalties is not one that can be settled once and for all; loyalties constantly shift as men perceive that their interests and aspirations are more fully represented by new groups. As Arnold Wolfers noted some years ago, "attention must be focused on the individual human beings for whom identification is a psychological event."[6] To the degree that human loyalties are divided between states and other groups, the latter can become significant global actors.

This is, in fact, what has happened. As Burton reminds us, "there is in contemporary world society an increasing number of systems—some basically economic, scientific, cultural, ideological, or religious—that have little relationship to State boundaries," and "whatever significance geographically drawn boundaries had, has been and is being greatly reduced by these developments."[7] Of the various transnational exchanges, some of the more important and well-known include teaching and research abroad, study abroad, overseas religious missions, military service abroad, tourism, work in multinational corporations, and participation in nongovernmental and international organizations.

Functional systems have spilled across nation-state boundaries and in some cases have defied the efforts of governments to regulate them. Citizens of many states find themselves linked in horizontal fashion, working together regardless of the wishes of governments. Thus, Jews in the United States, Israel, the Soviet Union, and Europe are linked by loyalties that transcend the interests of the states in which they reside. Leftist revolutionaries, industrial managers, international civil servants and others are linked

6. Arnold Wolfers, *Discord and Collaboration* (Baltimore: Johns Hopkins Press, 1962), p. 23.
7. Burton, *Systems,* p. 10.

in similar fashion though for different purposes. Individuals have become increasingly aware of the interests that they share with others in different states, have communicated these interests, and have developed new loyalties. In some cases these transnational affiliations have been organized and have acquired their own administrative hierarchies, thereby becoming non-state actors in a more formal sense.[8]

Several major trends have contributed to these developments. The proliferation and increasing potential destructiveness of thermonuclear weapons have made the prospect of war between the superpowers "unthinkable" and have contributed to the erosion of the great postwar ideological blocs. Conventional military force and intervention have become less effective in coping with certain problems, as evidenced by the French defeat in Algeria and the American debacle in Vietnam. As nuclear and conventional warfare have become more expensive to contemplate and less effective, new means of gaining influence, including guerrilla warfare, political terrorism, economic boycott, and political propaganda, have become more common, thereby permitting actors lacking the traditional instruments of power to exercise considerable influence and enjoy considerable autonomy. Even more frightening is the possibility that such actors may gain access to modern technology.

In addition, the diminution of the central ideological cleavage, the resurgence of Europe, China, and Japan, and the independence of a multitude of small and poor nation-states in Africa and Asia have led to the emergence of other cleavages, some global and many of a regional and local scope, and have therefore encouraged the "regionalization" or "localization" of international conflict. "The structure of the international system," Jorge Domínguez declares, "has been transformed through a process of fragmentation of the linkages of the center of the system to its peripheries and of those between the continental subsystems of the peripheries."[9] The new conflicts that have surfaced revolve around questions such as national self-determination, local border adjustment, economic inequality and exploitation, and racial or ethnic discrimination. These are questions that encourage the shifting of people's loyalties away from institutions that formerly held their affections.

At root, the twentieth-century emergence of new actors in the global system reflects the inability of territorially-limited nation-states to respond to, cope with, or suppress changing popular demands. Popular demands can be suppressed (and often are) by existing authorities; they can be

8. See Oran R. Young, "The Actors in World Politics," in James N. Rosenau, Vincent Davis, and Maurice A. East, eds., *The Analysis of International Politics* (New York: Free Press, 1972), p. 132.
9. Jorge I. Domínguez, "Mice that Do Not Roar: Some Aspects of International Politics in the World's Peripheries," *International Organization* 25:2 (Spring 1971), p. 208.

fulfilled by them; or they can lead to the emergence of new political structures designed to fulfill them. Thus, when a state can no longer guarantee the defense of its subjects, it may be conquered and eliminated as happened to eighteenth-century Poland. Conversely, the integration of existing units, like the merger of two corporations, or the creation of new nation-state actors such as the United States in 1776, Biafra (temporarily) in 1968, and Bangladesh in 1971, are partly the consequence of demands for a more capable and responsive performance of certain tasks—demands that were neither suppressed nor fulfilled.

Today the global system is complexly interdependent owing in part to improved communications and transportation. People's lives are being touched and affected ever more profoundly by decisions made outside their own national states. Their demands for justice, equality, prosperity, and independence tend to increase and further tax the capacity of existing nation-states. We are in the midst of a revolution of "rising expectations" in which the achievements of people in one corner of the system generate demands for similar achievements elsewhere. When these demands remain unanswered, they may lead to intense frustration. Thus, the frustration of large numbers of Arabs at continued Israeli occupation of Palestine and the failure of Arab governments to satisfy their claims have led to the creation of Palestinian terrorist and liberation groups, the organization and behavior of which are in part patterned after successful movements in Algeria, Cuba, and Vietnam.

In the contemporary world demands such as those for defense, full employment, or social reform place overwhelming burdens on the resources of poor states. Others, increasingly, are beyond the capacity of *any* single nation-state to fulfill. As Robert Keohane and Joseph Nye observe:

> It is clear that most if not all governments will find it very difficult to cope with many aspects of transnational relations in the decade of the 1970s and thereafter. . . . Outer space, the oceans, and the internationalization of production are only three of the most obvious areas in which intergovernmental control may be demanded in the form of new international laws or new organizations or both.[10]

One way in which national governments may seek to deal with transnational pressures is through the creation of specialized intergovernmental actors which acquire limited global roles. The emergence of regional agencies and organizations and those associated with the United Nations attests to the growth of large-scale functional systems with their own administrative overseers. Such organizations reinforce pre-existing linkages or

10. Robert O. Keohane and Joseph S. Nye, Jr., "Transnational Relations and World Politics: An Introduction," in Keohane and Nye, eds., "Transnational Relations and World Politics," special edition of *International Organization* 25:3 (Summer 1971), p. 348.

create new ones.[11] Intergovernmental organizations that have achieved some measure of autonomy, however, are often engaged in highly technical and relatively nonpolitical tasks. In those areas where governments resist transnational pressures, other groups may emerge.

Global Tasks

There are at least four general types of tasks that can be performed by actors:

1. *Physical protection* or security which involves the protection of men and their values from coercive deprivation either by other members within the group or by individuals or groups outside it.

2. *Economic development and regulation* which comprise activities that are intended to overcome the constraints imposed on individual or collective capacity for self-development and growth by the scarcity or distribution of material resources.

3. *Residual public interest tasks* which involve activities that are designed to overcome constraints other than economic, such as disease or ignorance, that restrict individual or collective capacity for self-development and growth.

4. *Group status* which refers to the provision of referent identification through collective symbols that bind the individual to others, provide him with psychological and emotional security, and distinguish him in some manner from others who are not members of the group. Such symbols are often grounded in ethnicity, nationality, class, religion, and kinship.

The behavior of actors in the global system involves the performance of one or more of the foregoing tasks in cooperation or competition with other actors responding to the actual or anticipated demands of their "constituencies." Although governments of nation-states customarily perform these tasks "domestically," tasks become relevant at the "international" level when a government acts to protect its citizens from externally-imposed change or to adapt them to such change. For example, the regulation of the domestic economy to create and sustain full employment is not itself an internationally-relevant task. When, however, tariffs are imposed on imports or the currency is devalued, the behavior acquires significance for the global system. Others outside the state are affected and made to bear the burdens of the "domestic" economic adjustment.

11. For a summary of many contemporary intergovernmental organizations, see John Paxton, ed., *The Statesman's Yearbook 1973–1974* (London: Macmillan, 1973), pp. 3–61; and Richard P. Stebbins and Alba Amoia, eds., *Political Handbook and Atlas of the World 1970* (New York: Simon & Schuster, 1970), pp. 437–513.

The suggested categories of tasks are, of course, in the nature of analytic pigeonholes, and many activities involve more than a single category. Most actors tend to perform several tasks for their members, but an actor may be specialized and perform only one type. The World Health Organization (WHO), for example, is largely concerned with upgrading global health standards (a residual public interest task). Armed mercenaries, on the other hand, are generally involved only in offering physical protection to those who require it and can pay for it. In practice different categories of tasks are often perceived as mutually supportive. Hence, national groups may believe that only by unifying their "nation" can they protect themselves, yet at the same time unification depends on self-protection.

Actors may add and drop tasks or enlarge and restrict them over a period of time. For example, only recently many "welfare state" policies have been initiated by nation-states or intergovernmental organizations, thereby enlarging the scope of activities involved in the residual public interest category. Previously, such services were offered, if at all, by groups such as the family, church, or political party. Technological change, the behavior of others, and the solution of old problems encourage demands for the performance of new tasks. Thus, modern technology and medicine, while solving problems that have bedeviled people for centuries, are partly responsible for growing global pollution and population pressures. If nation-states continue to cope only sporadically with these burgeoning problems, demands for pollution and population control may lead to the creation of significant intergovernmental and nongovernmental political structures. Indeed, in 1972 the United Nations for the first time began to turn its attention seriously to questions of world pollution control, and two years later it addressed itself to the specter of world hunger.

The increasing inability of modern nation-states to satisfy the demands of their citizens or to cope with problems that transcend their boundaries is partly the result of the growing complexity and specialization of functional systems as well as of the increase in the number of collective goods and benefits desired by individuals.[12] In contrast, states in the eighteenth century were concerned principally with providing physical protection for members and insulating subjects from externally-imposed change. Individuals were able to provide for their own economic and social needs either privately or through small groups such as the extended family. Only peripherally and sporadically was the larger collectivity called upon to undertake economic and social service tasks or even to provide group status. Political philosophers were largely preoccupied with identifying the

12. For an explanation of the difference between "collective" and "private" goods, see Mancur Olson, Jr., The Logic of Collective Action (Cambridge: Harvard University Press, 1965).

areas in which collective action was called for, and they tended to agree that these areas were narrowly circumscribed.

The increasing size and complexity of systems and institutions threaten individuals with a sense of helplessness in a world dominated by large impersonal forces where rapid change and "future shock" are common. Many small and new nation-states are only barely (if at all) able to provide physical security, economic satisfaction, or social welfare for their citizens. On the other hand, often they do provide their citizens with an emotionally-comforting sense of national identity and "in-group" unity. In this respect these states (as well as some nonstate units) can be seen as rather specialized actors in an increasingly interdependent world.[13]

The Panoply of Global Actors

We can identify at least six types of actors in the contemporary global system.

The first type is the *interstate governmental actor* (IGO) composed of governmental representatives from more than one state. Sometimes known as "international" or "supranational" organizations, depending upon their degree of autonomy, they include as members two or more national governments. Since the beginning of the nineteenth century, the number of such organizations has increased even more rapidly than has the number of nation-states.[14] Examples of this type of actor include military alliances such as NATO and the Warsaw Pact, universal organizations such as the League of Nations or the United Nations, and special purpose organizations such as the European Economic Community (EEC) and the Universal Postal Union (UPU). In 1972 there were at least 280 such actors in the international system.[15]

A second type is the *interstate nongovernmental actor.* Sometimes referred to as "transnational" or "crossnational," this type of actor encompasses individuals who reside in several nation-states but who do not represent any of the governments of these states. According to the *Yearbook of*

13. Occasionally, states may fail to provide even group status for inhabitants. Thus, in 1969–1970, it appeared that guerrilla organizations such as Al Fatah were largely providing physical protection and group status for many Palestinians in Jordan. When one prominent guerrilla leader was asked why his commandos permitted Jordan's King Hussein to remain on the throne and did not themselves seize the reins of government, he replied: "We don't want to have to take care of sewers and stamp the passports." Eric Pace, "The Violent Men of Amman," *The New York Times Magazine,* 19 July 1970, p. 42.
14. See J. David Singer and Michael D. Wallace, "Intergovernmental Organization in the Global System, 1815–1964: A Quantitative Description," *International Organization* 24:2 (Spring 1970), p. 277.
15. E. S. Tew, ed., *Yearbook of International Organizations* 14th ed. (Brussels: Union of International Associations, 1972), p. 879.

International Organizations, there were at least 2,190 such organizations in 1972 as compared to under 1,000 in 1958.[16] These groups are functionally diverse and include religious groups such as the International Council of Jewish Women, the Salvation Army, and the World Muslim Congress; trade unions such as the Caribbean Congress of Labor and the World Confederation of Labor; and social welfare organizations such as the International Red Cross or Kiwanis International. (*The Yearbook* may, in fact, not include the most significant of these groups because it omits multinational corporations and terrorist and revolutionary groups.) While many of these actors seek to avoid involvement in politically-sensitive questions, some behave autonomously and do become so embroiled. This is illustrated by the role of the International Red Cross in the Nigerian-Biafran civil war[17] and the conflict culminating in 1968 between Standard of New Jersey's subsidiary, the International Petroleum Corporation, and the government of Peru. The multinational corporation in particular is becoming a major transnational actor, rendering more obsolete the state-centric model of international interaction.[18]

A third type of actor is commonly known as the *nation-state.* It consists of personnel from the agencies of a single central government. Though often regarded as unified entities, national governments are often more usefully identified in terms of their parts such as ministries and legislatures. On occasion, the "parts" may behave autonomously with little reference to other government bureaucracies. "The apparatus of each national government," declares Graham Allison, "constitutes a complex arena for the intra-national game."[19] The ministries that make up large governments bargain with each other and regularly approach "national" questions with parochial or particularist views; each may view the "national interest" from a different standpoint. For instance, it has been alleged that the American Central Intelligence Agency has, on occasion, formulated and carried out policy independently and without the complete knowledge or approval of elected officials.

16. *Ibid.;* see also Angell, *Peace on the March,* pp. 129–46.

17. For a description of the rich variety of actors and actor-types involved in the Nigerian-Biafran war, see M. Davis, "The Structuring of International Communications About the Nigeria-Biafra War," paper delivered at the 8th European Conference, Peace Research Society (International).

18. See, for example, *infra.,* Chap. 8; Jonathan F. Galloway, "Multi-national Enterprises as Worldwide Interest Groups," paper delivered to the 1970 Meeting of the American Political Science Association; Galloway, "Worldwide Corporations and International Integration: The Case of INTELSAT," *International Organization* 24:3 (Summer 1970), pp. 503–19; Raymond F. Hopkins and Richard W. Mansbach, *Structure and Process in International Politics* (New York: Harper & Row, 1973), Chap. 12.

19. Graham Allison, *Essence of Decision* (Boston: Little Brown and Co., 1971), p. 144.

Fourth, there is the *governmental noncentral* actor composed of personnel from regional, parochial, or municipal governments within a single state or of colonial officials representing the state. Such parochial bureaucracies and officials generally are only peripherally concerned with world politics or, at most, have an indirect impact on the global political system. Occasionally, however, they have a direct impact when they serve as the core of secessionist movements or when they establish and maintain direct contact with other actors. In this context, the provincial officials of Katanga, Biafra, and in the 1860's the American South come to mind.

A fifth type is the *intrastate nongovernmental* actor consisting of nongovernmental groups or individuals located primarily within a single state. Again, this type of actor is generally thought of as subject to the regulation of a central government, at least in matters of foreign policy. Yet, such groups, ranging from philanthropic organizations and political parties to ethnic communities, labor unions, and industrial corporations may, from time to time, conduct relations directly with autonomous actors other than their own government. In this category, we find groups as disparate as the Ford Foundation, Oxfam, the Turkish and Greek Cypriot communities, the Communist Party of the Soviet Union, the Jewish Agency, and the Irish Republican Army.

Finally, *individuals* in their private capacity are, on occasion, able to behave autonomously in the global arena. Such "international" individuals were more common before the emergence of the nation-state, particularly as diplomatic or military mercenaries. More recently, one might think of the American industrialist Andrew Carnegie who willed ten million dollars for "the speedy abolition of war between the so-called civilized nations," the Swedish soldier Count Gustaf von Rosen who was responsible for creating a Biafran air force during the Nigerian civil war, or the Argentine revolutionary Ché Guevara.

Figure 2 relates actors to the tasks mentioned above and suggests the range of actors that exist in the global system and the principal tasks they perform. The entries in the matrix are illustrative and indicate that these actors at some point in time have performed these functions in ways relevant for the global system. Some categories may have many representatives; others only a few.

The Complex Conglomerate System

Our analysis up to this point enables us to return to the question of the structure and processes of the global political system. The contemporary global system defies many conventional descriptions of its structure as

	PHYSICAL PROTECTION	ECONOMIC	PUBLIC INTEREST	GROUP STATUS
INTERSTATE GOVERNMENTAL	NATO	GATT	WHO	British Commonwealth
INTERSTATE NONGOVERNMENTAL	Al Fatah	Royal Dutch Petroleum	International Red Cross	Comintern
NATION-STATE	Turkish Cypriot Government Officials	U. S. Dept. of Commerce	HEW	Biafra
GOVERNMENTAL NONCENTRAL	Confederacy	Katanga	New York City	Quebec
INTRASTATE NONGOVERNMENTAL	Jewish Defense League	CARE	Ford Foundation	Ibo tribe
INDIVIDUAL	Gustav von Rosen	Jean Monnet	Andrew Carnegie	Dalai Lama

Figure 2
Actors Defined by Membership and Principal Task

bipolar, multipolar, or balance of power.[20] These descriptions account only for the number of states and their distribution of power. "In particular," declares Oran Young, "it seems desirable to think increasingly in terms of world systems that are heterogeneous with respect to types of actor (i.e. mixed actor systems) in the analysis of world politics."[21]

We propose an alternative model of the contemporary global system which we shall call the *complex conglomerate system*.[22] The concept of "conglomerate" refers to "a mixture of various materials or elements clustered together without assimilation."[23] In economics the term is used to describe the grouping of firms of different types under a single umbrella of corporate leadership.

The principal feature of the complex conglomerate system is the formation of situationally-specific alignments of different types of actors using a variety of means to achieve complementary objectives. It is signifi-

20. See Morton Kaplan, *System and Process in International Politics* (New York: John Wiley & Sons, 1957).
21. Young, "The Actors in World Politics," p. 136.
22. See Hopkins and Mansbach, *Structure and Process,* p. 128.
23. *The Compact Edition of the Oxford English Dictionary* (New York: Oxford University Press, 1971), p. 516.

cant that many of these alignment "conglomerates" lack the formal structure of traditional alliances such as NATO and tend to be flexible and ideologically diffuse.

For example, until recently one could identify conglomerate alignments that are essentially adversarial on the issue of Angolan independence. On one side were the Angolan rebel groups, the U.N. General Assembly, Black African states like Tanzania, the Soviet bloc of states, and even the World Council of Churches; on the other side were Portugal, the United States, and several major international corporations. Another illustrative pair of alignments has formed over the question of the pricing of petroleum products and the ownership of petroleum-production and exploitation facilities in the Middle East. One one side in favor of the *status quo* are the major Western powers and the principal petroleum corporations, sometimes called "the seven sisters"; on the other side are the major oil producing states of the Middle East and elsewhere organized in a group called OPEC (Organization of Petroleum Exporting Countries), along with various Palestinian liberation groups, Egypt, and the Eastern bloc of states which perceive the oil question as linked to the Arab-Israeli conflict.

Figure 3 further suggests the range of alignments that characterize the complex conglomerate system.

In summary, we should stress that the complex conglomerate system exhibits several other characteristics in addition to the primary one relating to the existence of many autonomous actors of different types and their grouping into diffuse, flexible, and situationally-specific alignments:

1. The global system in traditional terms is steadily moving in the direction of multipolarity, with the breakup of the great postwar ideological blocs and the assumption of new global roles by Europe, Japan, and China. Concurrently, many new states have joined the system and the gap between the living standards of "haves" and "have nots" continues to widen. In addition, the Third World has begun to divide into resource-rich and resource-deprived states (the "Fourth World").

2. Weapons with the greatest destructive capacity are deemed unusable, and military intervention by nation-states is becoming increasingly expensive. Economic adjustment among the developed countries is rapidly joining security as a major preoccupation of developed-country policymakers. Additional conflicts involve questions like national self-determination, local border adjustment, economic inequality and exploitation, and racial or ethnic discrimination.

3. Many poor and small nation-states are unable to perform the tasks demanded of them by their populations.

4. Global problems such as oceanic pollution are emerging that transcend national boundaries and overwhelm the capacities of individual nation-states.

	INTERSTATE GOVERNMENTAL	INTERSTATE NON-GOVERNMENTAL	NATION-STATE	GOVERNMENTAL NONCENTRAL	INTRASTATE NON-GOVERNMENTAL	INDIVIDUAL
INTERSTATE GOVERNMENTAL	UN-NATO (1950)	UN-International Red Cross (Palestine)	EEC-Francophone African states	OAU-Biafra	Arab League-Al Fatah	Grand Mufti of Jerusalem-Arab League
INTERSTATE NONGOVERNMENTAL	UN-International Red Cross (Palestine)	Shell Oil-ESSO (1972)	USSR-Comintern (1920's)	IBM-Scotland	ITT-Allende opposition (Chile)	Sun-Yat-sen-Comintern
NATION-STATE	EEC-Francophone African states	USSR-Comintern (1920's)	"traditional alliances" (NATO)	Belgium-Katanga (1960)	North Vietnam-Viet Cong	U.S.-James Donovan
GOVERNMENTAL NONCENTRAL	OAU-Biafra	IBM-Scotland	Belgium-Katanga (1960)	N.Y. Mayor-Moscow Mayor (1973)	Algerian rebels-French Socialists (1954)	South African mercenaries-Katanga
INTRASTATE NONGOVERNMENTAL	Arab League-Al Fatah	ITT-Allende Opposition (Chile)	North Vietnam-Viet Cong	Ulster-Protestant Vanguard (1970)	Communist Party-USSR-Communist Party-German Democratic Republic	George Grivas-Greek Cypriots
INDIVIDUAL	Grand Mufti of Jerusalem Arab League	Sun-Yat-sen-Comintern	U.S.-James Donovan	South African mercenaries-Katanga (1960)	George Grivas-Greek Cypriots	Louis of Conde-Gaspard de Coligny (1562)

Figure 3
Alignments in a Complex Conglomerate System

5. Many means are available and are used to exert influence including conventional military force (nation-states), control of marketing facilities, pricing, and technology (multinational corporations), clandestine military force (terrorist and revolutionary groups), moral suasion (Roman Catholic Church), money and expertise (Ford Foundation), voting strength (Jewish community in the United States), and so forth.

6. Functional linkages create transnational perceptions of mutual interest and lead to regularized communication among status groups across state frontiers.

7. A high level of interdependence links diffuse groups in different nation-states and is fostered by modern communication and transportation facilities and complex production processes.

8. Nation-states are becoming increasingly permeable, that is, subject to external penetration.

9. The loyalties of peoples are increasingly divided among many actors and tend to shift depending upon the nature of the issue.

10. Discontinuities exist which are directly related to the salience of local issues and the level of political development of various regional systems.

In the next chapter we shall turn our attention to an historical example of a nonstate actor whose behavior had important consequence on global politics.

The Nonstate Actor in History:
The Case of *Jacobitism*[1]

FOUR

> To those who are accustomed to regard Jacobitism as a purely insular affair, a disproportionate amount of space may appear to have been devoted to the background of international politics, but my defence is that to understand the Movement properly, it must be viewed in the setting of the general European situation.[2]

Although political scientists are only beginning to recognize the impact that nonstate actors have on world politics, such actors have played important roles in the global system even during those eras when the state was recognized as the sole medium of sovereign behavior. Since men write history to agree with their theoretical predispositions, such actors have often been forgotten or at least not accorded the importance they deserve.

One such nonstate actor was the Jacobite movement which played a pivotal role in the "international" politics of Europe at various times between 1688 and 1746. The origins of Jacobitism date from the "Glorious" or "Bloodless" Revolution in Great Britain during which James II of England, Wales, and Ireland (or James VII of Scotland) was forced from the throne and the Stuart Dynasty ended by the English Parliament. A new relationship between king and subjects was established, based on the "contract theory" of government.

In essence, the Jacobite movement represented the efforts of those who continued to support the claims of James and the Stuarts to the thrones of England and Scotland and who allied with various European states to attain this goal.

1. The authors would like to thank especially A. Rhoda Urie upon whose work this chapter is based.
2. Sir Charles Petrie, *The Jacobite Movement: The Last Phase, 1716–1807* (London, Eyre and Spottiswoode, 1950), preface.

The revolution in 1688 was brought about by Parliament in its resistance to "the Prerogative of the Kings of England, their ancient claim to an undefined residuary power."[3] This prerogative King James wished to use to procure toleration for his fellow Roman Catholics, but "such a policy identified the cause of Roman Catholicism with the cause of despotism in the eyes of a people violently prejudiced against both."[4] Those who supported James and who became the Jacobites upheld the claim of the monarch that he ruled by "Divine right." (It was the doctrine wittily parodied by Alexander Pope as "the right divine of kings to govern wrong."[5]) Those who deposed the king followed John Locke in believing that a state's authority derived from a voluntary contract of its members and that any enfringement of the contract entitled the community to resist that authority.[6]

For all practical purposes the movement ended after 1745 when James's grandson, Prince Charles Edward Stuart, failed in his attempt to lead an army in rebellion against George II. The Battle of Culloden (the last battle fought on British soil) was the bloody termination to the Stuart hopes of restoration. As a sentiment, Jacobitism lingered on in Scotland, but after the failure of "Bonnie Prince Charlie," it had little effect on practical politics.

The Glorious Revolution

At this point a brief historical summary is appropriate. James's reign, which commenced April, 1685, seemed to begin quietly enough. The king, however, took the opportunity provided by an uprising in the western counties in July to begin enlarging the standing army. Although with this action Parliament could have no quarrel, the king's army now included officers whose presence was in violation of the Test Act of 1673. This act prevented anyone from holding a civil or military post or from voting in Parliament without taking both communion as a member of the Church of England and an oath denying the Catholic doctrine of transubstantiation. The stage was set for the struggle to come, in which James endeavored throughout his brief reign to secure the toleration he desired for fellow coreligionists.

The seventeenth century was one of religious struggles on the conti-

3. G. M. Trevelyan, *The English Revolution, 1688–89* (New York: Henry Holt and Co., 1939), p. 64.
4. *Ibid.*, p. 65.
5. Alexander Pope, *The Dunciad*, Book 4, 1. 189
6. Basil Williams, *The Whig Supremacy, 1714–60* (Oxford: Oxford University Press, 2d ed., 1962), pp. 4–5.

nent such as the Thirty Years' War. Apologists for James argue that he was a far-sighted ruler whose belief in religious toleration was far ahead of his time. But the country as a whole saw the king's actions as an attempt to impose the Pope's domination upon England. Spain and France were viewed as extensions of Papal power; the experience of the Spanish Armada was not forgotten, and France was at this time expanding its power in Europe.[7]

The struggle came quickly. Parliament was unwilling to permit officers in the army who did not comply with the Test Act. In contrast, James demanded the power to appoint civil and military personnel, whether Roman Catholic or not. This Parliament would not allow; it refused the king financial support for the army, and in turn the king prorogued Parliament and did not recall it.[8]

Without Parliament, James went his own way. It seemed ominous to England's Protestant majority that the standing army was concentrated each summer on Hounslow Heath for training. In Ireland, which had a separate army, most of the Protestant officers were dismissed and replaced by Catholics. In high places, too, similar changes were taking place. There occurred a "steady trickle of conversions among peers, lawyers, justices of the peace, mayors, place-holders of all kinds."[9] The Church of England was alienated, and a series of confrontations between it and the king took place.

Matters came to a head when, in July, 1688, a son was born to James. Until this time the heirs-presumptive to the throne had been James's Protestant daughters (by his first wife). With the prospect of the perpetuation of a Catholic dynasty, Protestants began to panic. The husband of James's eldest daughter Mary, William of Orange, who was Protestant and had his own claim to the throne through his mother, was now invited to England by a coalition of Protestant political leaders.[10] William had his own interests in the English succession, for with the perpetuation of a Catholic dynasty, he foresaw a period of peace between England and France that would be dangerous to him as Prince of Orange. He feared French expansion that would be a direct threat to his own country of Holland.[11]

In November, 1688, William landed at Torbay. The English gentry rallied to him, and there were desertions from James's own army and

7. Sir Charles Petrie, *The Jacobite Movement: The First Phase* (London: Eyre and Spottiswoode, 1950), pp. 49, 56–57, 60.
8. G. N. Clark, *The Later Stuarts 1660–1714* (Oxford: Oxford University Press, 1934), p. 116.
9. *Ibid.,* p. 118.
10. Trevelyan, *The English Revolution,* p. 101.
11. Petrie, *The First Phase,* pp. 59–60, 63.

court. James unsuccessfully sought a compromise with his enemies and then fled to France. Such a flight was tantamount to abdication.[12]

The Birth of Jacobitism

With James's flight to France, Jacobitism was born. Louis XIV received the exiled king at St. Germain-en-Laye, his chateau outside Paris, and established him there with a pension of 600,000 livres. In January, 1690, the English Parliament declared that "King James II, having endeavored to subvert the constitution of the kingdom by breaking the original contract between king and people . . . has abdicated the government."

Yet, though Parliament might get rid of James, it could not eliminate Jacobitism and the Jacobites (the seventeenth century was not equipped for the kind of efficient purging of opposition which the twentieth has seen). Large numbers of James's supporters remained in England, Scotland, and Ireland. At this time particularly the movement took the form of a government-in-exile. James was a usurped ruler trying to regain the country from which he had been exiled. Until their deaths, James II and his son regarded themselves as the rightful monarchs of Great Britain. They felt no Parliament could take from them the privilege of hereditary succession, whatever theories philosophers might dream up about contract between people and king and whatever revolutionary settlements parliaments might pass.

For the next sixty years the statesmen and rulers of Europe took cognizance of Jacobitism as an influential force. Although the court of the exiled Stuart kings had no territoriality—in fact its venue changed several times from this first refuge at St. Germain to the final one of the Palazzo Muti-Savorelli in Rome (given to James's son in 1718 by Pope Clement XI)—its presence influenced the European scene, in particular the resistance by England and other powers to France's expansionist aims in Europe.

The Anglo-French rivalry that dominated European politics in the eighteenth century and the conflicts that characterized this rivalry, including the War of the League of Augsburg (1688–1696), the War of the Spanish Succession (1702–1713), the War between England and Spain (1718–1720), and the War of the Austrian Succession (1740–1748), were crucial to Jacobite hopes. As long as James was in exile in France, or elsewhere in Europe, the British government could not rid itself of the specter of a Jacobite invasion or coup. Yet when the French king and the English king (or more properly, their respective ministers, Sir Robert Walpole and Cardinal Fleury) were in a state of detente, as they were between

12. *Ibid.*, p. 65.

1717 and 1740 (as a result of the Triple Alliance between England, France and Holland) no French help was given to the exiles. At such moments the exiles had to look to other nations with their own reasons for being displeased with English policies, as was the case of Sweden in 1717 and Spain in 1719.

Thus, after 1688 there existed a situation in which a group of people in one state (the Jacobites) looked towards an external authority (the Stuarts) for salvation and redress from their grievances against their own government. This external authority in alliance with other nation-states endeavored to give them this redress against what it considered illegitimate government and to restore itself to power with their help. The Jacobite court offers an example of a nonstate actor that, when circumstances permit, can ally or come in conflict with sovereign states. It was as if there were a spider stretching its web all over Europe, where the slightest touch on one strand of the web set the whole web quivering. Jacobite agents throughout Europe sought the restoration of the Stuarts to the throne of England.

The foreign policies of the rulers of Europe were bound up with the exiled James II and from 1701 with his son (known to his supporters as King James III of England, Ireland, and Wales and James VIII of Scotland, and to his opponents as the Pretender). One reason that Louis was prepared to shelter James in the first place was that Louis's enemy, William, was on the throne of England and, with the War of the League of Augsburg going on, French troops were fighting in Flanders. When James requested aid to organize an expedition to win back his kingdom, Louis recognized the possibility of occupying William's attention and troops in his newly-acquired kingdom and removing them from Flanders, one of the major theaters of the war.[13] James decided that Ireland would serve as a base from which to reconquer his kingdom since only Ulster had declared for William.[14] From Ireland help could be dispatched to Scotland where, although the Scottish Parliament (as yet independent of England) had recognized William, a number of James's supporters were in arms under James Graham of Claverhouse, Viscount of Dundee.[15]

King Louis gave James a contingent of French troops and money, but in return he demanded Irish regiments to aid him in his war on the continent. While lending James this aid, he also instructed his commanders not to be extravagant with the lives of French soldiers.[16] Thus it appeared that France's main interest in supporting the Jacobite effort was to keep the

13. See Clark, *The Later Stuarts*, p. 161.
14. See above, p. 3, cf. Petrie, *The First Phase*, p. 86.
15. Petrie, *The First Phase*, pp. 80 ff. see also, W. Ferguson, *Scotland 1689 to the Present: The Edinburgh History of Scotland* (New York: Praeger, 1968), pp. 3–4.
16. Petrie, *The First Phase*, p. 94.

English king and his government occupied at home so as to weaken their involvement in the continental theater of war. Indeed, it was a Jacobite complaint that Louis expected them to come out and be slaughtered for their king, just so that Louis could have a diversion in Britain.[17]

In all events the Scottish rising under Dundee failed when the latter was killed at Killiecrankie in July, 1689, so that there was little help to be looked for in Scotland. The war in Ireland lasted until the Battle of Aughrim, 1691, and was finally ended by the Treaty of Limerick. James himself fled to France after his defeat at the Battle of the Boyne in July, 1690.

This initial Jacobite adventure set the pattern for the many later attempts of the Stuarts to regain their throne. The strategy, which involved the rising of Jacobite sympathizers in Britain combined with an invasion by the exiled monarch with the help of foreign (usually French) forces, was pursued throughout the next fifty-five years of Jacobitism. The same pattern revealed itself in all the major Jacobite attempts: those projected for 1691–2 with English supporters, the 1708 attempt which was to have Scotland as its point of rising, the 1715 attempt which turned into the 1715 rebellion, the 1719 attempt, and the 1745 attempt which ended Stuart hopes forever. In large measure the relative success or failure of Jacobite efforts depended upon the state of affairs at any given moment of Anglo-French relations.

In addition to its involvement in Anglo-French politics, Jacobitism had a persistent effect on British domestic and foreign policy. Along with the major risings and expeditions were lesser schemes and plots, most of which never came to fruition or, if they did, were betrayed and their ringleaders apprehended. Yet even these caused a certain amount of political upheaval. There was also a certain amount of intrigue between the exiled court and ministers in high places in the British government, particularly in the early years of James's exile, for there was no certainty until 1714 that James might not be reestablished by Parliament. (It was only in 1714, after the reigns of William and Mary and James's half-sister Anne, that a complete dynastic change took place with the accession of George, Elector of Hanover.) As long as James's relatives were on the throne, intrigue between British ministers, particularly Tory ministers such as the Earl of Oxford and the Earl of Bolingbroke, and the exiled Stuarts at St. Germain was endemic. And at the beginning of James's exile there was scarcely an English minister whom William could trust. Whether for reasons of loyalty or fear for their fates in the event of counter-revolution, most had some contact, at least verbal, with St. Germain.[18]

17. G. H. Jones, *The Main Stream of Jacobitism* (Cambridge: Harvard University Press, 1954), p. 73.
18. Clark, *The Later Stuarts*, p. 126.

Jacobitism: 1690–1701

In the winter of 1691 plans were afoot for the first of the attempts to organize a rising of Jacobite sympathizers in England. In France preparations were going on for an invasion of England under the Comte de Tourville. James meanwhile issued a declaration that was printed and sent over to England, one of the many Stuart declarations in which James and then his son sought to win back their "subjects" to their proper loyalties. However, the invasion failed. Contrary winds prevented Tourville's squadron from meeting its transports, and an Anglo-Dutch fleet won a decisive victory at Cape la Hogue.[19]

Between 1694 and 1697 two more Jacobite plots were hatched in Britain.[20] The second of these, an assassination plot of 1696 against William as he returned from hunting, was linked to a planned uprising of Jacobite supporters with another invasion plan. The pattern is there. The uprising was organized by some English Jacobites of the minor gentry. Jacobite agents brought them commissions from James to muster soldiers, and they found recruits who promised to rise when the invasion occurred. Meanwhile, France supplied arms, soldiers and money, and James promised to come as leader with a French nobleman under his command, this time the Marquis d'Harcourt.[21] On this occasion, as on several subsequent occasions, the invasion force did not even leave France; for the plot against William was discovered, and it became obvious that the planned uprising would not take place.

In 1697 the War of the League of Augsburg was concluded by the Treaty of Ryswick. The peace proved a major setback to the Jacobites. By the terms of the treaty, Louis was forced to recognize William III as *de facto* king of Britain. England thus obtained the recognition of her new monarchy that had become a major objective during the war.[22] The treaty, however, also took cognizance of the Jacobites. Under its terms James's wife, Queen Maria Beatrice, was to be paid a jointure (fixed on her marriage by Act of Parliament at 50,000 pounds) for her own and her husband's maintenance. France, theoretically, was thereby relieved of the burden of supporting James. (In fact, the jointure was never paid since Britain kept demanding as a condition that James be removed from St. Germain. Then in 1702 the War of the Spanish Succession broke out between England and her allies and France, so it was not paid then either.)[23]

19. Jones, *Main Stream of Jacobitism*, pp. 23–28.
20. *Ibid.*, pp. 41–42.
21. *Ibid.*, pp. 46–48.
22. Clark, *The Later Stuarts*, p. 168.
23. Jones, *Main Stream of Jacobitism*, p. 53.

By this time the influence exerted by the exiled Jacobite court was emerging in a definite form. St. Germain-en-Laye was a little kingdom on alien soil. Several prominent Roman Catholics, fearing the revolution, had preceded James into exile, and with their aid he set up his own court almost immediately. It was modeled as closely as possible on the court of Whitehall from which James had been exiled.[24] The court had its own ministers, the first minister being given the title of Secretary of State, and it was known in France as "The Court of England." From St. Germain it conducted diplomatic relations with France and her allies, including the Vatican, Austria, and Spain.[25]

James's son carried on the traditions of his father. He was, in fact, a stickler for all forms and ceremonies at his little court, whether it was at St. Germain, Bar-le-Duc, Bologna, Urbino or Rome, which he made as like the English court as possible. English was the language and English food was served.[26] From this court the exiled kings, *de jure* kings of Britain, issued declarations to their subjects, sent agents to them, granted commissions in their name, and granted titles. Their supporters in return embarrassed the British government at intervals. For example, the Jacobites in Parliament made a point of voting in opposition to the government and published their own pamphlets. Other Jacobites rioted on the anniversary of James's birthday, drank toasts to "the king over the water," and in other symbolic ways kept the flame of Jacobitism burning.[27]

Another aspect of the eighteenth century on which Jacobitism exerted an influence transcending national boundaries was religion, as an institution rather than as a spiritual force.[28] Although James's dispute had been with the Church of England, four hundred of the clergy would not acquiesce in his overthrow. Since they had sworn on becoming members of the clergy of the Church of England to give allegiance to James II as their rightful king, they could not, they felt, swear allegiance to William as demanded by Parliament.

Known as *Non-Jurors,* these clergy continued loyal to James. In 1690 they were deprived of their benefices, and the schism began in the Church of England. The Non-Jurors regarded themselves as the true church in England. In Scotland, the Episcopal Church as a whole remained loyal to James and continued to pray for the Stuarts until 1788. Although the Church in the American colonies was under the jurisdiction of the Bishop

24. Petrie, *The First Phase,* p. 109.

25. See Jones, *Main Stream of Jacobitism,* pp. 19–20, 53.

26. H. Tayler, ed., *The Jacobite Court at Rome in 1719,* Scottish Historical Society, 3rd ser., vol. 31 (Edinburgh: Edinburgh University Press, 1938), pp. 115 ff. Also, P. Miller, *James* (New York: St. Martin's Press, 1971), pp. 262, 295.

27. See Jones, *Main Stream of Jacobitism,* pp. 43, 92–93.

28. Petrie, *The First Phase,* pp. 69 ff.

of London, it, too, remained loyal to James, and, when the colonies won their independence, it was to the Non-Juring Episcopal Church of Scotland that the first bishop of the American Episcopal Church came for consecration in Aberdeen. The Quakers in Pennsylvania also remained Jacobite adherents, and during the War of the Spanish Succession, Louis XIV gave orders to the French privateers not to attack their ships.

The influence of Jacobitism also could be seen in the European armies of the eighteenth century. When James retreated from Ireland in 1690, he retained an army of some size that was not disbanded until the Treaty of Ryswick in 1697. Thereafter its soldiers and officers were incorporated in the French, Spanish, and Neapolitan armies, so that fighting all over Europe were men whose political loyalties rendered them exiles and mercenaries; there was no place for them at home. These mercenaries were mainly Irish though they were joined after 1715 and 1745 by large numbers of Scots as well. In addition, England was deprived of the services of such skilled generals as the Duke of Berwick (James's half-brother who became a French citizen and one of Louis' generals), and ultimately of the French marshals MacDonald and MacMahon, the Prussian generals Keith and Mackensen, the Russian general Barclay de Tolly, and the Spanish general O'Donnell, Duke of Tetuan.[29]

The Second Phase: 1701–1715

The status of the exiled Stuarts was altered in 1701. In July, William persuaded Parliament to pass the first legal barrier against the return of the Stuarts in the Act of Settlement. Mary had died in 1695, and William had not remarried. He had no heirs, so that on his death the throne was to pass to Mary's younger sister, Anne. The last of Anne's surviving children, however, died in July, 1700. William thus had Parliament pass an act by which on Anne's death the throne would go to the nearest *Protestant* heir, in this case the Princess Sophia of Hanover, a granddaughter of James I, and not revert to the Catholic Stuarts.

James II died in September, 1701, and his son was immediately proclaimed King James III of England, Ireland and Wales, and VIII of Scotland. His accession to the throne (notwithstanding William's Act of Settlement) was publicly acknowledged by Louis, an act that enraged the English Parliament and provoked it into passing an Act of Abjuration and Attainder against the thirteen-year-old James. The Act accused him of high treason for calling himself *King of England* and made it a treasonable offense to correspond with him or to remit him money.[30] William himself

29. *Ibid.*, pp. 103–105.
30. *Ibid.*, p. 117.

died the following March (thrown from his horse which had stumbled on a molehill, so that thereafter Jacobite toasts were proposed to "the little gentleman in black velvet").

With the accession of Queen Anne and the presence of her nephew as *de jure* king across the water in France, Jacobitism took on a different tinge. It was no longer the case of a government-in-exile, a king trying to get back the throne he had lost. Now there was a king who had never had a kingdom, and who, as matters turned out, would set foot in the realm he claimed only once for a period of two months. Nevertheless, there continued the same pattern of projected risings in order to take advantage of domestic unrest in Britain, with an invasion by French forces.

Franco-Jacobite relations became close once more with the outbreak of the War of the Spanish Succession in 1702. The war largely resulted from French claims to the vacant Spanish throne, claims that were opposed by England, Holland and Austria in the name of the balance of power.

During the war, James remained in touch with many of the nobility and gentry of England and Scotland, while at the same time he waited for Louis to decide when the moment had come for another invasion that would divert British attention from the Netherlands. There was much coming and going among the court at St. Germain and England and Scotland. Several abortive schemes ensued. In 1703 Lord Lovat proposed that, if Louis would send 5,000 troops, 12,000 Scotsmen would "come out" for King James. Another scheme was proposed by Lord John Drummond in 1704. In the following year, Louis concluded that he could finally spare the troops for an expedition to Britain. He dispatched one Colonel Nathaniel Hooke, an Irish Catholic officer in the French service, to several of the nobility in Scotland. They proved, however, unwilling to move at this juncture because they feared that Louis intended to make a diversion in Scotland for no other purpose than the recall of English troops to deal with it and that the Jacobite leaders would thus bring out their men to be massacred for no good reason.[31] In view of the later history of French involvement with the Jacobites, they were probably correct in their suspicion. Yet another uprising in Scotland was planned for 1706 in the agitation that accompanied talks aimed at forming a union of the Scottish and English Parliaments.

This proposed union was prompted in part by England's fear of Jacobitism. In spite of William's Act of Settlement, many people expected that on Anne's death James would return and the succession would, in fact, be determined by civil war. Scotland had not been included in the Act of Settlement, but England wished to ensure that she would adhere to it.[32]

---

31. Jones, *Main Stream of Jacobitism,* p. 71. See pp. 67–71 for an account of those schemes.
32. *Ibid.,* pp. 73, 92.

Thus on May 1, England and Scotland were united as Great Britain, and Sophia, Princess of Hanover, and her Protestant successors became heirs to the crown of the united kingdom.

The 1706 uprising came to nothing, and a more serious venture was planned in 1708. Owing to the union, there was much discontent in Scotland. Louis also found himself hard-pressed by English forces under Marlborough in the Low Countries.[33] The French king thus provided James with five battleships, twenty privateers, 5,000 troops, and arms and money. The Pope also offered money if the landing were successful. Maréchal de Matignon was placed in charge of James's army, and the Chevalier de Forbin was the naval commander. One Charles Fleming was dispatched to Scotland to arrange signals between the French fleet and the Scottish Jacobites. James himself drew up a declaration to Scotland and set off for Dunkirk.

The attempt, however, failed. The British government, warned of the rising, hastily recalled troops from Flanders and alerted the fleet. The French ships overshot the Firth of Forth where they were supposed to land, and by the time they sailed back Admiral George Byng was there. With no signals from shore Forbin decided to make for home without attempting a landing. The British government now enacted repressive measures. Habeas Corpus was suspended, and there were many arrests in Scotland.[34]

Between 1710 and 1714, the last years of Anne's reign, the extent of Jacobite sympathy remaining in Britain was manifested in intrigue by high ministers of the Crown, particularly among the Tory ministers who came to power in 1710. The new Tory government included Jacobite sympathizers at the highest levels, including Robert Harley as Chancellor of the Exchequer and Henry St. John, Earl of Bolingbroke, as Secretary of State. The Tories, many of whom were Jacobites, wanted an end to the war as did Louis.[35] Such personages as Harley, Bolingbroke, the Duke of Ormonde, and even the Duke of Marlborough were prepared to consider inviting James to the throne after Anne's death. Yet, despite considerable correspondence and intrigue, nothing practical was accomplished for the *de jure* king. In April, 1713, the Treaty of Utrecht was concluded by which Louis XIV renounced the Pretender. James was forced to leave France and retired to Bar-le-Duc in Lorraine. Ultimately, the Tory government made no attempt to change the succession, and George I of the Protestant House of Hanover assumed the throne after the death of Anne in August, 1714.[36]

The change in dynasties was not accomplished, however, without resistance, and the ensuing unrest in Britain culminated in what is known

33. Petrie, *The First Phase*, p. 124.
34. *Ibid.*, pp. 125–128, see also, Jones, *Main Stream of Jacobitism*, pp. 78–82.
35. P. Miller, *James*, p. 130.
36. See Jones, *Main Stream of Jacobitism*, pp. 86–92 for an account of the intrigues and pp. 96–98 for the cabals even by the bedside of the dying queen.

as *The Fifteen* or the *First Jacobite Rebellion*. Much of the unrest was caused by King George's exclusion of the Tories from office and their replacement by anti-Jacobite Whigs. Leading Tories such as Harley, Henry St. John, the Duke of Ormonde, Lord Lansdowne, and others resumed their correspondence with James and began plans for an uprising. Gradually a reaction in England set in against the Hanoverian succession when it became obvious that the Whigs were dividing the spoils among themselves.[37] Some Jacobite gentry joined the Duke of Ormonde in his plans for a rebellion in the western counties, always well-disposed to James in England; in Scotland the Earl of Mar began to gather the Highland chiefs and the loyal nobility; there were riots and disorders throughout the country.[38] However, the flight of Henry St. John, Viscount of Bolingbroke, from England in March, 1715, after hints of impeachment for his dealings with James, followed by that of the Duke of Ormonde in July, left the English Jacobites leaderless.

In France, James was determined to seize the opportunity offered by the death of Anne and the unpopularity of George's actions. It seemed too good an opportunity to let pass. Although Louis XIV could not help him directly (after the long war he had little money, and the arms left by his reduced army could not be conveyed to James because of the efficient British spy system in Paris), he helped him indirectly and persuaded his nephew, the king of Spain, to give James a large sum of money. James received additional funds from the Pope, the Duke of Marlborough, supporters in England, and the Duke of Lorraine (who on Louis' death in September, 1715 became Regent of France for the young Louis XV). As in previous cases, James's strategy was to combine an invasion with a local uprising. The Earl of Mar in July requested arms for 20,000 men. In addition, Jacobite negotiations were underway with Sweden and Spain for money and arms.[39]

The rebellion failed. No foreign troops or arms were forthcoming. The Duke of Ormonde's flight in July, 1715 had left the Jacobites in the western counties not knowing what to do. The British government learned through its ambassador in Paris in July of plans for the uprising, and Admiral Byng was sent to watch the French channel ports. New regiments were added to the standing army, and garrisons were established in Bath and Oxford, known Jacobite towns. Those suspected of plotting with Ormonde, including six members of Parliament and two peers, were arrested, and, though Ormonde attempted to land in Cornwall, he did not do so when he learned of the arrests.[40]

37. *Ibid.,* p. 100.
38. Petrie *The First Phase,* pp. 154–59.
39. Jones, *Main Stream of Jacobitism,* pp. 106–8.
40. Miller, *James,* pp. 186, 190; Petrie, *The First Phase,* pp. 175–89; for an account of Mar's activities, also pp. 194–99.

Although the projected uprising in the western counties thus came to nothing, the rebellion went on in the north of England and Scotland. In September the Earl of Mar raised the Stuart standard at Braemar and managed to assemble an army of 16,000. An indecisive battle was fought at Sheriffmuir in November between Mar and the Duke of Argyll who had been sent against him with a small government force. On the same day as Sheriffmuir, the English Jacobites of the northwest, reinforced by a body of Lowland Scots and a detachment of Highlanders, were defeated at Preston in northern England.

James did go to Scotland, arriving at Peterhead on New Year's Day, 1716. By then it was too late. Mar's army was gradually drifting apart and was being pursued by a reinforced government army under General Cadogan. James thus returned to France in February, only to find that the Regent, the Duc D'Orléans (who had winked at his presence in France in September, hoping that the rebellion might succeed) now sought a detente with England. Louis XV, his ward, was not healthy, and, if he died, the French crown, in accordance with the terms of the Treaty of Utrecht (1713), would devolve on the Regent. Philip V of Spain, however, as lineal descendent, still had not given up hope of one day succeeding to the French throne. Orléans was therefore anxious to have England as an ally in order to secure for himself the rights promised by the treaty. James could not remain in France but had to proceed to the Papal state of Avignon.

The Final Phase of Jacobitism

The death of Louis XIV and the accession to power of the Duc D'Orléans as Regent for the young Louis XV marked a major change in France's relationship with the Jacobites, a change that illustrates how the Anglo-French interstate rivalry affected James and how he in turn exerted an influence upon it.

Louis XIV himself had sacrificed James to family interests by the Treaty of Utrecht, which had forced James to take up residence in Lorraine, but he had conveniently overlooked the Stuart's presence in France during preparations for the 1715 Rebellion. After Louis's death in September, 1715, the Regent too had overlooked James's presence in case his expedition should succeed. But, now that it had proved a failure, he was ready to sacrifice James. Hence, when a draft treaty was spoken of by England in which that state was prepared to guarantee Orléans right to the French throne in return for his guarantee of the Protestant succession of George I and his ousting of the Pretender from the Papal state of Avignon, Orléans was prepared to agree. As far as England was concerned, Avignon was still too close to home for comfort. As a result of English alliances, most of Europe was closed to James. He was thus forced to retire to Italy to the city of Bologna.

Since the Jacobites could look for no help from France after the Anglo-French treaty of November, 1716 (a treaty which became the Triple Alliance of 1717 when the United Provinces joined), James was forced to turn to other rulers who were willing to use him for their own ends against Britain and the House of Hanover. Charles XII of Sweden appeared to be such a candidate in 1717, and this was not the first time that Swedish assistance had been considered.[41] Charles had his own reasons for a grudge against the House of Hanover in its capacity as a German principality rather than as the ruling house in England.[42] Such an alliance was also welcomed by James because association with Protestant Sweden might remove the Jacobite reputation of being Papal servants.

A rather elaborate plot was thus concocted between the Jacobites and Swedish diplomats in London and the Hague. The plot was, however, exposed, and it made a good excuse for English participation in the Baltic against the Swedes. The Jacobites persisted, unsuccessfully seeking the cooperation of Sweden and Russia.[43] They appeared to be clutching at any straw. But the death of Charles XII of Sweden in 1718 put an end to their hopes of aid from this quarter.

Spain was the next power to which James turned. The chief adviser to the Spanish queen, Giulio Alberoni, wished to be a cardinal and desired the aid of a sponsor in Rome. James had considerable influence with the Pope and was prepared to use it for a *quid pro quo*. Alberoni gained his cardinal's hat, and James was promised aid when the opportunity arose. The opportunity arrived in 1717 when Spanish claims in Italy precipitated a war against Britain, France, Holland, and Austria.

Alberoni saw advantages in aiding James. He gave him a squadron of troops under the Earl of Ormonde to land in England and a second force under the Earl of Mareschal to land in Scotland. Meanwhile, one James Keith was sent to Avignon and Paris to collect the Jacobite exiles who had been there since the failure of 1715. Once again, however, the British government learned of the plot, this time from French sources, and sent forces into the west country where the landing was expected. As events turned out these troops were unnecessary. Setting out in March, 1719, Ormonde's force ran into a storm which destroyed the ships and forced the disembarkation of the troops. The Scottish force did land and joined up with the returned exiles who had collected some clansmen. But they were

41. Jones, *Main Stream of Jacobitism*, p. 125; Miller, *James*, p. 157.
42. Petrie, *The Last Phase*, p. 18; Miller, *James*, p. 223.
43. Petrie, *The Last Phase*, pp. 19–20; also Basil Williams, *The Whig Supremacy 1714–60*, 2d ed. (Oxford: The Clarendon Press, 1962), p. 174.

defeated by the government at Glenshiel. Thus ended the abortive Spanish expedition to Scotland to aid the Pretender.[44]

With the failure of this attempt and the reestablishment of peace in Europe in 1720, Jacobite hopes dimmed again. Nevertheless, the movement remained the cloud on the horizon which Sir Robert Walpole, who came to power in 1721, kept in his sight while he pressed for peace in the years that followed. Walpole believed that peace and prosperity could do the most to establish firmly the Hanover dynasty on the British throne. Peace was his way of dealing with the menace of Jacobitism and its implied threat to British stability. It proved to be a successful policy.[45]

James was now in exile in Rome, but his adherents kept up their scheming, their plots, their espionage, their contacts with the loyal or disaffected in Britain, always watching for signs of unrest at home and for any upset in the European balance of power, and casting around for help from Britain's enemies. The Jacobite schemes of 1722 and 1725 demonstrated their vigilance.

In 1720 England was rocked by a disastrous financial panic as a result of the bursting of the "South Sea Bubble."[46] The aftermath of the ruin of so many speculators was a period of great discontent with the government, and the Jacobites hoped to turn this hostility to their advantage. With the encouragement of James in Rome, both the Earl of Orrery in the House of Lords and Willian Shippen in the House of Commons made as much political capital as possible out of the failure of the South Sea scheme, hoping that the people could be stirred to rebellion and that James could come with troops and lead an invasion. The Scottish Jacobite leaders, including Lockhart, the Earls of Eglintone, Wigton, Lord Balmerino, and others, were also organized for such a possibility. James, in fact, issued commissions to several of the English Jacobite leaders in anticipation of the attempt. Casting about for aid, certain Jacobites now made approaches to Tsar Peter of Russia. Such assistance, however, was not forthcoming, and Walpole's system of alliances placed James in a difficult position.

Meanwhile, a widespread conspiracy led by the Bishop of Rochester to seize power when King George left the country on one of his frequent trips to Hanover was detected before it could be carried out. The Jacobites apparently planned to smuggle groups of officers into the country, win over the troops, and stir up election riots by playing on the mood of the people. But Walpole's system of peacetime alliances again paid off. Cardinal Dubois, the French foreign minister, revealed the plot to the British gov-

44. For an account of the Spanish intrigues and the 1719, see Jones, *Main Stream of Jacobitism,* pp. 137–42; and Petrie, *The Last Phase,* pp. 20–23.
45. Williams, *The Whig Supremacy,* pp. 182, 184–85, 186.
46. See *ibid.,* pp. 176–79 for an account of the activities of the South Sea Company and its failure.

ernment (for French intelligence easily obtained information of the activities of the Jacobite agents in Paris), and stern repressive measures were taken against the suspected ringleaders in England. The Habeas Corpus Act was suspended for a year, and the Duke of Norfolk, Lord North, and the Earl of Orrery were confined to the Tower of London; Christopher Layer, a lawyer, was arrested, as was Atterbury, the Bishop of Rochester, the leading Jacobite non-juring clergyman. Moreover, even had the plot not been detected in England, with England's system of alliances it had become almost impossible for James to leave Italy on an expedition to Britain, because any country through which he travelled would have reported his movements to the British government.[47]

Another opportunity seemed to present itself to the Jacobites in 1725. Europe was thrown into turmoil when France cancelled the engagement of the king to the Spanish Infanta. Out of this crisis grew two alliances, one involving Spain and Austria and the other France, Britain, Holland, and Prussia. Under these circumstances, Britain feared that Spain would again support James.

British fears were not groundless. There were definite plans for an expedition to Scotland which was in a state of unrest as evidenced by the Malt Tax Riots. However, at this moment, James's private affairs undid everything. A dispute erupted between James and his wife Maria Clementina, daughter of John Sobieski of Poland. Spain took the side of Clementina when she retired to a convent, and both Spain and the Pope suspended the pensions they paid to James. Thus, a bizarre domestic quarrel cost the Jacobites yet another opportunity.[48]

There was still plenty of intrigue but little major Jacobite activity in the remainder of the period of Walpole's peace. Jacobite hopes were roused when the War of the Polish Succession erupted in 1733, for any such disturbance in Europe always contained the possibility of some advantage to them. But Walpole managed to keep Britain neutral, and Jacobite activity remained dormant until the long period of peace for England, which Walpole had preserved so carefully, came to an end in 1739.

First, Britain was forced into the War of Jenkins' Ear with Spain in 1739, much against the will of Walpole who feared a Franco-Spanish alliance.[49] In the following year, the War of the Austrian Succession broke out. Although France and England were not officially at war until 1744, their troops fought one another as auxiliaries of Charles Albert of Bavaria and Maria Teresa of Austria respectively. Indeed, George II himself com-

---

47. See Jones, *Main Stream of Jacobitism,* pp. 144–45, 146, 150–52; and Petrie, *The Last Phase,* pp. 41–46.
48. Jones, *Main Stream of Jacobitism,* pp. 161–62, 165, 167.
49. Williams, *The Whig Supremacy,* p. 213.

manded an army of British, Hanoverians, and Hessians that defeated the French in the Battle of Dettingen in 1743.

As a consequence of Anglo-French hostility, Louis XV reverted to the policy of his father. If he could create a diversion in Britain, he could get British troops removed from the Low Countries, and what better way to create a diversion than by promoting the aims of James. With Europe in turmoil, Jacobite hopes had again risen and were stronger than they had been for a while. In addition, the exiled court found itself in a rare condition of prosperity owing to the death of John Sobieski who willed a large legacy to his grandsons, James's sons, Prince Charles and Prince Henry. James listened with interest to reports from his agents of Scottish Highlanders ready to rise up for him. Although the reports of these agents were misleading as was that of Louis's equerry whom he sent to England to see the state of Jacobite affairs there, they were believed, perhaps because it suited Louis to believe them.⁵⁰

Plans were set afoot. A Scottish Jacobite agent was sent to Rome to see if Charles would lead a French expedition. (James had already indicated that he considered himself too old for such an activity.) Leaving Rome secretly under the pretense of a hunting trip, Charles, who had been named his father's Regent, made his way to Avignon, then to Dunkirk where an invasion force was being assembled. But luck was against the expedition. (One is tempted to say as usual. The Stuarts were never fortunate with their weather.) Storms wrecked the fleet, and, what the storms did not destroy, British Admiral Sir John Norris did.

War was formally declared between England and France in March, 1744, but Louis postponed the expedition indefinitely. That might have been the end of the affair had not Charles taken matters into his own hands. Growing weary of waiting in Paris for the French king to decide to mount another expedition, he gathered a small force and procured two French privateers. These vessels, *Le Du Teillay* and *L'Elisabeth* were to carry him and seven companions to Scotland. There, Charles believed, his supporters, the Highland chiefs with whom his agents were in touch, would declare for him. Since England and Scotland were denuded of troops who were all in Flanders fighting the French, it seemed too good an opportunity to miss. Once he had led out his supporters, Charles thought, Louis would send help.

The failure of this adventure, which became known as the Second Jacobite Rebellion, destroyed Jacobitism as a political force. On the way Charles's escort ship was so badly damaged by a British naval vessel that it had to return to Brest. Charles sailed on, however, and landed in Scotland

50. The agents overestimated the readiness of the Highland chiefs to come out in rebellion, and Louis's equerry took too seriously the empty boasting of some English gentlemen at a hunting-meet.

with his retinue on July 25, 1745. There he was met with dismay by the Highland chiefs who had expected large-scale French military and financial assistance. Nevertheless, the prince won them over and initially led them to a series of striking victories. His forces captured Edinburgh, defeated the few troops that the government had available at Prestonpans, and marched into England where they reached Derby in December. The invasion of England caused panic in London.[51] Meanwhile, in October, the French and Jacobites concluded a treaty under which Louis was to assist Prince Charles and send him troops.[52] In compliance with the treaty, Lord John Drummond landed in Scotland in November with 1,100 Scots and Irish soldiers from French regiments.

By invading England Charles hoped to link up with an expedition that was being assembled in France under his brother, Prince Henry. However, weather prevented its sailing with Louis's 11,000 additional reinforcements. Moreover, the English army that had been recalled from Flanders continued to arrive in London between September and December. England was bitter that she should have been "stabbed in the back" by rebels while her troops were fighting abroad. At Derby, Charles found himself ringed in by three English armies; no word had reached him from France, nor had the English Jacobites come to his support. Thus he retreated to Scotland where his army fought an indecisive battle at Falkirk Moor in January, 1746. On April 16, 1746, the Jacobite army was crushed at Culloden by the Duke of Cumberland, second son of King George.

Only Louis XV profited from the uprising. The diversion created by Charles in Britain kept most of the English troops occupied for several months. The only French help that reached the Stuarts was 1,100 men and some supplies. The pattern of French aid to keep the English occupied at home had paid off more than either Louis XIV or Louis XV could have dreamed.

Prince Charles remained in Scotland for six months after his defeat at Culloden, lurking in the Highlands and the western islands with many daring escapes from Cumberland's soldiers. When he finally escaped to France, he was much feted in Paris; that is, until the French king wanted peace with England. By the Treaty of Aix-la-Chapelle signed in 1748 Charles was forced to leave France. Unlike his father, he did not go gracefully, and Louis had to arrest him first.[53]

For all practical purposes, Jacobitism was now dead. It lapsed into sentimental memory, carried on by little old ladies who, over teacups in

51. See, for example, R. Chambers, *History of the Rebellion, 1745–6* (Edinburgh: Chambers, 1869), p. 192. The day is known as Black Friday in the annals of British history.
52. W. B. Blaikie, *Itinerary of Prince Charles Edward Stuart*, Scottish History Society 23 (Edinburgh: Edinburgh University Press, 1897), p. 20.
53. Miller, *James*, p. 185.

Edinburgh, talked of the days when they had seen "Bonnie Prince Charlie," in songs of nostalgia and regret and wistful longings for a return of the Prince who would one day "come again." Charles did not stop intriguing, but the Elibank Plot and Charles' secret visit to London in 1753 were but wild chimerical schemes that find their fitting place in Sir Walter Scott's *Redgauntlet* rather than in political history.

Nonstate Actors in Three Regional Systems

PART II

Introduction[1]

We have suggested that the state-centric model is at best an historical anomaly and at worst a serious distortion of past and present global politics. It lacks both the descriptive and explanatory power to serve as the basis for meaningful research. Mainly, this is because of its exclusive concern with the "international" or interstate aspects of global politics. In its place we have substituted a model termed the complex conglomerate system. This model emphasizes the often critical roles played by nonstate actors that have the resources to influence nation-states and that align and come into conflict with them.

In Part II, we shall apply the complex conglomerate model to examine three regional systems—the Middle East, Latin America, and Western Europe—over a period of twenty-five years. Of particular interest to us is nonstate behavior in these systems. Hence, we have attempted to analyze not just nation-state behavior but "actor" behavior generally. We want to know, first, who (what actor or actors) did what (type of behavior) to whom (what actor or actors) in each of the regional systems over time. To this end, we have gathered "event" data for each region as reported in the *New York Times,* which has been demonstrated to be a reliable source for this kind of data. For each event that involves behavior (i.e., "action"), we

1. This brief introduction is a simplified discussion of the methods we have used to compile and analyze the data that serve as a basis for several of the following chapters. The advanced reader is strongly advised to refer at this juncture to the Appendix for additional details. Others may wish to omit the Appendix entirely.

have coded an *initiator,* the *behavior* of the initiator, a *target* of the behavior, and an *indirect target* (if any).[2]

Since it was physically impossible to review all relevant events in these regions over twenty-five years, 360 dates were selected at random for each region as a representative sample of the entire quarter-century (the representative character of the sample was tested and verified). The twenty-five years were divided into three time periods for each region, beginning and ending with watershed events that scholars agree were of major significance, and 120 random dates were coded for each period (*time slice*).

For coding purposes, actors were identified specifically by name and categorized as individuals, intrastate nongovernmental, governmental noncentral, nation-state, interstate nongovernmental (INGO), or interstate governmental (IGO). Later, in analysis, numerous specific actors were grouped into still other inductive categories. For example, Arab guerrilla groups in a single state might be classified as Intrastate Arabs, and corporations operating in several countries as Multinational Corporations. Each actor was also classified as either a nation-state or a nonstate actor (*nostac*).

We coded the behavior of actors in descriptive terms and in each instance further classified it as cooperative act (cooperative deed), cooperative word (verbal cooperation), participation, conflictful word, or conflictful act. Participation is a special category of behavior that does not evidence significant cooperative or conflictful "affect," or reach the "commitment" level of either word or deed. For example, the mere presence of a government representative at a general international conference would fall into this category. We also distinguished a separate category of violence within the broader category of conflictful act because of its obvious importance to world order. The categories thus combine two dimensions of

2. "Not only do events characterize the activity of any foreign policy actor, the generic term covers almost all foreign policy behavior in which a state or other actor might engage. . . ." Charles F. Hermann, "What Is a Foreign Policy Event?", in Wolfram F. Hanreider, ed., *Comparative Foreign Policy: Theoretical Essays* (New York: David McKay, 1971), p. 301. The logic behind the use of such data is explained by Charles McClelland:

> (A) country's external "performance characteristics" in dealing politically with a wide variety of situations and with other countries are conceived to be made up of combinations of "primary actions" that we categorize explicitly. These combinations of primary actions are expected theoretically to fit together with those of other countries in patterns of interaction. The purpose of the research is to discover if these theoretically expected characteristics and patterns make regular appearances in international relations. (Charles A. McClelland and Gary D. Hoggard, "Conflict Patterns in the Interactions Among Nations," in James N. Rosenau, ed., *International Politics and Foreign Policy* rev. ed., New York: Free Press, 1969, p. 712.)

COMMITTMENT AFFECT	"PARTICIPATE"	"DESIRE" "INTENT"	"ACTION"
Cooperation	PARTICIPATION	WORD COOPERATION	COOPERATIVE DEEDS
Conflict		WORD CONFLICT	CONFLICTFUL DEEDS

Figure 4

behavior—*affect* and *commitment*.[3] Affect refers to the disposition of the actor, and commitment refers to the level of resources that the actor invests in its action.

The basic units of analysis are dyadic combinations, that is, actor and direct target treated as a single unit. Therefore, a single event involving three direct targets is considered as three separate dyads (one for the actor with each target).

The coded data were crosstabulated and then subjected to a statistical technique known as factor analysis. Given the numbers and categories of actors and all the types of interactions among them, the task of analysis was obviously exceedingly complicated. The data set at this point looked a bit like "alphabet soup." Factor analysis helped us to sort out the alphabet soup into a smaller number of understandable "factors" or patterns of relationships among similar variables.

With the crosstabulated data and factor analysis in hand, we have sought the answer to the same series of questions about each regional system:

1. What were the major issues or "superissues" that dominated the politics of such region for the entire twenty-five-year period?

2. For each time slice, what was the rank order of importance of each superissue?

3. For each time slice, what were the specific issues that constituted each superissue?

4. For each time slice, how did different actors align and ally on different superissues?

5. For each time slice, to what extent were the superissues related to one another?

6. For each time slice, which actors were the most active and which were the most salient targets?

7. For each time slice, which actors were the major sources of conflict and violence (system *disrupters*) and which were the major sources of cooperation (system *supporters*)?

3. See Stephen A. Salmore, *National Attributes and Foreign Policy: A Multivariate Analysis,* unpublished Ph.D. dissertation, Princeton University, 1972.

8. For each time slice, what percentage of all dyads were cooperative, conflictful, and violent?

9. What were the answers to questions 2–8 for the quarter-century as a whole?

Our findings are presented in Chapters 5, 7, and 9 for the Middle East, Latin America, and Western Europe respectively. It should be emphasized that the narrative material in these chapters is derived from the event data themselves. The events described in text represent a sample of all the events that occurred. These chapters *do not,* and *are not intended,* to provide complete narrative histories. We compare the regions with one another in Chapter 11.

The regional system chapters are interspersed with three chapters (Chapters 6, 8, and 10) that are not directly derived from the data set. These chapters focus on particular nonstate actors that are central to the politics of the region analyzed in the preceding chapter in each case: for the Middle East, Palestinian guerrilla and liberation groups; for Latin America, the multinational corporation; and for Western Europe, the institutions of the European Economic Community.

The Middle East:
An Explosive Crossroads

FIVE

The area of the world that stretches from the coast of North Africa north of the Sahara eastward to the frontiers of Iran has had for centuries a unique political significance in global politics. In the western world it became known as *the Middle East* because of its historical and geographic role as the route from Europe to Asia. It links (or separates) three continents, Europe, Asia, and Africa, and dominates four major and increasingly important strategic bodies of water, the Mediterranean Sea, the Red Sea, the Persian Gulf, and the Arabian Sea.

Perhaps it is "an astonishing fact that the Christian, Jewish, and Islamic religions should have their origins in so small an area."[1] Yet, paradoxically, the Middle East has over and over again been the site of fierce clashes between uncompromising and messianic cultural heritages. Consider, in this connection, the history of Rome and of the Crusades. For political and geographic reasons, great empires fought across the area, and with the coming of European imperialism and global supremacy the region became the "lifeline of the British Empire," linking the metropole with the British bastions of India and Singapore and British colonial possessions in Black Africa.

During the twentieth century, the geopolitical significance of the region has increased immeasurably. The Suez Canal, which was opened towards the end of the previous century and which connected the Mediterranean and Red Seas, has become one critical focus of conflict. It was a major objective of General Rommel's armies which moved rapidly across North Africa during World War II in an attempt to sever the British Empire. The discovery of vast resources of petroleum, vital to modern

1. Wilfrid Knapp, *A History of Peace and War 1939–1965* (New York: Oxford University Press, 1967), p. 141.

technology, has added still another important dimension to the politics of the region.

In the last two decades, attention has been focused on the Middle East for an additional reason. Since the death of the Soviet dictator, Stalin, the arenas of probable conflict between the Soviet Union and the United States have been gradually limited, to such an extent that the East-West conflict has been transformed into detente. The frontiers of postwar Europe have been stabilized and institutionalized; American participation in the Vietnam War has ended, and the United States has retired from the Asian mainland. However, the Middle East has remained the one area where the possibility of a direct and catastrophic confrontation between the two superpowers has increased, and on at least three recent occasions, the Suez invasion of 1956, the Six-Day War of 1967, and the Arab-Israeli War of 1973, a collision between superpowers appeared ominously near. As Howard Sachar declares:

> It is accordingly the Eastern Mediterranean that has become the Balkan powder keg of the latter twentieth century. As in that earlier zone of tension, too, the fate of peace has been influenced not merely by the decisions and judgments of local regimes—in this case, Jerusalem, Cairo, Damascus, and Amman—but by the governments of major powers.[2]

The region has proved fertile ground for superpower penetration since it has been persistently divided along several dimensions, particularly those separating Arab from Jew. This major and dangerous division, and others, are the product of an historical train of events that began during World War I when the European Allies expelled the Ottoman Turks from the Arab lands. In their enthusiasm to wrest the region from Turkish control, Britain and France made a series of vague and often contradictory promises of self-government and independence to both Arab and Zionist leaders whom they wished to enlist as allies. But the European powers reneged on their promises to both Arab and Jew after the War, divided the region among themselves, and created a series of artificial state boundaries in the process. The most obdurate problem that grew out of this policy was the clash between Zionism, which generally established itself in the British Mandate of Palestine, and the displaced Arabs, who viewed the intrusion of European Jews with suspicion and hostility and as an alien culture in their midst. In addition, the artificial boundaries imposed by the powers fostered and at the same time thwarted various movements towards pan-Arabic unity and institutionalized conflicts among Arab rulers who sought regional unification and organization on their own terms. Arab nationalism was fueled by the colonial occupation and by the near-defeat of the Euro-

2. Howard M. Sachar, *Europe Leaves the Middle East, 1936–1954* (New York: Alfred A. Knopf, 1972), p. xv.

pean "protectors" during World War II. Moreover, the Arab-Jewish problem was exacerbated by the large-scale immigration of European Jews fleeing from the holocaust that the War brought to Europe. The Arab-Jewish dilemma was finally transformed and perpetuated by the establishment of the State of Israel in Palestine in 1948.

Our purpose in this chapter is not to review these or subsequent events in detail but rather to place the issues and actors in the Middle East since 1948 into a systemic perspective and to make some sense out of the complex web of interactions that constitute the regional system. We have divided our analysis into three time periods: 1948–1956, 1956–1967, 1967–1972. The divisions are based on the watershed events of the Suez War and the Six-Day War. As we shall see, each of the periods has a distinctive character of its own.

We found six superissues that appeared throughout the more than two decades we subjected to analysis. These are the *Arab-Israeli superissue* which included Arab-Israeli interaction either directly or indirectly; the *Colonial superissue* which related to European colonialism in the Middle East and North Africa; the *Inter-Arab superissue* which concerned the divisions among Arab regimes and the conflicting efforts of different regimes to exert influence over one another; the *Regime Stability superissue* which involved the survival of specific regimes threatened from within and without; the *Palestine superissue* which focused directly on the fate of the Palestinian Arabs; and the *Superpower superissue* which referred to the penetration and assertion of influence in the region by the United States and the Soviet Union, often in a Cold War context.

The Middle East 1948–1956:
Israeli Consolidation and Colonial Conflict

The *Arab-Israeli* and *Colonial* superissues dominated the Middle East between the creation of Israel and the Anglo-French invasion of Egypt in 1956. Each was more than three times as important as the next most salient superissue, *Regime Stability,* in terms of the amount of behavior for which it accounts ("explained variance"). Conflicts among Arab regimes and conflicts over Palestine were muted, and superpower involvement in the region remained at a low level. In sum, the Middle East between 1948 and 1956 was an arena of unremitting conflict between the Arab states and the newly-created State of Israel, and between the retreating European colonial powers and the impatient and dissatisfied Arab nationalists. The Cold War had not yet extended into the region and did not do so until 1955 when the Baghdad Treaty was signed and the Soviet Union began to supply Egypt with arms.

Table 1.   Ranking of Superissues by
Explained Variance 1948–1956*

1. Arab-Israeli	(1.48)
2. Colonial	(1.46)
3. Regime Stability	(0.47)
4. Inter-Arab	(0.37)
5. Palestine	(0.33)
6. Superpower	(0.20)

*Each time a superissue appears on a factor
it is given the "score" of the amount of the
total variance explained in the factor analysis by that factor. The "scores" are then
summed for each superissue. See Appendix,
pp. 310–11.

The *Arab-Israeli* superissue appeared on nine of the eleven factors
and involved 42 percent of the issues in the period. These issues included
guerrilla terrorism against Israel sponsored by Egypt from the Gaza Strip,
continuous conflict along the Jordanian and Syrian frontiers with Israel,
and controversy over the unyielding problems of control of the Jordan
River and the status of the city of Jerusalem. Nonstate actors played a key
role in this superissue. Guerrilla groups organized in Egypt and elsewhere
continued to harass Israel, which triggered Israeli reprisals particularly in
the Gaza Strip and on the West Bank of the Jordan River.

Indeed, guerrilla or *fedayeen* provocations were cited as a major
cause of Israel's decision to join France and Britain in the autumn of 1956
in a tripartite effort to cripple Egypt and depose President Gamel Abdul
Nasser. Their action followed upon Nasser's nationalization of the Suez
Canal, an act viewed in London and Paris as a devastating blow to their
strategic and prestige positions in the Middle East. The Anglo-French-
Israeli alliance was a complementary one, that is, each partner joined for
its own reasons. Israel, for its part, invaded the Sinai both in order to
secure the passage of Israeli ships through the Gulf of Aqaba and to
annihilate the guerrilla bases in the Gaza Strip. The Israeli policy of large-
scale retaliation for guerrilla raids had been adopted during the previous
year when David Ben-Gurion once again had become prime minister of the
Jewish State.

During the period under discussion Israel found dependable allies in
various American-based Jewish groups that sought to place political and
moral pressure both upon the United States government and the United
Nations and that provided direct political, material, and moral assistance
to the young Jewish State. The behavior of these intrastate nongovernmental actors exemplified one aspect of the complex conglomerate system,
the alignment of nonstate actors with selected governments on certain

*Table 2.   Major American-Based and Transnational Jewish
Groups Supporting Israel, 1948-1956*

American Zionist Council
American Jewish Committee
United Jewish Appeal
World Zionist Congress
The Jewish Agency
American Jewish Committee on Jews in the Moslem World
Rabbinical Council of America
National Council of Jewish Women
Hatsofeh
American Hebrew Congress
Mizrachi
Israeli Bond Organization
Hebrew Immigrant Aid Society
B'nai B'rith
Hadassah
American Joint Distribution Agency
American Committee for Judaism
Council of American Jewish Businessmen

issues. Some of the Jewish groups involved are shown in Table 2. As Table 2 suggests, the activities of the Jewish organizations were varied and overlapping, and during the early years of Israeli independence they proved to be staunch backers of the Zionist cause and important elements in the consolidation of Israel.

Still another major nonstate actor during this period was the United Nations and its agencies. The United Nations sought to separate the protagonists and to identify and force a cessation of the innumerable and persistent violations by both sides of the 1949 armistice agreements that had halted the first Arab-Israeli war. In this effort, the Israel-Jordan Mixed Armistice Commission played a particularly active and sensitive role, often condemning Israeli reprisals and in turn becoming the object of Israeli wrath.

The factor analysis revealed an intricate pattern of alignments on this superissue. Israeli support came from nonstate actors, the United States, and certain European governments. Arab support consisted largely of the Arab states themselves as well as nonstate Arab groups. Several major nation-states were actively neutral.

The second major superissue, *Colonialism,* appeared on eight of the eleven factors. During the period this superissue touched on such specific questions as revolution in Algeria, Moroccan and Tunisian independence, Egyptian nationalization of European interests in the Suez Canal, conflict over the British base in Egypt which was finally surrendered by treaty in 1954, and Libyan independence. In fact 36 percent of the issues had a Colonial content. At the center of the superissue were French efforts to

Table 3.   Arab-Israeli Cleavage 1948-1956: Major Coalitions*

Israeli Friends	Neutrals	Arab Friends
Israel	France	Egypt
United Kingdom	USSR	Jordan
United States	Canada	Syria
West Germany	United Nations	Intrastate Arabs
Intrastate Jewish	Saudi Arabia	Interstate Arabs

*To determine coalitions, we designated certain targets as "pivots" around which the superissue revolves. These "pivots" are underlined in the tables. All actors are scored in terms of their behavior towards the "pivot(s)." See Appendix, p. 311.

quell rising Arab nationalism in North Africa and British attempts to cope with Egyptian nationalism. Nonstate actors were crucial participants, particularly in North Africa where the French government and French-supported local administrators found themselves under attack by nationalist groups and political parties such as the Algerian National Liberation Front (FLN). The prominent role of nonstate actors was partly due to the facts that neither Morocco nor Tunisia attained full independence until 1956, and no indigenous independent government took power in Algeria until 1962.

A second set of colonial questions revolved around the issues raised by both Egypt's nationalization of the Anglo-French-owned Suez Canal and the Anglo-French-Israeli invasion of Egypt in 1956. Nationalization of the Canal was announced by Egypt's President Nasser in the city of Alexandria on July 26. This act proved to be a major turning point in Middle Eastern politics. It set the stage for the final retreat from the area by the two European colonial powers, and it provided an opportunity for American and Soviet entry into the region. Nasser's initiative was apparently triggered by the abrupt cancellation of an Anglo-American offer to finance the proposed Aswan High Dam. The nationalization was greeted in London and Paris as an intolerable affront to their prestige and political position in the area. For its part, the French government also viewed Nasser as an ally of the Algerian nationalist movement. An alliance was formed between France and Britain that later included Israel, the purposes of which were to oust the Egyptian leader and secure the canal. For Israel the crisis seemed an opportunity to tie the Arab-Israeli issue to the colonial question.

A climax of sorts was reached when Israeli forces invaded the Sinai Desert in the autumn of 1956 and did not halt until they stood on the shores of the canal. Under the transparent guise of protecting the canal, Anglo-French forces then landed at Suez, although not in time to prevent its being closed by the Egyptians' sinking of ships. Ultimately, under the combined pressure of the United States and the Soviet Union, the three were forced into a humiliating retreat, and a United Nations Emergency Force (UNEF) was dispatched to the canal. In effect, the event heralded the demise of Anglo-French influence in the Middle East and their replacement by the superpowers, the United States and the Soviet Union.

As the coalitions suggest, the major colonial powers (Britain and France) were by no means isolated. They found support among several of their fellow members of the North Atlantic alliance as well as several regional actors. Saudi Arabia's "procolonial" stance, for instance, testified to the abiding conservatism of that country's monarchy as well as to its close ties with the European consumers of petroleum. Israel's similar behavior, on the other hand, reflected a fundamental *quid pro quo* in which Israel supported European colonial pretensions in return for European support of Israeli survival. Regardless of Israeli motives, the Israeli position on this superissue accounts in part for Arab accusations that Israel was created as an "alien European island" in an Arab sea.

Of the lesser superissues, *Regime Stability* questions appeared on six of the factors. At least five regimes were threatened by internal or external forces. Yemen was rent by tribal conflict; the conservative monarchy of Jordan's King Hussein was threatened by pro-Nasser groups; Moroccan independence was followed by war in the Rif Mountains with Berber rebels; Israel was challenged by Arabs residing in that country; and in Egypt the monarchy of King Farouk was overthrown in 1952, and the regime of colonels which succeeded him was attacked by various extremist groups such as the Moslem Brotherhood. The Inter-Arab superissue appeared on four factors as did the *Palestine* question.

Finally, the *Superpower* superissue appeared on only three factors and accounted for little variance in behavior. In fact, as we have noted, the Middle East was for much of this period outside the main axis of East-West hostility. From about 1948 to 1954 regional questions were a "sideshow" for the superpowers, particularly the Soviet Union. Not until after the death of Stalin in 1953 did Soviet policy toward the Middle East begin to change, and Soviet penetration of the area did not begin in earnest until

Table 4. Colonial Cleavage, 1948–1956: Major Coalitions

Procolonial	Neutral	Anticolonial
United Kingdom	United States	Egypt
France		Morocco
Canada		Intrastate Arabs
West Germany		
Israel		
Syria		
Saudi Arabia		
Local North African Colonial Authorities		

Table 5. Superpower Alignments, 1948–1956

Pro-American	Neutral	Pro-Soviet
United States	Libya	USSR
United Nations	Jordan	
Canada	Intrastate Jewish	
France	Interstate Jewish	
West Germany		
Egypt		
Lebanon		
Israel		
Saudi Arabia		

1955 when the American-supported Baghdad Pact was being organized. Thus, for the period as a whole, the Soviet Union remained isolated, and actors behaved either as American friends or neutrals in the Cold War. Indeed, one particularly interesting neutral was American-based and transnational Jewish groups whose major interest was in the Arab-Israeli question. These groups were prepared either to support or to oppose the United States depending on whether or not American policy corresponded with their primary objectives. For much of the period, the United States continued to dominate the United Nations, a dominance that was most blatently revealed during the Korean War. The United States could count on the loyal support of its North Atlantic partners as well as the major state actors in the Middle East which were divided on other questions.

The relationships among the superissues themselves provide another means of emphasizing many of the points that have just been made. The higher the coappearance scores are among superissues, the greater their interdependence. Thus, the *quid pro quo* between Israel and the major colonial powers, France and Britain, is reflected in the high degree of coappearance between the first two superissues. In other words, when *Arab-Israeli* issues appeared on a factor they were usually accompanied by those of a colonial nature, and vice versa. Furthermore, the *Arab-Israeli* superissue, dominant in the period, exhibited a fairly high correspondence with all of the other superissues. The exception was the *Superpower* superissue, which showed a low coappearance with the remainder of the superissues, largely owing to the lateness of Soviet penetration of the region. The most surprising finding was the pervasiveness of the *Palestine* superissue. Even though it ranked next to last among the superissues for the period, the *Palestine* question provided an undercurrent to the other superissues, particularly the *Arab-Israeli* and *Regime Stability* superissues, and, when it surfaced, it did so in conjunction with the latter superissues.

As we turn from the pattern of issues that dominated the Middle East from 1948 to 1956 to the behavior of particular actors, the pivotal role of nonstate actors becomes even more impressive. Actors other than nation-

Table 6. Middle East Superissue Coappearance, 1948–1956*

	I	II	III	IV	V	VI
I. Arab-Israeli	–					
II. Colonial	.82	–				
III. Inter-Arab	.62	.67	–			
IV. Regime Stability	.67	.57	.40	–		
V. Superpower	.33	.22	.29	.44	–	
VI. Palestine	.62	.50	.50	.60	.57	–

*Coappearance indicates the degree to which superissues are related to each other. This is shown by the appearance of *different* superissues on the *same* factors. A coappearance score is determined by dividing the number of times two superissues *do appear* on the same factors by the number of times they *might appear* together. See Appendix, p. 311.

states were responsible for initiating 22 percent of the total activity in the period (based on dyadic analysis), and they were the targets of 27 percent of the activity. Tables 7 and 8 depict the twenty most active actors and the twenty most salient targets in the region during the period.

Tables 7 and 8 reveal considerable information about actors in the Middle East between 1948 and 1956. Of the twenty most important actors, seven were *nostacs*. Similarly eight of the most important targets were *nostacs*. Israel and Egypt, not unexpectedly, were both the focal actors and targets in the region. Israel ranked particularly high on both dimensions because its activity was distributed among several Arab foes, and at the same time it was a concentrated target of Arab behavior. France was the third most important actor and the fifth most important target, reflecting both its deep involvement in North Africa and the efforts of Moroccans, Tunisians, and Algerians to obtain independence. The United States was also an important initiator but significantly was an even more important target, as was the United Nations. Their very activity in the Middle East made them prime targets for various protagonists, who sought their support.

Among nonstate actors the most active were Arab independence groups in North Africa and guerrilla groups in Egypt and Jordan. These groups were also important targets, as were individuals acting on their own behalf. It is notable that financial institutions and corporations such as the Arabian-American Petroleum Company (ARAMCO), the Manufacturers Hanover Bank, and British Petroleum were significant targets.

The importance of nonstate actors becomes even clearer when we look only at "disruptive" or conflictful behavior. Of the ten actors which were most consistently disruptive, four were nonstate.[3] When we identify

3. It should be noted that disruptive-supportive scores do not reflect the total amount of conflictful or cooperative behavior but a ratio of one type to the other.

Table 7. The Most Active Initiators in the Middle East,
1948-1956*

	Israel	(206)
	Egypt	(186)
	France	(114)
(nostac)	United Nations	(99)
	United States	(70)
	United Kingdom	(63)
(nostac)	Intrastate Arab	(60)
	Jordan	(59)
	Syria	(58)
	Saudi Arabia	(48)
(nostac)	Intrastate Jewish	(43)
	Lebanon	(43)
(nostac)	Government Noncentral	(37)
(nostac)	Individuals	(33)
	West Germany	(30)
	USSR	(30)
(nostac)	Other Nonstate Actors	(26)
	India	(26)
(nostac)	Interstate Jewish	(25)
	Iraq	(24)

*Activity scores are calculated by multiplying the total number of an initiator's deed actions by 3, verbal actions by 2, and participative actions by 1 and then summing these. See Appendix, pp. 311-12.

Table 8. The Most Salient Targets in the Middle East,
1948-1956*

	Israel	(274)
	Egypt	(213)
	United States	(157)
(nostac)	United Nations	(153)
	France	(144)
	Saudi Arabia	(97)
(nostac)	Individuals	(81)
	Canada	(79)
(nostac)	Intrastate Arab	(65)
	Jordan	(64)
(nostac)	Government Noncentral	(62)
	United Kingdom	(58)
	Syria	(37)
	West Germany	(31)
(nostac)	Financial Groups and Corporations	(30)
	Lebanon	(29)
(nostac)	Political Parties	(24)
(nostac)	Other Nonstate Actors	(24)
(nostac)	Interstate Arab	(21)
	Iraq	(20)

*Salience scores are calculated by multiplying the number of deed actions received by a target by 3, verbal actions by 2, and participative actions by 1. These are then summed. See Appendix, pp. 311-12.

Table 9. Disruptive-Supportive Behavior, 1948-1956*

Disrupters		Supporters	
Intrastate Arab	(−48)	United States	(+40)
Other Nonstate Actors	(−18)	Saudi Arabia	(+40)
USSR	(−16)	United Nations	(+38)
Yemen	(−15)	Egypt	(+36)
Interstate Arab	(−9)	Israel	(+34)
Government Noncentral	(−9)	India	(+26)
Jordan	(−9)	West Germany	(+24)
Bulgaria	(−3)	Intrastate Jewish	(+23)
Turkey	(−2)	Ecuador	(+20)
Iceland	(−2)	Japan	(+20)
France	(−2)		

*Cooperative and participative behavior is assumed to be supportive of the system, and conflictful behavior is assumed to be disruptive. Disruptive-supportive behavior is calculated by subtracting conflictful activity scores from cooperative-participative activity scores. See Appendix, pp. 312-13.

an actor as disruptive, we do *not* mean that it was responsible for most of the conflictful actions but rather that its pattern of behavior was largely in this direction. Indeed, the two most disruptive actors were Intrastate Arab groups of the sort mentioned earlier as well as Other Nonstate actors, a category which included students from the University of Cairo and the Egyptian Student Union.

Our finding concerning the important role which nonstate actors, particularly Arab nationalists and terrorists in North Africa and Egypt, played in generating conflict is dramatized by looking merely at those actions which were violent in nature. Of all the violent acts committed in the Middle East in our sample between 1948 and 1956, 44 percent were committed by nonstate actors and 28 percent by intrastate groups, largely Arab, alone. In fact, intrastate Arab nationalists and guerrillas in Algeria, Morocco, Tunisia, Egypt, and Yemen were far and away the most violent actors in the system with Israel, France, and Egypt following, in that order.[4]

In summary, between 1948 and 1956 the Middle East was dominated by questions involving *Colonialism* and by the *Arab-Israeli* conflict. The old Arab proverb "the friend of my enemy is my enemy" did not necessarily hold true, since alignments shifted from superissue to superissue and foes in one sphere became collaborators in another. Finally, although non-

4. The reader should note that on the basis of event data we are unable to determine the magnitude of such violence, that is, the number of people hurt or property destroyed by the violent acts. Also, we have excluded from our analysis the two major wars of 1956 and 1967 because of the extensive and repetitive coverage of events in the region by the press at the time they occurred.

state actors were important initiators and targets of all kinds of behavior, they were particularly crucial in generating conflict and violence during the first period.

The Middle East 1956–1967:
The Nasser Era

In the period between the invasion of Egypt in 1956 and the eruption of the Six Day War between Israel and its Arab neighbors in June, 1967, issues in the Middle East became increasingly complex. The outstanding characteristic of the period was the rapid intensification of *Inter-Arab* cleavages based for the most part on a rivalry between "radical" and "conservative" regimes. A process of rapid political and ideological change had begun, bringing in its train a host of new divisions to the region. No longer were all Middle Eastern Arab states dominated solely by conservative monarchs or European colonialists. As a result, rivalry among Arab states reached its highest level yet as different leaders dueled and parried one another in the name of contrasting versions of Arab unity. Much of this conflict pivoted around Egypt and its charismatic leader, Gamal Abdul Nasser, who had emerged from the Anglo-French invasion of Suez as a hero of the Arabs and a challenge to other Arab leaders. Nasser had been one of the colonels who had overthrown King Farouk in 1954, and he had gradually eclipsed his colleagues to become the leader of the regime in Cairo. In addition, the period was characterized by the emergence of Israel as clearly the preponderant military power in the region, but this was coupled with the progressive political isolation of that state and its growing dependence upon the United States. As a consequence of increasing Soviet penetration of Egypt, Syria, and Iraq, and of increasing American support for Israel, questions involving the superpowers increased dramatically. The Cold War descended with full force upon the area. The period also witnessed the apex of *Colonial* questions, particularly in North Africa, as the French agony reached a climax, and the Europeans were finally driven out.

During these years, the *Inter-Arab* superissue became the most significant, closely followed by the *Arab-Israeli, Colonial, Regime Stability,* and *Superpower* superissues. The issue of *Palestine* remained relatively dormant. Thus five of the superissues acquired virtually equal importance in regional politics, a situation which contrasted with the comparative simplicity of the previous period when only two superissues dominated the region.

The leading superissue, *Inter-Arab* cleavages, appeared on ten of the thirteen factors and was involved in 35 percent of the issues. Some of the

Table 10. Ranking of Superissues by
Explained Variance, 1956–1967

1	Inter-Arab	(1.75)
2.5	Arab-Israeli	(1.19)
2.5	Colonial	(1.19)
4	Regime Stability	(1.14)
5	Superpower	(1.06)
6	Palestine	(0.21)

specific issues here were Nasserite penetration of Jordan and Lebanon (which culminated in the promulgation by the United States of the Eisenhower Doctrine in 1957 and Anglo-American landings in those countries the following year), Syrian-Egyptian interaction in the creation and ultimate dissolution of the United Arab Republic, Egyptian-Saudi Arabian conflict in the Yemeni civil war (during which Egyptian forces, supporting a radical regime, used poison gas against supporters of the deposed Yemeni royal family), Syrian-Turkish and Iraqi-Iranian border conflicts, Egyptian-Saudi Arabian competition over the fate of the British protectorate of Aden, and Iraqi attempts to seize oil-rich Kuwait. During the decade, alignments on this superissue shifted as specific regimes were overthrown or changed sides. Nonstate actors remained relatively unimportant to this "nation-state" superissue, although specific activities by Palestinian refugee and liberation groups and by Saudi Arabia's Yemeni royalist allies were obvious exceptions. Despite the complexity of the superissue a pattern of alignment did emerge: Saudi Arabian isolation in conflict with Egypt and a surprisingly large group of Egyptian supporters, including the United States and the Soviet Union which were competing for influence in Egypt.

More interesting, perhaps, than the adversaries on this superissue was the large bloc of "neutrals," many of which one might have expected to take sides. Syria, for instance, was a neutral because of the several changes that took place in the regime in Damascus. Its behavior was sometimes pro-Nasser and other times anti-Nasser. Arab IGO's, mainly the Arab League, sought to mediate conflicts among Arab regimes while Interstate Arab

Table 11. Inter-Arab Alignments, 1956–1967

Pro-Nasser	Neutral	Anti-Nasser
Egypt	Syria	Saudi Arabia
Iraq	United Nations	
Yemen	United Kingdom	
USSR	Kuwait	
United States	Israel	
Yugoslavia	Arab Intergovernmental	
Finance	Organizations	
	Interstate Arabs	

groups, notably the Palestinian organizations, sought to play one side off against the other in order to further their own interests.

As we have suggested, Nasser's Egypt was the pivot on which this superissue turned. Although Saudi Arabia was the only actor to oppose Nasser consistently, its isolation was more apparent than real. Saudi Arabia found allies on *specific* issues depending upon the threat which Nasser's pretensions seemed to pose to established regimes and other groups in the region. Even Syria and Iraq, generally close Egyptian allies, opposed Nasser on several occasions. At other times, Saudi Arabia was aided by oil-producing countries such as Kuwait. In fact, the anti-Nasser coalition in part depended upon an affinity between those states which produced petroleum and sought security for their profitable operations and those actors, particularly industrialized states, which required dependable petroleum resources.

The *Arab-Israeli* superissue, though still quite important, was involved in only 24 percent of the specific issues that arose and appeared in ten of the thirteen factors. It was manifested in such persistent questions as Jordanian-Israeli, Egyptian-Israeli, and Syrian-Israeli frontier incidents, and large-scale American assistance to Israel. Nasser's preoccupation with pan-Arab unity and his deep involvement in *Inter-Arab* issues such as the Yemeni civil war accounted in large measure for the decreased importance of the superissue. In effect, Israel was only one of several sources of major concern to Egypt at this time. In addition, Arab regimes, particularly Egypt's, succeeded in large measure in curbing the activities of unauthorized terrorists and Palestinian guerrillas and in this way lowered the incidence of Israeli reprisals. However, the superissue re-emerged with striking rapidity in 1967 when President Nasser ordered out the United Nations Expeditionary Force (UNEF) that had been stationed in the Sinai Desert between Egypt and Israel after the 1956 war. Simultaneously, Nasser closed the Gulf of Aqaba to Israeli shipping, thereby rendering the Israeli port of Elath useless and nullifying the only tangible Israeli gain that remained from the 1956 war. As one analyst observes: "When it was closed, the Israelis became fundamentally dissatisfied with the status quo. . . . In a least one respect, the Israeli calculations were like those of the Austrians in 1914 and the Japanese in 1941: The status quo had become so undesirable that military action seemed preferable."[5] On June 5, 1967 Israel launched a preemptive attack on Egypt, destroying much of the Egyptian air force on the ground and winning a crushing and decisive military victory which brought them to the shores of the Suez Canal in a mere six days.

5. Richard N. Rosecrance, *International Relations: Peace or War?* (New York: McGraw-Hill, 1973), pp. 246–47.

Table 12. *Arab-Israeli Cleavage, 1956–1967: Major Coalitions*

Israeli Friends	Neutrals	Arab Friends
Israel	France	Egypt
United States	USSR	Syria
West Germany		Jordan
Argentina		Lebanon
Turkey		
Other Intergovernmental Organizations		

Several aspects of this new pattern of coalitions are notable. In the first place, Israel was no longer firmly backed by the United Kingdom and still retained the support of only two major actors, the United States and West Germany. In retrospect, we see the first indications of future Israeli isolation. On the other hand, Intra- and Interstate Arab groups no longer appeared as major enemies of Israel. This is accounted for largely by their relative inactivity in this time period, an inactivity which stood in vivid contrast to their behavior in the previous period and in the period beginning after 1967.

During the second period, the *Colonial* superissue remained very important although somewhat less so than earlier. Between 1956 and 1967, it was involved in some 24 percent of the specific issues and appeared on eleven of the thirteen factors. Two major sets of issues emerged on the superissue—those concerning French North Africa and the European-Egyptian controversy over the Suez Canal.

During these years, France's North African dilemma had degenerated into a protracted civil war in Algeria. The questions of Morocco and Tunisia were resolved when these two countries received their independence in 1956. However, they thereafter became "sanctuaries" for Algerian rebels and nationalists who were able to flee across Algeria's borders after conducting military operations and could operate with relative impunity from Moroccan and particularly Tunisian border areas. As a result, several incidents ensued during the period entailing French "hot pursuit" of Algerians into these neighboring states as well as French bombing of suspected rebel concentrations across the borders. In France itself increasing instability marked the governments of the Fourth Republic when each showed itself equally incapable of resolving the frustrating and expensive problem of Algeria. In Algeria local French administrators and the French army began to behave more independently of Paris. Finally, in 1958, confronted by the threat of insurrection on the part of its own army, the French government of Pierre Pflimlin stepped down and invited Charles de Gaulle to come out of retirement and pick up once more the reins of government. De Gaulle's assumption of power and the subsequent demise of the Fourth Republic were enthusiastically greeted by both the French army and French settlers in Algeria who perceived any concessions by Paris to the Algerian nationalists as constituting "treason." But between 1958 and 1962 their enthusiasm waned and turned to odium as it became clear that de Gaulle was determined to permit Algerian independence. Indeed, before the drama could be completed de Gaulle himself was confronted by a second revolt on the part of the French army in Algeria, and his authority was challenged by the terrorism of the OAS (*Organisation de l'Armée Secrète*).

The second set of *Colonial* issues centered on the resolution of problems that had been created by the invasion of Suez at the end of the previous time period. These included the final withdrawal of the invaders from the area, the entry of a U.N. peacekeeping force, and the dredging of the canal in order to make it navigable once again.

Nonstate actors were particularly relevant to the *Colonial* superissue. In North Africa, the Algerian nationalists, especially the FLN, and the French settlers and local officials, including the terrorist organization, OAS, played key roles, both opposing French policy for different reasons. In the settlement of the Suez crisis, the United Nations provided a "cover" for Anglo-French withdrawal from the canal and thereby afforded the two countries a graceful path of retreat. For the period as a whole, the coalitions on the superissue were as shown in Table 13.

A fourth major superissue, *Regime Stability,* appeared on six factors and was involved in 19 percent of the specific issues. This superissue revolved around major threats to four regimes in the region: Jordan, Lebanon, Iraq, and Yemen.

In Jordan the regime of King Hussein was threatened by Palestinian refugees as well as by pro-Nasser elements. It was buttressed by both the United States and Great Britain. Lebanon was also threatened by supporters of Egypt's President Nasser, and an internal split developed that threatened to destroy that country's delicate confessional system. Ethnically divided between Christians and Moslems, Lebanese political stability depended upon these two groups' sharing political power and Lebanese ability to remain neutral in the thorny quarrels of the region. In addition, Lebanon, defended by only a small and poorly-equipped army, sought to remain aloof from Arab-Israeli hostilities. In 1958, 1963, and again in

Table 13. Colonial Cleavage, 1956–1967: Major Coalitions

Procolonial	Neutral	Anticolonial
United Kingdom	Egypt	Yemen
France	Tunisia	Intrastate Arabs
Jordan	Morocco	Secret Army
United Nations	Local North African	Organization
	Colonial Authorities	(OAS)

1964, Lebanese neutrality was threatened and the country was rent by the threat of civil strife. (Virtual civil war finally did engulf the country in the summer of 1975.) During this period, the gravest threat occurred in the summer of 1958 when a rising of Moslems and Druses under Saib Salam, Kamal Jumblatt, and Rashid Karami menaced the government of President Camille Chamoun. Chamoun called for and received American assistance in the form of marine landings on the beaches of Beirut.

Iraq, which had consistently followed a pro-British and pro-Western policy and had been the Arab anchor of the Baghdad Pact, fell victim to a bloody coup d'état in July, 1958 that took the lives of King Faisal II and the country's leading statesman, Nuri al-Said. Brigadier General Abdul Karim Kassem, the leader of the coup, governed as head of a left-wing regime until he too was killed in early 1963 in a coup that brought to power a military regime headed by Generals Abdul Salam Araf and Abdul Rahman Araf. This regime was also overthrown some years later. For much of the period Iraq was racked by insurrection on the part of an ethnic minority, the Kurds, who demanded self-determination for Kurdistan. (The Kurds are actually to be found in Iran, Turkey, and the Soviet Union as well.) War broke out between Iraq and the Kurds in 1961. A ceasefire was reached in February, 1964, but fighting resumed in April, 1965. In June, 1966 the Kurds accepted in principle a peace plan, but there was no final settlement at this time. (In fact, the Kurdish rebellion in Iraq did not finally end until March, 1975 when the government of Iran agreed to cease aiding the uprising.)

In Yemen, a series of abortive risings against the absolutist and theocratic rule of the Imam Muhammad al-Badr culminated in September, 1962 in the overthrow of the regime by army officers led by Colonel Abdallah al-Salal. The new revolutionary republican regime proceeded to establish close ties with Egypt's Nasser. Continued resistance to the new government by royalist followers of the Imam led to civil war in which the royalists were supported by Saudi Arabia and the republicans by Egypt. The civil war continued until late 1968. Indeed, the Yemeni civil war became a test of strength between the "progressive" Nasser and the "conservative" Saudis.

Nonstate actors were, of course, very significant in this superissue. Ethnic groups such as the Iraqi Kurds and the Lebanese Druses pointed up the potentially explosive nature of subnational separatism in the region, as well as the disparity between "nation" and "state" in several Middle Eastern countries.

The fifth major superissue, *Superpower* penetration, became markedly more prominent in the second period. It appeared on eight of the factors and was involved in some 21 percent of the issues which arose. In effect, the region, which had previously avoided the main consequences of the East-West confrontation, was now exposed to heated Soviet-American competition. Soviet-American penetration and rivalry made itself felt across the full spectrum of Middle Eastern issues. As we have seen, both powers supported Nasser at the time of the Suez invasion and sought to supplant the European colonialists as they retired from the region. The United States emerged as Israel's leading supporter; while the Soviet Union provided increasing material, moral, and political support to the Arabs, particularly Egypt, and the foundation of an Egyptian-Soviet alliance was laid. In addition, the United States consistently assisted conservative regimes threatened by internal and external difficulties, particularly those of Jordan and Lebanon. The pattern of alignments on the *Superpower* question is revealing. It suggests that the Soviet Union was no longer isolated in the region and that the United States was no longer receiving the unquestioned backing of its European allies in the Middle East. In this way, it reflected the general decay of world bipolarity and the loosening of postwar alliances that was beginning at the time.

Superissue coappearance scores indicated the virtually equal importance of the first five superissues and the increasing complexity of regional politics. *Superpower* penetration was very closely related to the *Arab-Israeli* cleavage. Israel became increasingly dependent upon American support, while the Soviet Union provided aid for various Arab clients. Moreover, both of these superissues were associated with *Inter-Arab* cleavages as well as with the remaining *Colonial* issues. On the one hand, the superpowers sought to augment their influence by taking sides in these quarrels, while on the other, propaganda battles between various, and often changing, Arab regimes were couched in terms of anticolonialism and fervor for the "Holy War" or Jihad against Israel.

Nation-state preponderance, especially reflected in pro- and anti-Nasserite visions of the Arab world, virtually eliminated the *Palestine* question during this period. Yet, despite its surface quiescence in the Middle East, the *Palestine* superissue managed to correspond to the other superissues of the period, particularly the *Arab-Israeli* and *Regime Stability* questions. A new and more politically aware generation had begun to mature in the squalid refugee camps in Jordan, Syria, and Lebanon.

Table 14. Superpower Alignments, 1956–1967

Pro-American	Neutral	Pro-Soviet
United States	Algeria	USSR
Israel	Yemen	Egypt
Jordan	United Nations	Iraq
Lebanon		
Syria		
Tunisia		
Morocco		

Table 15. Middle East Superissue Coappearance, 1956–1967

	I	II	III	IV	V	VI
I. Arab-Israeli	–					
II. Colonial	.76	–				
III. Inter-Arab	.86	.82	–			
IV. Regime Stability	.75	.59	.71	–		
V. Superpower	.88	.74	.74	.71	–	
VI. Palestine	.57	.40	.53	.60	.50	–

The relationship among the major superissues had thus changed markedly. This is not surprising in that the *Arab-Israeli* and *Colonial* superissues had dominated the first period but not the second. Instead, *Superpower* penetration, *Inter-Arab* divisions, and *Regime Stability* emerged as important factors in the Middle East, with Egypt under Nasser playing a catalytic role. Moreover, it was in part due to the emergence of a popular and ambitious regime in Egypt under the leadership of the charismatic Nasser, a regime more stable than most in the context of the region, that nonstate actors played a reduced role in the Middle East during this time.

Nonstate actors were less significant between 1956 and 1967 than they had been before. They were responsible for initiating 21 percent of the action dyads in the period and were targets of 24 percent of the activity. Tables 16 and 17 show the most active and most salient actors and provide evidence that some major changes occurred in the politics of the region. Six of the most active units were *nostacs*. Behavior on the part of such inter-governmental actors as the Arab League, the Three-Nation Commission on Yemen, and the Suez Canal Users' Association were more prominent than in the first period. Intrastate Arab groups ranging from the ethnic minorities of the Kurds and Druses to nationalist and terrorist groups such as the FLN and the Secret Army Organization in Algeria remained important initiators and targets.

The overall reduction in nonstate significance seems a result of two critical factors. The first of these is that the period was dominated by the highly successful pan-Arabic politics of Egypt's President Nasser. Egypt, which became both the leading initiator and target, succeeded in attaining an unprecedented position of dominance in the Arab world and even in channeling through Cairo or containing "irregular" Arab activity, for example, guerrilla raids against Israel. During much of the period Arabs believed that Nasser would be able to resolve the question of Israel on Arab terms and avoided recourse to "unauthorized" behavior. Nasser's enormous increase in prestige after 1956 had the general effect of increasing the legitimacy of established Arab regimes, notably that of Egypt, in the struggle with Israel. The second major factor involved in the reduction

*Table 16.   The Most Active Initiators in the Middle
East, 1956–1967**

	Egypt	(126)
	United States	(120)
	Israel	(75)
	Iraq	(64)
	Saudi Arabia	(55)
	Morocco	(54)
	France	(47)
	United Kingdom	(45)
	USSR	(43)
	Syria	(43)
(nostac)	United Nations	(42)
(nostac)	Intrastate Arab	(37)
(nostac)	Individuals	(35)
(nostac)	Arab Intergovernmental Organizations	(29)
	Algeria	(27)
	Jordan	(27)
(nostac)	Interstate Arab	(25)
	Lebanon	(25)
	Tunisia	(23)
(nostac)	Other Intergovernmental Organizations	(20)

*Table 17.   The Most Salient Targets in the Middle
East, 1956–1967*

	Egypt	(117)
	Israel	(93)
	United States	(81)
(nostac)	United Nations	(68)
(nostac)	Intrastate Arab	(59)
	Yemen	(59)
(nostac)	Individuals	(58)
	France	(52)
	Morocco	(49)
	Algeria	(45)
	Syria	(40)
	Jordan	(40)
	Iraq	(39)
	United Kingdom	(29)
	Tunisia	(27)
	Turkey	(25)
	Saudi Arabia	(23)
	USSR	(22)
	Lebanon	(22)
(nostac)	Other Intergovernmental Organizations	(20)

of nonstate behavior was the disappearance of nationalist rebellions in
North Africa after the independence of Morocco and Tunisia in 1956 and
of Algeria in 1962. The reduction in nonstate activity was accompanied by
an increase in the importance of these three new regimes. A final, but very
significant, change in activity and salience levels was shown in the greater

roles of the United States and the Soviet Union in the Middle East and the concomitant reduction in importance of France, Great Britain, and other Western European actors.

The pattern of behavior between 1956 and 1967 was generally more conflictual than in the earlier period as 38 percent of the dyads involved conflict in contrast to only 30 percent between 1948 and 1956; violence accounted for approximately the same percentage of dyads as in the first period. Although nonstate activity on the whole was down, nonstate actors remained among the leading disrupters in the system, particularly Intrastate and Interstate Arab groups. One major change from the first period was that four of the eleven principal supporters of the system were nonstate actors. Indeed, in terms of patterned cooperative behavior, the leading actors were the superpowers and certain nonstate actors, particularly the United Nations, NATO, the Arab League, and the Papacy. This suggests that the conflicts of the region were beginning to attract global concern and were becoming more deeply enmeshed in worldwide conflicts. The Middle East was no longer a periphery in any sense of the term.

The relative quiescence of nonstate actors during this period is further revealed by the fact that they accounted for only 29 percent of violent actions, though this is still a considerable percentage. The period witnessed a dramatic rise in anomic violence on the part of individuals who were not identified with any group. Fully 11.1 percent of all the violent actions in the system were initiated by such individuals in the form of terrorism, assassination, and other acts of protest. Among nation-states, France, Iraq, and Syria were the most violence-prone, attesting to the serious problems that these three states confronted.

In summary, the Middle East region between 1956 and 1967 became increasingly complex as five major superissues shared the attention of the participants. Alignments continued to show that "friends" and "foes"

Table 18. *Disruptive-Supportive Behavior, 1956–1967*

Disrupters		Supporters	
Iraq	(−32)	United States	(+56)
Saudi Arabia	(−25)	United Kingdom	(+39)
Interstate Arab	(−16)	USSR	(+33)
Jordan	(−15)	United Nations	(+26)
Intrastate Arab	(−13)	Arab Intergovern-	
France	(−11)	mental Organizations	(+25)
Syria	(−7)	Egypt	(+22)
Individuals	(−7)	Other Intergovern-	
Muscat and Oman	(−6)	mental Organizations	(+20)
Lebanon	(−5)	Finance	(+11)
Yemen	(−5)	Religious	(+11)
		West Germany	(+9)
		Israel	(+9)

shifted from issue to issue. Finally, the period was one of relative "nation-state dominance." Nonstate actors, while still very important, seemed to have a reduced impact on the system as a whole compared with the previous period.

The Middle East 1967–1972: Israel Beleaguered

After the conclusion of the Six-Day War in June, 1967, Israel stood victorious yet virtually isolated in the Middle East. The Jewish State had achieved a series of crushing military triumphs, none of which bore lasting political fruit. With only one major ally, the United States, it became increasingly clear that although Israel had won important territorial advantages—the West Bank of the Jordan River, the Sinai Desert up to the shores of the Suez Canal, the city of Jerusalem, and the Golan Heights overlooking Syria on the road to Damascus—it could not impose a military solution on the area.

For their part, the Arab regimes which had participated in the war, Egypt, Syria, and Jordan, became increasingly unstable as their policies appeared increasingly bankrupt. In Egypt, where President Nasser died in 1970 and was succeeded by Anwar Sadat, dreams of pan-Arabism were shunted aside in order to pursue the more pressing objective of recovery of the lands that Israel had occupied in 1967. Moreover, Egypt and the other Arab regimes were challenged by a new and major force in Middle Eastern politics, the Palestinian guerrillas. The guerrillas, organized on both an interstate and intrastate basis, believed that established regimes were either unable or unwilling to attain the goal of an independent Palestinian state. Although divided among themselves, the Palestinian groups were prepared to fight whomever they viewed as not supporting their cause whole-heartedly, whether Israel, the Arab states, or states outside the region. As a consequence, they posed a major threat to the stability of the region as a whole and to the stability of some Arab regimes, especially those in Jordan and Lebanon. Resorting in some cases to acts of assassination, hijacking, and random terrorism, they were clearly not under the control of any regime.

In part, the guerrillas were responsible for the revival of the *Palestine* superissue as a question apart from the *Arab-Israeli* struggle. Also, partly as a result of their behavior, the *Regime Stability* superissue remained important and troublesome.[6] Although *Inter-Arab* rivalry persisted, this

6. The legitimacy of the Palestinian cause was finally recognized by Arab states at the Rabat summit conference of October, 1974. There it was agreed that the Palestinian Liberation Organization should be given control over the occupied West Bank when Israel withdraws from it.

Table 19.   Ranking of Superissues by
Explained Variance, 1967–1972

1. Arab-Israeli	(1.25)
2. Superpower	(1.23)
3. Regime Stability	(0.97)
4. Inter-Arab	(0.80)
5. Palestine	(0.44)
6. Colonial	(0.06)

superissue became somewhat less significant as the Arab states sought to cope with the twin dangers of Israel and the Palestinians. Finally, *Superpower* penetration of the region reached unprecedented proportions. The Soviet Union sought to perpetuate its influence in Egypt as well as in Syria and Iraq; the United States, while continuing to assist Israel, sought to defuse what had become a potential arena of confrontation between itself and Moscow.

The *Arab-Israeli* superissue, which appeared on ten of the factors and was related to 37 percent of the issues, showed the effects of superpower penetration. Israel after 1967 found only one dependable ally and source of arms, the United States. In addition to the active opposition and hostility of the Arab states and the Soviet Union, Israeli occupation of Arab lands was the target of intensive criticism by the United Nations, and in U.N. debates, by the Afro-Asian bloc and others, such as Spain, Yugoslavia, and Cyprus. Along with guerrilla raids launched from Jordan, Syria, and Lebanon, between 1967 and 1970 Israel was confronted by an Egyptian war of attrition on the Suez Canal front, a war that was brought to an end as a result of a ceasefire plan offered by U.S. Secretary of State William Rogers. Increasingly frustrated in efforts to find a solution, Israel resorted to large-scale reprisals against Arab states alleged to be harboring guerrillas and terrorists. Israel also sought to placate the Arab populations in the occupied territories in order to prevent their allying with the Palestinian guerrillas and in order to consolidate its military control in the area.

The futility of the endless cycle of attack and counterattack was again revealed in October, 1973, when another major war engulfed the Middle

Table 20.   Arab-Israeli Cleavage,
1967–1972: Major Coalitions

Israeli Friends	Arab Friends
Israel	Egypt
United States	United Nations
	Interstate Arab
	USSR
	Jordan

East. Egypt and Syria launched attacks in the Sinai and the Golan Heights, respectively, on the eve of Yom Kippur, the holiest of Jewish holidays. Once again the military outcome proved inconclusive, although the increased proficiency of the Arab armies was now manifest. The alignments that prevailed on the superissue emphasize the virtual isolation of Israel and the elimination of active neutrals.

The second leading superissue, *Superpower* penetration, appeared on eight of the twelve factors and 31 percent of the issues. For its part, the United States, in addition to providing assistance to Israel, sought a solution to the *Arab-Israeli* question through the United Nations. It supported Gunnar Jarring's U.N. mission and in 1970 proposed a ceasefire to Egypt and Israel. The United States also extended political and material assistance to Jordan's King Hussein when in 1970 and 1971 his country fell prey to civil war and was threatened by an armed invasion from Syria. Finally, the United States became the object of intensive Arab pressure, particularly from Egypt, Saudi Arabia, and Lebanon, to modify its pro-Israeli stance.

For much of the period the Soviet Union acted as Egypt's "good friend," providing Cairo with a virtually uninterrupted flow of material and political assistance between 1967 and 1971 and gaining in return an unprecedented political and military foothold in the Middle East. In addition, the Soviet navy made its presence felt in the eastern Mediterranean, and the Soviet Union found itself the object of considerable world pressure concerning the vexatious question of Soviet restriction of Jewish emigration. (The influence of certain nonstate groups in the United States continued to be felt after the period under consideration as efforts to increase Soviet-American trade were thwarted in Congress as a consequence of the Soviet refusal to permit the free emigration of Soviet Jews.) Overall, between 1967 and 1972 the Middle East proved a critical exception to American-Soviet efforts to achieve a detente.

Alignments on *Superpower* questions showed that comparatively few Middle Eastern states were prepared to take sides consistently or actively. Moreover, the Palestinian groups, apparently believing that neither superpower was in favor of their cause, remained neutral, attacking both sides from time to time.

Regime Stability was the third most obdurate superissue during the

Table 21. Superpower Alignments, 1967–1972

Pro-American	Neutral	Pro-Soviet
United States	Iraq	USSR
Israel	Intrastate Jewish	Egypt
Lebanon	Interstate Arab	
United Nations		

period. It appeared on six of the factors and was involved in 22 percent of the issues. The regimes which found themselves most in jeopardy were those of Jordan, Lebanon, Iraq, Yemen, South Yemen, and, to a lesser extent, Egypt.

Jordan's and Lebanon's political crises revolved in large measure around the pent-up frustrations of the large Palestinian populations in those two countries. Commando activities in both countries represented a threat to sovereignty and stability, but the most dramatic collisions occurred in Jordan in 1969 and 1970. Palestinian fedayeen groups repeatedly and openly flouted the authority of the Hashemite monarchy and clashed with Bedouin army supporters of the king. In mid-September, 1970, the Jordanian army launched a full-scale offensive against the Palestinians, thereby plunging the country into virtual civil war. Bloody fighting went on for ten days in Amman and other principal cities of the kingdom until pressure from other Arab governments brought about a ceasefire on September 25, 1970. During the civil war, Syrian armored units invaded northern Jordan in order to aid the Palestinians but were driven back by the Jordanian air force. American and Israeli military maneuvers gave some indication that these two powers were preparing to intervene to save Hussein.

In Yemen the royalist-republican civil war continued even after the withdrawal of Egyptian troops from that country in August, 1967. Yemen's pro-Egyptian President al-Salal was deposed in a military coup in November and replaced by a three-man Presidential Council under Abdul Rahman al-Iryani. In December, a political moderate, General Hassan al-Amri, returned from Egypt where he had been detained and, with the assistance of Soviet aircraft, succeeded in blunting a royalist attack on the capital city of Sana. Although remnants of the royalist forces continued to threaten Sana, they were further weakened by the termination of Saudi Arabian assistance and internal dissension, and fighting ceased by the end of 1968.

While civil war raged in neighboring Yemen, Southern Yemen was also torn by civil strife. British control of what is now Southern Yemen had begun with the occupation of Aden in 1839 and had gradually extended northward as a result of British treaties with local rulers. Prior to granting the area its independence, Great Britain in the early 1960's had established the Federation of South Arabia, linking the colony of Aden with the sixteen sultanates that had been part of the Western Aden Protectorate. British plans for transferring power to the traditional leaders were thwarted by increasing nationalist agitation and terrorism on the part of radical elements. Between August and October, 1967 the sultanates were overrun by the forces of the radical National Liberation Front (NLF), and the traditional rulers resigned or fled. At the same time, a rival organization known as FLOSY (Front for the Liberation of Occupied South Yemen) fought the NLF and attacked the British in Aden. In November FLOSY lost the support of Egypt, and the NLF took power. Finally, the British surrendered the territory to the NLF on November 30, 1967, and Qahtan al-Shaabi became President of the People's Republic of South Yemen.

In Iraq, the Kurds, aided and abetted by the Shah of Iran, continued to pose a major threat to the stability of the regime. Meanwhile, in Egypt, Presidents Nasser and Sadat were challenged by extremists, particularly student groups, which demanded more vigorous prosecution of the war against Israel.

The *Inter-Arab* superissue, while remaining salient, became considerably less so after 1967. It appeared on only five of the factors and as part of 16 percent of the issues. The *Colonial* superissue also was virtually eliminated, appearing on only one factor and only 4 percent of the issues.

In contrast, the *Palestine* superissue increased in importance dramatically after the Six-Day War. Between 1967 and 1972 it appeared on four factors and 14 percent of the issues. (We will deal with the Palestinian movement in greater detail in Chapter 6.) An examination of the alignments involved in this superissue reveal that the Palestinian commando groups received relatively little political support from the Arab states except on a case-by-case basis. They were opposed, as a threat to regional and global stability and peace, by the superpowers, several Arab states, Israel, and the multinational petroleum companies. Finally, several allegedly "radical" Arab regimes actually behaved in a tepid, even neutral, manner towards the Palestinian groups during the period as a whole.

The virtual disappearance of the *Colonial* superissue was the most striking finding characterizing superissue coappearance in the third period. Those *Colonial* issues which did arise were highly idiosyncratic. This, in turn, affected the relationships among the remaining superissues. The close association of the *Arab-Israeli* superissue with *Superpower* penetration questions persisted in this time slice. The virtual isolation of Israel, except for the United States, and the continuous flow of Soviet aid to various Arab

Table 22. The Palestinian Superissue, 1967–1972

Procommando	Neutralist	Anticommando
Interstate Arab	Algeria	United States
(largely Palestinian)	West Germany	USSR
Egypt	United Kingdom	Jordan
Iraq	Sudan	Israel
	Libya	Lebanon
	Syria	Bahrein
	Saudi Arabia	Qatar
	Intrastate Arab	Trucial States
	Other Intergovern-	(United Arab Emirates)
	mental Organizations	Muscat-Oman
		Tapline Corporation
		Switzerland

regimes lent both of these superissues an East-West coloration, which was somewhat anachronistic in an era of lessening tensions elsewhere. *Regime Stability* questions remained associated with those of an *Inter-Arab* nature, even with Sadat's succession after the death of Nasser. The Hashemite monarchy of Jordan's King Hussein became a focus for issues of both types, a situation that became especially important with the rise to prominence of Palestinian groups. Not only did the *Palestine* question superimpose itself on the *Arab-Israeli* cleavage, but it also nearly toppled Hussein's monarchy in the civil war of 1970.

The years 1967 to 1972 clearly constituted an era of nonstate actors in the Middle East. During this period they initiated 28 percent of the dyads and were the targets of 34 percent of the activity. Nine of the twenty most active initiators and eight of the twenty-one (tie for twentieth place) most salient targets were nonstate. Interstate Palestinian guerrilla and liberation groups became the third most active initiators and the fourth most salient targets in the period, leaving no doubt as to their impact on the *Palestinian* and *Arab-Israeli* superissues.

In addition to the Palestinian guerrilla groups active both within and outside the region, other nonstate actors played significant roles in Middle Eastern politics. The United Nations, for example, became a leading target; while used as a forum to discuss Middle Eastern questions, protagonists vied for control of the "voice of global opinion." Small states sought through the United Nations a voice in the solution of world problems that they could not have in any other way at a time of increasing superpower intervention in the region. The United Nations itself became a more active direct participant in the politics of the region as highlighted by the ill-fated mission of Gunnar Jarring.

In the category *Other Nonstate Actors* were such organizations as the International Red Cross and the International Federation of Airline Pilots which attempted to mediate and exercise pressure in the face of the skyjacking of civilian aircraft by Palestinian guerrillas. Among Arab Intergovernmental Organizations, the most significant newcomer was the Organization of Petroleum Exporting Countries (OPEC), a group formed by Arab and non-Arab oil producing countries. OPEC sought higher prices for petroleum products and a better global bargaining position generally vis-à-

Table 23. Middle East Superissue Coappearance, 1967–1972

	I	II	III	IV	V	VI
I. Arab-Israeli	—					
II. Colonial	.18	—				
III. Inter-Arab	.40	0	—			
IV. Regime Stability	.63	0	.73	—		
V. Superpower	.78	.22	.46	.43	—	
VI. Palestine	.57	0	.22	.60	.50	—

Table 24. The Most Active Initiators in the Middle East, 1967–1972

	Israel	(249)
	Egypt	(138)
(nostac)	Interstate Arab	(101)
	Jordan	(85)
	United States	(58)
	USSR	(57)
(nostac)	Individuals	(48)
(nostac)	United Nations	(33)
	Iraq	(33)
(nostac)	Media	(30)
	United Kingdom	(24)
(nostac)	Intrastate Arab	(20)
	Lebanon	(19)
(nostac)	Other Nonstate Actors	(18)
	Yemen	(14)
	Algeria	(13)
	Libya	(13)
(nostac)	Intrastate Jewish	(12)
(nostac)	Arab Intergovernmental Organizations	(11)
(nostac)	Other Intergovernmental Organizations	(10)

Table 25. The Most Salient Targets in the Middle East, 1967–1972

	Israel	(186)
	Egypt	(135)
(nostac)	United Nations	(135)
(nostac)	Interstate Arab	(94)
	Jordan	(84)
	United States	(81)
	Syria	(48)
	USSR	(46)
(nostac)	Individuals	(35)
(nostac)	Media	(32)
(nostac)	Finance	(31)
	Lebanon	(31)
(nostac)	Intrastate Arab	(26)
(nostac)	Other Nonstate Actors	(18)
	Iraq	(16)
	United Kingdom	(14)
	Yemen	(14)
	Saudi Arabia	(13)
	Libya	(12)
	France	(9)
(nostac)	Arab Intergovernmental Organizations	(9)

vis major industrial consumers. Since the Arab-Israeli war of 1973, this intergovernmental cartel has emerged as a major force in the politics of energy.

The changed pattern of nation-state activity is also revealing. The extraordinarily high level of Israeli activity and salience was largely caused by the renewed importance of the *Arab-Israeli* and *Palestine* superissues. Israel was confronted by a veritable host of protagonists seeking its withdrawal from the territories occupied during the June 1967 war. Among Arab states, the increased activity and salience of Jordan confirmed the critical position of that state in regard to the *Palestine* question and Hussein's dilemma as his regime was buffeted by external and internal enemies. Moreover, the increased activity and salience levels of the Soviet Union reflected the growing importance of superpower penetration; it is notable that for the first time the Soviet Union's levels were virtually the same as those of the United States. The Soviet Union had become a formidable arbiter of political outcomes in the region and would have to be consulted before the conclusion of any major political agreements.

Regional interaction in the period was more conflictual than at any other time; even excluding the 1967 war, fully 40 percent of all dyadic activity involved conflict of some kind. Even more striking was the fact that only 31 percent of the dyads involved cooperation as compared to 50 percent and 43 percent respectively in the two earlier periods. Violence also increased; over 13 percent of all dyads involved violent behavior compared to 9 percent and 8 percent respectively in the previous periods. The increases in conflict and violence appear to be related to the increased activity of nonstate actors, particularly the Palestinian groups. Indeed, although Israel was responsible for the largest number of violent acts, Egypt and Palestinian groups such as Fatah and the Popular Front for the Liberation of Palestine were tied as the second most violent. Moreover, much of Israeli-initiated violence was in response to terrorist provocations and attacks. Another Arab liberation organization, the National Front for the Liberation of South Yemen, was also a major contributor to regional violence. As Table 26 shows, among the leading disrupters were Israel,

Table 26. *Disruptive-Supportive Behavior, 1967–1972*

Disrupters		Supporters	
Israel	(−85)	United States	(+50)
Interstate Arab	(−39)	Media	(+10)
Other Nonstate Actors	(−8)	Finance	(+9)
Chad	(−6)	Trucial States	(+8)
Arab Intergovernmental		Muscat and Oman	(+8)
Organizations	(−5)	France	(+7)
Intrastate Arab	(−4)	Sweden	(+7)
Syria	(−4)	United Kingdom	(+6)
Algeria	(−3)	Spain	(+5)
South Yemen	(−3)	Yemen	(+4)
Six actors tied with	(−2)	Sudan	(+4)

Arab nonstate groups, and certain radical Arab regimes. In contrast, American behavior was largely cooperative. Overall, nonstate actors were leading disrupters but were generally not responsible for behavior that supported the system.

In summary, the leading characteristics of the Middle East between 1967 and 1972 were a rapid rise in the importance of certain nonstate groups and greater system conflict and violence. These behavior patterns were related to the increased importance of three superissues: *Palestine, Arab-Israeli,* and *Superpower* penetration.

The Middle East
As A Complex Conglomerate

Our discussion of the Middle East to this point reveals that the region epitomizes what we termed in Chapter 3 the complex conglomerate system. During the twenty-five year period we investigated, there were shifting alignments on several major superissues. A number of nation-states in the region, notably Jordan, Lebanon, and Yemen, were extremely porous. They exhibited chronic instability and were subject to diverse external and internal pressures. Influence in the region was exerted in a variety of ways ranging from traditional military force to economic blockade and covert terrorism. The persistently important role of nonstate actors, particularly those organized on an interstate basis, suggest the growth of complex linkages in the region as well as the existence of divided loyalties on the part of many individuals.

Contrary to what might be expected in a bipolar world, the Middle East was not characterized by a single dominant cleavage. Whereas two superissues, *Arab-Israeli* and *Colonial,* were prominent in the system during the first phase, five superissues were of virtually equal importance between 1956 and 1967. In the final period, there were two leading superissues, *Arab-Israeli* and *Superpower,* and three other superissues were of somewhat lesser significance, including the question of *Palestine.*

Our analysis also indicates that alignments shifted on each superissue over time as well as across superissues. Thus on the *Arab-Israeli* superissue, Israel was practically alone after 1967 in contrast to earlier periods, and Egypt was joined by both the Soviet Union and the United Nations. In addition, the United Nations, which in two of the periods was to be found in alignment with the United States on *Superpower* questions, opposed the United States on the *Arab-Israeli* superissue. Even the superpowers themselves were aligned on the *Inter-Arab* superissue between 1956 and 1967, and on the question of *Palestine* between 1967 and 1972. The complexity of issues and alignments is perhaps best illustrated by the behavior of the Arab states. While they appeared relatively united on the *Arab-Israeli* question, they were hopelessly divided on at least four other superissues. It is clear that the existence of Israel is not, nor has ever been, sufficient to prevent severe conflicts among Arab states.

As for alignments of other nonstate actors: On *Arab-Israeli* questions, Israel could generally find support among world Jewish groups and organizations, while the Arab states were aided by various Arab groups and individuals. Such Arab groups, however, tended to remain neutral on the *Inter-Arab* superissue and on *Superpower* questions, and were actively opposed by most of the principal regional and global actors on the matter of Palestine. Arab nationalist groups in North Africa were also leading opponents of French colonialism in the Middle East.

Superissue coappearance scores remind us just how pervasive the *Arab-Israeli* superissue was, even if it was often evoked only for rhetorical purposes by the various Arab states and groups. Indeed, scores for the more than two decades suggest that "if Israel did not exist, the Arabs would have had to invent it" to mask a multitude of divisions among themselves. While the *Arab-Israeli* superissue has the highest average issue coappearance for the twenty-five years we have examined, questions of *Inter-Arab* rivalry, *Regime Stability,* and *Superpower* penetration were also significantly interrelated. Some of these linkages can be illustrated by American policy, which has always sought to increase the power of putative voices of moderation in the region, especially Jordan's Hussein and Saudi Arabia's Faisal (and his successor, King Khalid). In the latter case, the importance of Arab petroleum for the economically developed countries is manifest. In attempting to end the Arab oil embargo and secure Arab-Israeli peace after the 1973 war, Secretary of State Henry Kissinger again tried to woo moderate Arabs such as Sadat and Faisal away from their more radical allies such as Libya and Syria. In this way he sought to link *Inter-Arab* rivalries to the *Arab-Israeli* question. By warning them of the dangers of Soviet penetration, he was also trying to link them to the *Superpower* question. The oil embargo itself was illustrative of important aspects of the complex conglomerate model as Arab states acted to "punish" American

Table 27. Middle East Superissue Coappearance, 1948–1972

	I	II	III	IV	V	VI
I. Arab-Israeli	—					
II. Colonial	.65	—				
III. Inter-Arab	.65	.65	—			
IV. Regime Stability	.64	.47	.63	—		
V. Superpower	.67	.46	.56	.54	—	
VI. Palestine	.59	.38	.44	.60	.52	—

Table 28. The Most Active Initiators in the
Middle East, 1948–1972

	Israel	(530)
	Egypt	(450)
	United States	(258)
(nostac)	United Nations	(174)
	Jordan	(171)
	France	(168)
(nostac)	Interstate Arab	(135)
	United Kingdom	(132)
	USSR	(130)
	Iraq	(121)
(nostac)	Intrastate Arab	(117)
(nostac)	Individuals	(116)
	Saudi Arabia	(111)
	Syria	(109)
	Lebanon	(87)
(nostac)	Intrastate Jewish	(62)
	Morocco	(61)
(nostac)	Governmental Noncentral	(51)
(nostac)	Arab Intergovernmental	
	Organizations	(50)
	Yemen	(50)

Table 29. The Most Salient Targets in the
Middle East, 1948–1972

	Israel	(553)
	Egypt	(465)
(nostac)	United Nations	(356)
	United States	(319)
	France	(205)
	Jordan	(188)
(nostac)	Individuals	(174)
(nostac)	Intrastate Arab	(150)
	Saudi Arabia	(133)
	Syria	(125)
(nostac)	Interstate Arab	(115)
	United Kingdom	(101)
	Yemen	(90)
(nostac)	Governmental Noncentral	(84)
	Lebanon	(82)
	USSR	(81)
(nostac)	Finance	(79)
	Canada	(79)
	Iraq	(75)
	Morocco	(56)

and European support of Israel. In this way they tried to turn public opinion against nonstate Jewish and other groups in the United States and Europe. As a result, millions of Americans found themselves waiting in line for the gasoline they had previously taken for granted, while various corporations were forced to alter their production and marketing procedures. Throughout, the role of the multinational oil corporations remained obscure. They appeared to be "covering up" an extremely successful attempt to "play both sides against the middle" as they demanded higher prices for their products while delaying Arab expropriation of their property.

Although *Colonial* questions were of lesser importance as time went on, the role that they, too, played in fostering a rhetoric as well as a reality that often obscured *Inter-Arab* rivalry is significant. Finally, the question of *Palestine* became prominent in the period of 1967–1972 in a fashion that illustrated significantly the volatile effects that the activities of nonstate Palestinian guerrillas could have for the stability of particular regimes, most notably that of Hussein in Jordan. Furthermore, the imposition of the *Palestine* question on the dominant *Arab-Israeli* cleavage reminds us that if peace is to come to the Middle East, some resolution of the status of displaced and dispossessed Palestinian refugees must be found.

Turning once more to the actors themselves, we find that of the twenty most active initiators and salient targets from 1948 to 1972, six and five, respectively, were nonstate. The most important *nostacs* overall were Interstate and Intrastate Arab groups, including those shown in Table 30. Underscoring the significance of Intrastate and Interstate Arab groups is the fact that their behavior was the most consistently disruptive of that of any actors in the region. Because of their "contribution," the region as a whole exhibited greater amounts of conflict and violence during those periods of time (1948–1956 and 1967–1972) when nonstate actors were most active.

On the other hand, certain types of nonstate actors, notably intergov-

Table 30. Major Nonstate Arab Groups in the Sample

Interstate	Intrastate
Palestinian Liberation Organization	Kurdish rebels (Iraq)
Palestine Refugee Office	Druse rebels (Lebanon)
National Front for the Liberation of the Arabian Gulf	Syrian Popular Resistance Movement
Front for the Liberation of Occupied South Yemen	Egyptian National Front
	Yemeni royalists
Action Committee on U.S.–Arab Relations	Yemeni republicans
Al Fatah	Saiqa
Popular Front for the Liberation of Palestine	Moslem Brotherhood
	Turkish Peoples' Liberation Army
Palestine Commando Movement	Arab Organization of Sinai
Arab Higher Committee for Palestine	Lebanese Higher Committee for Palestinian Affairs
	National Liberation Front (Algeria)
	Moroccan Liberation Party

Table 31. *Disruptive-Supportive Behavior, 1948–1972*

Disrupters		Supporters	
Intrastate Arab	(−65)	United States	(+146)
Interstate Arab	(−64)	United Nations	(+65)
Israel	(−42)	Egypt	(+56)
Jordan	(−27)	United Kingdom	(+54)
Iraq	(−25)	West Germany	(+34)
Other Nonstate Actors	(−22)	Liberia	(+26)
Yemen	(−16)	Intrastate Jewish	(+26)
Chad	(−6)	Other Intergovern-	
France	(−6)	mental Organizations	(+26)
Bulgaria	(−5)	Sweden	(+25)
		Finance	(+25)

ernmental organizations like the United Nations, were consistently among the leading supporters in the system. Among nation-states, Israel, Jordan, Iraq, Yemen, and France were generally disruptive, while the United States, Egypt, and Britain were among the most supportive actors.

In conclusion, our analysis suggests that the complex conglomerate label is suitable for the Middle East, none the least in that nonstate actors have been significant participants in the politics of the region throughout the period under review. Moreover, especially in view of the responsibility of some of them for conflict and violence, an understanding of their behavior is even more important than mere activity levels might suggest. If peace is to come to the Middle East, it will entail more than a simple agreement among nation-states; it will require the approval or demise of powerful groups that are not currently controlled by nation-states.

The Palestinian Resistance
and Middle East Politics

SIX

Palestinian "liberation" or "terrorist" organizations have had a dramatic, if not sustained, impact on world politics for several years. The nature of the movement precludes the existence of much information about it, but its activities, including the assassination of Arab leaders, the hijacking of aircraft, the harassing of Israelis and their supporters abroad, and flamboyant raids in the Middle East itself, have attracted popular interest and concern. The organizations have mobilized a highly educated Arab stratum and have restored the "Palestine question" to public consciousness.[1] The issue revolves around demands for the creation of a "state" that would be home to the Palestinian "nation" by those Arab inhabitants of what was known as Palestine before the creation of the State of Israel. The symbolic and material importance of these groups, both in terms of Arab-Israeli and inter-Arab relations, demonstrates the growing salience of nonstate actors in world politics.

The Palestinian movement consists of several major organizations as well as a host of splinter groups, some acting clandestinely and others openly, some using violence and others primarily political agitation. Some of the groups are organized substantially within single Arab states, while others are predominantly transnational. The movement is loosely united around the goal of liberating Palestine, but within the movement can be found individuals who openly profess Marxism-Leninism as well as Trotskyite, xenophobic Pan-Arabic, and Fanonistic views. The groups range from those that are prepared to overthrow any and all of the existing

---

1. One survey suggested that only 6 percent of the membership was illiterate, whereas 54 percent had primary education, 32 percent secondary education, and 8 percent university training. *Le Monde* (weekly), 16 July 1969, p. 32; see also, *New York Times,* 9 March 1969, p. 3.

regimes in the region to those that have been organized by and act on behalf of particular regimes.

The origins of the movement can be traced as far back as 1948 (and perhaps even earlier).[2] A corporate sense of Palestinian national identity was largely nonexistent before the emergence of Israel, and Palestinian elites were organized primarily along sectarian and family lines. The trauma of mass exodus by Arabs from Palestine in 1948–1949 and the grim experience of surviving in crowded refugee camps scattered throughout the region in an anomalous international limbo provided the conditions for political ferment. Freed from the traditional social structure that had inhibited national consciousness and political organization under the British Mandate, the children of the refugees adopted the symbol and myth of an independent Palestine as a first principle of their political catechism.

The Six Day War
and the Transformation
of the Palestine Issue

Despite growing national consciousness, it was not until the destruction of the regular Arab armies by Israel in June, 1967 that the Palestine problem became the focal question of regional politics.

Between 1956 and 1967, the question of an independent Palestinian entity remained essentially dormant. The most characteristic feature of Middle Eastern politics in this decade was that "more Arab states were at each other's throats at once than ever before."[3] Regional issues such as the Iraqi revolution of 1958 and the subsequent feud of Iraq's Kassem with Egypt's Nasser, the Lebanese civil war of 1958, the rapid dissolution of the United Arab Republic (a union of Egypt and Syria) between 1958 and 1961, the Sudanese civil war, and the Yemeni civil war precluded a united Arab stand against Israel.

The Palestinians themselves served as "good soldiers" for the various Arab regimes and were manipulated first by one and then another of these regimes in the name of inter-Arab politics. Al Fatah, the first of the major Palestinian organizations, was formed in 1956–1957. It was largely dependent upon Syria and was used by that country after 1961 as a means of competing with Egypt's Nasser. In contrast, the Palestinian Liberation Organization (PLO) was established in Cairo in 1964 in order to provide

2. See Michael Hudson, "The Palestinian Resistance Movement: Its Significance in the Middle East Crisis," *The Middle East Journal* 23 (1969).
3. Malcolm Kerr, *The Arab Cold War, 1958–1967* (London: R.I.I.A., 1967), p. 127.

President Nasser with leverage over the Palestinians. This group purported to be the "official" voice of Palestinian nationalism.[4]

Before the Six Day War, the liberation organizations reflected the main lines of interstate rivalry for leadership of the pan-Arabic movement. Damascus Radio labeled PLO leader Ahmed Shuqayri "an agent for President Abdul Nasser" who had turned his organization into "a machine obeying the orders of certain regimes to cripple its revolutionary effectiveness and independence."[5] Fatah viewed the PLO as an ineffective Egyptian-controlled organization which Cairo was using to *restrain* Palestinian activities against Israel.

The destruction of the Arab armies by Israel in June, 1967 brought the Palestine problem to the fore. The prophecy of inevitable confrontation with Israel, regardless of national consequences—a prophecy that was essentially fulfilled in October, 1973—was escalated through the dynamics of inter-Arab competition into the crucial test of regime legitimacy.

From the perspective of the liberation organizations, the Six Day War had several major consequences, some which strengthened their position and others which endangered it. The first consequence of the war was to increase the autonomy, prestige, and size of the guerrilla groups, so that from a position of relative obscurity they were rapidly transformed into formidable political contestants at the regional level. The second consequence, however, was a proliferation of guerrilla groups, a development which had the effect of weakening the Palestinian movement as a whole.

Let us first turn to the way in which the war strengthened the movement. Prior to the war, the Palestinian organizations lacked both a convincing politico-military strategy and an adequate manpower pool from which to recruit. Until the June defeat, the principal Arab regimes and elites, even Palestinian nationalists, regarded the conventional Arab armies as the shield against Israeli "aggression" as well as the sword with which to recover Palestine. After large-scale domestic expenditures on defense and Soviet assistance, by the mid-1960s these armies were confidently regarded as sufficient to defeat Israel in the absence of great power intervention. The Palestinian activists' strategy was to catalyze the decisive confrontation, leaving the task of ultimate liberation in the hands of the national armies. For its part, Cairo created the PLO expressly to prevent Palestinian activities that were not compatible with the conventional strategy.

The defeat suffered by the armies of Egypt, Syria, and Jordan in June radically transformed the existing relationship between national governments and guerrillas. Following the war there was not only a military but also a political vacuum. The ensuing competition among Arab regimes for

4. See Shahrough Akhavi, "The Middle East Crisis," in Alan M. Jones, ed., *U.S. Foreign Policy in a Changing World* (New York: David McKay, 1973), p. 205.
5. *New York Times,* 15 June 1965, p. 1.

the loyalty of the Arab masses provided the Palestinian organizations with an invaluable wedge to increase their political autonomy. Israel's victory shattered the prestige both of conservative and radical Arab governments, and, during the weeks that followed, the authority and credibility of established national governments were further undermined as the deception which they had practiced became known. The inability of "legitimate" Arab leaders to coordinate policy *after* the defeat (revealed, for example, in a three-month delay in holding a proposed summit conference) created new opportunities for "irregular" leaders to seize the initiative and gain popularity throughout the Arab world. Moreover, the 1967 defeat at last destroyed the myth of "Arab unity," which was already in question as a consequence of the breakup of the United Arab Republic in 1961. Also, the success enjoyed by the Algerian guerrillas in 1962 and the examples of guerrilla movements in Cuba and Vietnam created a new faith in revolution *from below* in contrast to the previous belief in decisive action by established Arab regimes working together. The Palestinian cause came to be viewed apart from the main Arab-Israeli struggle, and a constant motif of Palestinian politics since 1967 has been the prevention of an Arab-Israeli settlement that would sacrifice the "sacred cause."

The war had the additional effect of providing the Palestinian groups with an enormously increased pool of potential manpower. When they renewed their call for armed resistance against Israel in October, 1967, the guerrillas could recruit from a greatly enlarged Palestinian refugee population. As of May, 1967, some 330,000 refugees, largely those who had fled or had been forced from their homes in 1948–1949, subsisted in U.N. refugee camps in Jordan, Syria, and Lebanon. After June, more than one million Palestinians found themselves under Israeli rule, and in an atmosphere of rapidly changing political allegiances the idea of a movement of national resistance based on the local population was more appealing. The prestige of the guerrilla movement, particularly of Fatah, was enhanced by the "battle" of Karameh in March, 1968, when an Israeli armored column trying to destroy guerrilla bases on the eastern bank of the Jordan met strong resistance from the guerrillas. During the remainder of 1968 volunteers and contributions to the resistance increased dramatically.

By February, 1969, when (as we shall see) Fatah at last succeeded in dominating the PLO, the movement had acquired an ideology, formidable resources, and an articulated strategy. Terror was now to be used to demonstrate Palestinian power and to goad Israel into counterterror against Arab civilians in the occupied territories, thereby expanding the pool of militant fedayeen.[6] The results of this strategy were limited, how-

6. See Sharabi Hisham, *Palestine Guerrillas: Their Credibility and Effectiveness* (Washington, D.C.: Center for Strategic Studies and International Studies, 1970), p. 38.

ever, since Israeli authorities consciously sought to curb excessive reactions by Israeli citizens and security forces.[7]

Over the years the major resistance groups that survived the June War proved to be more autonomous than the commando groups that had operated from Gaza in 1955–1956 and from Syria and Jordan in 1965–1967. They still depended, of course, upon Arab regimes for political and material support and paid a price in the form of government interference in their activities. Nevertheless, it became far more difficult for Arab governments to manipulate the guerrilla groups openly.

The persistence of interstate Arab cleavages after 1967 provided further opportunities for Palestinian liberation groups to increase their autonomy and their bargaining leverage by jockeying for support among the divided Arab governments.[8] While the Arab states were superficially united against Israel, they remained divided among themselves on numerous issues. Inter-Arab schisms were accentuated by the failure of diplomatic pressure to bring about an Israeli withdrawal from the territories occupied in June, 1967 and the accession to power of "radical" regimes in Libya and the Sudan in 1969.

On the one hand, Egypt, Jordan, and Lebanon, as "frontline" states, seemed prepared to reach a political accord with Israel in order to retrieve their "lost" territories and to lessen their vulnerability to Israeli military preponderance. Such a solution would have included recognition of the Jewish State itself and would have violated the fundamental interests of the Palestinian groups. These governments were unwilling to permit an irredentist Palestinian movement whose behavior was unpredictable and destabilizing for the region as a whole to dictate the terms of a political settlement.

In contrast, Saudi Arabia, Kuwait, and Libya (until September, 1969) perceived their interests primarily in terms of protecting vital petroleum exports and maintaining tolerable relations with the Western powers on which their economic prosperity depended. These governments, however, also sought to prevent their isolation from the remainder of the Arab world and to protect their domestic political positions. For these reasons, they agreed in 1967 to provide a yearly financial subsidy to Egypt and Jordan in exchange for unimpeded petroleum exports to the West. They also attempted to "buy off" the Palestinians by channeling financial aid to Fatah primarily, which was regarded as the least threatening of the fedayeen organizations.

A third group that included Syria, Algeria, and Iraq (after 1968) publicly rejected all proposed nonmilitary solutions to the Arab-Israeli

7. See David Waines, *The Unholy War* (Wilmette, Ill.: Medina University International, 1971), pp. 175–80.
8. See Malcolm H. Kerr, *Regional Arab Politics and the Conflict with Israel*, RM-5966-FF, Rand Corporation (October 1969).

conflict and advocated a war of popular liberation against Israel on the Vietnamese model. For this purpose they strongly, though not unconditionally, supported the Palestinian movement. In practice, Syrian and Iraqi support of the Palestinians depended on the internal stability of the respective regimes, and Algerian enthusiasm waned after 1969 as a consequence of President Boumedienne's increasing concentration on national economic development.

Fission and Fusion
in the Palestine Movement:
The Politics of Disunity

In some respects, then, the Middle East provided an environment in which an autonomous Palestinian liberation movement might flourish. Yet, factionalism within the movement itself proved a principal source of embarrassment and weakness. "Alliances were formed and broken; conflicts over authority were resolved, only to erupt again. Steps toward unity were offset by the proliferation of autonomous groups that formed around individual leaders or represented the interests of various Arab states."[9] Indeed, the problem of organizational rivalry proved so vexing that the history of the Palestinian movement after 1967 was largely one of attempts at unification. Internal cohesion in the movement seemed to be "a practical and theoretical prerequisite of liberation."[10] During the period at least twelve major groups emerged. They are listed in Table 32.

Fatah

Fatah, the oldest of the groups, became the largest and most significant of them as well. Before June 1967, Fatah had sought to increase tension along Israel's borders in order to embroil the Arab countries in a decisive confrontation with Tel Aviv. Its military arm, Al-Assifa (The Storm), launched its first guerrilla operations against Israel in early 1965, largely from bases in Jordan.[12]

Fatah's relative success was due in part to an eschewal of pan-

9. William B. Quandt, Fuad Jabber, and Ann Mosely Lesch, *The Politics of Palestinian Nationalism* (Berkeley: University of California Press, 1973), p. 53. Also, see pp. 52–123 for a detailed discussion of this aspect of the Palestinian movement.
10. *New York Times,* 16 November 1967, p. 1.
11. From Quandt, Jabber, and Lesch, *The Politics of Palestinian Nationalism,* p. 66.
12. Ehud Yaari, *Strike Terror: The Story of Fatah* (New York: Sabra Books, 1970), p. 73.

Table 32. *Major Palestinian Commando Groups: Summer, 1970*[11]

Commando Groups	Major Sources of Aid
I. Large Groups (5,000–10,000 armed men)	
1. Palestine National Liberation Movement—Fatah	Diverse (Libya, Syria, Kuwait, Saudi Arabia, Algeria, private Palestinians)
2. Palestine Liberation Army (PLA) Popular Liberation Forces (PLF)	Arab League through Palestine Liberation Organization (PLO)
3. Vanguards of the Popular Liberation War (Saiqa)	Syrian Baath Party
II. Middle Groups (1,000–3,000 armed men, including militia)	
4. Popular Front for the Liberation of Palestine (PFLP)	Iraq
5. Popular Democratic Front for the Liberation of Palestine (PDFLP)	Syria
III. Small Groups (100–500 armed men)	
6. Popular Front for the Liberation of Palestine-General Command (PFLP-GC)	Syria; later Libya and Iraq
7. Arab Liberation Front (ALF)	Iraq
8. Organization of Arab Palestine (OAP)	UAR
9. Action Organization for the Liberation of Palestine (AOLP)	UAR, Kuwait
10. Palestinian Popular Struggle Front (PPSF)	Miscellaneous
11. Popular Organization for the Liberation of Palestine (POLP)	UAR, miscellaneous
12. Al-Ansar	Arab Communist Parties

Arabism *per se,* which it saw as a distraction from the primary task of combatting Zionism. Fatah explained the loss of Palestine as a case of classical imperialism and depicted the Palestinians as "the wretched of the earth" who could achieve liberation only through the destruction of the imperialist system.[13] But the emphasis was on a simple, if rather vague, nationalism. The aim was the establishment of a new nation-state to give expression to an emergent Palestinian national consciousness. Fatah avoided detailing what such a nation-state would be like in order not to dilute its mass appeal. The group's greatest achievement was to convince large numbers of Palestinians of the feasibility and desirability of a people's war of liberation against Israel.

Support for Fatah reflected a growing disillusionment with Israel's

13. See Emile A. Nakhleh, "Anatomy of Violence: Theoretical Reflections on Palestinian Resistance," *The Middle East Journal* 25 (Spring 1971), pp. 187–88.

Arab neighbors by Palestinians and a belief that, rhetoric notwithstanding, the Arab regimes were seeking to manipulate the Palestinians for their own national interests. To Fatah this meant that Palestinian liberation could be secured only if the Palestinians shed their dependence on Arab governments. In addition, Fatah's "ideological neutrality," its concentration on the Palestinian question, enabled the group to seek and receive assistance from several Arab regimes simultaneously.

As the largest of the Palestinian groups, Fatah consistently sought to resist the process of fission that rent the movement and to assert control over the movement as a whole. Thus in November, 1967, Fatah called upon the PLO to disband and turn over its funds.[14] In the autumn of 1968, Fatah attempted to absorb two smaller groups, the Palestine People's National Liberation Front and the Free Palestinians' Movement. These efforts proved abortive, and during this period Fatah was itself weakened by the breakaway of a new leftist group calling itself the Popular Struggle Front.[15]

In February, 1969 Fatah's efforts finally met with a measure of success when it took control of the Palestine National Assembly and had its own leader, Yasser Arafat, elected chairman of the PLO. In the spring of 1969, it was also joined by several other groups in forming the Palestine Armed Struggle Command (PASC), whose purpose ostensibly was to improve military coordination. However, the Popular Front for the Liberation of Palestine (PFLP) spurned the new coordinating group.

Another major effort to unify the Palestinian movement under Fatah's leadership took place in early 1970. In January Arafat announced that the number of independent commando groups had been reduced from 33 to 23. Promising that Fatah would not seek the liquidation of rival groups, Arafat compared Fatah's role in the liberation of Palestine with that of the Viet Cong in Vietnam, and attributed Fatah's prominence to its single-minded nationalism.[16] It was a spurious analogy, of course, because the Viet Cong organization was a cohesive politico-military structure led by a small Marxist-Leninist party that was not rent by acrimonious tactical and ideological dissensions like those still dividing the Palestinians. Indeed, the continuing lack of coordination within the movement as a whole was pointed up during the following month by the skyjacking of a Swiss airliner by a small group that had broken away from the PFLP. Nevertheless, in the face of intensive world criticism, all the other Palestinian groups condemned the action as irresponsible.[17]

Additional divisions were revealed in a pair of seminars held in Cairo

14. *Free Palestine* 1:1 (October 1969), p. 2.
15. *Arab Report and Record*, no. 17 (September 1–15, 1968), p. 272.
16. *Arab Report and Record*, no. 2 (January 16–31, 1970), p. 81.
17. *New York Times*, 24 February 1970, and *Arab Report and Record*, no. 4 (February 15–28, 1970), pp. 138–39.

in March, 1970 to discuss Palestine. At the first of these, Fatah's proposal for the creation of a united movement was turned down by the Popular Front and the Democratic Popular Front because of Fatah's rejection of doctrinaire Marxism. Moreover, at this time new splits arose within Fatah itself when Arafat was challenged by Salah Khalaf. Khalaf declared that Fatah had associated itself too closely with China and not closely enough with the Soviet Union and that it should follow the example of the PFLP in attacking Israeli interests throughout the world.[18] Khalaf also charged that Fatah had been too friendly with the Jordanian and Lebanese governments.

The Palestine Liberation Organization

In general the PLO proved to be the least militant and independent of the various Palestinian groups. Governed by an executive committee under Shuqayri, the PLO organized a Palestine Liberation Army (PLA). However, until the organization was taken over by Fatah in 1969, it was led by an older generation of Palestinians who continued to view the struggle against Israel in the context of conventional military victory by the Arab states. For the most part, its rhetoric was fiery and its bureaucracy unique; but it was a rather passive group for all that.[19] Shuqayri's dictatorial leadership and passive dependence on Egypt led to efforts to oust him in 1966. The struggle for power in the PLO resulted in several organizational changes that did little to ease internal strains. In December, 1967, Shuqayri finally fell from power.

The jealousy and hostility existing between Fatah and the PLO did not disappear after Shuqayri's fall. The PLO refused to appear at a conference in January, 1968, summoned by Fatah and attended by the representatives of thirteen guerrilla groups. It continued to claim that it was an umbrella organization of the resistance and not merely another sectarian group. As a counter to the Fatah initiative, the PLO executive committee under Yahya Hammuda called for a meeting of the Palestine National Assembly (PNA), a parliamentary-style body of Palestinian representatives, to unify guerrilla activity.[20]

PLO efforts to become *primus inter pares* achieved some success when it was announced in May, 1968 that the Palestinian National Assembly would indeed convene in Cairo. In the Assembly, the PLO was given 50 seats, Fatah 38, and the Popular Front 10. The Cairo meeting of July 1–17 seemed to presage a PLO-Fatah reconciliation. The Assembly

18. *The New Middle East,* no. 20 (May 1970), p. 10.
19. See Walter Laqueur, *The Road to War* (Baltimore: Penguin Books, 1968), p. 67.
20. *Arab Report and Record,* no. 3 (February 1–15, 1968), p. 42. See also Y. Harkabi, *Fedayeen Action and Arab Strategy,* Adelphi Papers no. 53 (London: Institute for Strategic Studies, 1968).

rejected *U.N. Security Council Resolution 242* and endorsed armed struggle as the means to liberate Palestine. (Resolution 242 called for Israeli withdrawal from occupied territories and the guaranteeing of Israeli boundaries.) Yet while a military council was created, the Assembly was unable to agree on the composition of an executive committee for the movement, and Fatah declared its disappointment with the proceedings.[21] Despite Fatah's wariness, the PLO set up a Supreme Palestine Planning Council in Beirut under Dr. Yusif Sayegh to seek political and propaganda coordination among the liberation groups.[22]

Shortly after the Cairo meeting, the PLO was rent by a mutiny on the part of its military arm, the PLA, which spurned an attempt by the PLO executive committee to replace General Subhi al-Jabiri as its commander.[23] The PLO's weakness worked to the advantage of Fatah, and this advantage was turned into victory when Arafat himself was elected chairman of the PLO in February, 1969.

The Leftist Palestinians

While Fatah espoused mainly a simple nationalism, other commando groups emerged with more radical leanings. These groups took seriously the argument that the Arab-Israeli conflict and the strategy of guerrilla warfare constituted part of a larger struggle against Western-oriented bourgeois regimes within and without the Arab world and against Western "imperialism" in general.

The antecedent of the major "leftist" commando groups was a group called the Arab Nationalist Movement (ANM) which emerged in the 1950's under Dr. George Habash, a Palestinian of Greek Orthodox origin and a graduate of the American University of Beirut. In the late 1950's and early 1960's, the ANM was supported by Egypt, but Egyptian efforts to bind the group ever more closely to Cairo were resisted, particularly by younger intellectuals who began to develop a Marxist-Leninist orientation. By early 1968 part of the ANM had united with several smaller groups, including Naif Hawatmah's Vengeance Youth, Wajih al-Madani's Heroes of the Return, and Ahmad Jibril's Palestine Liberation Front (PLF), and had formed a group called the Popular Front for the Liberation of Palestine (PFLP) under Habash.

The PFLP differed from Fatah in several respects. Where Fatah

21. *Arab Report and Record,* no. 9 (May 1–15, 1968), p. 128; no. 10 (May 16–31, 1968), inside cover; no. 13 (July 1–15, 1968), p. 199; no. 14 (July 16–31, 1968), p. 214.
22. *Arab Report and Record,* no. 19 (October 1–15, 1968), p. 315; no. 20 (October 16–31, 1968), pp. 339–40 and back cover.
23. *Arab Report and Record,* no. 14 (July 16–31, 1968), p. 216; no. 15 (August 1–15, 1968), p. 234; no. 21 (November 1–15, 1968), back cover.

argued that violence against Israel could precede political organization, the PFLP emphasized the need for unity before struggle. Second, insofar as the PFLP perceived the struggle for Palestine as part of the larger question of domestic political and social revolution throughout the Arab world, the group was anathema to most Arab regimes and did not receive the same level of support as its larger and more conservative rival. Nevertheless, its clear ideological line proved attractive to intellectuals and gave the group a greater impact than its size suggested. Third, the PFLP maintained that, since Zionism was part of world imperialism, terrorism against Israel's non-Arab supporters as well as struggle against Arab regimes that did not render unquestioning support to the Palestine cause was necessary and would be effective.[24] Fatah and the PLO rejected these claims.

Like the other Palestinian groups, the PFLP also suffered divisions. In October, 1968, while Habash was imprisoned in Syria, Hawatmah, a self-proclaimed Trotskyite, sought to seize control of the organization. Habash regained control of the PFLP after he was released by his supporters on November 3 of the same year.[25] That same autumn the PFLP was deserted by Jibril who formed his own group called the PFLP-General Command and by Ahmad Za'rur who formed a group called the Organization of Arab Palestine (OAP). The most important split in the PFLP, however, occurred in February, 1969, when the radical followers of Hawatmah broke away and formed the Democratic Popular Front for the Liberation of Palestine (PDFLP). The ensuing bitterness led to armed clashes in the streets of Amman between the supporters of the two factions which Fatah sought to mediate.[26]

Habash termed his rivals the victims of "infantile leftism" who wished to overthrow Arab governments when they should be focusing their resources on the struggle with Israel. For his part Hawatmah condemned the PFLP's terrorist operations outside the Middle East, including the skyjacking of commercial aircraft, a tactic also practiced by Jibril's PFLP-General Command. Ideological differences between the two radical groups were not, though, as fundamental as the personal animosity between the two leaders, Habash and Hawatmah. William B. Quandt accurately describes the differences and similarities in their views:

> Both the PFLP and the PDFLP appreciate the limits of armed struggle in the absence of fundamental social and political changes in the Arab world. George Habash . . . , however, stresses that armed struggle can

24. See Robert Anton Mertz, "Why George Habash Turned Marxist," *Mid-East,* August 1970, pp. 32–36.
25. *Arab Report and Record,* no. 19 (October 1–15, 1968), pp. 315–16; no. 20 (October 16–31, 1968), p. 340.
26. *Arab Report and Record,* no. 1 (January 1–15, 1969), p. 19; no. 2 (January 16–31, 1969), p. 43 and front cover; no. 3 (February 1–14, 1969), p. 65; no. 4 (February 15–28, 1969), pp. 73–74, 89. See also Gérard Chaliand, *La Résistance Palestinienne* (Paris: Editions de Seuil, 1970).

help to mobilize and educate the masses, and accuses his rival, Nayif Hawatmah of the PDFLP, of following a strategy of first building a political movement, then educating the people, then fighting. The two groups nonetheless agree that the Palestinians cannot achieve their objectives until social and political revolutions have occurred in most of the Arab world. The slogan of noninterference in the affairs of the Arab countries is rejected by both Habash and Hawatmah. . . . The regimes in Lebanon, Jordan, and Saudi Arabia are all branded as reactionary, and both the PFLP and the PDFLP have made no secret of their belief that they should eventually be overthrown. These groups also have often been critical of the so-called progressive regimes in Syria, Iraq, Algeria, and the UAR, all of which they see as dominated by the "petite-bourgeoisie."[27]

Owing to their radicalism and sectarian tactics, the PFLP and PDFLP remained largely isolated, opposed both by other Palestinian groups and by most of the Arab regimes. In time the PFLP-Fatah schism proved to be the most serious division within the Palestinian movement. Both groups, for example, sought to take credit for the same guerrilla operations including market bombings in Jerusalem in November, 1968,[28] the destruction of a pipeline in Haifa, and an explosion near Jerusalem's Wailing Wall during the following year.[29]

The PFLP claimed that Fatah was a reckless and undisciplined organization that strayed from authentic guerrilla warfare and made itself and its supporters conspicuous targets for Israeli reprisals. The Fatah-PFLP rivalry increased as a consequence of fighting that broke out in November, 1968 between units of the Jordanian army and a guerrilla unit. The fighting ended when agreement was reached between the guerrillas involved and the Amman government. The PFLP rejected the armistice, insisting that King Hussein's regime must be toppled before a successful war of liberation against Israel could be launched. This view was in sharp contradiction to the Fatah-PLO policy of seeking a *modus vivendi* with Hussein.[30]

The fact that tactical differences also divided Habash from the other major Palestinian groups became even more evident after an attack in February, 1969 on an Israeli jetliner in Zurich. Fatah denounced the Zurich raid as counterproductive and explained that its operations were designed to avoid civilian casualties. The PFLP declared that it would attack Jewish property anywhere in the world, a threat which it began to carry out zealously.[31] The use of terror in occupied territories had already

27. Quandt, Jabber, and Lesch, *The Politics of Palestinian Nationalism*, p. 99.
28. *Arab Report and Record*, no. 22 (November 16–30, 1968), front cover and p. 383.
29. *Arab Report and Record*, no. 12 (June 16–30, 1969), p. 270.
30. *New York Times*, 6 November 1968, p. 1.
31. See Oriana Fallaci, "A Leader of the Fedayeen: We Want a War Like the Vietnamese War," *Life Magazine* (June 12, 1970), p. 34; also, "Strategy for Revolution: Popular Front for the Liberation of Palestine," in Russell Stetler, ed., *Palestine: The Arab-Israeli Conflict* (San Francisco: Ramparts Press, 1972), pp. 168–89.

complicated the Palestinian search for popular support because of Israeli restrictions on the local population. Thus a grenade attack in Hebron in October, 1968 led the Arab mayor of the city to express publicly his regret to Moshe Dayan.[32] In fact, similar attacks often resulted in greater Arab than Israeli casualties.[33]

Habash and the PFLP naturally resisted Fatah's efforts to coordinate the Palestinian movement, and the PFLP's separate operations continued to embarrass the other groups. When the PASC was formed in the spring of 1969, the PFLP refused to join and carried out the destruction of a section of the Aramco oil pipeline. Since the pipeline brought Saudi Arabia some $150 millions in revenue annually and Saudi Arabia was a prominent financial contributor to Fatah, Fatah publicly apologized for the movement as a whole and demanded that PASC condemn the act. Indeed, all Arab states except Algeria took pains to characterize the incident as contrary to Arab interests.[34] Again, in defiance of the other groups, in the summer of 1969 the PFLP carried out a series of terrorist acts outside the Middle East, including two firebomb attacks on stores in London which had dealings with Israeli's ZIM shipping line. On August 28 Habash warned of further assaults on Jewish establishments in London and elsewhere.[35] His warning was followed by a series of grenade attacks on an El Al office in Brussels and on Israeli embassies in Bonn and the Hague.[36]

The Palestine National Assembly reconvened in Cairo in September. Arafat was reelected chairman of its Executive Committee, and the PASC came under his direction. The Assembly announced that it would follow a policy of noninterference in the affairs of Arab states provided they did not obstruct the Palestinian revolution. The PFLP, however, again boycotted the Assembly.[37] Further organizational reforms ensued. In November a secret Palestinian Revolutionary Council (PRC) was set up to include members of the central committees of Fatah, the Popular Struggle Front, and a small group called al-Ard. The Council's purpose was to further guerrilla activities within the occupied territories in the face of intensive Israeli security measures. These measures proved so unsuccessful that Fatah disbanded its terrorist cells in occupied territories on November 26, 1969.

The waning days of 1969 witnessed more conflicts within the Pales-

32. *New York Times,* 10 October 1968, p. 4.
33. Habash also condemned Fatah's acceptance of financial assistance from "reactionary" regimes.
34. *Arab Report and Record,* no. 10 (May 16–31, 1969), p. 214; no. 11 (June 1–15, 1969), pp. 241, 250; no. 12 (June 16–30, 1969), p. 270.
35. *Arab Report and Record,* no. 16 (August 16–31, 1969), p. 353.
36. In addition to questioning the prudence of the Popular Front's activities, Fatah and the PLO were displeased with the publicity that the PFLP was receiving, *New York Times,* 17 September 1969, p. 23.
37. *New York Times,* 2 September 1969, p. 8; *Arab Report and Record,* no. 17 (September 1–15, 1969), p. 376.

tinian movement. A guerrilla clash with the Lebanese Army in November forced Arafat to seek a negotiated settlement with the Lebanese in Cairo. The settlement was turned down by the PFLP, which claimed that it had not been represented at the parley.[38]

Confounded by continuing internal schisms and bedeviled by growing difficulties with certain Arab regimes, the Palestinian movement made its most ambitious attempt to date to achieve cooperation within its ranks by creating the Unified Command of Palestinian Resistance (UCPR) in February, 1970. The Unified Command seemed particularly significant because, in addition to the original seven member groups that constituted the Palestine Armed Struggle Command, it included the previously independent PFLP and the Democratic Popular Front (PDF) which had suspended its participation in PASC earlier.[39] Formation of the UCPR was a direct response to a crisis in Jordan. The Jordanian government had issued a decree prohibiting the carrying or shooting of weapons in cities. Fearing a clash with the Jordanian army, the Palestinian groups sought to close ranks. In addition to coordinating guerrilla defenses against Amman, the UCPR was to end disturbances caused by its members. The UCPR issued a twelve-point order-of-the-day that implicitly admitted that guerrilla indiscipline was at the root of tension with Jordan.[40] Similar steps in disciplining the movement were taken in Lebanon by the Higher Committee for Palestinian Affairs (HCPA), an organization of representatives of Palestinian groups in that country.[41]

While the UCPR was to complement PASC, it was not to be able to overcome ideological, tactical, and personal differences in the movement or to enforce the discipline it was demanding. Shortly after its formation, there were a series of PFLP attacks on American property in Lebanon and two incidents of sabotage in Istanbul carried out by a group called the Popular Struggle Front (PSF).

The National Commando Groups

As a consequence of the growing influence of the Palestinian liberation groups after 1967, several Arab regimes sought to bolster their flagging positions by creating their own groups. The most notable of these was Saiqa, established in 1968 by the Syrian Baath party. Generously supported by the Syrians, Saiqa grew quickly in 1969 and 1970. Despite its relatively large size, however, Saiqa never became politically important because of its dependence on civilian Baathist politicians in Damascus.

38. *Arab Report and Record,* no. 21 (November 1–15, 1969), p. 474.
39. *Arab Report and Record,* no. 4 (February 15–28, 1970), p. 136.
40. *Arab Report and Record,* no. 4 (February 15–28, 1970), p. 137.
41. *New York Times,* 27 February 1970, p. 1.

They sought to use the group domestically as a counterweight to the political ambitions of Baathist members of the Syrian Army, principally General Hafiz al-Assad. When Assad took power in late 1970, he was able to seize control of Saiqa as well.

The second major state-sponsored group was organized in 1969 by the Iraqi Baathists, bitter enemies of their Syrian colleagues. This group, the Arab Liberation Front (ALF), never gained much influence in the Palestinian movement.

Chronic squabbling among the Palestinians so disgusted President Muhammar al-Qaddafi of Libya, an outspoken supporter of the guerrillas, that he declared at Tobruk on March 31, 1970, that Palestinian cohesion might become a condition for his country's continued support of the movement.[42] The disarray was summarized by Professor Walid Khalidi in an address to the seminar:

> (We) have found that the fedayeen were no less shortsighted than were the Arab Governments. The fedayeen have split into nationalists, Marxist-Leninists, left-wingers, and even Baathists. Each faction claims to be the one true spokesman for the Palestinian and some go even further and fight the others. . . .[43]

The Palestinian Movement and Regime Stability

Based on quantitative data, we concluded in the previous chapter that the *Palestine* and *Regime Stability* superissues were closely related. A qualitative analysis of the Palestinian question also confirms this generalization.

However autonomous the Palestinian movement became in certain respects, the support of certain "front-line" Arab regimes and at least the tacit acquiescence of others were always indispensable for its survival. Despite initial hopes, the Palestinian struggle did *not* conform to the Vietnamese, Cuban, or Algerian models of popular wars of liberation. Although Fatah sought briefly after June, 1967 to develop a climate of civil disobedience in the occupied territories and to create an incipient clandestine network, its attempt to bring about a general insurrection was an abject failure. The principal reasons for this failure lay in the fear of local Arabs that open revolt would provide Israel with a rationale for their wholesale ejection, in the compactness of the theater of operations, and in the tight Israeli military control of both the West Bank and the Gaza Strip. Thus, as early as September, 1967, a group of professional and business leaders in the Arab community began to discuss the possibility of a settlement with Israel that would involve a new Palestinian state separate from

42. *The New Middle East,* no. 20 (May 1970), p. 47.
43. *Ibid.,* p. 9.

Jordan.[44] In February, 1970, the mayor of Hebron called for the creation of a "Palestinian entity" on the West Bank, declaring that Arab refugees were being used as pawns by the Arab governments and that guerrilla activity prevented peace in the Middle East.[45] In September, 1970 one observer declared: "Indeed, never have the fedayeen organizations been so unpopular in the occupied areas as in the past few weeks; never has the cleavage been so great between the Palestinians living under Israeli control and those outside of Palestine, who claim to represent all Palestinians."[46] The losses suffered by the guerrillas in Jordan shortly thereafter only emboldened West Bank Palestinians to take further initiatives in defiance of the fedayeen groups.

Under these conditions, the Palestinian organizations had no recourse but to engage in commando-style, hit-and-run raids *across* the ceasefire lines. Their inability to maintain effective forces in the Israeli-occupied territories or in Israel itself made the existence of accessible sanctuary areas imperative. Such sanctuaries, necessary for recruitment, training, and logistics, had to be located in the front-line states: Jordan, Syria, and Lebanon. The attitude of these countries was made even more crucial by the fact that, without the support of Palestinians in occupied territories, the major source of guerrilla strength was Palestinian refugees housed in camps in these three states. The unique grievances of the refugees made them receptive to mobilization. As one commentator observes:

(W)hat does distinguish these people is the loss of those things which constitute a heritage—the home which provides privacy for one's family . . . the land and property which belonged to one's ancestors . . . and a nationality and pride in that nationality.[47]

Free movement in Jordan, Syria, and Lebanon was vital to the guerrillas, but an inevitable tension arose between the fedayeen and the three regimes because of the operational requirements of large-scale paramilitary organizations and the Israeli tactic of retaliating against sanctuary states after guerrilla raids. The pressure on host regimes to restrain guerrilla activities remained high as a consequence of Israel's undisputed military preponderance on the "eastern" front after June, 1967.

Other interests of the sanctuary states and the Palestinian movement were by no means identical or even congruent. After 1967 the objectives of the Arab regimes vis-à-vis Israel involved liberation of occupied territories,

44. *New York Times,* 9 September 1967, p. 9.
45. *New York Times,* 18 February 1970, p. 12.
46. *The New Middle East,* no. 20 (September 1970), p. 18.
47. "Human Rights and the Palestinian," *Mid-East* 7 (December 1967), p. 15. See also James A. Michener, "What To Do About the Palestinian Refugees," *The New York Times Magazine* (September 27, 1970), p. 23.

regime stability at home, and, in some cases, reduction of inter-Arab hostility. Ultimately, those regimes prepared to reach a political compromise with Israel would have to recognize that nation-state's right to exist and accept either an isolated independent Palestinian state on the West Bank or the return of that area to Jordan. All of these possibilities remained inimical to the avowed objectives of the Palestinian guerrillas who sought the liberation not only of occupied territories, but of Israel itself, with the ultimate goal of assuming political power over the entire area. In addition, the Palestinian movement remained largely indifferent to questions of Arab regime stability except as they related to the attainment of Palestinian objectives. Indeed, as we have noted, certain groups actively sought the overthrow of "reactionary" regimes. It was natural, therefore, that the degree and type of support which regimes were prepared to afford the Palestinians was influenced by more than simply the merits of the Palestinian cause. The internal stability of a regime, its capacity to resist Israeli reprisals, and its relations with its Arab neighbors (as well as other national, economic, social, and political factors) were also significant variables.

During much of the period, Jordan and Lebanon, both small states with conservative regimes threatened by acute domestic cleavages, behaved similarly towards the guerrillas. While the Jordanians acknowledged the justice of the Palestinian cause, they hesitated to provide political or military assistance. Indeed, Jordan did not endorse the Palestinian goal of liberating Israel, and on several occasions King Hussein indicated his willingness to recognize the existence of Israel as part of a final political settlement.[48] Moreover, Jordan's attitude towards the Palestinian objective of liberating the West Bank remained ambiguous. Jordan considered the territory an integral part of the Hashemite kingdom and was sensitive to any suggestion that it might be made permanently independent of Amman. Hussein would only concede the West Bank population a right to determine its own future *after* Jordanian authority had been restored there. The main pillar of Hashemite and monarchical support derived from the Bedouin tribes on the East Bank, not from the Palestinians.[49]

The most important service Jordan could render the Palestinians was to permit them sanctuary and freedom of movement, and, as guerrilla operations within Israel became impossible, the guerrillas did view Jordan as an indispensable base of operations. Yet as Israeli search-and-destroy tactics and air strikes stepped up against the Jordanian sanctuary, sending refugees eastward and causing severe economic dislocation, the costs to

48. *New York Times,* 22 June 1967, p. 1; and 26 July 1967, p. 9.
49. Despite Jordanian resistance, an Arab summit conference held in Rabat, Morocco, in October, 1974 decided that a Palestinian state under the PLO should be established in the West Bank after Israel withdraws.

Amman became prohibitive. Thus in 1970 and 1971, the Jordanian army began to intercept guerrilla units en route to Israel.[50] In addition, Amman came to view the Palestinians as a serious threat to Jordanian sovereignty.[51] Within the teeming refugee camps, the guerrillas had actually established a parallel administrative and governing hierarchy, and by 1970 Hussein was no longer willing to tolerate expedients that placed restrictions on his regime. Amman's uneasiness was increased by the fact that certain guerrilla groups such as Saiqa were sponsored by Arab regimes that were hostile to the monarchy.

Like Jordan, Lebanon evidenced disquiet over the prospect of an independent Palestinian state even though in the abstract this would relieve the Lebanese of the burden of a large refugee community. Unlike Jordan, Lebanon had no potential territorial quarrel with the Palestinians who did not claim areas of Lebanon as part of Palestine. Beirut held the guerrillas at arm's length for other reasons. One of these was that Lebanon's population was half Christian, largely Maronite and Greek Orthodox, and this significant sector did not view the Palestinian cause with particular favor. A second reason was that Lebanon, with an army of only 12,000 troops, feared that Israeli reprisals might lead to a loss of territory in the south and dislocate its economy which was heavily dependent on tourism. Hence Beirut endorsed United Nations Security Council Resolution 242 and the related principle of a political settlement with Israel, a position which placed the regime in conflict with Palestinian aims.[52]

After Jordan, Lebanon was the most important sanctuary available to the fedayeen. However, Beirut ultimately sought to restrict guerrilla base areas and operations along Israel's border, especially after the Jordanian civil war. Lebanon's sovereignty, like Jordan's, was threatened by the establishment of parallel governing hierarchies in fourteen of the fifteen refugee camps and in large areas in southern Lebanon.[53] Also, when guerrilla operations were shifted to Lebanon after the fedayeen defeat in Jordan, Israeli retaliations menaced the tourist trade and the agricultural productivity of the south. By 1971 Lebanese villagers in the south began to demand the cessation of guerrilla activities. In addition, the machinations of the guerrillas threatened to upset the country's delicate confessional system in which political power was equally divided between Christians and Moslems. Finally, Beirut grew sensitive to the possibility that the leftist Palestinian groups might seek to overthrow the regime itself.[54]

50. *New York Times,* 1 June 1971, p. 3.
51. *New York Times,* 26 July 1971, p. 22.
52. *Arab Report and Record,* no. 12 (June 16–30, 1968), p. 167.
53. *New York Times,* 28 December 1968, p. 25.
54. By 1974, Lebanon had become the major Palestinian sanctuary for attempts to prevent a successful conclusion to Henry Kissinger's efforts to negotiate a Middle Eastern settlement. Consequently, Lebanon had again become a target of large-scale Israeli reprisals.

As the most influential of the Arab states, Egypt's position was crucial to the Palestinians. Egypt, however, while repeatedly declaring the fedayeen cause "lawful and just," also denied to the movement unlimited political and material support. After 1967 Egypt pursued the limited aims of achieving a return of the Sinai and other occupied territories, while restricting Soviet influence in the Arab world. Such objectives seemed to allow for the *de facto* existence of Israel. While Egypt declared that any political solution would have to take Palestinian rights into account, this did not necessarily imply recognition of the Palestinian goal of the destruction of the Jewish state.[55] Egypt was prepared to provide "moderate" guerrilla groups with limited arms, money, training, military intelligence, and broadcast time on Radio Cairo. But, this assistance fluctuated and was withheld when it suited Cairo's purposes. Probably the most important aid that Egypt rendered the Palestinians prior to the 1973 "Yom Kippur" war was indirect: the Egyptian "war of attrition" on the Sinai front which coincided with fedayeen tactics of gradually "bleeding" Israel. Despite Palestinian objections, the war of attrition ended in 1970 when Nasser accepted the American cease-fire plan.

On the other hand, Egypt's position of leadership in the Arab world made it difficult for Nasser, and later Sadat, to abjure the guerrillas completely. Following the June 1967 war Nasser's prestige suffered, and Yasser Arafat and his followers emerged as the heroes of the Cairo mob, a major factor in Egyptian politics. Nasser also found it expedient to lend the guerrillas support so as not to stimulate greater opposition to him among radical Arab regimes, and to keep the Palestinian movement from emerging as the unrivalled champions of the Arab struggle against Israel. In addition, Egypt found the movement useful as an instrument to pressure Israel into making diplomatic concessions.

Overall, the Egyptian leadership continued to believe that conventional warfare was the only feasible way to pursue Arab objectives, a view which seemed in part to be borne out by the events of October, 1973. Moreover, Anwar Sadat was not committed to Nasser's goal of pan-Arabism. Sadat's willingness to pursue a moderate nationalist policy was rewarded after October, 1973, when negotiations with Israel, mediated by Henry Kissinger, led to a mutual pullback in the Sinai. Such an "Egypt-first" policy could only be antagonistic to the Palestinian movement and its aspirations, and the policy triggered a desperate attempt on the part of certain groups to prevent a permanent settlement with Israel.

The relations of the monarchical and oil-rich states—Kuwait, Saudi Arabia and Libya—with the Palestinians were largely restricted to selective financial aid until a military coup which threw out King Idris in 1969 transformed Libya into a militant supporter of the guerrillas.

55. *New York Times,* 30 August 1970, p. 12.

Kuwait, like Saudi Arabia and Libya, was concerned with avoiding both isolation in the Arab world and Western reprisals, as well as with preventing disruption of the flow of petroleum. Kuwait financed specific fedayeen groups from both public and private sources and declared that it would approve of no political settlement that was not acceptable to the "Palestinian people." In May, 1968, the Kuwait government enacted a two-percent tax on gasoline sales and cinema tickets to support the guerrillas. This support supplemented a three-and-one-half percent deduction from the salaries of the large population of Palestinians residing in the country that was already being donated.

Saudi Arabia, governed by the conservative King Faisal, was a cautious benefactor of only "moderate" Palestinian organizations, that is, groups which it viewed as neither a threat to the political stability of the Saudi monarchy nor to the country's vast oil reserves. Ideologically opposed to radical republicanism and communism in the Middle East, Faisal sought to make Fatah dependent upon Saudi contributions partly to prevent the organization's being controlled by Egypt and Syria, which Faisal perceived as hostile to his kingdom. Faisal's opposition to Egyptian pretensions to leadership was apparent in the open support that Saudi Arabia rendered the royalist faction during the Yemeni civil war of 1967. Always concerned about the unreliability of the leftist Palestinian groups, the Saudi government was outraged by the PFLP Tapline incident of May, 1969. Saudi Arabia denounced the Palestinian extremists and demanded that they be purged, and, as we have seen, Fatah publicly apologized to Faisal for the episode.[56] Saudi financial assistance to the Palestinians (reportedly $100,000 per month) was sufficiently important to persuade Arafat to pay periodic visits to Jedda in 1970, particularly after one quarterly payment to the PLO was withheld.[57]

Saudi Arabia's political support of the guerrillas remained inconsistent. The Saudis, for example, welcomed the Rogers's ceasefire plan and voiced their hope for "an era of stability and tranquility in the region." In May, 1971, Faisal emphasized to the American Secretary of State that a political settlement with Israel was possible if the latter withdrew from territories occupied in June, 1967.[58] Moreover, Faisal was prepared to back his fellow-monarch, King Hussein, during Jordan's trial with the guerrillas in the summer of 1971.[59] While seeking to mediate the Jordanian-Palestinian quarrel, Faisal was determined not to permit Hussein's overthrow by the leftist guerrillas whom he feared and detested. At the same time, he sought a reconciliation with Egypt and Syria. In general, the

56. *New York Times,* 31 May 1969, p. 14; and *Arab Report and Review,* no. 11 (June 1–15, 1969), p. 233.
57. *Arab Report and Review,* no. 15 (August 1–15, 1970), p. 462.
58. *Daily Star* (Beirut), 3 October 1971, p. 1.
59. *New York Times,* 23 July 1971, p. 9.

Saudis aimed to become principal spokesmen for the Arab nations while preventing the struggle with Israel from becoming an excuse for regional instability. To some degree Faisal ultimately succeeded in this policy after the Yom Kippur war when he took the lead in the Arab restrictions of petroleum exports to Israel's Western supporters.

Libya, Syria, Algeria, and Iraq proved over a period of time to be the most militant supporters of the Palestinian movement. Their relations with the fedayeen, however, were also profoundly affected by internal politics.

Libya, as we have mentioned, became a firm backer of the fedayeen after a military coup brought Muhammar al-Qaddafi to power.[60] Yet the assertively militant posture of the Tripoli junta on the question of liberating the Palestinian "homeland" did not go so far as to support guerrilla warfare as the *only* Arab strategy. Qaddafi frequently criticized the tactics and ideology of certain Palestinian groups, and, his revolutionary rhetoric notwithstanding, at times he seemed to be more intent on engineering a confederation with Egypt and Syria than achieving the defeat of Israel. Indeed, Qaddafi's brand of Moslem fundamentalism and his view of Palestinian liberation through the lenses of pan-Arabism suggest that to him the fedayeen were at most auxiliary forces in the conflict with Israel. Thus Qaddafi condemned the Palestinians for holding parochial views of the Arab-Israel struggle. He argued that Palestine was not analogous to Vietnam because the Palestinian question was a matter for all Arabs, not just the Palestinians, whereas Vietnam was a matter for the Vietnamese to settle by themselves.[61]

Although Tripoli rendered moral, political, and material assistance to the Palestinians, its relationship with them was complicated by Qaddafi's antipathy towards the PFLP. Libya professed little enthusiasm for the extra-regional terrorist acts of this group and permitted its press to criticize it. Ideologically, Qaddafi was at odds with the PFLP because he viewed Marxism-Leninism as alien to Islam. On several occasions, therefore, leftist guerrillas in Libya were arrested or deported. In January, 1971, Qaddafi termed the PFLP and PDF "deviationist, secessionist organizations" that were preoccupied with Marxist-Leninist dogma to the detriment of the movement as a whole. After the PDF retorted that the Libyan leader was siding with American imperialism, Qaddafi demanded that the leftist groups be purged by the PLO.

Qaddafi's mistrust of leftist groups was reinforced by his conviction that they were largely responsible for the chronic disunity of the Palestinian resistance. As a zealous advocate of pan-Arabic unity, he became increasingly frustrated with the "radical" Palestinians. During the Jordanian crisis

60. See Eric Rouleau, "Oil and Monarchy Don't Mix," *Africa Report* 14 (November 1969), pp. 24–27.
61. *Arab Report and Review,* no. 15 (August 1–15, 1970), p. 463.

of June, 1971, he absolved both Fatah and Hussein of blame for the civil war, whose blame he placed instead upon the "eastward-looking extreme leftists and the westward-looking extreme rightists."[62]

Qaddafi's public criticism of the guerrillas engendered hostility towards him even among moderate Palestinians. Some described him as a "young and inexperienced . . . dictator" who criticized the Palestinians because of pressure from "his masters, the Egyptians and other Arab heads of state." Many Palestinians were openly annoyed by what they saw as Qaddafi's unqualified admiration of Egypt's Nasser, which seemed to be reflected in Qaddafi's acceptance with Egypt of the Rogers's ceasefire plan in the summer of 1970.

As in the case of Libya, Iraq's policy, while generally strongly supporting the guerrillas, was influenced by leadership changes. During the remainder of 1967 after the June war, Baghdad appeared to render the Palestinians unqualified assistance, even permitting its troops in Jordan to join in commando attacks.[63] In addition, the Baghdad regime encouraged pro-fedayeen demonstrations, raised funds for the PFLP, PDF, and Fatah, and endorsed the idea of a war of national liberation.

Iraq's position began to waver, however, after a coup d'état in July, 1968, brought to power Ahmed Hassa Bakr and the Baath Party.[64] In the spring of 1969, the new regime began to demand that the guerrillas coordinate their activities more closely with Iraqi security forces. More importantly, Iraq requested that the fedayeen in that country place themselves under the aegis of the newly-created Arab Liberation Front (ALF). Holding power tenuously while keenly aware of Iraq's history of political turmoil and coups, Iraq's Baathist politicians were apprehensive lest an organized force such as the Palestinian guerrillas meddle in the country's internal affairs and hold the balance of power during a political crisis.[65] This concern was manifested in May when the guerrillas were told to restrict their training to camps near the frontier—in the Rutbah area near Jordan—and to stop sponsoring public rallies or collecting funds.[66]

In spite of these restrictions, Iraq continued to serve as a relative bastion of support for the guerrillas. In September, 1969 Baghdad refused to send a delegation to the Islamic summit conference because the PLO had not been guaranteed a right to speak. Iraq also censured Lebanese

62. *The New Middle East,* no. 22 (July 1971), p. 8.
63. *New York Times,* 21 October 1967, p. 12; 13 November 1967, p. 4; 24 March 1968, p. 21.
64. For a discussion of Iraq's domestic problems, see Abbas Kelidar, "Shifts and Changes in the Arab World," *The World Today* 24 (November 1968), p. 508.
65. See Michael Feld, "Growing Realism Among the Revolutionaries," *The New Middle East,* no. 29 (February 1971), p. 27.
66. *Mid-East* 9 (May–June 1969), p. 26; *New York Times,* 15 June 1969, p. 17.

actions against the commandos in September, publicly pledged its support to the Palestinians in the United Nations General Assembly, and vowed to protect the guerrillas during a Lebanese-guerrilla confrontation in October. In December the government passed a law requiring Palestinian residents to pay a three percent tax to the PLO and the next month began large-scale deliveries of arms to the guerrillas.[67]

When civil war erupted in Jordan in June, 1970 between the Palestinians and Hussein, Iraq dispatched Vice-President Saleh Mahdi Amash to Amman in order to reconcile the two sides. After mediation failed, Baghdad indicated that its 12,000 troops stationed in Jordan were at the disposal of the Palestinians. In addition, Iraq rejected the Roger's Plan and charged that Egypt's acceptance of it meant that Cairo had forsworn Palestinian liberation.[68]

As the Jordanian civil war continued, however, Iraq chose the path of caution, which proved a major factor in King Hussein's ability to decimate the guerrillas in his country.[69] Although Iraq sent its Vice-President and Chief of Staff to visit guerrilla forces in Jordan and carried on a vituperative radio campaign against Hussein, it turned down fedayeen appeals to intervene militarily. In fact, Iraqi forces in Jordan permitted Hussein's troops to pass through their positions.

Iraq's caution at this time appears to have been the product of a fear of foreign intervention coupled with concern about domestic instability. Vice-President Hadran Takritti, who had headed the military committee that supervised the Iraqi contingent in Jordan and who had opposed Iraqi intervention, was removed from office in an attempt by President Bakr to appease the militant civilian wing of his Baath Party.

Syria's relations with the Palestinian movement, like Libya's and Iraq's, varied with internal conditions. After the June war, Syria reiterated its support of a people's war of national liberation as the appropriate strategy for freeing Palestine. Rejecting the possibility of a political settlement with Israel, Syria's Baathist leadership underscored its militance by boycotting the Khartoum summit meeting and training fedayeen for service on Jordan's borders.[70]

Nevertheless, Damascus remained selective in its support of guerrilla groups. In March and April, 1968, members of the radical PFLP were arrested and their arms confiscated. This move apparently stemmed from

67. See *New York Times,* 1 September 1969, p. 4; 23 September 1969, p. 27; 10 January 1970, p. 1; 24 January 1970, p. 7; 12 February 1970, p. 1.
68. *Arab Report and Review,* no. 14 (July 16–31, 1970), p. 429; *New York Times,* 27 July 1970, p. 14.
69. *Arab Report and Review,* no. 17 (September 1–15, 1970), pp. 492–93, 516; no. 18 (September 16–30, 1970), p. 539.
70. *New York Times,* 30 July 1967, p. 22; 30 August 1967, p. 1; 18 September 1967, p. 3; 21 October 1967, p. 4.

the concern of the Syrian Baathists about their former domestic rival, the Arab Nationalist Movement (ANM), which constituted the core of the PFLP. Of still greater significance was the creation and support by the civilian wing of the Syrian Baath Party of its own guerrilla organization, Saiqa. Syria's rejection of the possibility of peace with Israel, and United Nations Security Council Resolution 242 was compatible with fundamental Palestinian views.[71] In addition, Syria publicly turned down Secretary of State Rogers' ceasefire plan of July, 1970. Yet Damascus seemed to adopt this position largely for domestic consumption and pressed its brief against Egyptian acceptance with little vigor or conviction.

If Syria was privately disposed to go along with Nasser on the American plan, a moderate position became untenable when Jordan was plunged into civil war in September, 1970. Early in that month Damascus accused Amman of plotting the liquidation of the Palestinian resistance and pledged its assistance to the guerrillas. When its prophecy seemed to come true and the beleaguered commandos publicly called for aid against Hussein's army, Syria responded by supporting (perhaps even initiating) an abortive armed invasion of Jordan.[72] The invasion had mixed results. On the one hand, Syrian prestige in the Arab world soared, particularly when its action was contrasted with the inertia of its Baathist rivals in Iraq. On the other hand, confronted by a threatened American intervention and with its tank column bloodied by Jordanian aerial attacks, Damascus was forced to withdraw the contingent without preventing Jordan from crushing the guerrillas. Indeed, the commitment of a tank force lacking air support and its enforced withdrawal created the conditions for political backlash in Syria and led to the overthrow of the civilian Baathists of Jedid and President Atassi by the military wing of the Baathists under General Assad. Assad himself was known to be out of sympathy with Saiqa, and his adversaries claimed that he wished to see the guerrilla movement destroyed and a political settlement reached with Israel.[73]

In light of these developments, the Palestinians could take little comfort from Syria's verbal criticism of Hussein's final crackdown on the guerrillas and the resultant closing of the Syrian-Jordanian frontier. Although Syria severed diplomatic ties with Jordan in August, 1971, this seemed less a substantive weakening of Hussein than a response by Assad to pressure from Iraq, Algeria, and Syrian militants. No major military buildup took place at this time in southern Syria.[74]

General Assad's skepticism about the guerrillas was indirectly revealed by his decision in 1971 to join in a loose confederation with Egypt

71. *The New Middle East*, no. 22 (July 1970), p. 8.
72. *New York Times*, 21 September 1970, p. 1.
73. *New York Times*, 16 October 1970, p. 1.
74. *New York Times*, 14 August 1971, p. 5.

and Libya, since Egypt (the most influential of the three) was then known to favor a political settlement with Israel.[75] Syria's later participation in the attack on Israel in the autumn of 1973 suggested that Damascus had revised its views about the efficacy of conventional military pressure on Israel. Finally, Syria's willingness to negotiate with Israel in 1974 boded ill for the ultimate fate of the Palestinian movement, given the fact that Syria had theretofore been the most secure of guerrilla sanctuaries.

Perhaps the most consistent supporter of the Palestinian revolutionaries throughout this period was Algeria. The possibility of Algerian assistance, however, was limited by the simple fact of geography; it is more than 1,100 miles from Israel. Both before and after the June War, the regime of Houari Boumedienne extolled the Palestinian cause and the efficacy of revolutionary war. Algeria repeatedly denounced the various peace proposals and opposed interference in the Palestinian movement, including the actions of Jordan and Lebanon and the creation of small state-sponsored guerrilla groups such as Saiqa.[76] As early as 1970, Palestinians were attending officer training in Algeria with the same status as Algerian cadets. Algerian military and financial support of the guerrillas also proved to be relatively generous.

In addition to their sincere sympathy for the Palestinians, Algerian policy, it seemed, was influenced by several factors. These included geographic safety from Israeli reprisals, the experience of a successful revolutionary war against France, and a desire to divert attention from problems of internal economic development.[77]

The Fruits of Disunity:
Civil War in Jordan

By 1970 divisions within the Palestinian movement were no longer merely frustrating joint efforts against Israel but were also generating grave friction with the governments of Lebanon and Jordan. The Palestinian cause suffered a major setback when Egypt accepted the American ceasefire proposal in the summer of 1970. The ambushing of an Israeli school bus on May 22, resulting in eleven Israeli deaths, was condemned by Fatah and led to heavy Israeli shellings of Lebanese border areas and Israeli incursions across the frontier. In response, the Lebanese Cabinet banned the firing of rockets from Lebanon and the planting of explosives near the

75. *New York Times,* 21 August 1971, p. 18.
76. See *New York Times,* 30 July 1967, p. 12; *Arab Report and Review,* no. 6 (March 16–31, 1968), p. 69; no. 7 (April 1–15, 1969), p. 138; *The New Middle East,* no. 30 (March 1971), p. 4.
77. See J. Gaspard, "Algerian Mentor Gives a Helping Hand," *The New Middle East,* no. 33 (June 1971), pp. 33–34.

border. The PFLP declared that it would resist Lebanon's attempt "to impose tutelage on commando activity in the name of coordination."[78] In effect, the indiscipline of certain groups was placing in jeopardy Palestinian relations with the sanctuary states.

The seventh meeting of the Palestine National Assembly, which lasted from May 30 to June 4, made an attempt to prevent matters from further deteriorating.[79] Pleas for unity by the representatives of Fatah and others, however, fell on deaf ears as the PFLP boycotted the conclave.

A decision was reached at the meeting to set up (1) a central committee responsible for the overall direction of Palestinian affairs, (2) a unified military command to replace the PASC, and (3) liaison committees to foster closer relations with the Lebanese and Jordanian governments. The unified military command, with Arafat at its head, was made up of the eleven groups represented on the central committee. It divided all guerrilla activity and training into geographic areas, each with its own commander. Each group retained the right to withdraw from the command, but in the meantime the command was to enforce discipline upon groups that carried out operations endangering the security of the movement.[80] The real agency for coordination, though, was to be the central committee on which all major groups were represented. Its six-man secretariat consisted of Arafat (Fatah), Habash (PFLP), Issam Sartawi (AOLP), Hawatmeh (PDFLP), Dhafi Jumayanni (Saiqa), and Kamal Nasser (PLO).

The efficacy of the new organizational structure was soon put to the test. Shortly after the Assembly session ended, the PFLP and PDFLP instigated serious fighting with the Jordanian army.[81] By this time King Hussein, buttressed by Bedouin loyalty to the Hashemite throne, was convinced that commando operations in his country could only lead to Israeli reprisals and so contribute to unrest among the Palestinian refugees in Jordan. Such developments, he felt, posed a threat to national stability and to the throne itself.

On June 15, the new central committee announced that it was assuming all responsibility for the direction of the Palestine resistance and was placing all military and popular forces under its command. Nevertheless, Habash and Hawatmeh and their radical groups, having gained prestige as a consequence of the fighting, demanded that King Hussein disband his special forces and relieve a number of prominent military commanders and political figures. In addition, the PDF criticized an attempt by the central committee to set up a four-man committee to mediate the crisis, calling it interference in the internal affairs of the resistance.[82]

78. *New York Times,* 23 May 1970, p. 5.
79. *Arab Report and Record,* no. 10 (May 16–31, 1970), p. 312.
80. *Arab Report and Record,* no. 11 (June 1–15, 1970), pp. 343–44.
81. *The New Middle East,* no. 22 (July 1970), pp. 8–10.
82. *Arab Report and Record,* no. 12 (June 16–30, 1970), p. 373.

Pressure continued to mount on the dissidents to conform. On June 26, an obviously irritated Yasser Arafat warned Habash that "our masses cannot anymore tolerate an extremist demagogue who does nothing to change the *status quo*."[83] Egypt's President Nasser then reached an understanding with Hussein and Arafat to curb Habash and Hawatmeh,[84] and in July the central committee and the Jordanian government reached an accord which did not include the demands that had been made by the radicals.[85]

This accord was aborted, however, by a series of explosive events that rocked the Middle East in September. In the already tense atmosphere created by episodic fighting that had gone on between the Jordanian army and the guerrillas since June, the PFLP carried out a series of dramatic skyjackings. During the summer, the PFLP and PDFLP had apparently decided that the moment was at hand for the launching of a full-scale assault on the Jordanian regime. When the passengers and aircraft were held hostage in Jordan in defiance of the regime, the government perceived a threat to national sovereignty and the army experienced a sense of acute humiliation as it was forced to stand by helplessly.

Fatah sought to minimize the damage caused by the PFLP by negotiating an agreement with the International Red Cross for the release of the hostages. A central committee meeting on September 12 decided to release both the aircraft and hostages, but the PFLP, in defiance of the majority, blew up the jetliners. The central committee responded by suspending the membership of the PFLP, condemning the skyjackings, and warning against further activities that harmed the revolution.[86]

The Jordanian army now moved against the guerrillas with savage fury until an agreement ended the fighting on September 27. The civil war in Jordan proved a disastrous defeat for the militant guerrillas as they were pushed out of Jordan's cities into the north and suffered large-scale casualties and losses of equipment. The guerrilla decline was reflected in the sudden cessation of military activity against Israel. Indeed, several of the smaller commando groups, including the ALF, were virtually eliminated by the civil war.

The principal cause of the September debacle was the PFLP's behavior. This behavior again revealed Palestinian disunity and organizational indiscipline. In addition to providing King Hussein with an excuse to decimate the guerrillas, the skyjackings elicited criticism throughout the Arab world, the Soviet Union, and the world community. In the final analysis, the political, material, and moral defeat for the Palestinian movement far outweighed the release of a few imprisoned guerrillas.

83. *New York Times,* 27 June 1970, p. 1.
84. *The New Middle East,* no. 22 (July 1970), p. 8.
85. *New York Times,* 11 July 1970, p. 8.
86. *Daily Star* (Beirut), 13 September 1970, p. 2; *New York Times,* 14 September 1970, p. 3.

During the remainder of 1970 and for much of 1971, internecine strife among the Palestinians was greater than Arab-Israeli conflict. The movement reached its lowest point since the June war. On January 4, 1971, the PFLP and Saiqa, referring to Fatah, condemned "unilateral acts and a trend towards autocracy by certain sections of the resistance movement."[87] Renewed fighting with the Jordanians further increased tension among the guerrilla groups. Thus the PFLP refused to abide by a ceasefire negotiated with Jordan on January 14, which was to involve disarming the guerrilla militia in Amman. Instead, the PFLP called for the overthrow of Hussein.[88] Fatah in turn charged that the PFLP was in collusion with Hussein to undermine the resistance, and a Fatah leader, Kamal Adwan, warned that force would be used to prevent the revolution from being diverted from the struggle with Israel. He branded Habash "an adventurer who wants to make good his inferiority complex."[89] Simultaneously the PDFLP criticized both sides, charging that Fatah was isolating the resistance from the Jordanian masses and that the PFLP was displaying "adventurist tendencies" that gave Jordan "pretexts for liquidating the resistance and disarming the people."[90]

Against this background, a meeting of the Palestine National Assembly was summoned to meet on February 27 in order to consider "serious problems." At this moment the commander of the Palestinian Liberation Army (PLA), General Abdal-Yahya, apparently decided to challenge Arafat and made a bid for power. Citing the "lamentably deteriorating commando movement" and the need for unity in order to bring the PLO from the brink of collapse, Yahya urged all guerrilla formations to merge into the PLO and asked the Assembly to form a new collective leadership.[91] Yahya pursued his course throughout February, demanding the dissolution of existing Palestinian organizations and their unification under a single command as well as the establishment of a special committee to investigate alleged errors that the movement had made.[92]

Arafat's position seemed secure, however, as the Assembly adopted the so-called "Arafat Plan" which proposed a measure of guerrilla unification in the political, military, and propaganda fields. The Fatah leader stressed that this should be "unity in the real sense and not only some kind of coordinated work."[93] While no meaningful fusion took place, agreement was reached to prohibit skyjackings.[94] Shortly thereafter a committee was named to discuss the "Arafat Plan," and Arafat in a goodwill

87. *Arab Report and Record,* no. 1 (January 1–15, 1971), p. 48.
88. *New York Times,* 18 January 1971, p. 4.
89. *Arab Report and Record,* no. 2 (January 16–31, 1971), p. 78.
90. *Ibid,* p. 78.
91. *Daily Star* (Beirut), 28 January 1971, p. 1.
92. *Daily Star* (Beirut), 18 February 1971, p. 5.
93. *Free Palestine,* February 1971, p. 1.
94. *Arab Report and Record,* no. 5 (March 1–15, 1971), p. 156; *The New Middle East,* no. 31 (April 1971), p. 50.

gesture appointed a Saiqa officer as guerrilla commander in Lebanon.

As usual, not all groups were satisfied with the eighth meeting of the Assembly. Both the PFLP and PDFLP viewed it as an abject failure, and the PFLP declared that before approving the "Arafat Plan" it was necessary to agree upon who were the movement's enemies and who were its friends—a demand that reflected the PFLP's aversion to "reactionary" regimes, notably the Jordanian monarchy.[95] Yahya's followers also ridiculed the results of the meeting and urged that a new Assembly be established in June along with a single politico-military command to enforce standardization of equipment, training, and planning.[96]

In the midst of this confusion, Jordan and even Syria took steps to bring the guerrillas under control. Hussein vowed to launch a "final crackdown," and the PLO sought to defuse the situation by denying Jordanian charges that the guerrillas had carried out acts of sabotage in Amman, Zerqa, and Ruseifah. But to the PLO's chagrin, the PFLP promptly stepped forward and took credit for the very acts which the PLO was disclaiming![97] In Syria the regime took steps to purge leftist elements from the guerrillas in that country by confiscating arms and placing Saiqa under closer government control.

With events in Jordan entering another critical phase, the Palestine National Assembly reconvened on July 7, 1971. Owing to persistent ideological differences, Arafat conceded that a loosely federated movement had become preferable to any more tightly organized movement. However, confronted by mounting Jordanian hostility, the Assembly indicated that all the guerrilla groups had agreed to join a single command under Arafat. It was also announced that the Action Organization for the Liberation of Palestine, the Arab Palestine Organization, and the Popular Struggle Front would merge with Fatah. Further impetus toward coordination was provided by the severe financial shortage then being experienced by the guerrillas.[98] The meeting of the Assembly concluded earlier than planned when King Hussein decided to unleash his army against the guerrillas in an effort to drive them once and for all from Jordan. The disunited Palestinians were again routed, and their acute frustration was revealed in an interview with Fatah's Salah Khalaf:

> These are the facts—the facts of the butchery of September. Now what took place following the events of September? After September, an evaluation of all the confrontations and plots against the movement . . . should have been undertaken . . . so that the forces of the revolution would take a unified course of action against the counterrevolutionary

95. *Daily Star* (Beirut), 1 March 1971, p. 4; 13 March 1971, p. 1.
96. *New York Times*, 29 May 1971, p. 20.
97. *New York Times*, 3 June 1971, p. 3.
98. *Arab Report and Record*, no. 13 (July 1–15, 1971), p. 366.

plots. The truth is that the resistance movement did not conduct any such evaluation and did not undertake any attempt to learn from the mistakes that preceded September. In all honesty, the Central Committee of the resistance continued . . . to conduct laborious meetings, which were governed neither by systematic thought nor logic. . . . Their task should have been directed towards defining a clear program around which all the various fedayeen organizations would unite to confront the massive assault on them by the Jordanian regime.[99]

With the Palestine resistance crushed for the moment by Jordan and confined largely to southern Syria where it was closely watched by Syrian authorities, Egypt and Saudi Arabia sought to mediate between Amman and the guerrillas. After two months of Saudi and Egyptian effort, a meeting was scheduled in Jedda on September 16. Squabbling within the movement nevertheless persisted even in the midst of defeat, and Jordan also proved reluctant to participate. On September 3, the PFLP criticized the proposed meeting, and Habash called for an underground war of revolutionary violence to overthrow Hussein. Relegating the struggle with Israel to second place, the PFLP leader exclaimed that "the resistance battle against the reactionary regime is the central battle facing the resistance movement now."[100] The PFLP pledged as well to undermine any agreement that might be reached at Jedda.[101] In fact the Jedda conference was not held, because the Palestinian delegation failed to appear. Arafat explained its absence as caused by the presence in the Jordanian delegation of an intelligence officer allegedly responsible for planning the July offensive against the guerrillas.[102]

Confronted by the intransigence of both sides, Saudi Arabia and Egypt rescheduled the Jedda meeting and warned both parties that measures would be taken against them if they failed to appear. Saudi Arabian foreign minister Omar Saqqaf told Amman that the Saudi frontier with Jordan would be closed and that Saudi aid to Hussein would cease if the Jordanian representative did not attend; a similar threat was conveyed to Fatah. Under intensive pressure, then, both sides appeared in Jedda for three days of talks, which, however, proved to be fruitless.[103]

Terrorist violence in the Middle East now erupted with greater intensity. In October an unsuccessful attempt was made on Arafat's life, probably by members of his own organization. Shortly thereafter Jordanian Premier Wasfi Tal, who had abetted Hussein's expulsion of the fedayeen from Jordan, was shot and killed by Palestinians in Cairo. The assassination was carried out by a new group which referred to itself as "Black

99. *Free Palestine,* September-October 1971, p. 6.
100. *New York Times,* 6 September 1971, p. 1.
101. *New York Times,* 9 September 1971, p. 1.
102. *New York Times,* 10 September 1971, p. 1.
103. *New York Times,* 17 September 1971, p. 1.

September," a reference to the Jordanian civil war of September, 1970. For the time being, the murder of Tal seemed to end all hopes of a rapprochement between Amman and the Palestinian movement. The words of Salah Khalaf seemed to be as applicable as ever: "We had twelve organizations, which meant twelve different strategies and twelve different guns pointing in twelve different directions. From all that, our ills grew."[104]

Conclusion

Although the Palestinian organizations did not succeed in creating the conditions for successful revolutionary warfare in the Middle East—a fact increasingly attested to by ever greater resort to indiscriminate terror such as the atrocities committed at the Munich Olympics and at the Rome and Athens airports—they vividly illustrate the growing significance of certain nonstate actors in contemporary global politics. From an historical perspective, their most lasting accomplishment may have been to restore a Palestinian dimension to the Arab-Israeli conflict, a dimension that had been notably absent between 1949 and 1967. They focused world attention on the Palestinian diaspora. After all, the Palestinian people provide an outstanding case of a "nation" without a "state" or even a territory of its own. There is little doubt that the Palestinians must be represented in any conclusive peace talks with Israel.

The failure of the movement to attain the commanding role which it sought can be found initially in the ideological, tactical, and personal rivalries that cleaved it and secondarily in the suspicions of established Arab regimes. In large measure, the posture of these regimes toward the guerrillas has been one of "divide and rule" through the establishment or support of selected groups, rather than one of direct confrontation with the movement as a whole (with the obvious exception of Jordan). Over time the Palestinian movement itself came to mirror many of the cleavages dividing the Arab states from one another as well as the traditional social and political divisions in Palestinian society.

The Jordanian catastrophe did not obliterate the commandos although it severely weakened them. In particular, they retained a capability of operating from southern Lebanon, an area which acquired the name of "Fatahland" in Israel. Guerrilla operations in Lebanon in early 1972 prompted severe Israeli reprisals, including the virtual, if temporary, occupation of certain areas in the south. They also occasioned attempts by the Lebanese Army in the summer to control guerrilla behavior in order to bring an end to Israeli reprisals. However, Black September's murder of

104. *Arab Report and Record,* no. 8 (April 16–30, 1971), p. 213.

eleven Israelis at the Munich Olympics in September triggered another wave of reprisals by Israel, and further Lebanese attempts to restrict the guerrillas proved singularly unsuccessful. That their influence persisted is revealed by the fact that the Egyptian-Syrian attack on Israel in October, 1973 was, in part, the result of efforts by regular Arab regimes to regain the initiative from the guerrillas who during previous months had dominated the public imagination. By the spring and summer of 1974 commando operations from southern Lebanon seemed bent on disrupting the delicate negotiations for peace in the area that were being coordinated by American Secretary of State Kissinger.

Lack of acquaintance with the behavior of the Palestinian organizations not only makes it difficult to understand what has transpired in Middle Eastern politics since 1967 but also obscures the domestic evolution of several of the nation-states of the region. The role of the guerrillas in this period illustrates the growing linkages between "domestic" and "international" politics in the area and the diminished importance of national boundaries as significant explanatory variables.

In short, though their existence has been brief, the Palestinian groups have profoundly affected the Middle East. They have fostered new attitudes by creating new myths, symbols, and norms focusing on the Palestinian national entity. They have provided the Arab world with a cause which it desperately needed after the humiliation of 1967. They have modified the objectives, policies, and tactics of the Arab states which feared them, yet could not dispense with them. And they have promoted a form of regional pluralism and transnationalism by linking groups in several states in the pursuit of a single political goal.

Latin America:
The Janus Face of Conflict

SEVEN

In one sense, the state-centric model seems eminently applicable to the regional politics of Latin America.[1] Unlike much of the so-called Third World, the nation-states of Latin America (with only a few exceptions) have been formally independent for over 150 years. Like the United States, they represent the "second generation" of nation-states, the initial spin-offs of the colonial empires established by first-generation mother countries in Europe. But the state-centric model obscures the most significant factors affecting Latin America's involvement in world affairs: the domestic political turmoil that has threatened most governments from within, and the additional challenge of external "penetration." In these respects, Latin American states have been far from the "billiard balls" implied by the state-centric model.

During the nineteenth and early twentieth centuries, domestic political instability in Latin America reflected a simple hierarchical social structure. A small elite, recruited primarily from landowning circles, ruled, and the vast majority of citizens was isolated from effective participation in nearly all aspects of "national" life. Political issues, such as conservatism vs. liberalism, centralism vs. federalism, and clericalism vs. anticlericalism, often masked a merely "personalist" struggle for power and influence among members of the elite, which was refereed by an equally opportunistic military. Lacking a popular base, in most countries regimes rose and fell with remarkable frequency, and only an occasional *caudillo* managed to occupy the presidential palace for any appreciable length of time.

While early governments were unstable partly because politics repre-

1. Our data set included the twenty traditional Latin American countries as well as the Bahamas, Guyana, Jamaica, Trinidad and Tobago (after independence) plus British Honduras (Belize) and Puerto Rico.

sented little more than internecine conflict at the top of the social structure, a surfeit of popular participation became a problem after the onset of industrialization. As Latin America moved into the twentieth century, gradual economic development accelerated urbanization and laid the basis for fundamental social changes. Notable among the changes were the emergence of the "middle sectors,"[2] an urban working class, an expanded *lumpenproletariat,* and large numbers of peasant marginals who left the countryside to eke out a subsistence existence in city slums. Politics became more complex. Almost everywhere, the middle sectors eventually succeeded in wresting control of political institutions away from the landed oligarchs, with the acquiescence of the military and the support of organized labor as well as other citizens lower down the social scale. However, as John J. Johnson expresses it, once in office the middle sectors faced the "herculean task" of keeping ahead of the fires that they themselves had lighted.[3]

The nationalism of the middle sectors proved an asset in gaining power but a distinct liability in exercising it. Greater identification with the nation on the part of lower-class citizens implied a right to make demands, and increasing social communication within and across national boundaries led to what came to be described as a "revolution of rising expectations."

Middle-sector governments were hard-put to fulfill their promises of a better life for all and a reduction of foreign penetration and dependence. Among other problems, policy-makers had to face the undiminished economic and residual political power of the upper classes (including a new industrial, commercial, and financial elite), the reluctance of the middle class to help pay for social reforms, and the continued apparent need for trade concessions as well as public and private investment from abroad. The situation was further complicated by modernization in the military, which produced a "technocratic" officer corps dedicated to economic development, fearful of domestic unrest, and impatient with "inept" civilian politicians. Besieged from all quarters, middle-sector governments either collapsed under the pressure or achieved at best painfully incremental change.

A second major factor that has conditioned regional politics has been external penetration. Douglas A. Chalmers comments:

> One of the most enduring features of Latin American linkages has been the predominance of one other nation—a colonial power to begin with [Spain or Portugal], and then a dominant commercial one [Great Britain],

2. John J. Johnson coined the term "middle sectors" in his book, *Political Change in Latin America,* Stanford, Cal.: Stanford University Press, 1958, to avoid the label "middle class" for a heterogeneous social stratum of bureaucrats, teachers, technicians, managers, clergy, military, and such. In his view, the middle sectors "do not fulfill the central condition of a class: their members have no common background of experience" (p. 3).
3. Johnson, *Political Change,* p. 195.

and finally, despite the growing importance of international markets and agencies, the United States. One might say that with marginal exceptions, for five hundred years each Latin American polity has been in someone's sphere of influence.[4]

The notion of spheres of influence has long been deemed consistent with a state-centric view of world affairs. Yet an obvious implication of spheres of influence is that some states are more "sovereign" than others.

Moreover, as Chalmers points out, much of the influence that has prevailed over the years has been the product of "linkages" between discrete "linkage groups." Within Latin American societies, such groups as the military, intellectuals, commercial elites, and guerrilla bands have developed their own special ties with the outside world. Chalmers notes, as well, that the Latin American pattern has been moving in the direction of "a differentiated and specialized international set of linkage groups." Among these external groups are various interstate governmental organizations (IGO's) such as the Organization of American States (OAS), the Economic Commission for Latin America (ECLA), the International Monetary Fund (IMF), the World Bank (IBRD), the Andean Common Market (ANCOM), and the so-called Group of 77 (now over 100 members) less-developed countries that has mapped strategy for meetings of the United Nations Conference on Trade and Development (UNCTAD). External groups also include interstate nongovernmental organizations (INGO's) such as the multinational corporation, to mention one that has been the focus of growing concern (see Chapter 8). In addition, a "bureaucratic" perspective on foreign policy reminds us that even such supposed agents of governments as aid missions, military attachés and advisers, and the CIA often pursue at least semi-independent courses of action in the field. Finally, a prominent feature of Latin American linkage patterns is that external groups are often *physically* present on the nation's home ground. The concept of "penetrated" societies thus is not an abstraction but an entirely accurate description of concrete reality.

Our analysis of the Latin American regional system falls into three time periods. The first, from 1948 through 1958, begins with the signing of the OAS Charter and closes with the fall of the Batista regime in Cuba. The second period from 1959 to October 9, 1967, includes the consolidation and attempted export of the Cuban Revolution, and ends with the death of Ernesto "Che" Guevara in Bolivia. The third and last period, from October 10, 1967, through 1972, spans part of the Johnson Administration and the initial term of the Nixon administration, years of increasing divergence between the United States and Latin America.

4. Douglas A. Chalmers, "Developing on the Periphery: External Factors in Latin American Politics" in James N. Rosenau, ed., *Linkage Politics* (New York: The Free Press, 1969), p. 71.

Seven superissues appeared in the twenty-five years under consideration. The *Security* superissue included traditional territorial disputes as well
as subversive activities by domestic groups with direct or indirect cross-
national linkages. *Peronism* concerned the internal evolution and foreign
policy of the Peronist movement in Argentina. *Castroism* similarly focused
on the internal politics of Cuba and external repercussions of the Cuban
Revolution. *Regime Stability* involved the efforts of Latin American governments to survive in the face of a variety of challenges at home and
abroad. The *Democracy-Dictatorship* superissue related to the contest between the Latin American democratic left and authoritarian regimes of
both the right and the left. *External Assistance* concerned extraregional
public and private, bilateral and multilateral "aid" for Latin American
development. Finally, the *Trade and Integration* superissue involved Latin
America's exports and imports, as well as common markets and free trade
areas within the region.

A Decade of Strife
and Ideological Competition:
1948–1958

Regime Stability was by far the dominant superissue in the decade 1948 to
1958, as indeed it was throughout the twenty-five-year period. This superissue was roughly twice as prominent as the next four, closely related superissues, which in rank order are: *Security, Democracy-Dictatorship, External Assistance,* and *Peronism.*

The *Regime Stability* superissue appeared in eleven of thirteen factors
and included 59 percent of the issues in the first period. It clearly highlighted the importance of nonstate actors such as political parties, labor
unions, student groups, and peasant organizations that served as vehicles
for newly emergent social sectors in the domestic politics of the region. For
its part, the military often, at least temporarily, stood between new groups
and the exercise of power.

Regime Stability had two major dimensions over the decade. In sev-

*Table 33. Ranking of Superissues by
Explained Variance, 1948–1958*

1. Regime Stability	(3.81)
2. Security	(2.09)
3. Democracy-Dictatorship	(1.86)
4. External Assistance	(1.76)
5. Peronism	(1.48)
6. Trade and Integration	(0.37)
7. Castroism	(0.18)

eral of the more developed South American countries where the middle
sectors were already a decisive factor in politics, governments encountered
severe difficulties in managing economic growth and especially in accom-
modating the demands of organized labor. Fluctuating prices for copper
and nitrate, runaway inflation, chronic unemployment and strikes plagued
successive Chilean governments. Sluggish commodity sales, inflation,
strikes, and official corruption in Brazil made a nightmare of Getulio
Vargas's 1950 "comeback" as a democratically-elected president. He committed suicide in frustration four years later. Meanwhile, in Argentina,
Juan Perón established a unique regime with the fervent support of urban
labor, the *descamisados* ("shirtless ones"), to whom he catered as had no
previous Argentine government. Perón, however, fell to a military coup in
1955, in the wake of economic strains and other events that we shall
examine in our discussion of the *Peronism* superissue below.

The period under consideration also brought significant political
change to several countries in Central America and the Caribbean. Reformist President José Remón of Panama was assassinated in 1955. In

Elsewhere in Latin America during this period, domestic instability
derived primarily from the struggle of reformist middle-sector parties and
their allies against conservative regimes that represented the last bastions
of an earlier era in Latin American politics. In Venezuela, the Pérez
Jiménez dictatorship filled a political vacuum that was created by the military's overthrow of an *Acción Democrática* government in 1948, but AD
returned to power in 1958 when the military deposed Pérez. Riots swept
the Colombian capital of Bogotá in 1948 following the assassination of
Liberal Party figure Jorge Eliécer Gaitán, and guerrilla warfare (*La Vio-
lencia*) between Conservatives and Liberals persisted in the countryside
during the Conservative dictatorship of Laureano Gómez. General Rojas
Pinilla toppled Gómez in 1953 and established a dictatorship of his own,
which lasted until 1958. The year 1952 witnessed a massive outbreak of
violence in Bolivia that claimed some 3,000 lives. MNR (*Movimiento
Nacionalista Revolucionario*) leader Víctor Paz Estenssoro returned from
exile and, with initial backing from tin miners and peasants, embarked on
an unprecedented series of economic and social reforms. Conflict between
conservatives and the political forces of the moderate left also continued in
Peru throughout this period. A *modus vivendi* between the conservative
government of President Bustamente y Rivero and the APRA party of
Haya de la Torre broke down in 1948. The *Apristas* retreated into exile or
the underground during the military dictatorship of Manuel Odría, and
Haya himself had to seek asylum in the Colombian embassy in Lima from
1949 to 1954. Odría eventually decided to step down, however, and the
next president, Manuel Prado, legalized the *Apristas* in return for their
support in the elections of 1956.

The period under consideration also brought significant political
change to several countries in Central America and the Caribbean. Reformist President José Remón of Panama was assassinated in 1955. In

1956 another assassin's bullet ended the longstanding (since 1933) personal rule of Anastasio Somoza in Nicaragua, although his two sons continued the Somoza dynasty. A full-scale civil war erupted in Costa Rica in 1948 when the incumbent conservative regime refused to honor the election of a candidate supported by the reform-minded *Liberación Nacional* party. Party leader José ("Pepe") Figueres rallied students, professionals, and workers and, after two months of bitter fighting, succeeded to the presidency. Free elections following a military coup elevated a close associate of Figueres, Ramón Villeda Morales, to the presidency of Honduras in 1957.

In Guatemala the middle-sector government of Jacobo Arbenz became increasingly responsive to Communist influence and succumbed to an invasion in 1954 sponsored by the United States. The leader of the invasion, Carlos Castillo Armas, remained in control until his assassination in 1957. Conservative General Miguel Ydígoras Fuentes won the election of 1958. Civil strife also escalated in Cuba after Fulgencio Batista overthrew the middle-sector *Auténtico* government of Prío Soccarrás in 1952. Fidel Castro's rebel band landed in the Sierra Maestra in 1956 and began a guerrilla campaign that three years later brought down the Batista dictatorship and ushered in the Cuban Revolution.

The second-ranking superissue between 1948–1958 was *Security,* which appeared on ten factors and involved 26 percent of the issues. One leading issue here concerned the machinations of exile groups which plotted the overthrow of regimes in their homeland, while enjoying the shelter and often direct support of rival governments abroad. Central America and the Caribbean, in particular, were hotbeds of exile activity and the locus of several interstate conflicts that triggered the collective security provisions of the Rio Treaty.[5] Two of these episodes, in 1948 and 1955 respectively, involved attacks by conservative Costa Rican exiles under the auspices of the Somoza regime. When Costa Rica brought the first case before the OAS, Nicaragua countered that the Figueres government itself was harboring a "Caribbean Legion" of antidictatorial exiles from Nicaragua, Honduras, and the Dominican Republic. An OAS investigating committee confirmed both Nicaragua's support of the original attack and the existence of the Caribbean Legion. These findings were the basis for an OAS Council resolution that called upon the two governments to refrain from additional hostilities. The OAS also dispatched a group of military officers from five member states to oversee the closing of the border and the disarming of exiles on both sides. Some months later the two governments signed a "Pact of Amity" drafted by the OAS Council.

5. These disputes are discussed in detail in Jerome Slater, *The OAS and United States Foreign Policy* (Columbus: Ohio State University Press, 1967), pp. 64–83.

The pact notwithstanding, in 1954 an armed clash, growing out of Nicaragua's massing of troops on the border, was narrowly averted when the United States pointedly sent six air force planes on a "goodwill visit" to the Costa Rican capital. Then, in January, 1955, anti-Figueres exiles crossed into Costa Rica from Nicaragua. The OAS Council proceeded cautiously to avoid, in Jerome Slater's words, "the outright opposition of a number of dictatorships." Ultimately, however, it authorized military aid to Costa Rica, a step which constituted an historical precedent for the inter-American system.[6] When an OAS "presence" on the scene failed to stop attacks by rebel aircraft, the Council gave its approval to a U.S. "sale" of four fighter planes at $1 apiece to Costa Rica. A threat to impose further OAS sanctions against Nicaragua persuaded Somoza to order the invaders to return.

Not long after the first Costa Rica-Nicaragua episode, the OAS became involved in several Caribbean disputes that derived from the efforts of a revived Caribbean Legion to topple the Trujillo dictatorship in the Dominican Republic. In 1949 the United States brought the problem of rising tensions in the area to the Inter-American Peace Committee, which issued a report stressing the principle of nonintervention. Nevertheless, Haiti and the Dominican Republic invoked the Rio Treaty in January, 1950. Trujillo charged that Cuba, Guatemala, Haiti, and Costa Rica were marshaling Legion forces for an invasion of his country. Haiti accused Trujillo of assisting exiles to overthrow the Estimé government in Port-au-Prince. The OAS verified Cuban and Guatemalan complicity in an earlier invasion and appointed a committee to foster negotiations between the parties and to see to the control of exiles. These steps brought a measure of calm to the Dominican situation for the rest of this period.

Another *Security* issue, a territorial dispute between Honduras and Nicaragua, reached the level of armed border clashes in 1957. The OAS again sent a committee to the scene, which obtained a ceasefire and supervised the withdrawal of troops from the area in question. While OAS joint military teams patrolled the border, the committee proceeded to mediate a settlement. Both parties eventually agreed to submit their claims to the International Court of Justice and to abide by its decision.

Within the Cold War context of the times, a third, highly controversial *Security* issue involved the alleged threat of Communism in the Western Hemisphere. The inter-American alliance embodied in the Rio Treaty was, of course, only one of several organized around the world by the United States in connection with its postwar policy of containment. From the outset, most Latin American governments proved willing to condemn "international Communism" at regular intervals, but they were wary of

6. *Ibid.*, p. 73.

being drawn directly into the East-West struggle. A U.S. attempt to elicit enthusiastic Latin American support for the Korean War effort met with a cool reception at the Fourth OAS Meeting of Consultation of Ministers of Foreign Affairs in Washington. Colombia alone actually contributed troops, and Latin governments paid little heed to a recommendation emanating from the Washington meeting that they enact new laws to curb subversives.

Such was the background when the organization was asked to consider the case of Guatemala in 1954. Relations between the United States and Guatemala had been steadily on the decline since 1944 when Juan José Arévalo came to power. Arévalo's movement involved a classic coalition led by the middle sectors among such diverse social groups as lower-ranking civil servants, intellectuals and students, some professionals, industrial workers and laborers on "modernized" plantations, and numerous military and police officers. The new president embarked on an ambitious reform program, including proposals for division of large landholdings and controls on foreign investment. These proposals posed a threat especially to United Fruit and also to other U.S. private companies that controlled railroads and electric power. From Washington's standpoint, things went from bad to worse after Arbenz became president in 1951 and permitted the Communists to assume prominent roles at all levels of government. Verbal attacks against the United States increased, and the Agrarian Law of 1952 expropriated major portions of United Fruit's private domain.

At the Tenth Inter-American Conference, held in Caracas in March, 1954, U.S. Secretary of State John Foster Dulles pressed for OAS subscription to the "Dulles Doctrine," a rather vague declaration to the effect that "domination or control" of an American government by the "international Communist movement" would call for "appropriate action in accordance with existing treaties." In apparent contradiction, the declaration also disavowed any intention to "impair the inalienable right of each American state freely to choose its own form of government and economic system." The U.S. initiative was obviously aimed at Guatemala, and most Latin American delegations voted for it reluctantly and only after they had extracted a *quid pro quo.* In return, Washington had to agree to attend another conference at Rio later that year to consider Latin American grievances over aid and trade.

The Guatemalan situation came to a head in mid-May, following Arbenz's order of a large shipment of Soviet-bloc arms. While ostensibly seeking another OAS conference under the Dulles Doctrine, the United States was, in fact, preparing the invasion force of Guatemalan exiles led by Castillo Armas, with the active support of the governments of Honduras and Nicaragua. The exiles crossed the border from Honduras on June 18. As Slater explains:

The strategy of the United States in the period immediately following the invasion was to give the attacking forces sufficient time to overthrow the Arbenz government, while preventing that regime from obtaining assistance from either the U.N. or the OAS. To this end it was necessary for the OAS to take just enough action to justify the exclusion of the U.N., but not so much as to endanger the success of the Castillo Armas coup.[7]

Guatemala made a serious error in this respect by appealing simultaneously to the Inter-American Peace Committee and the United Nations Security Council, thus complicating the question of which organization had jurisdiction. Before this question could be resolved, the Guatemalan army joined the rebellion and the Arbenz regime collapsed.

A final *Security*-related issue that materialized from 1948 to 1958 concerned the claims of a growing list of Latin American states to various forms of jurisdiction over territorial waters extending beyond the traditional three-mile limit to as much as 200 miles from shore. The issue was far from academic since the limit of territorial waters presumably governed not only the movement of warships and other surface vessels but also the right to conserve and exploit fisheries, seabed, and subsoil resources. In particular Peru and Ecuador evidenced a determination to enforce their claims by seizing U.S. private fishing vessels off their coasts. For its part, the United States government found itself crosspressured, on the one hand, by the Defense Department and the offshore fishing industry which argued for maintenance of the three-mile limit; and, on the other, by the Interior Department and the inshore fishing industry which lobbied for an extension of the limit to curb competition from foreign fleets in home waters. Without much success, the State Department continued to cast about for some compromise solution.

During this period, the *Security* superissue, like *Regime Stability,* had a distinct nonstate dimension. It included exile groups such as the Caribbean Legion, U.S. private companies such as United Fruit in Guatemala and the inshore and offshore fishing industries, countervailing bureaucracies at the highest level of the United States government, and interstate organizations, the United Nations and especially the OAS. The latter organization became involved in every *Security* issue except that of territorial waters, which fell within the purview of successive U.N. conferences on the law of the sea. Indeed, the following table of "strong supporters" and "weak supporters" of the OAS reads like a "who's who" of the principal protagonists in the main disputes between 1948–1958. The fact that we could distinguish only varying degrees of support also suggests that even those actors which were on the receiving end of OAS condemnatory resolutions and threatened sanctions were on the whole favorably disposed toward the organization.

7. *Ibid.,* pp. 122–23.

Table 34. Attitudes Toward The OAS,
1948–1958

Strong Supporters	Weak Supporters
Costa Rica	Nicaragua
United States	Guatemala
Honduras	Costa Rican Rebels

Some readers, aware of the stereotype of the OAS as a rubberstamp for the United States, may be uncomfortable regarding it as essentially a nonstate actor. To be sure, OAS effectiveness in mediating conflict situations has derived in large part from U.S. moral and material support. It is no accident that the organization's greatest successes in peaceful settlement have been in Central America and the Caribbean, areas of traditional U.S. strategic and economic involvement. Yet the stereotype underestimates the extent to which success depended in each instance upon the face-saving element involved in OAS "collective legitimization" of U.S. policies, both for the United States and parties to disputes.[8] It also neglects both the day-to-day independence of OAS negotiating committees on the scene and the dynamics of decision-making in the organization. Again we must quote Slater:

> While the United States obviously exercises great influence within the OAS and occupies a central role in the collective decision-making process, . . . it does not *dictate* policy. Rather it bargains, negotiates, and compromises, and although it can usually in effect veto action it strongly opposes, it by no means invariably gets its own way. . . . Moreover, insofar as the United States exercises leadership in the OAS, it usually acts as the broker of the organization, seeking consensus and leaning over backward to bring its position into line with the majority of the Latin American states.[9]

As Slater argues, the *real* reason for a decisive OAS role in peaceful settlement has been, not U.S. dominance, but the convergence of U.S. interest in the maintenance of *stability* in hemisphere affairs with Latin American interest in the preservation of *sovereignty*.[10] Put another way, an active OAS role in peaceful settlement has been seen as quite consistent with—even necessary for—a viable regional system of independent nation-states. This insight also helps explain the relative ineffectiveness of the organization in dealing with the Communism issue. Most Latin American

8. On the "collective legitimization" function of the OAS, see Jerome Slater, "The Limits of Legitimization in International Organizations: The Organization of American States and the Dominican Crisis," *International Organization* 23:1 (Winter 1969), pp. 48–72.
9. Slater, *Foreign Policy*, pp. 274–75.
10. Slater, "The Limits of Legitimization," p. 51.

governments have been willing to condemn "Communism" in the abstract, Soviet machinations in the Western Hemisphere, and (as we shall see) *concrete* manifestations of Cuban subversion. But many of them have been uneasy with resolutions such as the Dulles Doctrine that have implied a judgment about the internal character of regimes. Such judgments, they have felt, are violations of the nonintervention principle that itself derives from state sovereignty.

Democracy-Dictatorship was the third-ranking superissue from 1948 to 1958. Many of the middle-sector parties that were in and out of power during this period were not only nationalist and reformist but also strong proponents of political democracy, hence the label "democratic left" that has often been attached to them. Devotion to the democratic ideal was particularly characteristic of parties that acknowledged an ideological debt to Haya de la Torre in Peru, including (in this period) *Acción Democrática* in Venezuela, *Liberación Nacional* in Costa Rica, and the Liberal Party in Honduras. The *Auténticos* in Cuba, the Arévalo administration in Guatemala, and successive governments in Uruguay were also dedicated supporters of democracy.

Alignment patterns vis-à-vis Colombia, Cuba, the Dominican Republic, Nicaragua, and Venezuela—five countries where dictators held sway for most of the period—suggest the range of government and nonstate actors on both sides of the superissue:

Table 35. Democracy-Dictatorship Coalitions, 1948–1958

Prodictatorship	Neutral	Antidictatorship
Colombia	United States	Castroites
Cuba	OAS	Media
Dominican Republic	USSR	Other Cuban Parties
Nicaragua	Cuban "Small" Business	Cuban Communist Party
Venezuela		Costa Rica
United Nations		Cuban Students
FRG		AD Party
U.S. Business		Venezuelan Communists
Panama		Colombian Liberal Party
		Cuban Workers

Notable is the presence of the United States in the "neutral" column, a position that in part reflects Washington's defense of Costa Rica in its disputes with Nicaragua and U.S. abandonment of Batista in the closing months of the Castro revolution. Otherwise, the United States had excellent relations with dictatorial regimes, which were staunchly anticommunist and generally dependable supporters of U.S. policies. In addition, the OAS appears as a "neutral," mainly indicating the organization's even-handed approach to peaceful settlement problems that involved Nicaragua and the Dominican Republic. The cooperation of U.S. Business in Latin America with dictators will come as no surprise, and the Federal Republic of Germany is a step higher in the same category by virtue of its commercial ties with dictatorial regimes. The "pro" characterization for the United Nations is primarily a measure of the overall support for the world organization by dictatorial regimes (including support for the U.N. action in Korea) rather than the other way around.

The *Democracy-Dictatorship* cleavage had ramifications far beyond the confines of internal political systems. For one thing, it was a source of repeated verbal conflict between the two kinds of regimes. Moreover, as we have noted, hostility often spilled over into the encouragement of exile plots. Lastly, prodemocracy governments sought without much success to have clauses incorporated into inter-American agreements that could be used as weapons against dictatorship. Latin American democrats failed in their effort to frame the Rio Treaty so as to place violations of democratic principles on a par with other "threats to the peace." On their insistence, the Bogotá Conference accepted Article 5(d) of the OAS Charter, making the maintenance of "representative democracy" a binding obligation of member states. Yet the conference neither clarified the exact nature of the Charter democratic norm nor provided enforcement procedures. In addition, by 1958, the downfall of so many longstanding dictators (Vargas, Perón, Odría, Pérez Jiménez, Rojas Pinilla and Batista) made it seem that the "twilight of the tyrants" was at last at hand.[11] This trend had a significant impact on U.S., OAS, and various Latin American unilateral policies in the next period.

The fourth-ranking superissue from 1948 to 1958 was *External Assistance,* which appeared on eight factors and 21 percent of the issues. In this period, *External Assistance* for Latin American development meant primarily capital flows from the United States. Much to the chagrin of some Latin American governments, Washington insisted on classifying both public and private investment as "aid." Substantial private capital flowed into the region in these years, and, aside from the clash in Guatemala, there were few serious threats to U.S. companies.[12]

Public aid was another matter. The United States provided grants and training to the Latin American military. Latin Americans, however, had hoped for a Western Hemisphere equivalent of the Marshall Plan, which was not forthcoming. European revival had a higher priority in Washington, and U.S. decision-makers believed that private investment would be adequate for Latin America's needs if governments in the area would establish the proper climate for it. In addition, Washington strongly dis-

11. Tad Szulc's book, *The Twilight of the Tyrants* (New York: Holt, 1959), captured the spirit of the times.
12. The MNR government's nationalization of the tin mines in Bolivia, with a pledge of compensation, did not prove a major burden on relations between La Paz and Washington.

approved of Latin American deviations from "sound" economic practices. These included state-owned industries as well as state development and trading corporations (seen as competing with private capital), the promotion of heavy industry as opposed to agriculture, and the maintenance of "inefficient" industries through high tariffs.[13]

These attitudes surfaced regularly in official circles during the Truman and Eisenhower years. Fearing that the program would undercut Latin American incentive to welcome foreign capitalists, various business groups initially objected even to Point IV technical assistance. Under the first Eisenhower Administration, Secretary of the Treasury George Humphrey also made a determined effort to phase out Exim Bank[14] lending to Latin America. This effort failed in the context of the Caracas Conference and the follow-up economic meeting in Rio in 1954. With the support of the Senate Banking and Currency Committee, the State Department succeeded in getting a modest expansion in the Exim Bank's role. The only other concession to Latin American demands at this stage was the establishment of the International Finance Corporation, an international fund designed to aid foreign private investment projects.

In the mid-1950's a number of leading American senators began to question U.S. Latin American policies in general, including prevailing assumptions about aid. They criticized the Eisenhower Administration for supporting reactionary governments in Latin America, for catering too directly to U.S. business interests, and for neglecting the need for increased public assistance. Foreshadowing the Alliance for Progress, there also emerged a new congressional interest in aid for "social development." As early as 1956–1957 Senator Smathers of Florida managed to tailor legislation to ensure that a small amount of separate funds and the newly created Development Loan Fund could be used for this purpose in Latin America. Nevertheless, the Eisenhower Administration stoutly resisted this trend until after the establishment of the Inter-American Development Bank (IDB) in 1958.

Since U.S. aid was primarily designed to further U.S. influence in Latin America, it is appropriate to examine alignment patterns with the United States as a "pivot."

Table 36 confirms the prominent U.S. role in the OAS, as well as the fundamentally cooperative nature of Washington's relations with three leading Latin American countries: Chile, Brazil, and Mexico. Nicaragua

13. R. Harrison Wagner, *United States Policy Toward Latin America: A Study in Domestic and International Politics,* (Stanford: Stanford University Press, 1970), pp. 18–19. Our discussion of Truman-Eisenhower aid policies draws heavily on Wagner's analysis.
14. The Export-Import Bank was established in 1934 to encourage U.S. foreign trade. Loans or guarantees are extended primarily to private borrowers and are normally tied to purchases of U.S. goods.

Table 36.   Attitudes Toward the United States, 1948–1958

Pro-United States	Neutral	Anti-United States
U.S.	Venezuela	Cuba
OAS	Bolivia	Guatemala
Chile		Argentina
Honduras		Mexican Workers
Individuals		Cuban Castroites
Brazil		
Mexico		
Uruguay		
Nicaragua		
Ecuador		

also appears in the "pro" column, suggesting that the OAS (to which, we should recall, Nicaragua gave only "weak support") was an effective "lightning rod" for any anti-U.S. sentiment generated by Washington's backing of Costa Rica in 1948 and 1955. Venezuela's presence as a "neutral" reflects that country's criticism of U.S. oil import quotas, and Bolivia's, resentment over U.S. efforts to dictate the terms of a domestic economic stabilization plan in 1957. Turning to the "anti" category, we see that the United States alienated Cuban Castroites by supporting Batista, and then angered Batista by withdrawing support at the eleventh hour. Guatemala appears for obvious reasons, and Argentina, as a result of Perón's "independent" foreign policy (see below). Mexican Workers deviated from their government's cooperative posture because of U.S. controls over migrant labor (the "wetback" issue).

Peronism ranked fifth among the superissues and was involved in nine factors and 21 percent of the issues. The Perón era had a profound impact on Argentine politics and society, and an important regional side as well. Internally, as Robert J. Alexander comments:

> The fundamental significance of the Perón regime was that it transferred political and economic power in Argentina from the rural landholding class to the lower and middle classes of the cities. The votes which Perón received in successive elections came largely from the agricultural laborers, the urban industrial and transportation workers and, to a much less degree, from the white-collar workers and other middle-class elements.[15]

Perón had numerous assets in his first term of office, including his beautiful and politically astute wife Eva, support from a substantial sector of the Argentine military, a thriving *Peronista* party with control of most of organized labor, and a vague ideology of *"Justicialismo"* that regime propa-

15. Robert J. Alexander, *Prophets of the Revolution* (New York: Macmillan, 1962), p. 252.

gandists represented as a "Third Position" between capitalism and communism and between materialism and idealism. With his political position secure, Perón proceeded to shift the Argentine economy away from agriculture into industry and to enact extensive social and labor legislation.

Fervent nationalism, limited pan-Latin Americanism, and strident anti-Americanism were the keynotes of Perón's foreign policy. The Argentine government acquired ITT's telephones and British-owned railways, and it managed to pay off the entire outstanding foreign debt. Argentina entered into modest economic union agreements with Chile, Paraguay, and Bolivia. *Peronista* military and labor attachés actively sought to influence their contacts in other Latin American countries, while ATLAS, a hemisphere-wide *Peronista* labor confederation, competed with the democratic ORIT and the communist CTAL. Relations with Washington had been strained ever since World War II, when the United States had levied sanctions against Argentina's shelter of Axis subversives and had sided openly with the opposition during the election that brought Perón to power. Thereafter, Perón seized every opportunity to adopt a militantly "independent" posture. For example, after the United States had informed the Bogotá Conference that it would not fund an inter-American bank, Argentina offered to do so alone (a promise Perón could not keep).

In the early 1950's grave economic difficulties arose mainly from a drastic decline in food production. These difficulties in Argentina started a chain of events that led to the regime's demise. Perón had to seek U.S. economic aid. Inflation swept Argentina, and "unauthorized" strikes became frequent occurrences. Eva's death in 1952 robbed Perón of his best political adviser, while his romantic pecadillos in the role of "merry widower" scandalized both the good ladies of Argentina and the military. The government closed the prestigious newspaper, *La Prensa*. *Peronista* mobs sacked and burned the Jockey Club, the symbol of the Argentine oligarchy. Finally, interpreting the formation of a small Christian Democratic party as evidence of a Roman Catholic conspiracy, Perón clashed with the Church; he arrested priests, dismissed Catholic university professors, legalized divorce and prostitution, abolished several religious holidays, and exiled two Buenos Aires bishops. This last action brought excommunication from the Vatican and precipitated an abortive military coup. Another coup three months later, on September 16, 1955, was successful.

Alignments on the *Peronism* superissue involved a wide range of actors (see Table 37). For much of the period, the United States was in tacit alliance with various groups in Argentine society against Perón. The Vatican joined the active opposition when the Argentine Church came under official attack. On the other hand, French and German commercial relations were basically supportive of Perón. Argentine labor appears as

Table 37. *Peronism Alignments, 1948–1958*

Pro-Perón	Neutral	Anti-Perón
Argentina	British Media	Anti-Peronists
Peronists	Individuals	Argentine Parties
Ecuador	Argentine Labor	Argentine Media
Chile	UK	Argentine Church
France		Vatican
Panama		United States
FRG		

"neutral" because of the strikes that troubled the regime's closing years.

Trade and Integration was the sixth superissue, and appeared on five factors and involved 4 percent of the issues. A leading actor in the trade debate during this period was the Economic Commission for Latin America. ECLA's Executive Secretary, Raúl Prebisch, propounded the "declining terms of trade" thesis that the prices of Latin American commodities would not increase as rapidly as the prices of finished goods from the industrialized countries. Prebisch's prescription was "import-substitution" industrialization in the region, more public aid from the United States, as well as a removal of tariff and nontariff barriers to Latin American trade, commodity price stabilization agreements, and Latin American economic integration. The commodity pricing issue came to the fore in the late 1950's regarding a proposed International Coffee Agreement. The Eisenhower Administration was initially dubious about the legitimacy of interfering with the price mechanism inherent in the free world market. But the administration was more receptive to negotiations after the riots that greeted Vice-President Nixon's visit to Caracas. Economic integration, too, made some headway with the signing of the landmark Multilateral Treaty on Free Trade and Central American Integration in 1958.

Castroism, the seventh-ranking superissue, appeared on only two of the factors and involved 3 percent of the issues. As we have noted, the first period covered just the revolution against Batista.

Coappearance scores illuminate some of the relationships *among*

Table 38. *Latin American Superissue Coappearance, 1948–1958*

	I	II	III	IV	V	VI	VII
I. Security	—						
II. Peronism	.74	—					
III. Castroism	.17	0	—				
IV. Regime Stability	.76	.80	.31	—			
V. Democracy-Dictatorship	.82	.76	.29	.96	—		
VI. External Assistance	.67	.47	.20	.63	.70	—	
VII. Trade and Integration	.40	.43	.29	.63	.59	.77	—

Table 39.   The Most Active Initiators
in Latin America, 1948–1958

	United States	(112)
	Cuba	(101)
	Argentina	(79)
(nostac)	Other Parties	(75)
	Guatemala	(69)
	Bolivia	(59)
(nostac)	Individuals	(55)
	Brazil	(51)
	Chile	(51)
	Mexico	(45)
(nostac)	Castroites	(39)
(nostac)	OAS	(38)
(nostac)	Labor	(37)
(nostac)	Governmental Noncentral	(36)
	Costa Rica	(36)
(nostac)	Media	(32)
	Venezuela	(32)
	Haiti	(30)
(nostac)	Catholics	(29)
	Nicaragua	(29)

Table 40.   The Most Salient Targets in Latin
America, 1948–1958

(nostac)	Individuals	(147)
(nostac)	Other Parties	(98)
(nostac)	Media	(85)
	United States	(85)
	Argentina	(75)
(nostac)	Labor	(71)
(nostac)	Communists	(55)
	Cuba	(55)
	Brazil	(51)
(nostac)	Extra-Regional Business	(46)
(nostac)	United Nations and Other IGO's	(46)
(nostac)	MNC's	(40)
	Guatemala	(35)
	Costa Rica	(33)
(nostac)	Castroites	(32)
(nostac)	Latin Business	(28)
	Bolivia	(28)
	Chile	(28)
	Mexico	(27)
(nostac)	OAS	(25)

superissues. *Regime Stability* was almost perfectly associated with *Democracy-Dictatorship,* indicating the primary ideological dimension of the decade's internal political struggles. *Democracy-Dictatorship* was also clearly related to *Security,* a fact mainly reflecting exile activities. Another relationship here was the support prodemocracy governments gave to OAS anti-Communist resolutions because of their opposition to dictatorships generally. Moreover, rather ironically in view of the foregoing, all three superissues were involved in the regular characterization of the democratic left as "Communist-influenced." This characterization was made by their military and conservative opponents as a justification for coups and repression. *Peronism,* too, had strong *Regime Stability, Democracy-Dictatorship,* and *Security* aspects, the last deriving from attempts by the Perón government to spread its doctrine abroad and by Argentina's "Third Position" on the Guatemala question. Finally, *External Assistance* and *Trade and Integration* coappeared at a relatively high level because the subjects of aid and trade were usually linked both in ECLA doctrine and at regional meetings like the 1954 Rio conference.

A summary look at actors and targets points up the significance of nonstate actors. Nonstate actors initiated 36 percent of the dyads in this period and were the targets of 53 percent of the actions. In addition, as Tables 39 and 40 show, of the actors occupying the first twenty activity ranks, eight were *nostacs.* Among the twenty most salient targets, eleven were *nostacs.* The tables also highlight the tremendous importance of various intrastate groups—especially political parties—and IGOs and INGO's.

Disruptive-supportive scores help define the impact different kinds of actors had on the Latin American regional system from 1948 to 1958. Nearly twice as many *nostacs* were disruptive as were supportive, and all of the disruptive nonstate actors were domestic in origin. The United States was the system's leading supporter, while the two main disrupters (Cuba and the Castroites) testify to the magnitude of the revolution that brought Castro to power. IGO's were supporters as were most political parties. The military and the media were, in their unique ways, equally disruptive.

Taken as a whole, the Latin American system during this decade was remarkably conflictful though not especially violent. Conflict words or

Table 41. Disruptive-Supportive Behavior, 1948–1958

Disrupters		Supporters	
Cuba	(−66)	United States	(+68)
Castroites	(−29)	Other Parties	(+27)
Governmental Noncentral	(−22)	Cultural Groups	(+23)
Military	(−18)	OAS	(+20)
Media	(−18)	United Nations and Other IGO's	(+14)
Labor	(−15)	Mexico	(+11)
Haiti	(−14)	Brazil	(+11)
Demonstrators, Rebels,		Honduras	(+10)
Terrorists	(−13)	Colombia	(+10)
Panama	(−11)	Uruguay	(+10)
Students	(−7)		
Chile	(−7)		

actions represented no less than 44 percent of the dyads, with violence accounting for 6 percent of the total.

The Long Shadow
of the Cuban Revolution:
1959–1967

The Cuban Revolution was indisputably the single most significant development in Latin America during the entire period of our analysis. The Castroist challenge further polarized Latin American domestic politics between the left and the right and elicited a two-pronged response at the regional level: an effort to isolate the Cuban "virus" coupled with a positive attempt to support incremental change as an alternative to radicalism. The period 1959–1967 closed with the failure of Che Guevara's guerrilla campaign in Bolivia, which symbolized the end of active export of Castroism from Cuba. Ironically, by 1967 the forces of the democratic left, the supposed alternative to Castroism, were also in disarray, with the military in several key countries moving from a "guardian" role to the direct exercise of power.

From 1959 to 1967, *Regime Stability* was again the dominant superissue. *Castroism* soared from last to second rank, and was closely followed by *Security*. *Democracy-Dictatorship* dropped from third to fourth rank. Despite the Alliance for Progress, *External Assistance* slipped to fifth rank. United States accession to Latin American demands for public aid somewhat "defused" the superissue. After Perón's fall, *Perionism* moved down from fifth to sixth rank, but the superissue did not disappear altogether. *Trade and Integration* occupied the seventh and last rank.

The top-ranking superissue, *Regime Stability,* was involved in all twelve factors and a striking 61 percent of the issues in the period.

As in the previous decade, governments in those countries where the middle sector already played a prominent role in politics encountered severe difficulties in managing demands. Organized labor continued to be a

Table 42.   Ranking of Superissues by Explained Variance, 1959–1967

1. Regime Stability	(6.53)
2. Castroism	(4.54)
3. Security	(4.51)
4. Democracy-Dictatorship	(2.56)
5. External Assistance	(1.39)
6. Peronism	(0.71)
7. Trade and Integration	(0.12)

major political force, and greater popular participation generated more demands from the lower social sectors as well. Governments found their plight aggravated by chronic economic problems, the specter of radicalism raised by the Cuban Revolution, and the emergence of a "technocratic" military devoted to "order" and economic development. Professionalism in the military led to more, not less, military intervention in politics, as military officers grew increasingly confident of their own ability to rule and contemptuous of civilian corruption and "indiscipline." Further complicating matters were interservice rivalries and policy differences within the military establishments themselves.[16]

In Argentina following Perón's overthrow, the *Peronistas* were outlawed, and in 1958 formal control of government passed to one branch of the middle-sector Radical Party led by Arturo Frondizi. As president, Frondizi set about the delicate task of reintegrating Perón's former supporters into the political system. But Frondizi made the fatal political mistake of allowing the Peronist Front to run its own congressional and local candidates in the elections of 1962. When the *Peronistas* won over one-third of the votes, more than any other single party, the military revolted. Although the military reluctantly allowed Vice-President José María Guido to succeed to the presidency, he had to contend with a continuous threat of civil war between *legalista* and *gorila* military factions over the issue of whether new elections (with the *Peronistas* excluded) should be held in 1963. The *legalista* faction prevailed, and elections brought the somewhat more conservative branch of the Radical Party to power under Arturo Illía. But Illía, too, was unable to govern for long. Significantly, it was former *legalista* General Juan Onganía who spearheaded a coup that overthrew Illía in 1966. At this time Onganía announced that the military would stay in office indefinitely.

The Argentine military's decision was obviously influenced by events in Brazil. President Jânio Quâdros's sudden resignation in 1961 faced the Brazilian military with the succession of Vice-President João Goulart, a Vargas protegée whom they profoundly mistrusted. To avert a coup, Goulart agreed to share authority in a quasi-parliamentary arrangement with the conservative Brazilian Congress. When this system soon proved unworkable, the presidential system was restored; Goulart then began to rally support in an effort to maneuver around a stalemate over his reform program in Congress. He called for the enfranchisement of illiterates and the legalization of the Communist Party. Moreover, in the name of reform, he urged labor to strike and encouraged enlisted men to make their influence felt in the armed forces. Meanwhile, Goulart attempted to implement

16. For further background on coups in individual countries during this period, see especially Edwin Lieuwen, *Generals vs. Presidents: Neo-Militarism in Latin America* (New York: Praeger, 1964).

a series of controversial measures by decree, including an ambitious agrarian reform program, and he adopted a "neutral" foreign policy stance toward Cuba and Cold War issues in general. Interservice rivalries for a time prevented the military from unified action. The increasingly radical course of the Goulart government, however, brought the country to the brink of civil war, and the military finally staged a successful coup in late March, 1964. Having at last seized power, the military proceeded to construct the "corporatist" regime that governs Brazil to the present day.

In 1964 the armed forces also assumed the helm of state in Bolivia. The efforts by President Paz Estenssoro to reform the ailing Bolivian tin industry brought him into direct conflict with the tin miners and their leader, Juan Lechín, an old associate of Paz and heir presumptive to the presidency. When Lechín persisted in his candidacy prior to the 1964 election, the president had him expelled from their common political party, the *Movimiento Nacionalista Revolucionario* (MNR). Paz opened up additional divisions in party ranks by his decision to change the constitution so that he could run for a second term. Discovery of an assassination plot next prompted Paz to exile a number of political figures, including Lechín and former president Hernán Siles. Student riots and a new series of strikes in the tin mines ensued, setting the stage for a coup led by generals René Barrientos Ortuño and Alfredo Ovando Candia.

Two *golpes* of considerable significance occurred in the Central American countries of Guatemala and Honduras in 1963. In Guatemala the military overthrew the conservative Ydígoras government as a preventive measure, for fear that former president Arévalo might win the election scheduled for December, 1963. Three years later new elections returned the country to civilian rule under the reformist leadership of President Julio César Méndez Montenegro and his *Partido Revolucionario*. The cause of reform suffered a crushing defeat in Honduras, however, when a coup replaced the Villeda Morales administration with an old-style military dictatorship headed by Colonel Osvaldo López Arellano.

A coup in Ecuador in 1963 was something of a special case since the Ecuadorian political system had not developed to a point where middle-sector rule was as yet a central issue. The target president, Julio Carlos Arosemena, was a moderate conservative who aroused the ire of the military because of both his conciliatory attitude toward Cuba and his habitual drunkenness.

Elsewhere in Latin America, political instability continued to arise from the efforts of reformist middle-sector parties to make an initial break in the traditional pattern of upper-class dominance. In Peru, Haya de la Torre's long-awaited opportunity to run for the presidency in 1962 ended in frustration. No candidate received the requisite one-third of the votes cast, and the military intervened rather than accept Haya's probable selection by Congress. Fernando Belaúnde Terry and his middle-sector Popular

Action party won new elections held in 1963 and proceeded with a reform program that was very similar to that advocated by the *Apristas*.

The year 1962 witnessed the first free elections in the Dominican Republic after Trujillo's fall. Juan Bosch and the Dominican Revolutionary Party (PRD) won the election, but the Bosch administration ran into determined resistance from a rightist military establishment, the business-professional-landholding elite, and the Church. Bosch was ousted by a coup after only seven months in office, and conservative elements, which had been prominent in the governments of the immediate post-Trujillo period, temporarily regained control. Another coup in April, 1965, however, sparked a civil war between the rightist military and Bosch supporters (the "constitutionalists"). The latter were led by Colonel Francisco Caamaño and included civilians ranging from the middle to the far-left of the political spectrum. Fearing that a constitutionalist victory might result in a "second Cuba," Washington landed troops and stalemated the conflict. Shortly afterwards, the OAS authorized the creation of an Inter-American Peace Force and the United Nations sent its own representative to the Dominican Republic. Intricate negotiations were "mediated" by various OAS groups and the OAS Secretary-General, the U.N. representative, and a succession of presidential "troubleshooters" dispatched by the Johnson Administration. Eventually they raised an interim government under Héctor García-Godoy. Former President Joaquín Balaguer defeated Bosch in the elections of 1966.

The Dominican crisis of 1965–1966 was unprecedented in its complexity, none the least in that it involved not only U.S. military intervention but also two leading interstate governmental actors. Yet from another standpoint, it represented merely an extreme example of the Latin American pattern of internal divisions coupled with external penetration. Consider the main threats to Dominican stability, that is, those actors "conflicting" with different Dominican governments in these years as shown in Table 43.

Table 43. Threats to Stability in the Dominican Republic, 1959–1967

Venezuela
Individuals
OAS
Bosch Supporters
Dominican Castroites (including Fourteenth of June)
Haiti
Dominican Military
Dominican Students
National Civic Union
United States
Dominican Church and Roman Catholics
International League for the Rights of Man

It is significant that only three nation-states were among the threats. As we shall see when we examine the *Security* superissue, the United States emerged as a belated but nonetheless key opponent of the Trujillo regime; Venezuela brought the formal complaint that enabled the OAS to levy sanctions against Trujillo, and Haiti became embroiled in a bitter dispute with the Bosch administration. The Fourteenth of June was a Dominican youth movement that leaned to Castroist ideology and violence during the 1965–1966 crisis. The National Civic Union was a political party (upper- and middle-class constituency) that opposed Trujillo and ran its own candidate in the elections of 1963. The International League for the Rights of Man protested Trujillo's treatment of political prisoners.

Guerrilla activity constituted still another dimension of political instability in Latin America from 1959–1967. This brings us to the second-ranking superissue, *Castroism*. *Castroism* was involved in all twelve factors and 46 percent of the issues in these years.

Within months after Fidel Castro came to power, the Cuban Revolution took a radical turn. Although Castro had originally pledged to restore the 1940 Cuban constitution and to hold free elections, he indefinitely postponed a return to democracy. Moreover, he allowed the Moscow-oriented *Partido Socialista Popular* to supplant his own Twenty-sixth of July Movement and former democratic left elements in the revolutionary government and army. Alienated by these developments, and by Castro's clash with the Church and his steady regimentation of the Cuban economy, massive numbers of upper- and middle-class Cubans joined former supporters of the Batista regime in exile. At the same time, relations between the Castro government and the United States rapidly deteriorated over the issue of nationalization of U.S. private enterprises in Cuba. The Eisenhower Administration cut the Cuban sugar quota in mid-1960 and began preparations for an exile invasion on the Guatemala model. The Kennedy Administration finally launched this invasion with disastrous results in 1961 (the Bay of Pigs episode). Even as Castro burned his bridges with the United States he drew closer to the Soviet Union and the Eastern bloc. The Cuban Premier characterized himself as a "Marxist-Leninist" in 1961, and four years later he officially designated the revolutionary party as the Communist Party of Cuba. Soviet pressure was a major factor in the Castro government's decision in 1963 to reverse its early emphasis on industrialization and give major attention to agriculture. Nevertheless, Castro carefully maintained a degree of independence from the Soviet Union, symbolized by his several purges of old-line Communists and his occasional public criticism of Moscow's policies.

Through 1967, one important measure of Castro's independence from the Soviet Union was his subscription to a doctrine of "armed struggle" in Latin America. This doctrine was really much closer to the

Peking line. Its principal exponents were Che Guevara and his admirer, French intellectual Régis Debray. They argued that Latin America was ripe for social revolutions and that guerrilla movements in the countryside would be the main catalysts of such revolutions. The Castro regime made expediential shifts toward the Soviet "peaceful road to socialism" position, most notably at a Havana conference of Latin American Communist parties in late 1964. On that occasion, the Cubans accepted a communiqué which recognized the right of each national Communist party to select its own strategy and condemned "all factionalist activity." Yet armed struggle was again the central theme at two additional meetings convened in Havana, the Tricontinental Conference (January, 1966) and the First Latin American Peoples' Solidarity Conference (July–August, 1967).

The extent to which Castro gave material assistance (as distinct from inspiration and moral support) to Latin American guerrilla movements in this period remains a matter of debate. Certainly Cuba became a refuge and training center for many radical exiles from throughout the hemisphere, and modest shipments of arms and money did flow to some rebel groups. At the same time, however, most guerrilla movements were *primarily* indigenous. The exception was Guevara's own expedition to Bolivia, which indeed might have been more successful had it been less of an alien enterprise.

From 1959 to 1967, guerrilla violence of some kind erupted in virtually every Latin American country, though in no case was the Guevara-Debray vision fulfilled. Aside from Bolivia, among those countries hardest hit were Venezuela, Colombia, Peru, and Guatemala. In Venezuela, the Movement of the Revolutionary Left (MIR) split off from the AD party in 1960 and in 1963 merged with the Forces of National Liberation (FALN). Revolutionary violence reached a crescendo prior to the 1964 elections. Violence abated when the elections were held without serious incident and President Rómulo Betancourt turned over power to his elected AD successor, Raúl Leoni—the first such constitutional transition in Venezuelan history. The Colombian situation, involving the National Liberation Army (ECN), was in some respects merely an extension of violence that had plagued the Colombian countryside for generations. Camilo Torres, a prominent Catholic priest and intellectual, became the leading martyr of the Colombian revolutionary cause when he was killed in guerrilla action. In Peru as in Venezuela, a Movement of the Revolutionary Left spun off a key democratic-left party, in this instance APRA. An entirely separate revolutionary movement, organized by Hugo Blanco and much less influenced by Castroist ideology, was an outgrowth of peasant unionization in the Peruvian sierra. The two most significant guerrilla groups in Guatemala were the *Movimiento Armado del 13 de Noviembre* (MR-13) and the *Fuerzas Armadas Rebeldes* (FAR), led by Marco

Antonio Yon Sosa and Luis Augusto Turcios respectively. Turcios's death in an automobile accident in 1966 was a severe setback to the revolutionary left. Moreover, rightist vigilante groups, including the notorious *La Mano Blanca,* emerged to match leftist violence with terrorism of their own.

The OAS considered the Castroist threat in a series of meetings beginning in 1960. Once again the organization had to confront the thorny problem of passing judgment on the internal political character of a member government, although the Castro regime's alleged external subversive activities had no parallel in the earlier case of Guatemala. The Seventh Meeting of Foreign Ministers in San José, Costa Rica (August, 1960) convened shortly after Castro's acceptance of a "figurative" offer by Chairman Khrushchev to defend Cuban independence with Soviet missiles. Venezuela and several other democratic-left governments indicated that they were still willing to give the Castro regime the benefit of the doubt. The meeting did, however, condemn Sino-Soviet machinations in the Western Hemisphere and declared that "the inter-American system" was "incompatible with any form of totalitarianism."

Sentiment at the Eighth Meeting of Foreign Ministers in Punta del Este, Uruguay (January, 1962) was less ambivalent, since it took place after the orientation of the Revolution was clearly established and only two months following Castro's "I am a Marxist-Leninist" speech. On this occasion, a majority of the foreign ministers resolved that "Marxism-Leninism" was "incompatible with the inter-American system" and on this ground excluded the "Government of Cuba from participation" in the OAS. By this time, most of the democratic-left contingent, including Venezuela, had reluctantly concluded that the Castro government had become a dictatorship of the left. Nevertheless, six governments—Argentina, Bolivia, Brazil, Chile, Ecuador, and Mexico—abstained on the resolution with the "technical" objection that exclusion of a member government was not among the sanctions available to the OAS under the Rio Treaty.

Later in 1962, the OAS again dealt with Cuba in the context of the Missile Crisis. Member governments were unanimous in giving "collective legitimization" to the United States "quarantine." But, three of the governments that had abstained on the earlier exclusion measure—Bolivia, Brazil, and Mexico—abstained on part of the resolution in this instance that appeared to authorize military action against missiles already present in Cuba.

Owing to the context of the Cuban Missile Crisis, OAS "sanctions" were directed primarily at the Soviet Union rather than the Castro government, which accounted for the level of unanimity achieved. Divisions of opinion reappeared at the Tenth Meeting of Foreign Ministers in Washington (July 1964), held upon Venezuela's complaint (verified by an OAS investigating team) that Cuba had been shipping arms to Venezuelan

Table 44. Alignments on Castroism, 1959–1967

Pro-Castro	Neutral	Anti-Castro
Cuba	Cuban Labor	Anti-Castroites
Castroites	Haiti	United States
USSR	Venezuela	Individuals
Eastern Bloc	Argentina	Cuban Church and Roman
United Nations		Catholics
Egypt		U.S. Business
British Aircraft Industry		OAS
		Guatemala
		United Kingdom
		U.S. Media
		Uruguay
		U.S. Democratic Party
		Puerto Rico

terrorists. By a vote of 14–4–1, the meeting ordered member states to sever diplomatic relations and trade with Cuba. Mexico alone refused to comply with the OAS directive.

In the light of our previous discussion, alignments on Cuba are largely self-explanatory. Among the "antis," Guatemala appears not only because of terrorist problems but also because the Ydígoras government provided a training ground for the Bay of Pigs invasion. Uruguay expelled the Cuban ambassador and protested that Cuban militiamen had fired on a refugee sequestered in the Uruguayan Embassy in Havana. Puerto Rican authorities resented Cuban support of the Puerto Rican independence movement. In the "neutral" column, Cuban Labor was divided over the question of Communist infiltration in the early days of the revolution. Haiti was slightly "neutral" solely because it released several members of an alleged Cuban invasion force. On the "pro" side, the United Nations provided Cuba with a forum for complaints about the United States and the OAS. Egypt's Nasser was a neutralist leader whom Castro attempted to woo. The British Aircraft Industry provided Cuba with commercial planes and a BOAC air link to Nassau. Lastly, it should be noted that our sample captured not a single interaction between Mexico and Cuba throughout the period, which suggests that Mexican "neutrality" on *Castroism* amounted to little more than a matter of casting votes on OAS official occasions.

Security was the third-ranking superissue, appearing on all twelve factors and involving 45 percent of the issues from 1959–1967.

OAS meetings on the Cuban problem, which we examined briefly above, were part of the *Security* superissue as well. There was a subtle change in the character of OAS involvement after the Missile Crisis of 1962. By this time Castro had been effectively isolated, and the actual settlement of the crisis was a product of bilateral negotiations between Washington and the Kremlin, with U.N. Secretary-General U Thant playing a secondary mediating role. Thereafter, the United States sought to confine OAS action to "periodic, symbolic anti-Cuban gestures" and actually resisted the demands of several Central American and Caribbean countries for a more aggressive policy. Washington feared that such a policy would open up too many divisions in the inter-American system and possibly provoke another confrontation with Moscow.[17]

Nevertheless, the *Castroism* superissue found an "echo" of sorts in the United States intervention against a perceived threat of "another Cuba" in the Dominican Republic in 1965.[18] The dilemma of OAS member governments that were outraged at Washington's unilateral *fait accompli* was acute: either "multilaterize" the intervention or forego whatever influence the organization might have over the ongoing situation. In the end, a majority of member governments chose the former course of action, but votes on a succession of OAS resolutions indicated how deeply divided the organization was. For instance, creation of the Inter-American Peace Force (IAPF) required the vote of the representative of the defunct Dominican government that had been deposed by the "pro-Bosch" coup! Chile, Mexico, Peru, Uruguay, and Venezuela regularly abstained.

Slater terms the OAS role in the crisis "peripheral" to that of the United States, but he adds that "it would probably be incorrect to conclude that the outcome of the crisis would have in no way differed if the organization had not become involved at all." OAS involvement appeared to be a major factor in restraining Washington from a full-scale military attack against the pro-Bosch rebels in the first weeks after the intervention. And to the detriment of its own image, the organization once again served as a lightning-rod, deflecting criticism away from the United States. In addition, OAS *de facto* recognition of the constitutionalists as equal participants in negotiations gave them a degree of status and legitimacy that they otherwise would have lacked.[19] The OAS Inter-American Commission on Human Rights was credited with reducing acts of terrorism and easing the plight of political prisoners. The Commission also joined the OAS electoral assistance and observation mission, a U.N. group, and some seventy American liberals in verifying that ballots were properly cast and counted in the elections of 1966.

Other nonstate actors, too, made important contributions to the Dominican case. The U.N. mission helped counterbalance the conservative bent of the IAPF and most OAS negotiators, since U.N. representative Mayobre's sympathies clearly lay with the constitutionalists. The Papal Nuncio successfully negotiated a ceasefire. Voluntary organizations such as

17. Slater, *The OAS*, pp. 142–74 *passim*.
18. See Yale H. Ferguson, "The Dominican Intervention of 1965: Recent Interpretations," *International Organization* 27:4 (Autumn 1973), pp. 517–48.
19. Jerome Slater, *Intervention and Negotiation: The United States and the Dominican Revolution* (New York: Harper & Row, 1970), pp. 100–103.

the International Red Cross and CARE provided much-needed humanitarian relief to citizens of strife-torn Santo Domingo.

Prior to the 1965 Dominican case, U.S. relations with the British over British Guiana and with Brazil also had strong *Security* and *Castroism* overtones. The Kennedy Administration was profoundly concerned about the election of Cheddi Jagan in British Guiana in 1961. Jagan was reported to have "Marxist" leanings, and Washington ultimately convinced the British to institute a system of proportional representation that, in late 1963, tipped the balance to Jagan's opponent, Forbes Burnham. Meanwhile, the United States grew increasingly disturbed about what it perceived as Castroist tendencies in the Goulart government in Brazil. The coup against Goulart in 1964 thus came as a great relief to the Johnson Administration, which enthusiastically recognized the new regime and developed a warm relationship with the Brazilian military in the ensuing years. Brazil contributed a large contingent to the OAS force in the Dominican Republic.

We now return to 1959 to pick up the thread of other *Security* issues that were only indirectly related to the *Castroism* superissue. Before the course of the Castro government had been firmly established, the Cuban Revolution triggered yet another series of exile invasions in the Caribbean.[20] In April, 1959, a group led by Panamanian politician Roberto Arias landed and was immediately apprehended in Panama. The expedition had originated in Cuba, but an OAS investigating committee found no evidence of Cuban government involvement. A month later Nicaragua complained of an invasion from Costa Rica that was allegedly abetted by "international communism." After a two-week delay during which the rebels surrendered, the OAS investigated and found no concrete indication of complicity in the plot by the governments of Costa Rica or Cuba. Finally, in mid-summer, the Trujillo regime reported that it had been the target of several small-scale exile invasions emanating from Cuba, and it charged that Venezuela and Cuba were planning further aggression. In this instance the OAS decided, rather than to consider the Dominican complaint as such, to convene the Fifth Meeting of Foreign Ministers in Santiago, Chile (August, 1959), for the purpose of reviewing tensions in the Caribbean generally. Most delegations at the meeting reiterated their support for the nonintervention principle. Although there was an unsuccessful exile invasion of Haiti from Cuba during the conference itself, the frequency of this kind of incident declined afterwards.

The territorial dispute between Honduras and Nicaragua flared up again in November, 1960, after the World Court decided in favor of Honduras, and the Nicaraguan government demanded a long period of

20. Discussed in Slater, *The OAS*, pp. 83–97.

time to comply with the award. A full-blown crisis was averted, however, when the two parties agreed to allow a joint commission chaired by the President of the Inter-American Peace Committee to administer the territory in question for six months, provide for relocation of residents, and undertake a careful survey of boundaries. This was an unprecedented task for the OAS, and the organization effectively completed it.

An additional territorial dispute between Bolivia and Chile erupted in 1961. Bolivia initially protested Chile's diversion of Río Lauca waters for irrigation purposes. Then in 1963 it made settlement of this problem contingent upon a reopening of the longstanding question of a Bolivian outlet to the Pacific. When talks under the auspices of the OAS Council collapsed, Bolivia temporarily withdrew its representative from the Council to dramatize its claim. For the same reason, President Barrientos refused to attend a 1967 Summit Meeting at Punta del Este. Yet Bolivia did return to the Council, and the dispute eventually became quiescent.

Panama invoked the Rio Treaty against the United States in early 1964, following the death of several Panamanian citizens in Canal Zone riots. The OAS quickly arranged for bilateral talks mediated by the Peace Committee, but Panama insisted that there should be a parallel investigation of its charge of "aggression." President Johnson broke the deadlock in December by announcing his willingness to negotiate a new treaty governing the status of the canal.

An overview of attitudes toward the OAS from 1959–1967 reflects the divisive effect of the *Castroism* superissue, the Río Lauca controversy, the 1965 Dominican crisis, and the sanctions levied against the Trujillo regime in 1960. Whereas in the 1948–1958 period we could detect only different degrees of support, in this period Cuba, the Dominican Republic, and Mexico were definitely hostile to the OAS, and Bolivia and Chile were

Table 45.   Attitudes Toward the OAS, 1959–1967

Pro-OAS	Neutral	Anti-OAS
OAS	Individuals	Cuba
Brazil	Bolivia	Dominican Republic
United States	Chile	Bosch Supporters
Honduras		Mexico
El Salvador		
Costa Rica		
Nicaragua		
Guatemala		
Peru		
Argentina		
Panama		
Colombia		
Venezuela		
Paraguay		

ambivalent. The Individuals category in the "neutral" column also captures increasing criticism of the organization by independent commentators. At the same time, most hemisphere governments, including both democracies and dictatorships, continued to support the organization in general, as an instrument for peaceful settlement and a modest curb on unilateral behavior by the United States.

Other *Security* issues in these years did not come before the OAS. These included several disputes between South American countries. The British successfully arbitrated an Andean boundary controversy between Argentina and Chile in 1966, but the disputants were unable to agree as to which country had proper claim to three islands in the Tierra del Fuego. Negotiations between Argentina and Uruguay deadlocked over possession of a sandbar in the Río de la Plata. Finally, Venezuela and Guyana became engaged in a border dispute arising out of revelations that a nineteenth century arbitral award to British Guiana may have been "fixed" at the time by the British.

The fourth-ranking superissue from 1959 to 1967, *Democracy-Dictatorship,* was involved in ten factors and 23 percent of the issues.

To Latin American democratic-left governments, the overthrow of Batista provided final confirmation that the twilight of the tyrants was at hand, and at the 1959 Santiago conference they moved to institutionalize a prodemocracy role for the OAS. At their insistence, the conference took several steps to achieve this end, but only initiatives related to human rights produced much in the way of results. An Inter-American Commission on Human Rights was established, and, through its investigation of complaints and publication of reports, the Commission subsequently made a modest contribution to the welfare of particular individuals suffering political repression.

Despite the lack of progress in what might be termed the juridical approach to promoting democracy, the OAS was a key actor in a confluence of events that led to the demise of the Trujillo regime. By 1960 Trujillo had become the primary symbol of dictatorship for militant Latin American democrats, and even the United States had begun to regard him as a tyrant in the Batista mold who might provoke a Castroist revolution in the Dominican Republic. In that year, Trujillo himself provided his opponents with an opening by personally instigating an unsuccessful plot to assassinate President Betancourt of Venezuela. When the origins of the plot came to light, the Sixth Meeting of Foreign Ministers at San José (August, 1960) voted unanimously to levy sanctions against the Dominican regime. These sanctions included severence of diplomatic relations and cessation of arms shipments. Although the United States had already stopped arms shipments, the Eisenhower Administration initially argued in vain that the OAS should merely use the threat of sanctions to pressure

Trujillo into holding elections. Once it became clear that a majority of governments favored a more direct approach, however, the United States not only acquiesced in the decision to enforce sanctions but went beyond it and ended preferential treatment of Dominican sugar exports. Some months later, with strong U.S. backing, the OAS Council formally extended sanctions to embrace a variety of economic measures.

On May 30, 1961, Trujillo was assassinated, and the Kennedy Administration and the OAS made the lifting of sanctions conditional upon a genuine democratization of the Dominican regime. In November the United States went so far as to send a naval task force to Dominican waters, which forestalled resistance from various *Trujillista* elements and paved the way for the establishment of a Council of State and the election that brought Bosch to power.

The early Kennedy years marked the peak of U.S. unilateral support for democracy in Latin America.[21] "New Frontier" decision-makers initially concluded that the United States should lend moral and material support to the Latin American democratic left, which then appeared to be in the ascendent, and to offer the best hope that change in the area would assume the character of peaceful reform (evolution) rather than violent revolution (chaos). From this orientation flowed the Kennedy policy of nonrecognition of "unconstitutional" governments in Latin America. United States pressures, as we have seen, were a major factor in ushering in the Bosch government in the Dominican Republic, and they were also principally responsible for the Peruvian military's scheduling of elections in 1963. However, Washington did not respond vigorously to coups in Ecuador and Guatemala in 1963. The military in Honduras and the Dominican Republic interpreted apparent U.S. indifference as a green light to move against Villeda Morales and Bosch respectively. Although the Kennedy Administration did strongly condemn the Honduran and Dominican *golpes,* its policy of deterrence was no longer credible. Moreover, the administration was entirely unsuccessful in forcing "Papa Doc" Duvalier to abandon the Haitian presidency at the end of his constitutional term in May, 1962. Following Kennedy's death, President Johnson's Assistant Secretary of State for Latin American Affairs, Thomas A. Mann, reversed the Kennedy policy, placing a higher priority on anti-Communism than on democracy or social progress.

Only a handful of governments adhered to the "Betancourt Doctrine," the Latin American equivalent of the Kennedy nonrecognition

21. For details on Kennedy and Johnson administration policies relating to the promotion of democracy in Latin America, see Yale H. Ferguson, "The United States and Political Development in Latin America: A Retrospect and a Prescription" in Ferguson, ed., *Contemporary Inter-American Relations: A Reader in Theory and Issues* (Englewood Cliffs, N.J.: Prentice-Hall, 1972), pp. 348–91. Also see Lieuwen, *Generals vs. Presidents.*

policy, and the United States gave but cautious encouragement to proposals for multilateral prodemocracy action. Urgent appeals from democratic governments menaced by the military in 1962–1963 finally resulted in an OAS call for a Meeting of Foreign Ministers. The meeting was never actually convened, largely because prodemocracy ranks by then were decimated. When Duvalier's regime appeared (incorrectly) to be on the verge of collapse, the United States suggested that the OAS ought to consider establishing a trusteeship over Haiti. There was little enthusiasm in the organization for such a task. On the other hand, the OAS did investigate a dispute between Haiti and the Dominican Republic that was an offshoot of the psychological campaign against Duvalier. Dominican troops massed on the border with Haiti in purported response to the Duvalier government's unauthorized search for Haitian refugees in the Dominican embassy in Port-au-Prince and Duvalier's complicity in a *Trujillista* plot to assassinate President Bosch. The report of the OAS committee criticized both governments: Haiti for the embassy incident and the Dominican Republic for allowing its embassy to serve as a center for subversive activities against Duvalier.

External Assistance was the fifth superissue in the second period. It was involved in nine factors but only 13 percent of the issues.

The Alliance for Progress was the material side of the Kennedy Administration's policy of support for the Latin American democratic left. The administration reasoned that the democratic left would need a massive infusion of capital from abroad to succeed in the face of rightist obstructionism and Castroist revolutionary threats. Hence the United States promised at least two billion dollars a year over ten years in public and private funding for the goals of democratic government and socioeconomic reform embodied in the 1961 Charter of Punta del Este. This target for aid was more than met, although it soon became clear that the other goals of the Alliance were overly ambitious.

One of the early features of the Alliance was U.S. acceptance of the idea of national planning that had long been advocated by ECLA. Latin American countries were each to draft a ten-year development plan for submission to ad hoc committees composed of an equal number of OAS Panel of Nine experts (the "Nine Wise Men") and outside experts. Upon approval, these plans were to serve as the basis for allocation of aid from a variety of sources. Only a handful of countries actually drafted acceptable plans, however, and even these proved to be of questionable value.

In any event, with so few Latin American plans forthcoming, the Alliance lost much of the limited inter-American character it had initially had. The Panel of Nine had virtually no control over aid, and the biannual meetings of the OAS Inter-American Economic and Social Council (IA-ECOSOC) were unable to exercise meaningful supervision. Therefore in

1963, the IA-ECOSOC accepted the recommendation advanced in independent reports by former Presidents Kubitschek of Brazil and Lleras Camargo of Colombia to create an Inter-American Committee of the Alliance for Progress (CIAP). Ironically, as it emerged CIAP closely resembled the framework for the Alliance that had originally been proposed by the United States. Washington had reasoned that Latin Americans would find pronouncements from a multilateral institution that they dominated more acceptable than those emanating from AID. But in 1961 a majority of Latin American governments had opted instead for the Panel of Nine approach, preferring to continue their bilateral aid relationships with the United States to a more highly multilateralized program. Two years later, with the Alliance rapidly losing momentum, they reconsidered.

CIAP has proceeded to set "guidelines" for development assistance, and its role was enhanced by a provision that the U.S. Congress attached to foreign assistance legislation beginning in 1966, to the effect that U.S. aid must be consistent with CIAP's recommendations. Nevertheless, CIAP has never evolved into a multilateral master of the Alliance. In part this is because it has customarily framed its recommendations in very general terms. In addition, from the start CIAP suffered from the relatively small size and limited professional competence of its staff.

Apart from development assistance, the Kennedy Administration continued but shifted U.S. aid to the Latin American military away from conventional defense to counterinsurgency, where the emphasis has remained.

Table 46 is consistent with many of the major developments during this period that we have surveyed. Argentina has now moved into the "pro" column, and Panama, into the "anti." Brazil's appearance among the "anti's" reflects the tumultuous Goulart years and contrasts with Brazil's strong support of the OAS (and, indirectly, the United States) during the

Table 46. *Attitudes Toward the United States, 1959–1967*

Pro-United States	Neutral	Anti-United States
United States	Dominican Republic	Cuba
OAS	USSR	Cuban Castroites
Argentina	Peru	Bosch Supporters
Chile	British Guiana	Panama
Mexico	Uruguay	Individuals
United Nations		Venezuelan Leftists
El Salvador		Brazil
Puerto Rico		Cuban Labor
Cuban Refugees in United States		
Bolivia		
Panama Media		
American Legion		
United Kingdom		

Dominican intervention. Bolivia, Chile, and Mexico maintained friendly relations with the United States, despite their less-than-enthusiastic attitudes toward the OAS. Panama Media's "pro" stance stems from its praise of U.S. willingness in 1960 to fly the Panamanian flag at various locations in the Canal Zone. Among the "neutrals," the Soviet Union was cooperative in the latter stages of the Cuban Missile Crisis. Peru began to question the International Petroleum Company's (IPC) concession, which would be a major factor in the military coup of 1968. British Guiana reflects the Jagan controversy and U.S. support of Burnham. Uruguay criticized Washington's unilateral intervention in the Dominican Republic.

The sixth-ranking superissue from 1959 to 1967 was *Peronism,* which appeared in only five factors and a mere 6 percent of the issues. Leaving political and economic chaos behind him in Argentina, Perón sought asylum in several Latin American countries and eventually took up residence in Spain. There he entertained a succession of Peronist leaders from Argentina, who carried home Perón's dicta as to strategy and his promises that their aging leader would one day make a triumphal return.

Trade and Integration was the last superissue in this period and was involved in but two factors and 1 percent of the issues. Despite the relatively low level of "activity" generated, Latin American economic integration made considerable headway. The most successful experiment along these lines was the Central American Common Market (CACM), which vastly expanded and diversified zonal commerce and generated such institutions as the Central American Development Bank and a monetary council. The Latin American Free Trade Association, brought into existence by the 1960 Montevideo Treaty, also expanded commerce within its zone. However, most of this expansion was in traditional foodstuffs and raw materials, and member countries continued to gear their industrialization programs almost exclusively to domestic markets. Still another integration scheme got underway in 1967, with the founding of the Caribbean Free Trade Association (CARIFTA).

Coappearance scores for the 1959–1967 period as a whole testify to the close relationship among the five most important superissues: *Regime*

Table 47. Latin American Superissue Coappearance, 1959–1967

	I	II	III	IV	V	VI	VII
I. Security	—						
II. Peronism	.59	—					
III. Castroism	1.00	.59	—				
IV. Regime Stability	1.00	.59	1.00	—			
V. Democracy-Dictatorship	.91	.67	.91	.91	—		
VI. External Assistance	.86	.58	.86	.86	.95	—	
VII. Trade and Integration	.29	.29	.29	.29	.33	.36	—

Stability, Castroism, Security, Democracy-Dictatorship, and *External Assistance.*

Nonstate actors in these years were even more prominent initiators and only slightly less significant targets than they had been in the first time slice. Reflecting the ever-increasing complexity of Latin American societies and domestic political conflicts, the entire period calls to mind Samuel P. Huntington's maxim that "development" often involves political "decay."[22] Nonstate actors initiated 38 percent of the dyads and were the targets of exactly half of the actions. Of the actors occupying the first twenty activity ranks, eleven were *nostacs.* Among the twenty most salient targets, twelve were *nostacs.* Cuba surpassed the United States in total activity. Labor was a slightly more active initiator than Other Political Parties. The OAS was a more active initiator than all but five nation-states, and a more salient target than all but two nation-states. Extraregional Business made its first appearance on the activity table, and Multinational Corporations (MNC's), their first appearance on the target table.

Turning to disruptive-supportive scores, we find once again that nearly twice as many nonstate actors were disruptive as were supportive. The United States again was the system's leading supporter, followed (interestingly enough) by the Soviet Union. Intergovernmental organizations and multinational corporations were also supportive. In contrast to the first period, no leading Latin American nation-state appeared on the list of supporters, a result of the Latin American nationalism that would blossom in the years to come (manifested in this time slice with respect to Cuba and the 1965 Dominican case). Cuba was by far the leading disrupter in the system, and the impact of the Cuban Revolution is still more significant when one considers as well the disruptive roles of Anti-Castroites, Castroites and Demonstrators, Rebels, and Terrorists (DRT's). We might note too that Labor was an even more disruptive actor than was the Military.

The second period was similar to the first in that it was quite conflictful, though not particularly violent. Conflict words and actions accounted

22. See Samuel P. Huntington, *Political Order in Changing Societies* (New Haven: Yale University Press, 1968), especially Chap. 1. Huntington remarks: "A basic and frequently overlooked distinction exists between political modernization defined as movement from a traditional to a modern polity and political modernization defined as the political aspects and political effects of social, economic, and cultural modernization. The former posits the direction in which political change theoretically should move. The latter describes the political changes which actually occur in modernizing countries. The gap between the two is often vast. Modernization in practice always involves change in and usually the disintegration of a traditional political system, but it does not necessarily involve significant movement toward a modern political system" (p. 35).

Table 48. *The Most Active Initiators in
Latin America, 1959–1967*

	Cuba	(355)
	United States	(329)
(nostac)	Labor	(121)
(nostac)	Other Parties	(118)
	Brazil	(118)
	Argentina	(103)
(nostac)	Governmental Noncentral	(94)
	Dominican Republic	(87)
(nostac)	OAS	(83)
(nostac)	Individuals	(72)
	Venezuela	(68)
(nostac)	Castroites	(56)
	Chile	(54)
	USSR	(52)
(nostac)	Demonstrators, Rebels, Terrorists	(48)
(nostac)	Cultural Groups	(48)
(nostac)	Extra-Regional Business	(45)
(nostac)	Anti-Castroites	(39)
	Guatemala	(39)
(nostac)	Students	(38)

Table 49. *The Most Salient Targets in
Latin America, 1959–1967*

	United States	(266)
	Cuba	(250)
(nostac)	OAS	(198)
(nostac)	Individuals	(141)
(nostac)	Media	(113)
	Argentina	(100)
(nostac)	Labor	(99)
	Dominican Republic	(97)
(nostac)	Other Parties	(95)
	Brazil	(87)
(nostac)	Governmental Noncentral	(72)
(nostac)	United Nations and Other IGO's	(70)
(nostac)	Castroites	(69)
	USSR	(64)
(nostac)	Demonstrators, Rebels, Terrorists	(59)
(nostac)	MNC's	(52)
(nostac)	Students	(47)
	Chile	(47)
(nostac)	Catholics	(40)
	Bolivia	(39)

Table 50. Disruptive-Supportive Behavior, 1959-1967

Disrupters		Supporters	
Cuba	(−115)	United States	(+109)
Other Parties	(−34)	USSR	(+44)
Labor	(−33)	Cultural Groups	(+30)
Venezuela	(−32)	UN and Other IGOs	(+28)
Governmental Noncentral	(−26)	El Salvador	(+19)
Dominican Republic	(−25)	Honduras	(+18)
Anti-Castroites	(−23)	MNC's	(+17)
Castroites	(−20)	Costa Rica	(+12)
Military	(−20)	Guatemala	(+11)
DRT's	(−18)	Other Religious	(+7)

for 46 percent of the dyads, an increase of 2 percent over the figure for 1948–1958. Violence remained constant at 6 percent of the total.

The Decline of the "Special Relationship": 1967–1972

The Nixon Administration completed the process, begun by President Johnson when he entered the Vietnam quagmire, of moving Latin America from near-the-top to near-the-bottom of the list of U.S. foreign policy priorities.[23] Most important, Nixon's policy-makers scaled down the U.S. estimate of the security threat, which had always provided the principal rationale for U.S. involvement in hemisphere affairs. With the Soviet-American detente, the ebb of Castroist subversion, and an increase in Latin American nationalism, they believed it was time to strive for a "low profile" in the hemisphere. Latin America, they reasoned, would profit from a little calculated neglect behind the rhetoric of a "mature partnership" and a "nuts-and-bolts" approach to issues of aid and trade. The United States could thus devote its attention to trouble-spots like Southeast Asia and to the related, primary task of reshaping U.S. relations with the Soviet Union, China, Europe, and Japan. At least until the energy crisis of 1973, Henry Kissinger's conception of an emerging quintipolar world clearly assigned only residual significance to the developing countries, Latin America included.

For their part, Latin American governments responded to their declining special relationship with the United States by increasing cooperation among themselves and with extra-regional developing countries, as well as by cultivating an ever-wider network of political and commercial

23. For an in-depth analysis of Nixon policies and full documentation, see Yale H. Ferguson, "An End to the 'Special Relationship': The United States and Latin America," *Revista/Review Interamericana* (Inter-American University of Puerto Rico) 2:3 (Fall 1972), pp. 352–87.

ties with Europe, Japan, and Communist governments. Of particular significance was the coordination of policies regarding aid and trade in several multilateral contexts. These included CECLA, an irregular meeting of Latin American government representatives, that summarized basic Latin American demands in the 1969 *Declaration of Viña del Mar,* and the so-called *Group of* 77 developing countries that caucused prior to UNCTAD II (October, 1970) and UNCTAD III (April–May, 1972). Another important trend, foreshadowing the worldwide concern about primary commodities that grew out of the energy crisis, was the participation of some Latin American producing countries in the Organization of Petroleum Exporting Countries (OPEC) and the Organization of Copper Exporting Countries (OCEC). Moreover, reacting explicitly or implicitly to the warnings of "dependence" theorists whose ideas gained broad currency in this period, various Latin American nation-states sought a greater measure of control over multinational corporations and other forms of foreign private investment (see Chapter 8). From 1967 to 1972, this policy thrust was a preoccupation especially of the governments of Peru and Chile, and it found multilateral expression in a path-breaking foreign investment code adopted by the new Andean Common Market (ANCOM).

Regime Stability maintained its front-ranking position among the superissues in the third period. *Security* displaced *Castroism* in the second rank, and *Castroism* dropped to third. *External Assistance* rose from fifth to fourth rank, reflecting not really its increased importance, but the total disappearance of the *Democracy-Dictatorship* superissue. For the same reason, *Peronism* climbed from sixth to fifth rank, and *Trade and Integration* from seventh to sixth.

Regime Stability appeared in all eleven factors and 61 percent of the issues from 1967 to 1972. In this period, the struggle of democratic-left parties against old-style dictatorships was no longer an issue. Rather, instability involved primarily an extension of one pattern from the second time slice: this was the contest between civilian politicians and military establishments inclined to exercise power themselves.

In Peru, considerable uncertainty about the terms of an agreement

Table 51. Ranking of Superissues by Explained Variance, 1967–1972

1. Regime Stability	(3.36)
2. Security	(2.65)
3. Castroism	(1.38)
4. External Assistance	(0.98)
5. Peronism	(0.54)
6. Trade and Integration	(0.21)
7. Democracy-Dictatorship	(0)

negotiated by President Beláunde regarding the International Petroleum Company's future rights to Peruvian oil provided the military with an opportunity to seize control in October, 1968. General Velasco Alvarado proceeded to implement a series of reforms by decree which buttressed his claim that his military government was presiding over a genuine "revolution." These reforms included the nationalization of oil, an innovative foreign investment code, and an extensive agrarian reform program.

Prior to the elections of 1968 in Panama, an opposition coalition in Congress impeached President Robles on the grounds that he was improperly intervening in the electoral process. Arnulfo Arias, the leader of the opposition, subsequently won the election but was deposed by the military after a mere eleven days in office. Colonel (later General) Omar Torrijos emerged as the strong man of the new military regime.

The winner of the 1968 elections in Ecuador was the eccentric José María Velasco Ibarra, whose previous four terms had all been aborted by coups. Two years later, with the military's blessing, Velasco temporarily assumed dictatorial powers. But the military overthrew him again in early 1972 in order to avert the probable victory of radical reformer Assad Bucaram and his Popular Forces Alliance in elections scheduled for June of that year. On this occasion, the military indicated that it intended to remain in charge for an indefinite period.

Bolivian politics was thrown into renewed turmoil when President Barrientos (who had legitimized his rule by winning the election of 1966) was killed in a helicopter crash in April, 1969. His civilian vice-president, Siles Salines, succeeded to the presidency, only to be deposed shortly thereafter by Barrientos's former associate, General Ovando. Ovando's regime then fell in October, 1970 to a *golpe* staged by leftist military forces under Colonel Juan José Torres. Finally, another coup led by rightist Colonel Hugo Banzer Suárez toppled Torres's self-proclaimed "popular nationalist" government in August, 1971.

In Uruguay, *Tupamaro* guerrilla violence and a desperate economic slump clouded the elections of February, 1972, which saw a leftist Broad Front win one-fifth of the total vote. The conservative victor, Juan María Bordaberry, imposed a program of stringent austerity. Strikes and more guerrilla violence ensued, setting the stage for the end of Uruguayan democracy. (With military support, in 1973 Bordaberry disbanded Congress and began systematic political repression.)

At the same time, events were moving toward a restoration of civilian rule in Argentina. After six frustrating years in power, in 1972 the military decided to schedule elections for March, 1973, with the *Peronistas* freely allowed to participate. In November, 1972, Juan Perón himself returned to select Héctor Campora as his party's standardbearer. (Campora won the election but soon yielded the presidency to Perón.)

If anything could upstage the return of Perón, it was the political developments in Chile beginning with the 1970 electoral victory of "Marxist" Salvador Allende Gossens and his Popular Unity coalition. Urban squatters, peasants, and especially industrial workers provided most of the votes necessary for Allende to win the three-cornered race of that year, but they could not provide him with the power to rule. From the outset Allende was very much a minority president seeking to achieve radical change in a most unpropitious domestic setting. The Chilean middle class was particularly vulnerable to the economic dislocations of the Allende period, and in the end it was they who were principally responsible for bringing him down. For a time, the military tolerated Popular Unity assaults against foreign corporations and the domestic oligarchy, land seizures in the countryside and urban slums, and an ongoing political stalemate between the executive, legislative, and judicial branches of government. However, the generals ultimately felt compelled to respond to the massive street demonstrations of middle-class citizens in Santiago and the strikes of shopkeepers, professionals, and truck owners that threatened the country with economic collapse. Christian Democrats conducted an unbridled campaign of protest to capitalize on middle-class discontent. Moreover, Popular Unity workers were involved in some of the strikes that plagued the Chilean economy, and Allende was under constant criticism in his own movement to the effect that he was conceding too much to the opposition.

Whatever the internal situation in Chile, no explanation of the difficulties that beset the Allende government would be complete without reference to the roles of multinational corporations and the United States government.[24] The copper companies, including Anaconda and Kennecott, reacted to nationalization of their operations in Chile by urging the Nixon Administration to adopt a hard line toward Chile and by instituting a series of court challenges to prevent the sale of Chilean copper abroad. ITT went still further. It initially offered the Nixon Administration a large sum of money prior to the 1970 election to be used to stop Allende from coming to power. We shall review the formal Nixon policy regarding expropriations in connection with the *External Assistance* superissue at a later point. Suffice it to say here that there was also a clandestine side to this policy in Chile. Although the Nixon Administration did not accept ITT's initial offer, the CIA seriously considered and rejected a plan to allocate $350 thousand of its own to bribe Chilean legislators in an attempt to prevent Allende's selection by Congress when no candidate received the requisite majority of votes in the election proper. But the CIA apparently

24. See especially the exchange between Elizabeth Farnsworth and Paul E. Sigmund in "Chile: What Was the U.S. Role?" in *Foreign Policy,* No. 16 (Fall 1974), pp. 126–56. See also Anthony Sampson, *The Sovereign State of ITT* (New York: Stein & Day, 1973), chap. 11.

did spend some $8 million (worth $30–$50 million on the Chilean black market) from 1970 to 1973 in support of the opposition to Allende (including the crippling truckers' strike). The money was used to organize demonstrations and otherwise to disrupt the Chilean economy. ITT came back into the picture in late September, 1970, when William Broe, the CIA's chief for clandestine activities in Latin America, this time approached the company with a plan to create economic chaos in Chile before the upcoming congressional runoff elections. ITT reluctantly turned the plan down, mainly because of doubts that other companies could be persuaded to cooperate. A year later, in October, 1971, ITT submitted to the State Department a *Chile White Paper,* proposing an escalation of U.S. economic sanctions against Chile. The Nixon Administration did not react with much enthusiasm to the proposal, perhaps because CIA "dirty tricks" already underway were deemed sufficient.

An overview of leading actors affecting Chilean regime stability from 1967 to 1972 offers another dramatic illustration of the Latin American pattern of domestic political schisms cum external penetration. It should be remembered that Table 52 covers the closing years of the Christian Democratic government as well as most of the Allende period. United States' strong support for Christian Democratic President Eduardo Frei Montalva is part of the explanation for categorizing the United States as a "supporter." Another consideration was the fact that the Nixon Administration made a determined effort to keep its *public* relations with Allende on a "cool but correct" basis. Brazil's support reflected solely an amicable meeting between President Frei and Brazilian President Costa e Silva. The IMF appeared as a "supporter" because of its relatively flexible approach to Chilean balance-of-payments problems. It is noteworthy that all the major overt threats to stability were by nonstate actors.

The second superissue from 1967 to 1972 was *Security,* which was involved in ten of the factors and 54 percent of the issues.

Table 52. Regime Stability: Chile, 1967–1972

Supporters	Threats to Stability
United States	Multinational Corporations (Anaconda,
USSR	Kennecott, ITT)
United Kingdom	Students (Marxists, anti-Marxists)
Brazil	Chilean Parties (Christian Democrats,
Peru	Popular Unity, Communists, Socialists)
IMF	Chilean Business (landowners,
	truckers, banks, shopkeepers,
	professionals)
	Chilean Labor
	Individuals
	Chilean Church and Roman Catholics

The Nixon Administration's generally optimistic view of the status of hemisphere security rested upon the presumed intentions of Moscow and Peking to establish "respectable" links with Latin American nationalist governments rather than to support revolution and upon the apparent failures of Latin American guerrillas. Latin American urban terrorism, kidnappings, assassinations, and hijackings continued and even increased in this period, mainly in Chile, Uruguay, and Argentina. (In Argentina, not even Perón could stop the violence perpetrated by the Trotskyite People's Revolutionary Army and the older leftist group, the *Montoneros,* as well as the rightist Argentine Anti-Communist Alliance.) However, most observers interpreted this unrest as a byproduct of social strains in specific countries, not as a manifestation of transnational subversion.

Despite the improving outlook for security, which the Nixon Administration regarded as providing a low profile option for the United States, the low profile was frustrated in part because it did not include a drastic overhaul of certain pre-existing high-profile security policies such as the hard line on Cuba. Nor did detente and greater multipolarity make U.S. decision-makers any less concerned with other adverse developments in their country's traditional sphere of influence in Latin America. The Nixon Administration's hostility to Allende was *primarily* a function of the threat he posed to U.S. private economic interests. But one might speculate as well about the extent to which Washington's attitude represented a defense of U.S. prestige, a simple visceral reaction to "Marxism," and/or an expression of genuine fear about a security threat to Chile's Latin American neighbors.

This period was a relatively quiescent one for the OAS in the security field. In 1970–1971, the OAS General Assembly grappled with the institution of political asylum as it affected the ability to control political terrorism. The OAS at length produced a convention that defined only the kidnapping of diplomats as an international "crime" and that maintained the right of national governments to refuse extradition if they judged that the act committed was essentially "political" in nature. Several conservative governments, including Brazil's, found the document inadequate and boycotted the session that approved it.

The "Soccer War" between El Salvador and Honduras during the summer of 1969 provided evidence that the OAS could still act to mediate a "traditional" interstate conflict. In this case, the threat of inter-American sanctions raised at an emergency Meeting of Foreign Ministers and the personal diplomacy of Secretary General Galo Plaza Lasso were instrumental in obtaining both a ceasefire and El Salvador's military withdrawal from Honduras. OAS observers patrolled the boundary between the two countries, and the Inter-American Commission on Human Rights investigated charges of mistreatment of foreign nationals by both sides.

Several draft treaties on the Panama Canal negotiated by the Robles government were a casualty of the political turmoil and coup of 1968. Pressures for a settlement gradually mounted on Torrijos, but little real progress resulted from ongoing talks with the United States until after the United Nations Security Council met in Panama in March, 1973. (The United States and Panama signed a "declaration of principles" governing future negotiations in February, 1974.)

There was also some movement in the U.S. position on territorial waters during these years. Seizures of U.S. fishing vessels off Ecuador and Peru continued, and in early 1971 Ecuador complained to the OAS of U.S. "economic aggression" when Washington reacted to seizures by cutting off arms credits. In May, 1972, the United States managed to conclude a temporary agreement concerning shrimping rights with Brazil. Meanwhile, looking to the U.N. Law of the Sea Conference scheduled for 1974, the State Department advanced a possible compromise: (1) the extension of sovereign jurisdiction to twelve miles, with international guarantees of free passage; and (2) coastal state exercise of yet-to-be-defined special rights over such matters as fishing, pollution and safety regulations, and the exploitation of natural resources within an additional "coastal zone" of up to 200 miles.

Castroism was the third-ranking superissue. It appeared on eight of the factors and included 29 percent of the issues from 1967 to 1972. Compared with the second time slice, this superissue had become considerably less important.

Castro's speech of August 22, 1968 expressed support for the Soviet intervention in Czechoslovakia. It signaled a major shift in Cuban foreign policy. Afterwards, Castro drew closer both to the Soviet Union and to Latin America. He muted the call to armed struggle, commented favorably on the expropriations and reforms instituted by the Peruvian and Bolivian military governments, and lauded Allende's victory at the polls in Chile. The Cuban regime was preoccupied with grave economic problems at home, typified by a succession of disappointing sugar harvests. Moreover, Guevara's defeat in Bolivia appeared to be a final factor in convincing Castro of the inefficacy of additional exhortations to revolutionary violence. Cuba was officially accepted as a member of COMECON (the Soviet bloc's economic grouping) in July, 1972.

Despite these developments, the Nixon Administration consistently opposed any major change in the *status quo* regarding Cuba. It repeatedly warned the Soviet Union that it would not tolerate the use of Cuba as a base for missile-carrying submarines, which in Washington's interpretation was a violation of the agreement that resulted from the 1962 Cuban Missile Crisis. Contrary to the expectations of some observers, Washington did not move decisively to end the OAS boycott of Cuba after normalization of

U.S. relations with Peking and the conclusion of a hijacking pact with the Cuban government in 1972. Explanations for this intransigence seemed to lie in the utility of Cuba as a financial liability for the Soviet Union, President Nixon's personal antipathy toward Castro, and a politically influential constituency in the United States (conservative Congressmen, businessmen, sugar importers, and the Cuban exile community) to whom Castro remained anathema. (However, inaugurating a "new hemisphere dialogue" early in 1974, Kissinger did agree to leave the question of inviting Cuba to participate entirely to the OAS membership, and the OAS eventually voted in the summer of 1975 to lift sanctions imposed at the multilateral level.

External Assistance was the fourth superissue, appealing on eight factors and involved in 22 percent of the issues in the third period.

The Nixon Administration inherited a foreign aid program that was already under severe attack in Congress. In the past, bilateral programs of both military and development assistance had enjoyed the bipartisan support of moderates, and a voting majority had been constructed on the basis of trade-offs between liberals and conservatives. What was unique about the situation facing Nixon was the sudden hardening of conservative opposition to development aid in the wake of expropriations and the growing dissatisfaction with military *and* bilateral development aid among liberals and moderates who were uneasy about U.S. identification with repressive regimes.

With Congressional discontent mounting, there were several significant changes in the U.S. foreign aid program. First, development aid was steadily multilateralized as the U.S. channeled more and more of approximately the same total through international lending agencies. By 1970, U.S. bilateral loans represented only 16.4 percent of total AID, Inter-American Development Bank, and World Bank lending, compared with 48.5 percent in 1965. Second, AID assistance was concentrated in three countries (Brazil, Chile before Allende, and Colombia), and in two ostensibly social development sectors (agriculture and education). Third, Congress created the Inter-American Social Development Institute (renamed the Inter-American Foundation in 1972), a U.S. government corporation to fund Latin American private-sector experimental projects directly contributing to social development. Fourth, President Nixon acceded to Latin American demands for an end to "additionality" provisions that limited aid purchases to a specific list of U.S. exports, and he "untied" aid funds for expenditure anywhere in the Western Hemisphere (though still not in Europe and Japan). Finally, drawing on the *Peterson Report,* in 1971 Nixon proposed a number of reforms in the administration of U.S. assistance, including the replacement of AID with two new semi-public "independent" institutions.

The Nixon Administration's reform proposals remained a dead letter in Congress, and the Senate dramatized its general dissatisfaction by temporarily killing the administration's aid bill in 1972. Foreign aid came back from the grave on that occasion, but it was clear that it would continue to face tough sledding on Capitol Hill. Over the long run the best hope for its survival appeared to be the large stake that the U.S. business community still had in aid subsidies. (In 1973, Congress directed AID to give greater stress to the needs of the poor majority in the developing countries, paralleling a similar emphasis at the World Bank under Robert McNamara's leadership.)

UNCTAD III strongly endorsed the U.N. Second Development Decade target of a minimum of 1 percent of gross national product (GNP) for public and private capital transfers from the developed countries (0.07 percent for "official development assistance," which consisted of food aid plus bilateral and multilateral financial assistance). The U.S. total in recent years has been only about .03 percent of GNP, and appropriations even for U.S.-pledged contributions to multilateral programs have lagged well behind those of other donor states. UNCTAD III also raised other aid-related questions concerning International Monetary Fund Special Drawing Rights (SDR's), the new paper reserves for international monetary transactions. The developing countries argued that SDR's should not be allocated on the basis of national income and trade as in the past, but should be "linked" in some way to their requirements to finance imports for development. This was a proposal that the Nixon Administration viewed with considerable skepticism.

Although they supported the UNCTAD target, Latin American governments formally maintained in the 1969 Viña del Mar Declaration and elsewhere that foreign private investment should not be counted as "aid." From 1968 to 1972, there seemed to be an emerging consensus that such investment should be limited to certain sectors of the economy and that it should assume appropriate forms in order to serve better the interests of the nation-state. The most ambitious code to date regarding the treatment of foreign private capital (modeled on the Peruvian code) was enacted by ANCOM in mid-1971.

Soon after President Nixon took office, expropriations with the threat of little or no compensation in Peru, Bolivia, Ecuador, Chile, and Guyana touched off a bitter internal dispute within the U.S. executive branch as to the proper response. State Department officials held that efforts to protect private business abroad would have only marginal success and might do irreparable damage to U.S. relations with Latin American governments. The State Department especially opposed any policy that would involve automatic withholding of aid to the governments in question. On the other hand, Treasury Secretary John B. Connally, with the backing of Exim

Bank President Henry Kearns, argued for an automatic cutoff on the grounds that protection of private interests is a legitimate national interest of the United States. In their view, punishment of errant governments would serve as a lesson to others that might be tempted to a similar "irresponsible" course of action.

From mid-1971 to early 1972 the hard line gradually gained ascendance, and the position eventually dictated by the White House stopped just short of the automatic cutoff desired by the Secretary of the Treasury. On January 19, 1972, the White House issued the following statement:

> Under international law, the United States has a right to expect that the taking of American property will be nondiscriminatory; that it will be for a public purpose; and that its citizens will receive prompt, adequate and effective compensation from the expropriating country.
>
> Thus when a country expropriates a significant United States interest without making reasonable provision for such compensation to United States citizens, we will presume that the United States will not extend new bilateral economic benefits to the expropriating country unless and until it is determined that the country is taking reasonable steps to provide adequate compensation or that there are major factors affecting United States interests which require continuance of all or part of these benefits.[25]

The statement also confirmed that in such cases the United States would "withhold its support from loans under consideration in multilateral development banks," a policy that Congress subsequently incorporated into the Gonzalez Amendment to foreign assistance legislation.

At the outset, although aid already "in the pipeline" continued to flow, the Nixon Administration denied any new authorizations of bilateral development or military aid to Peru, Bolivia, Ecuador, Chile, and Guyana pending satisfactory settlement of outstanding claims. The Treasury also ordered U.S. officials in the World Bank, the IDB, and other international credit institutions to oppose or abstain on further loans to these governments for the time being. The White House made it clear to the Chilean government that the administration would regard the terms offered to the copper companies as the principal initial test of Allende's desire for amicable relations with the United States. When Allende refused to pay and went on to nationalize other U.S. companies, U.S.–Chilean relations deteriorated into open hostility. Symbolically, Washington then decided to continue aid to the Chilean military while other funds dried up. This was a clear sign that the United States was prepared to support those elements in Chile that had the power to oust Allende.

Attitudes toward the United States once again mirrored some of the

25. *New York Times,* 20 January 1972, pp. 1, 4.

Table 53.   Attitudes Toward the United States, 1967–1972

Pro-United States	Neutral	Anti-United States
United States	Peru	Individuals
Panama	Anti-Reelection	Peoples Pro-
OAS	Committee (Dom. Rep.)	gressive Party
Chile	Cuba	(Guyana)
Costa Rica	Brazil	Bolivian Students
British Guiana (Guyana)		Mexico
Bolivia		Argentine Labor
U.S. Airlines		
MNC's (petroleum)		
Nicaragua		
Ecuador		
Inter-American Press		
Association		
United Nations		

concerns of the period. An interesting dichotomy emerged between co-operative governments and dissident *nostacs* in the cases of Guyana and Bolivia, although the immediate aftermath of the Guevara episode did make the Bolivian government's behavior appear more cooperative than it was, for example, with respect to the expropriation of Gulf Oil. Panama's presence on the "pro" side of the table reflects negotiations over the canal. Chile was "pro" because of Washington's support for Frei and its generally "correct" overt relations with Allende. Ecuador's overall "pro-U.S." orientation outweighed serious frictions over territorial waters. Continued bickering over migrants and especially over Washington's virtual closing of the border during "Operation Intercept" (designed to dramatize its concern about drug traffic) were sufficient to push Mexico temporarily into the "anti" column. Peru appeared among the "neutrals" because of controversies over the IPC and territorial waters, and Velasco's independent nationalist foreign policy. Significantly, Castro's cooperation with the United States on hijacking overshadowed his relatively low-key criticism of the Nixon Administration. Also important, Brazil aligned with other Third World governments against the United States on most aid and trade issues.

   Trade and Integration, the sixth superissue from 1967 to 1972, was involved in only one factor and a scant 4 percent of the issues.

   Although this superissue generated comparatively few "events," some of these involved highly significant developments. The developed countries agreed in 1970 at UNCTAD III to a system of generalized preferences for the developing countries' manufactures and semi-manufactures. Europe and Japan quickly implemented partial preferences, but a protectionist-minded Congress blocked U.S. compliance. Moreover, much to the chagrin of Latin Americans, their countries' goods were not exempted from the temporary 10 percent surcharge President Nixon imposed on imports in mid-1971.

A limited commodity agreement on cocoa was negotiated in 1972 upon the urging of UNCTAD III. Two other such agreements existed at this stage that governed tin and coffee. Only the last had U.S. support. The OPEC model—a cartel of producing countries acting jointly against consumers—gained increasing attention during this period. A parallel organization for copper (OCEC) in late 1972 voted to boycott Kennecott in retaliation for that company's efforts to block sales of Chilean copper.

The Central American Common Market was almost scuttled by Honduras's withdrawal after the Soccer War, and LAFTA made little progress. The most interesting experiment in Latin American integration during this period was ANCOM, which arose out of an agreement that was signed in May, 1969, by Bolivia, Chile, Colombia, Ecuador, and Peru (Venezuela signed in 1973). As we have noted, ANCOM adopted an innovative investment code. An equally important milestone was the conclusion of ANCOM's first sectoral agreement in 1972, which provided for the complementary division and assignment among member countries of some seventy-three basic metal-mechanical industries.

Coappearance scores from 1967 to 1972 illustrate the already mentioned "wash-out" of the *Democracy-Dictatorship* superissue and the decline in *Castroism*. There was still a clear relationship between *Security* and *Castroism* and between *Regime Stability* and *Castroism,* but no longer at the previous levels. *Security* and *Regime Stability* were considerably more interrelated than *Regime Stability* and *Castroism. External Assistance* coappeared regularly with *Security,* less with *Regime Stability,* and even less with *Castroism. Trade and Integration* remained a markedly independent superissue.

During this time slice, nonstate actors for the third successive period increased their prominence as actors, with a corresponding increase in their involvement as targets as well. *Nostacs* initiated 40 percent of the dyads and were the targets of 52 percent of the actions. As the following tables

Table 54. Latin American Superissue Coappearance, 1967-1972

	I	II	III	IV	V	VI	VII
I. Security	—						
II. Peronism	.43	—					
III. Castroism	.89	.50	—				
IV. Regime Stability	.95	.53	.84	—			
V. Democracy-Dictatorship	0	0	0	0	—		
VI. External Assistance	.89	.17	.75	.84	0	—	
VII. Trade and Integration	.18	0	.22	.17	0	.22	—

Table 55. *The Most Active Initiators in Latin America, 1967–1972*

	United States	(152)
	Chile	(104)
	Mexico	(51)
	Peru	(43)
(nostac)	Castroites	(42)
(nostac)	Individuals	(40)
(nostac)	DRT's	(39)
(nostac)	Labor	(37)
(nostac)	Students	(36)
(nostac)	Governmental Noncentral	(36)
	Bolivia	(35)
(nostac)	Cultural Groups	(34)
	Argentina	(34)
	Cuba	(33)
(nostac)	Other Parties	(32)
	Brazil	(32)
(nostac)	OAS	(27)
(nostac)	MNC's	(22)
(nostac)	United Nations and Other IGO's	(18)
	El Salvador	(18)

Table 56. *The Most Salient Targets in Latin America, 1967–1972*

	United States	(139)
(nostac)	MNC's	(63)
(nostac)	Individuals	(61)
	Chile	(54)
(nostac)	Latin Business	(47)
(nostac)	Media	(46)
	Cuba	(45)
(nostac)	Cultural Groups	(41)
	Bolivia	(41)
	Argentina	(38)
(nostac)	Students	(37)
(nostac)	Labor	(36)
(nostac)	OAS	(36)
(nostac)	Castroites	(34)
(nostac)	Governmental Noncentral	(30)
(nostac)	Other Parties	(27)
	Brazil	(26)
	Nicaragua	(25)
(nostac)	Extra-Regional Business	(24)
(nostac)	United Nations and Other IGO's	(22)
	Peru	(22)

indicate, of the actors occupying the first twenty activity ranks, eleven were *nostacs* (the same number as the second period). Among the twenty most salient targets, thirteen were *nostacs*.

The United States regained its position as the most active initiator. Chile was the second most active initiator, attaining the rank formerly occupied by Cuba. Mexico returned to the activity table, this time to the third rank, and Peru made its first appearance on both the activity and salience tables. Castroites, in fifth rank, were much more active than Cuba, testifying to the new domestic orientation of the Castro government. Significant, too, was the fact that Anti-Castroites disappeared from the activity table. Demonstrators, Rebels, and Terrorists (DRT's) climbed from fifteenth to seventh rank as initiators, and the OAS slipped from ninth to seventeenth rank. Other Parties were the least notable of active intrastate nongovernmental actors. They dropped from fourth to fifteenth rank, which points up their inability to make a substantial contribution to the "institutionalization" of demands. Multinational Corporations (MNC's) made their first appearance on the activity table, and they were more salient targets than any single nation-state except for the United States. Latin Business appeared for the first time, as a target in the fifth rank. This reflected such events as acquisitions by multinationals, foreign loans, and nationalizations.

As for actor behavior: Once again nearly twice as many nonstate actors were disrupters than were supporters, and the United States was plainly the system's leading supporter. Again, too, intergovernmental organizations were supporters, as was Latin Business. Brazil and Mexico returned to the supporter list, but at relatively low levels. Among the disrupters was Chile which supplanted Cuba as the main disrupter. Indeed, neither Cuba nor Anti-Castroites were among the disrupters. Peru appeared primarily because of the IPC controversy, Argentina and Uruguay mainly because of internal strife, and El Salvador appeared as the "aggressor" in the Soccer War. Students, DRT's, and Labor were all more disruptive than was the Military.

The third period was slightly less conflictful than the second but a shade more violent. Conflict accounted for 44 percent of the dyads, 2 percent less than 1967–1972. Violence increased from 6 percent to 8 percent of total dyads.

Table 57. *Disruptive-Supportive Behavior, 1967–1972*

Disrupters		Supporters	
Chile	(−28)	United States	(+60)
Students	(−26)	OAS	(+17)
DRT's	(−21)	Cultural Groups	(+14)
Labor	(−19)	United Nations and Other IGO's	(+12)
Individuals	(−18)	Colombia	(+12)
Argentina	(−16)	United Kingdom	(+11)
Military	(−13)	Panama	(+10)
Peru	(−9)	Brazil	(+10)
Castroites	(−8)	Mexico	(+9)
El Salvador	(−8)	Latin Business	(+8)
Uruguay	(−8)	USSR	(+8)

Latin America as a Complex Conglomerate

No single superissue or overall system pattern during the quarter-century can be adequately understood without reference to nonstate actors. Coappearance scores for the 1948–1972 period emphasize the centrality of *Regime Stability* and *Security,* which were not only themselves associated, but were also significantly linked to other superissues. What we are dealing with here is *both* the "international" dimension of "domestic" strife *and* the "domestic" dimension of "international" strife. Indeed, *Regime Stability* and *Security* are so intimately connected that in this context the distinctions between domestic and international wither away to a degree far exceeding the notion of "linkages." This is the "Janus face of conflict" to which we referred in our chapter title. *Regime Stability* was by far the dominant superissue in all three periods, and *Security* was significant throughout as well. The pattern of coappearance would doubtless have been still more striking had *Castroism* and *Democracy-Dictatorship* also remained important over the entire time span. *Trade and Integration* was obviously the most consistently independent superissue, evidencing a relatively weak relationship with other superissues over the twenty-five years.

Between 1948 and 1972 nonstate actors initiated a significant 37 percent of all dyads and were the targets of fully 52 percent of all actions. Of the twenty most active initiators, nine were *nostacs*. In addition, thirteen of the twenty most salient targets were *nostacs*. The United States and Cuba were overwhelmingly the most prominent actors and targets. But, a wide range of "domestic" groups and the OAS were important on both lists; the U.N. and Other IGO's as well as Multinational Corporations, Latin Business, and Extra-Regional Business appeared among the most salient targets. Only four nation-states were more active initiators than the OAS, and only two were more salient targets. However potent their actions

Table 58. Latin American Superissue Coappearance, 1948–1972

	I	II	III	IV	V	VI	VII
I. Security	–						
II. Peronism	.60	–					
III. Castroism	.78	.39	–				
IV. Regime Stability	.94	.65	.79	–			
V. Democracy-Dictatorship	.70	.65	.55	.75	–		
VI. External Assistance	.81	.42	.68	.78	.68	–	
VII. Trade and Integration	.25	.31	.27	.38	.47	.48	–

when they did act, it is interesting that the Military in Latin America neither initiated nor received sufficient actions to be among the top twenty in either category. (It should be remembered with regard to this point that the military *in power* is regarded as a nation-state actor.)

Turning to disruptive-supportive scores, we find the Military and five

Table 59. *The Most Active Initiators in Latin America, 1948-1972*

	United States	(593)
	Cuba	(489)
(nostac)	Other Parties	(225)
	Argentina	(216)
	Chile	(209)
	Brazil	(201)
(nostac)	Labor	(195)
(nostac)	Individuals	(167)
(nostac)	Governmental Noncentral	(166)
(nostac)	OAS	(148)
(nostac)	Castroites	(137)
	Mexico	(125)
	Bolivia	(120)
	Guatemala	(112)
	Venezuela	(109)
(nostac)	DRT's	(104)
	Dominican Republic	(103)
(nostac)	Cultural Groups	(99)
(nostac)	Students	(91)
	Peru	(91)

Table 60. *The Most Salient Targets in Latin America, 1948-1972*

	United States	(490)
	Cuba	(350)
(nostac)	Individuals	(349)
(nostac)	OAS	(259)
(nostac)	Media	(244)
(nostac)	Other Parties	(220)
	Argentina	(213)
(nostac)	Labor	(206)
	Brazil	(164)
(nostac)	MNC's	(155)
(nostac)	United Nations and Other IGO's	(138)
(nostac)	Castroites	(135)
	Chile	(129)
(nostac)	Governmental Noncentral	(124)
	Dominican Republic	(112)
	Bolivia	(108)
(nostac)	Latin Business	(102)
(nostac)	Extra-Regional Business	(98)
(nostac)	DRT's	(96)
(nostac)	Students	(96)

Table 61. Disruptive-Supportive Behavior, 1948–1972

Disrupters		Supporters	
Cuba	(−184)	United States	(+237)
Labor	(−67)	Cultural Groups	(+67)
Castroites	(−57)	USSR	(+55)
DRT's	(−52)	United Nations and Other IGO's	(+54)
Military	(−51)	OAS	(+36)
Governmental Noncentral	(−50)	MNC's	(+26)
Students	(−49)	Honduras	(+24)
Chile	(−39)	Mexico	(+23)
Dominican Republic	(−35)	Costa Rica	(+23)
Venezuela	(−31)	Colombia	(+18)

other *nostacs* in the disruptive column, contrasting with only three *nostacs* listed as supporters. The United States and Cuba were the region's leading supporter and disrupter respectively. Other than Cuba, nonstate actors were the most consistently bent upon overturning the *status quo*. With the possible exception of Castroites, all the disruptive nonstate actors were those customarily associated with "domestic" politics. On the other hand, intergovernmental actors and multinational corporations joined nation-states as system supporters. Confirming what has often been said about its fundamental conservatism, the Soviet Union emerged as the third most important supporter. Mexico was the only major Latin American nation-state supporter, and this was despite its absence from the list of the top-ten supporters in the second time slice. Chile and the Dominican Republic appeared as disrupters for obvious reasons. Venezuela appeared because of the Venezuelan government's lengthy battle with guerrillas and its role in precipitating OAS sanctions against Castro and Trujillo.

The Latin American regional system was highly conflictful, though not especially violent, over the twenty-five years as a whole as well as during each of the three periods. From 1948 to 1972 conflict was involved in fully 45 percent of all actions, and violence accounted for 7 percent of all dyads. What makes Latin America unique, we should stress again in closing, is not only the high level of conflict as such, but the "Janus face" sources of conflict in "domestic" and "international" systems that are so fused as to be virtually indistinguishable.

The Multinational Corporation versus Latin American Governments: *Who Is at Bay?*

EIGHT

Among nonstate actors in global politics, perhaps only terrorist groups have generated comparable concern—and none as much controversy—in recent years as the multinational corporation.[1] The problem of the multinationals has permeated emerging multipolar relationships within the developed North (DC-DC), as evidenced by Jean-Jacques Servan-Schreiber's warning about the American challenge to Europe,[2] Washing-

---

1. The amount of literature on the multinationals that has appeared since the late 1960s is staggering. Those readers seeking an introduction to the subject might want to start with some of the following works and others cited elsewhere in this chapter: Louis Turner, *Invisible Empires* (New York: Harcourt, Brace, Jovanovich, 1971); *Multinational Corporations and the Third World* (London: Allen Lane, 1974); Stefan H. Robock and Kenneth Simmonds, *International Business and Multinational Enterprises* (Homewood, Ill.: Irwin, 1973); Mira Wilkins, *The Emergence of Multinational Enterprise* (Cambridge: Harvard University Press, 1970); James W. Vaupel and Joan P. Curham, *The Making of Multinational Enterprise* (Cambridge: Harvard University Press, 1969); Jack N. Behrman, *National Interests and the Multinational Enterprise* (Englewood Cliffs, N.J.: Prentice-Hall, 1970); Charles P. Kindleberger, ed., *The International Corporation: A Symposium* (Cambridge: MIT Press, 1970); Charles P. Kindleberger, *American Business Abroad* (New Haven: Yale University Press, 1969); Courtney C. Brown, ed., *World Business: Promise and Problems* (New York: Free Press, 1970); entire issue of *The Annals of the American Academy of Political and Social Science* 403 (September 1972); entire issue of *International Studies Quarterly* 16:4 (December 1972); and two articles from *International Organization* 25:3 (Summer 1971)—Louis T. Wells, Jr., "The Multinational Business Enterprise: What Kind of International Organization?" (pp. 447–64) and Raymond Vernon, "Multinational Business and National Economic Goals" (pp. 693–706).
2. Jean-Jacques Servan-Schreiber, *The American Challenge* (New York: Atheneum, 1968). See also Edward A. McCreary, *The Americanization of Europe* (Garden City, N.Y.: Doubleday, 1964) and Kari Levitt, *Silent Surrender: The Multinational Corporation in Canada* (New York: St. Martin's Press, 1970).

ton's successful pressuring for some relaxation in Japanese barriers to foreign investment, and the contribution of the multinationals' currency juggling to a series of monetary crises in the early 1970's. The multinational corporation has been a major issue, as well, in the "new bipolarity" (DC-LDC) between the "developed" North (the "haves") and the "developing" South (the "have-nots").

Paradoxically, suspicion of the multinationals as purveyors of the policies of their home governments and also as independent entities responsible only to themselves has been a common denominator of both DC-DC and DC-LDC relations. As Peter Drucker comments: "For the first time in 400 years—since the end of the sixteenth century when the word 'sovereignty' was coined—the territorial political unit and the economic unit are no longer congruent."[3] The problem has been somewhat more acute in the DC-LDC context precisely because the nation-state tends to be weaker in the developing world and thus all the more susceptible to multinational intimidation. Borrowing from the title of Raymond Vernon's well-known book on the multinationals, "sovereignty" might be presumed to be "at bay" in direct proportion to the actual strength of the "sovereign" units that are being threatened.[4] In this respect, it is not reassuring that the $3 billion of value that each of the top-ten multinationals adds every year exceeds the GNP of about eighty member-states of the United Nations.[5] Moreover, productive capacity is only one, and perhaps not the most meaningful, gauge of the viability of sovereign units. Third World governments are also often pitifully weak from an internal political standpoint.

Latin America has been a key region in the evolution of the DC-LDC variant of the controversy over multinationals for several reasons, not the least because of a heavy concentration of foreign investment in the area and highly publicized clashes between foreign corporations and nationalist governments in such countries as Chile and Peru. Even more important, certainly for our purposes, has been the emergence in Latin America (and among students of Latin America) of a sophisticated body of theory revolving around the central concept of "dependence." Among other things, dependence theorists have focused on an alleged *growing* imbalance between developing-country governments and the multinationals. As traditional interstate security concerns continue to diminish, their analyses suggest, it is probable that the Latin American "Janus face of political

3. Peter F. Drucker, "Multinationals and Developing Countries: Myths and Realities," *Foreign Affairs* 53:1 (October 1974), p. 133.
4. Raymond Vernon, *Sovereignty at Bay: The Multinational Spread of U.S. Enterprises* (New York: Basic Books, 1971). See also Vernon, "The Multinational Enterprise: Power Versus Sovereignty," *Foreign Affairs* 49:4 (July 1971), pp. 736–51.
5. Joseph S. Nye, Jr., "Multinational Corporations in World Politics," *Foreign Affairs* 53:1 (October 1974), p. 153.

conflict" will have an increasingly significant transnational economic dimension.

The aim of this chapter is not to offer an in-depth discussion of the issues raised by the multinational corporation on a global basis or even in Latin America. Nor can we hope to assess here all of the implications, strengths, and weaknesses of the vast literature on dependence, which, in fact, deals with much more than just the multinational challenge (for instance, with a Latin American "style" of "problem-solving" that has often relied on imported "solutions"). Rather, we shall attempt to examine some of the advantages and disadvantages of the multinational "presence" in Latin America. We shall look at a few of the policy options available to Latin American governments that wish to reassert the primacy of national objectives under conditions of penetration and of greater interdependence in the world economy generally. As we shall stress, the range of such options and their prospects for adoption with at least limited success are somewhat greater than it is often assumed. Ironically, beyond unilateral policies, one approach to lessening dependence on the multinationals is the acceptance of greater dependence on other developing-country governments: in short, countering the threat posed by a leading interstate nongovernmental *nostac* with the creation of new intergovernmental organization *nostacs.*

The General Nature
of the Multinational Corporation

Delineating the multinational challenge is in some respects easier than arriving at a precise definition of the multinational corporation itself. Many companies, of course, have long been exporting goods and services to foreign countries. Perhaps the most distinguishing feature of the "modern" multinational corporation is that it maintains a "significant" presence involving direct investment abroad. This definition allows us to see that some multinationals have been in existence about as long as companies engaged in simple export activities. As Joseph S. Nye reminds us:

> . . . it is sometimes forgotten that the American multinational corporation arose in the nineteenth century . . . that it was not (then or later) located primarily in the Caribbean and Latin America; and that it had already created fear of a *défi américain* in Europe at the turn of the century. In fact, U.S. direct foreign investment was as large a percentage of GNP (7 percent) in 1914 as in 1966.[6]

6. *Ibid.*, p. 163.

The number of multinational corporations has increased dramatically in the post-World War II period. Paralleling a similar concentration of economic power in the domestic economies of the developed countries, a relatively small number of companies have succeeded in dominating foreign private investment activity in general. In 1966, for example, 3,400 U.S. firms had some 23,000 foreign affiliates, but 298 of these enterprises accounted for 53 percent of the total assets and 66 percent of the sales of foreign affiliates of U.S. companies.[7] Multinationals based in the United States together represented 55 percent of total direct foreign investment in 1970, while European companies represented 37.5 percent, Canadian 3.9 percent, Japanese 2.6 percent, and Australian 0.4 percent.[8]

As these figures which focus on size and nationality suggest, the multinational corporation is a phenomenon of considerable variety.[9] Some multinationals do a major portion of their business abroad; others are only peripherally so engaged. The pattern of peripheral engagement is illustrated by the activities of multinationals that are not involved in extractive industries in the developing countries. Peter F. Drucker reports:

> Confidential inside data in my possession on about forty-five manufacturers, distributors and financial institutions among the world's leading multinationals, both North American and European, show that the developed two-thirds of Brazil—from Bello Horizante southward—is an important market for some of these companies, though even Brazil ranks among the first twelve sales territories, or among the major revenue producers, for only two of them . . . otherwise not even India and Mexico—the two "developing" countries with the largest markets—ranks for any of the leading multinational companies in my sample ahead even of a single major sales district in the home country, be it the Hamburg-North Germany district, the English Midlands, or Kansas City.[10]

Some multinationals have operations in a great many countries; others in only one or several countries. A network spanning many countries, not surprisingly, seems to be characteristic of the larger firms. Nye states, "There are currently some 200 large multinational corporations which operate simultaneously in twenty or more different nations and are joined together by a common ownership and management strategies."[11]

Of the numerous other distinctions that might be made between multinational companies, three stand out as perhaps the most important. First is the *type of enterprise:* extractive (Anaconda Copper), agriculture

7. David H. Blake and Robert S. Walters, *The Politics of Global Economic Relations* (Englewood Cliffs, N.J.: Prentice-Hall, 1976), p. 81.
8. *Ibid.,* p. 77.
9. An excellent analysis of the distinctions among multinational corporations, upon which we have drawn, is in *ibid.,* pp. 80–88.
10. Drucker, "Multinationals and Developing Countries," p. 122.
11. Nye, "Multinational Corporations," p. 152.

(United Brands), manufacturing (Ford Motor Co.), service (Hilton Hotels, Inc.), financial (Chase Manhattan Bank), or conglomerate (ITT). Moreover, each category includes several different subtypes (for instance, extractive industries: oil, copper, tin, bauxite, and so forth). The classic pattern of multinational investment has been in extractive industries, agriculture, and the service industries of public transportation and utilities. In recent years, however, the other categories have attracted a greater share of foreign investment. From 1960 to 1972, U.S. direct foreign investment in manufacturing increased from 35 percent to 42 percent of the total. During the same period, although steadily increasing in book value, investment in the extractive industries declined from 43 percent to 35 percent of the total. Other investment, mainly in service and financial categories, held constant at around 22 percent of the total.[12]

A second distinction among the multinationals relates to *ownership*. Is a particular subsidiary wholly-owned by a foreign firm, or is it a joint venture with local private and/or public participation? If it is a joint venture with local capital, does the foreign company have a controlling or only a minority interest? In the case of the so-called fade-out joint venture,[13] for how long is foreign participation contemplated?

A third major distinction concerns the *degree of autonomy* that subsidiaries have vis-à-vis the parent firm. Howard Perlmutter, for instance, has classified intracompany relationships as *ethnocentric, polycentric,* or *geocentric*.[14] Ethnocentric firms are clearly identified with the nationality of the parent company in terms of decision-making authority and perspectives. This description would fit most multinational corporations today. Polycentric enterprises reflect the nationality of the host country and allow subsidiaries considerable decision-making leeway. Geocentric companies strive for a genuine international outlook, with "collaboration" between headquarters and subsidiaries designed to yield policies of benefit to company fortunes worldwide. Only a few multinationals (the major oil companies, for example) as yet have a true global strategy. Nevertheless, most analysts agree that there is likely to be a definite trend toward geocentricity among many of the larger firms in the years to come.[15] Indeed, some would argue that geocentricity is desirable as a means of increasing the benefits flowing to the world economy from the transnational organization of the multinationals. In other words, efficiency would be gained from the

12. 1960 statistics from Blake and Walters, *Global Economic Relations,* p. 79; 1972 statistics from U.S. Department of Commerce, *Survey of Current Business* 53:9 (September 1973), pp. 24–25.
13. Simply stated, a fade-out joint venture is one in which foreign participation declines to zero over a number of years, following a predetermined schedule.
14. Howard V. Perlmutter, "The Tortuous Evolution of the Multinational Corporation," *Columbia Journal of World Business* 4:1 (January–February 1969), p. 12.
15. On this point, see Nye, "Multinational Corporations," p. 164.

capacity of multinationals to overarch inward-looking nation-states, the economies of which are in fact highly interdependent.

Once again, we should emphasize that a single multinational company may have subsidiaries of more than one type, and ownership patterns and/or organizational practices may vary accordingly. Furthermore, none of the categories we have advanced fit neatly with the Japanese model of subsidiaries acting essentially as "subcontractors" for parent firms. In this model, actual parent firm investment and formal management control are low; but subsidiaries rely heavily on parent firms for technology and assistance in management, and they contract in advance to sell the parent almost all of their production.

The Multinational Corporation in Latin America: Investment Patterns and "Benefits"

Some statistics regarding U.S. investments illuminate recent patterns of multinational activity in Latin America. Between 1965 and 1972, the book value of total U.S. direct private investment in the Western Hemisphere (excluding Canada) increased from $10.9 billion to $16.6 billion. During the same period the Western Hemisphere share of all U.S. direct foreign investment declined from 22 percent to 17 percent, reflecting an increased flow to the European Economic Community (13 percent to 17 percent). In 1972, five countries accounted for 60 percent of the book value of all U.S. investment in the Western Hemisphere: Venezuela ($2.7 billion), Brazil ($2.5 billion), Mexico ($2.0 billion), Panama ($1.4 billion), and Argentina ($1.4 billion).[16] From 1965 through 1972, the share of U.S. investment in Western Hemisphere extractive industries declined from 46 percent to 38 percent, while investment devoted to manufacturing increased from 27 percent to 33 percent. Other investment, mainly in service and financial categories, increased only slightly from 27 percent to 28 percent.[17]

Optimistic analysts marshal an impressive array of arguments concerning the contribution of multinational investment to Latin America.[18] The first and most obvious contribution is investment capital itself, whether in the form of new capital or reinvested profits. Most analysts, however, place greater stress on some of the *effects* flowing from foreign investment rather than on Latin America's need for capital *per se*. Indeed, Drucker maintains that "developing countries have . . . more capital than they can productively employ." What they lack, he argues, is "the full ability to

16. *Survey of Current Business*, pp. 26–27.
17. *Ibid.*, pp. 24–25.
18. Most of these arguments are regularly advanced to support multinational investment in the developing countries generally.

mobilize their resources, whether human resources, capital or the physical resources." In Drucker's view, multinational investment can provide a "trigger" that will help mobilize resources with a sort of "multiplier effect."[19] Manufacturing concerns, he points out, have a particular stake in the general economic development of the countries in which they operate and thus may well regard their investment as "pump priming" rather than "fuel."[20] Insofar as foreign enterprises do prime the pump, the indirect benefits of such investment should be conceived as extending far beyond the direct benefits that flow from the activities of particular companies.

According to the defenders of the multinational corporation, the direct benefits are substantial. Multinational enterprises are the prime source of new technology for many countries. Such technology stimulates the production of new products and makes for the most efficient use of labor. The multinationals also provide vital managerial skills, pass on these skills to nationals through management training programs, and generate additional employment at submanagerial levels. Moreover, foreign companies are major taxpayers, helping to boost host government revenues.

Another central line of argument in support of the multinationals centers on their contribution to Latin America's exports. Subsidiaries of U.S. companies in the early 1970's accounted for about 35 percent of total exports from the region and 41 percent of Latin America's exports of manufactured goods.[21] David H. Blake and Robert S. Walters observe: "Most available data seem to indicate that the subsidiaries of multinational corporations are more effective in exporting their products, especially manufactured products, than are domestic firms."[22] The multinationals, the argument continues, possess the technology that gives birth to new products[23] and the necessary links to the world market that can assist Latin America in increasing its competitive advantage in production based on low labor costs.[24] John Diebold maintains, as well, that in encouraging development aimed at production for export, foreign firms aid in fighting the runaway inflation that plagues many Latin American countries. Export-oriented industries have an incentive to dampen inflation because higher costs make their products less marketable abroad.[25]

19. Drucker, "Multinationals and Developing Countries," p. 124.
20. *Ibid.,* p. 126.
21. Blake and Walters, *Global Economic Relations,* p. 98. These authors cite Herbert K. May, *The Contribution of U.S. Private Investment to Latin America's Growth* (New York: The Council for Latin America, 1970), p. 19 as the original source for these statistics.
22. Blake and Walters, *Global Economic Relations,* p. 99.
23. John Diebold forecasts that "the biggest expansion in developing countries' manufacturing for export during the period of 1972–92 may well take place in new products." ("Why Be Afraid of Them?" *Foreign Policy,* no. 12 [Fall 1973], p. 86.)
24. Drucker, "Multinationals and Developing Countries," pp. 28–29.
25. Diebold, "Why Be Afraid of Them?" p. 83.

Finally, in a more general vein, some analysts point to certain present and potential advantages of the multinational corporation in bridging nation-state boundaries and ideological differences. Raymond Vernon summarizes "the viewpoint of the managers of most multilateral enterprises":

> The record of modern states does not unequivocally command the nation state as the chosen instrument for man's earthly salvation . . . the shortsighted, destructive, antisocial measures of states in their dealings with other states, and even with their own people, are painfully apparent at times. The undermining of the state system, therefore, can readily be seen by concerned managers as a contribution to the welfare of mankind.[26]

Similarly, Blake and Walters remark: "The coordinated worldview of the international firm . . . stands in vivid contrast to the fragmented worldview of the international organization whose management has little authority and whose member states often disagree not only on the means to achieve objectives but also on the substance of the objectives themselves."[27] The multinationals, Blake and Walters suggest, may help in some respects to promote integration and cooperation among states and other nongovernmental actors, and may "contribute to the establishment of a common regional culture and life style."[28]

The Dependence Critique of the Role of the Multinational Corporation

Writers on "dependence"[29] question many of the assumptions of optimis-

---

26. Raymond Vernon, "Does Society Also Profit?" *Foreign Policy,* no. 13 (Winter 1973–74), pp. 112–13.
27. Blake and Walters, *Global Economic Relations,* p. 108–9.
28. *Ibid.,* p. 115.
29. See especially the following by Osvaldo Sunkel: "The Crisis of the Nation-State in Latin America: Challenge and Response" in Yale H. Ferguson and Walter F. Weiker, eds., *Continuing Issues in International Politics* (Pacific Palisades, Cal.: Goodyear, 1973), pp. 352–69; "Big Business and 'Dependencia': A Latin American View," *Foreign Affairs* 50:3 (April 1972), pp. 517–31; and "Transnational Capitalism and National Disintegration in Latin America," *Social and Economic Studies* (University of the West Indies, Jamaica) 20:1 (March 1973), pp. 132–76. The entire issue of *Social and Economic Studies* in which Sunkel's article appears is devoted to dependence theory. See also "Dependency Theory: A Reassessment," entire issue of *Latin American Perspectives,* 1:1 (Spring 1974); Julio Cotler and Richard R. Fagen, eds., *Latin America and the United States* (Stanford: Stanford University Press, 1974); Susanne Bodenheimer, "Dependency and Imperialism: The Roots of Latin American Underdevelopment," *Politics and Society* 1:3 (May 1971), pp. 327–57; André Gunder Frank, *Capitalism and Underdevelopment in Latin*

tic analysts concerning the alleged benefits that flow from multinational investment in Latin America. They regard the multinational corporation as, at best, a potential threat that must be carefully controlled by governments, and, at worst, an entity that is absolutely incompatible with "genuine" national development.

The concept of dependence covers a wide range of links between dominant "have" and subordinate "have-not" countries, but we are interested here in that aspect of dependence theory which approaches political and social matters primarily from an economic perspective. Even with this qualification, we are faced with essentially two schools of thought, which (for want of better terminology) are often labeled *Marxist* and *non-Marxist*.[30] Marxist writers tend to view dependence in the framework of Lenin's theory of imperialism as a "natural" advanced stage in the development of world capitalism. Moreover, they are less sanguine about the possibilities of reaching an accommodation with foreign firms and, indeed, are inclined to argue that the only hope for a marked reduction in dependence lies in socialist revolutions. Non-Marxist thought is a logical extension of the economic doctrines propounded by ECLA and its Executive Secretary, Raúl Prebisch, in the 1950's and 1960's. The tenets of non-Marxist theory, especially, have gained increasing currency in Latin American official circles, and in UNCTAD, for which Prebisch served as Executive Secretary after he left ECLA. This acceptance has prompted Marxists to complain that what should be a "radical" set of doctrines has, in fact, been co-opted by the "establishment."[31] Nevertheless, it is significant that however much the two schools differ as to the reasons for capi-

America (New York: Monthly Review Press, 1967); James D. Cockcroft, André Gunder Frank, and Dale L. Johnson, *Dependence and Underdevelopment: Latin America's Political Economy* (Garden City, N.Y.: Doubleday, 1972); Keith Griffin, *Underdevelopment in Spanish America: An Interpretation* (Cambridge, Mass.: MIT Press, 1969); North American Congress on Latin America, *Yanqui Dollar: The Contribution of U.S. Private Investment to Underdevelopment in Latin America* (NACLA, 1971); Celso Furtado, *Economic Development of Latin America* (Cambridge, Eng.: Cambridge University Press, 1970); Miguel S. Wionczek, *Inversión y technología extranjera en América Latina* (Mexico: Joaquín Mortíz, 1971); Fernando Enrique Cardoso, *Dependencia y desarrollo en América Latina* (Mexico: Siglo Veintiuno Editores, 1969), and Cardoso, "Dependency and Development in Latin America," *New Left Review* 74 (July-August 1972), pp. 83–95; and Theotonio Dos Santos, *El nuevo carácter de la dependencia* (Santiago, Chile: Cuadernos de CESO, 1968).

30. Sunkel himself makes the Marxist/non-Marxist distinction in his "Transnational Capitalism," pp. 136–37. Although some writers are hard to classify, Sunkel, Furtado, and Pinto, for example, belong rather clearly in the non-Marxist category; and Frank, Quijano, and Bodenheimer, among the Marxists.

31. See, for example, André Gunder Frank, "Dependence is Dead, Long Live Dependence and the Class Struggle: A Reply to Critics," *Latin American Perspectives* 1:1 (Spring 1974), p. 90.

talist expansion and the ways it might be overcome, both advance basically the same assessment of the multinational threat in the present context.

ECLA's contribution to regional economic theory centered on the implications of the prevailing "international division of labor" that assigned to Latin America the role of supplying primary commodities to, and importing finished goods from, the industrialized countries of the world. Prebisch stressed that foreign-owned extractive industries and agriculture constituted monopoly "enclaves" within host countries. These enclaves, he pointed out, had little direct relation to local economies, but the exports they produced were vital to the position of host countries in world trade. Foreign enterprises in these categories earned exhorbitant "excess" profits which were repatriated to home countries. This made for a serious drain on the balance of payments of host states. The economic welfare of Latin American countries was not only dependent upon decisions made by foreign firms but, in a more general sense, upon the notorious vicissitudes of the world market for primary commodities. Finally, Prebisch argued, the "terms of trade" between developed and developing countries were gradually worsening; the price of primary commodities was steadily declining while the costs of finished goods were rising. Prebisch's prescription was an "import substitution" policy for Latin American economic development, emphasizing industrialization at home to produce for local consumption those goods that had previously been imported. In this fashion, according to Prebisch, Latin America would vastly improve its balance-of-payments position and indirectly lessen dependence on traditional exports controlled by foreign enterprise.

Dependence theorists have taken up where Prebisch left off. Their concern has been with the consequences of a policy of import substitution that most Latin American countries have, in fact, adopted. Far from lessening dependence, import substitution has increased it, because much of the industrialization that has resulted took place under the aegis of additional foreign investment. Today, multinational dominance of manufacturing and service sectors raises the traditional problem of dependence in a new, and in some respects, even more serious form.

The extent of foreign control of most Latin American economies can be illustrated by the case of Chile prior to Salvador Allende's election as President in 1970. At that time, over one hundred U.S.-based corporations had operations in Chile. This included twenty-four of the largest U.S. multinational corporations. In addition to copper and nitrates, foreign corporations were involved in the following:

1. Machinery and equipment, 50 percent foreign control (including Xerox, National Cash Register, ITT, GE);
2. Iron, steel, and metal products, 60 percent foreign control (including Bethlehem and ARMCO Steel, Koppers, Kaiser, Singer, Hoover);
3. Petroleum products and distribution, over 50 percent foreign control

(Standard Oil of N.J., IBEC, Gulf, Mobil);

4. Industrial and other chemicals, 60 percent foreign control (Dow, Monsanto, W. R. Grace);

5. Rubber products, 45 percent foreign control (General Tire, Firestone);

6. Automotive assembly, 100 percent foreign control (including Ford, GM, Chrysler);

7. Radio and television, nearly 100 percent foreign control (RCA, Phillips, General Telephone and Electronics);

8. Pharmaceuticals, nearly 100 percent foreign control (American Cyanamid, Pfizer, Parke-Davis);

9. Office equipment, nearly 100 percent foreign control (Sperry Rand, Remington, Xerox);

10. Copper fabricating, 100 percent foreign control (Phelps Dodge, Northern Indiana Brass Co., General Cable);

11. Tobacco, 100 percent foreign control (British-American Tobacco Co.);

12. Advertising, 90 percent foreign control (J. Walter Thompson, McCann-Erickson, etc.).[32]

Under such conditions, it is difficult not to agree with dependence theorists who insist that governments find that basic economic decisions with important political and social ramifications are being made by foreign firms. Such firms, they allege, chart the development destinies of host countries or, at the very least, fundamentally limit the options available to national planners.

The ITT episode in Chile[33] supports another allegation, that some multinationals still meddle nefariously in local politics, acting in tacit alliance with foreign governments. In this connection, critics also often point to the example of the Johnson Administration's withholding of aid to Peru in order to provide the International Petroleum Company with bargaining leverage in its negotiations with the Peruvian government before the 1968 military coup.[34] Moreover, whatever the desires of the companies or of the host state, foreign governments occasionally use the multinationals as

32. From the chapter "The Multinationals" in *The Chilean Road to Socialism* edited by Dale L. Johnson. Copyright © 1973 by Dale L. Johnson. Copyright © 1973 by Doubleday & Company, Inc. Reprinted by permission of Doubleday & Company, Inc. See also Stephen F. Lau, *The Chilean Response to Foreign Investment* (New York: Praeger, 1972).

33. For a brief discussion, see *supra*, pp. 175–76.

34. See Richard Goodwin, "Letter from Peru," reprinted in Yale H. Ferguson, ed., *Contemporary Inter-American Relations: A Reader in Theory and Issues*, pp. 439–64; Charles T. Goodsell, *American Corporations and Peruvian Politics* (Cambridge: Harvard University Press, 1974); George M. Ingram, *Expropriation of U.S. Property in South America: Peru, Bolivia, and Chile* (New York: Praeger, 1974); Adalberto J. Pinelo, *The Multinational Corporation as a Force in Latin American Politics: A Case Study of the International Petroleum Corporation in Peru* (New York: Praeger, 1973); and Dolph W. Zink, *The Political Risks for Multinational Enterprise in Developing Countries: With a Case Study of Peru* (New York: Praeger, 1973).

instruments to support official policy goals; for instance, the Trading with the Enemy Act forbids U.S. companies abroad to export to certain communist countries. This legislation effectively restricts the independence of Latin American states to export what they want to whomever they choose.

Several leading writers on dependence, most notably Chilean economist Osvaldo Sunkel, have conceived of increasing multinational penetration as part of a broader process of "marginalization" with both "international" and "domestic" dimensions.[35] According to this analysis: "Internationally," there is a widening gap or "polarization" emerging between "center"—"have" and "peripheral"—"have-not" countries. The domestic corollary is a pattern of "internal colonialism" between the "modern" cities and the "traditional" countryside, with the "zones of misery" (the slums ringing major cities) constituting a type of intermediate zone. Foreign investment, Sunkel and others maintain, has helped to create and sustain a clientele "domestic" elite whose attention is focused away from the development needs of their own countries. This elite has little incentive to concern itself with policies that would spur indigenous entrepreneurs, widen local markets, redistribute income, or otherwise bring the masses into full participation in national life. The elite is content with the *status quo,* whereby the countryside services the cities, which, in turn, direct their primary energies (via the foreign firms) abroad.

A key part of the marginalization thesis is that this process is increasing because of the special nature of multinational expansion in host countries. The multinationals are discouraging the emergence of genuine national enterprises not only by pre-empting the most dynamic sectors of the economy but also by absorbing local capital that might be used to finance local companies. From 1957 to 1965, for example, U.S.-based manufacturing concerns raised 40 percent of their capital from local sources.[36] Because they have been regarded as excellent credit risks, the multinationals have naturally received preference from local lending agencies, none the least from branches of such institutions as the First National City Bank of New York (whose funds, it should be emphasized, are raised from local sources). Another practice of the foreign firms that discourages native enterprises is the coopting of local talent through managerial and worker-training programs.

An even more important consideration, in terms of an increase in marginalization, is the fact that a significant part of multinational expansion has continued to involve the acquisition of already-existing local companies. Of the subsidiaries (on which data are available) established

35. Sunkel's fullest development of this thesis is in "Transnational Capitalism." See also William G. Tyler and J. Peter Wogart, "Economic Dependence and Marginalization: Some Empirical Evidence," *Journal of Inter-American Studies and World Affairs* 15:1 (February 1973), pp. 37–45.
36. United Nations, Economic Commission for Latin America, *Economic Survey of Latin America, 1970* (New York: United Nations, 1972), p. 277.

between 1958 and 1967 by the 187 largest U.S.-based multinational corporations 42 percent were formed through purchases of local enterprises.[37] Typically, after purchase, the multinational firm has proceeded to replace local management with a structure that is top-heavy with foreign professionals, while unneeded local professionals have been "discarded." In addition, regardless of whether the company is an entirely new or an acquired enterprise, the multinational enterprise customarily relies on a capital-intensive technology in the production process rather than on a labor-intensive technology that might be more suitable to a developing economy. Hence, dependence theorists argue, contrary to the usual claims, the multinationals actually generate unemployment.

Another criticism made by writers on dependence is that import substitution under the aegis of foreign firms has exacerbated the balance-of-payments problem in Latin America. Statistics for Latin America as a whole show that the "income received" as an outflow from U.S. private investment has been of such a magnitude that it has more than offset new U.S. private investment, and the net capital flow to Latin America has been nil or worse even when U.S. public development loans and grants are added into the total.[38] Part of the multinational corporation's negative contribution to Latin America's balance of payments has, of course, been simple repatriation of profits. Between 1960 and 1968, profits repatriated averaged 94 percent in mining and petroleum, 48 percent in manufacturing, and 57 percent in other enterprises.[39] Another aspect has been the purchase by subsidiaries of goods, services, and technology from parent companies, normally at inflated prices as an artificial means of reducing local "profits" to lessen tax liability in host countries. A large percentage of multinational manufacturing firms are "finishing touch" industries whose very existence depends on a steady stream of component parts from parent corporations. But it is demonstrable that foreign enterprises in general have a greater propensity and financial incentive to import than their native counterparts and thereby to ignore potential local sources of supply.

Dependence theorists question, as well, the proposition that the multinationals' negative impact on the balance of payments is more often than not offset by their supposedly unique contributions to Latin America's exports.[40] These writers do not deny that the multinationals account for a major percentage of exports, or that Brazil, for example, has built an

37. Ronald Müller, "Poverty Is the Product," *Foreign Policy,* no. 13 (Winter 1973–74), p. 88.
38. See, for example, the AID-prepared chart on "U.S. Disbursements to the Latin American Republics" for the years 1962–67 in Ferguson, *Contemporary Inter-American Relations,* p. 429.
39. ECLA, *Economic Survey of Latin America, 1970,* p. 275.
40. On the relationship between the balance of payments and exports, see Frank Falero, Jr., "Foreign Investment and the Balance of Payments: Some Negative Implications for Developing Countries," *Inter-American Economic Affairs* 28:2 (Autumn 1974), pp. 77–85.

impressive export capacity based on a policy of encouraging foreign investment.[41] What they do deny is that foreign firms are more effective as
exporters than local enterprises. Ronald Müller, a U.S. student of the
multinational corporation, summarizes his findings in this regard (based on
a detailed econometric analysis):

> . . . relative to local firms, MNC subsidiaries performed significantly
> better only in . . . three countries (Argentina, Brazil, and Mexico) and
> only in terms of export sales to other Latin American countries. In con-
> trast, for exports to the rest of the world, where one would expect the
> technological and marketing superiority of the MNC's to be most crucial,
> their export performance was not significantly different from domestic
> enterprises. For the remaining countries of the region, the MNC's were
> outperformed on exports to the rest of the world by firms which had sub-
> stantial domestic participation, while on exports to other Latin-American
> countries, the MNC's performed no differently than their domestic
> counterparts.[42]

An important reason why foreign firms have made no greater contribution to exports than they have is that subsidiaries are often reluctant to
compete with the parent corporation in the external market. Indeed,
Müller found that 79 percent of multinational subsidiaries in the Andean
countries were prohibited by their parents to engage in exporting.[43] Moreover, the multinationals carried over their policy into licensing agreements
with local firms, forbidding them to use the technology shared under such
agreements to produce exports.[44] (This policy has not only curbed exports
but has also clearly limited the "diffusion effect" that supposedly results
from the introduction of foreign technology into the developing economy.)
Finally, Müller notes that the contribution of multinational exports to
local economies has been minimized by the practice of exporting products
mainly to parent corporations at low prices. Of the firms he examined, 75

41. See Celso Furtado, "The Brazilian 'Model'," *Social and Economic Studies*
20:1 (March 1973), pp. 122–31. Furtado observes: "Brazil's high rate of
growth in industrial production attained in the last five years (1968–72) after
a period of seven years of relative stagnation (1961–67), has been obtained
through a very successful governmental policy which aims at attracting the
MNC and fostering the expansion of the branches of such corporations already
installed in the country. By various means the government has been guiding the
process of income distribution (in favor of the upper and middle classes) in
order to produce the demand profile most attractive to the MNCs" (p. 127).
Undeniably, the costs of this policy, both in terms of political repression and
general neglect of Brazil's poor majority, have been great. See also the following
from *The World Today* 29:11 (November 1973): Albert Fishlow "Brazil's
Economic Miracle" (pp. 474–80); and Peter Flynn, "The Brazilian Development Model: The Political Dimension" (pp. 481–94).
42. Müller, "Poverty Is the Product," pp. 93–94.
43. *Ibid.*, p. 93.
44. *Ibid.*, p. 91.

percent sold exports only to other subsidiaries of the parent at prices averaging 40–50 percent less than the prices being received by local firms.[45]

Writers on dependence also qualify their acceptance of the argument that multinational corporations are making an invaluable contribution to host governments' revenues through taxation. Their doubts relate, in part, to the accounting devices that foreign firms regularly employ to evade taxes. We have already mentioned the practice of overvaluing imports from parent companies as a means of reducing "profits" in the host country so that extra payments can be channeled abroad tax-free. Another device is the overvaluation of existing investment, which takes advantage of national laws that normally link the percentage of profits that may be repatriated without taxation to the value of the enterprise involved. Not surprisingly, dependence theorists also decry the fact that a number of countries have granted various tax incentives in order to attract foreign investment.

A final criticism of the multinationals is that the bulk of their production is tailored to the demands of consumers in the developed countries. Extractive industries drain host countries of irreplaceable natural resources. Manufacturing for local markets often takes the form of relatively expensive consumer goods that only can be afforded by upper-income groups whose desire for these items is "artificially" stimulated by means of advertising. Prices are driven up by the monopoly status of foreign manufacturing enterprises. A corollary of the charge that the wrong kinds of goods are being produced is that goods that would be more suited to the special conditions prevailing in developing countries are not being produced. Perhaps the most eloquent exponent of this proposition is Ivan Illich, who has regularly inveighed against the encouragement of frivolous consumption by the upper classes as opposed to the production of items of real value to the Latin American masses. The Latin American peasant, unlike the U.S. farmer in the Midwest, Illich argues, does not need and cannot afford an expensive automobile. What he needs is a "mechanical donkey" that will give years of trouble-free service, but no such "donkey" is rolling off multinational assembly lines.[46]

The Multinationals at Bay: Nation-State Options to Reduce Dependence

Dependence theory has itself met with some skepticism, mainly from a few North American scholars who have criticized the Marxist perspective linking dependence with imperialism and blaming virtually all the ills of Latin

45. *Ibid.,* p. 94.
46. Ivan Illich, "Outwitting the Developed Countries," *New York Review of Books* 13:8 (November 6, 1969), p. 21.

American societies on foreign domination.[47] It has also been suggested that writers on dependence in general present far too extreme an indictment of the multinational corporation and that they fail to appreciate that dependence/nondependence should be conceived as a continuum. According to these critics, the reality of interdependence should lead to a perception that some sort of accommodation with the multinationals is both possible and desirable.

Criticism along these lines is no doubt well-founded, except perhaps insofar as it evidences a regrettable tendency to lump the two schools of dependence thought together and therefore to give insufficient credit to the sophistication especially of some non-Marxist writers such as Sunkel. Moreover, whatever the merits and deficiencies of dependence theory, it is clear that many Latin American governments are finding the concept of dependence a useful spur to action and that they are seeking to meet the challenge of the multinationals in anything but a doctrinaire fashion. Their efforts are part of a worldwide trend. As C. Fred Bergsten observes:

> . . . virtually every country in the world, big or small, industrialized or developing, Communist or non-Communist, Left or Right—is levying increasingly stringent requirements on foreign firms. . . . Few countries any longer ask the simplistic question: "Do we want foreign investment?" The issue is how to get foreign investment on the terms which are best for them, and indeed to use the power of the firms to promote their own national goals.[48]

With reference to Latin America, Sunkel predicts a "new era of hard bargaining and negotiations" and of "pragmatic and detailed consideration of specific cases."[49] Strong currents of economic nationalism are moving, and innovative policies are emerging even in countries that have customarily been regarded as paralyzed by chronic political instability or otherwise quite content with the *status quo*.

Expropriation with full, partial, or no compensation ("confiscation") represents one approach that will no doubt continue to be employed in cases where foreign involvement in particular industries is no longer tolerable. The extractive industries, often involving companies with long and none-too-savory reputations in host countries, are likely to be the main (but not the only) targets. If a government is able and willing to pay

47. See, for example, David Ray, "The Dependency Model of Latin American Underdevelopment: Three Basic Fallacies," *Journal of Inter-American Studies and World Affairs* 15:1 (February 1973), pp. 4–20; and Robert A. Packenham, "Latin American Dependency Theories: Strengths and Weaknesses," paper delivered at the 1973 Meeting of the American Political Science Association.

48. C. Fred Bergsten, "Coming Investment Wars?" *Foreign Affairs* 53:1 (October 1974), p. 136.

49. Sunkel, "The Crisis of the Nation-State," p. 368.

"prompt, adequate, and effective" compensation for expropriated companies, the repercussions can be lessened. Otherwise, expropriation is a relatively radical step that can cloud the general climate for new investment from abroad and strain relations with foreign governments. For this reason, expropriation will probably be used sparingly except by self-styled "revolutionary" governments.

Consider the example of Peru after the military seized power in 1968:[50] By the end of 1973, eleven U.S. companies had been nationalized, among them the IPC, the Cerro de Pasco Corporation (copper), and firms engaged in the fishmeal industry. Faced with statutory requirements for better housing and with labor disputes, Cerro de Pasco offered to sell its operations to the Peruvian government in 1972, but no price acceptable to both parties could be found. The decision to nationalize the fishmeal industry came after the General Fisheries Law (1971) had supposedly established dependable new guidelines and, as a dramatic departure from these guidelines, was especially upsetting to businessmen inside and outside Peru. The Peruvian government insisted that the desperate plight of the fishing industry caused by a shift in the Humboldt Current obviously made this a special case. The United States reacted much less harshly to expropriations in Peru than to those in Allende's Chile, apparently because the Peruvian military declared themselves to be firmly anti-communist and also evidenced a willingness to allow foreign investment a continued (albeit much modified) role in the national economy. Negotiations between Washington and Lima dragged on until February, 1974, when the Peruvian government agreed to pay a modest $76 million in compensation for five expropriated companies (excluding the IPC) whose claims were still outstanding.

Expropriation will probably be used sparingly not only because it is an extreme step but also because Latin American governments have many other options in dealing with the multinational challenge. To avoid expropriation, they may exclude all new foreign investment from certain sensitive sectors of the economy, limit totally foreign investment that would threaten an undue concentration of economic power in a particular sector, and/or require some existing foreign companies to phase out operations over a substantial period of time. As an example of this last approach, the Caldera administration in Venezuela announced its intention to nationalize the Venezuelan oil industry in 1983 and 1984, with book value compensation when existing concessions are due to expire. (The current Pérez government speeded up the timetable to January 1, 1976.) President Caldera set minimum production levels for the industry prior to takeover, established fines for insufficient production, and required foreign oil companies

---

50. Our summary is drawn from Robert H. Swansbrough, "The Politics of Independence: The Ideology and Foreign Policy of Peru's 'Realistic' Revolutionaries." Unpublished mss., n.d.

to deposit large sums of money with the Venezuelan government as a guarantee of satisfactory performance.

The joint venture, which is a common phenomenon even in the relatively freewheeling investment climate of Brazil, is a form of ownership that ensures local private and/or public participation. Mexico added teeth to its long-standing policy of "Mexicanization" in 1973, by providing that foreigners normally cannot control more than 49 percent equity in any new business enterprise. (A national commission is empowered to adjust the percentage as circumstances may require.)[51] The "fade-out" joint venture is a central feature of the 1970 General Law of Industries promulgated by the Velasco government in Peru, with an additional provision that increasing national participation over the years in certain industries will be accomplished by distributing company shares to workers. Another practice that is widespread is the establishment of job quotas for nationals. Argentina, for example, requires that 85 percent of management and other top-level personnel be Argentine.

Another measure designed to increase benefits to host countries is a policy of boosting the "domestic content" of products, that is, requiring more stages of the production process to be located in host countries. Mexico has announced plans to limit the amount of technology that may be purchased abroad by companies, reportedly to ensure that Mexicans will not buy outmoded technology and to force them to develop their own. A number of countries are outlawing parent-company restrictions on the use of technology by subsidiaries and on subsidiaries' distribution of technology to local firms. More governments, too, are demanding a larger share of company profits through taxation and are adopting stricter controls on the repatriation of original investment and profits. (Of course, a possible danger inherent in requiring reinvestment of profits is ever-greater expansion of foreign firms in the host economy.) Yet another approach is to encourage exports by banning parent-company limitations on subsidiaries in this regard and even by insisting that companies commit themselves to export as the price of their entering the economy initially or of maintaining their investment once they are established.

In a somewhat different vein, Peru has forced oil companies seeking new concessions to contract that all future disputes affecting these investments will be settled in local courts without recourse to diplomatic protection from abroad.

It should be stressed that most of the policy options discussed above are not mutually exclusive. On the contrary, the great range of possible policies, which can be employed singly or in combination, allows host governments considerable leeway in tailoring foreign investment to meet

51. See "Mexico: Law on the Promotion of Mexican Investment and the Regulation of Foreign Investment," *International Legal Materials* 12:3 (May 1973), pp. 643–49.

specific needs in various sectors of their economies. Moreover, restrictive policies can be "sweetened" by linking them to certain incentives. Brazil, for instance, provides special assistance and attaches less-stringent conditions to companies investing in underdeveloped areas of the country. Mexico allows multinational corporations to maintain 100 percent foreign ownership if the firm exports 100 percent of its production. Peru exempted oil companies making new investment from the codes governing other foreign enterprises.

Thus far we have considered policies that can be implemented by governments unilaterally within their own borders. Many of these policies would obviously be more effective if several governments were to adopt them as a cooperative strategy, if only to make it more difficult for developed-country firms and governments to isolate and make an example of one or more countries whose restrictions they disliked. The Common Investment Code of the Andean Common Market,[52] adopted in 1971, rests in part on this premise. From another standpoint, the governments involved—Bolivia, Chile, Colombia, Ecuador, Peru, and (after 1973) Venezuela—deemed such a code to be an absolute necessity for ANCOM, since previous economic integration schemes in Latin America had suffered from the fear that foreign multinational corporations would be the principal beneficiaries of a wider market.

The Andean Code (modeled on the Peruvian code) restricts new foreign investment to sectors not competitive with domestic industry, demands the establishment of local majority ownership and control of all enterprises within fifteen to twenty years (this figure varies by country), bans parent-company restrictions on the use of technology, and limits the repatriation of capital to the original investment when foreign firms disengage from an enterprise. Companies that export 80 percent or more of their output are exempted from the provisions relating to local majority participation. The code also includes provisions that permit member countries to make a limited number of exceptions to the rules.

How successful the Andean Code will be over the long haul remains to be seen. Aside from the question of whether new investment from abroad will be forthcoming in the amounts desired by individual countries, there is some doubt as to the long-range clarity and stability of the Andean rules of the game. Member governments have been making liberal use of discretionary clauses, and domestic political changes over time could make for critical shifts in policy. As we have noted, Peru has waived its own code and that of ANCOM to pave the way for new concessions to the oil

52. See Edward S. Milenky, "Developmental Nationalism in Practice: The Problems and Progress of the Andean Group," *Inter-American Economic Affairs* 16:4 (Spring 1973), pp. 49–68; and William P. Avery and James D. Cochrane, "Innovation in Latin American Regionalism: The Andean Common Market," *International Organization* 27:2 (Spring 1973), pp. 181–224.

industry, and nationalization of the fishmeal industry represented a major departure from previously-announced plans. The Banzer government in Bolivia has increasingly leaned toward Brazil, where decidedly more liberal policies for foreign investment prevail. Moreover, the 1973 coup in Chile brought to power a regime whose continued participation in ANCOM is itself uncertain (though probable, until and unless Chile moves decisively into the Brazilian orbit), and whose eagerness to reattract foreign capital after the Allende period may lead to agreements that are difficult to reconcile with the code.

ANCOM is an interesting experiment in another respect concerning the multinational enterprise. Member governments have pledged themselves to the establishment of "local" multinational companies to serve as the future "grid" of the system, and the Andean Development Corporation was assigned the task of helping to fund these companies. To date, however, ANCOM multinational projects are still in the planning stage.

ANCOM has attempted to set *general* standards for treatment of multinational corporations within a single subregion. The Organization of Petroleum Exporting Countries (OPEC) presents quite a different model, a worldwide cartel of producing countries in a single industry acting jointly against consumers, with multinational corporations serving as intermediaries.

Clearly, we are entering a new era in world trade, although exactly *how new* an era is the question of the hour. There is considerable debate as to whether OPEC is or is not the precursor of numerous developing-country cartels. Another question is how likely these cartels are to work anywhere nearly as well as the one that brought the developed countries to their knees in the winter of 1973.[53]

The developing countries overwhelmingly endorsed the OPEC model at a meeting of "nonaligned" states in Algiers in September, 1973 and at a United Nations special assembly dealing with economic matters in April–May, 1974. Furthermore, there is evidence that, at least in this respect, they are beginning to practice what they preach. Three major coffee producers, Brazil, Colombia, and the Ivory Coast (which account for 56 percent of world production), are boosting prices through Cafe Mundial, a multinational coffee-marketing corporation which they created in September, 1973. Seven bauxite-producing countries, including Jamaica and Guyana and, incidentally, Australia (which account for 63 percent of world production), formed a permanent organization in March, 1974. The

53. See, for example, C. Fred Bergsten, "The Threat from the Third World," *Foreign Policy*, no. 11 (Summer 1973), pp. 102–24; Zuhayr Mikdashi, "Collusion Could Work," *Foreign Policy*, no. 14 (Spring 1974), pp. 57–68; Stephen D. Krasner, "Oil Is the Exception," *Foreign Policy*, no. 14 (Spring 1974), pp. 68–84; C. Fred Bergsten, "The Threat Is Real," *Foreign Policy*, no. 14 (Spring 1974), pp. 84–90; and William J. Levy, "World Oil Cooperation or International Chaos," *Foreign Affairs* 52:4 (July 1974), pp. 691–713.

following May, Jamaica, which currently supplies 60 percent of the U.S. market, forged ahead of its associates to triple the taxes and royalties it charges to mining companies. The Organization of Copper-Exporting Countries—Chile, Peru, Zaïre, and Zambia (which account for 80 percent of world production)—met to set prices in April, 1974. Earlier, in late 1972, this organization had boycotted Kennecott in retaliation for the company's attempts to prevent the sale of Chilean copper in Europe.

Where international commodities go from here is anyone's guess, although it is certain that things will never be quite the same again. A great deal depends upon how much unity is achieved and *sustained* among producers of how many commodities, and particularly how successful producers of certain *different* commodities are in avoiding destructive competition. Bergsten states, "Concerted action by copper, tin, and bauxite producers would sharply reduce the risk to each that cheaper aluminum or tin would substitute for higher-priced copper, or vice versa. An alliance among the producers of coffee, cocoa, and tea could preempt substitution by drinkers around the world."[54] As Bergsten cautions, however, confrontation is a high-risk strategy for all concerned, from which there may emerge "no winners." Developed and developing countries alike would be losers if a series of confrontations were to lead to worldwide economic collapse, or if "drinkers of the world" were to turn exclusively to martinis!

Ironically, far from suffering at least in an immediate sense from the emergence of cartels, the multinational companies involved have been reaping windfall profits by passing on higher prices (and then some?) to consumers. On the other hand, there does appear to be a trend toward the nationalization of the oil companies, which some observers predict will ultimately be disadvantageous to producing countries. Unless they succeed in developing adequate refining and marketing facilities, they will still be dependent upon international oil companies, whose services will not come cheap. It will also be much more difficult to maintain a common price level when countries are competing directly with one another. In any event, what happens in the oil industry will doubtless continue to provide lessons to governments engaged in other cartels.

Toward a New Relationship Between the Multinational Corporation and the Nation-State in Latin America

How will multinational corporations respond to economic nationalism in contemporary Latin America? One possibility, of course, is that they will gradually phase out most of their operations in the area and search for more favorable investment opportunities elsewhere. Such a foreign private

54. Bergsten, "The Threat from the Third World," p. 111.

investment boycott of Latin America *might* have a positive impact on the area. As Albert O. Hirschman points out:

> . . . the Latin American continent is now well supplied with both "light" and "basic" industries. . . . A boycott of Latin America by international investment might reveal the strength and resilience and ability to *fare da sé* in a great number of areas which the Latin American industrial establishment has acquired, in much the same way in which the two world wars permitted its then fledgling industries to take vigorous steps forward. Perhaps Latin America really needs at this point a sort of "economic equivalent of war," a measure of insulation, that is, from the advanced economies that would permit it fully to deploy the potential for entrepreneurship, skills and capital formation which it has acquired over the past twenty-five years of continuing intimate contact.[55]

Should an investment boycott occur, the consequences would depend largely upon how Latin Americans themselves would react. Would the "potential for entrepreneurship, skills and capital formation" of which Hirschman speaks actually materialize? Would Latin American entrepreneurs meet the need for products tailored to the domestic environment? Would they bring more citizens into productive roles in national economies? Would they make the most of labor-intensive technology and develop new industries to increase exports of manufactured and semimanufactured goods in competition with the developed countries? Would Latin American governments widen markets by lowering trade barriers between countries and planning complementary industries? These are important questions, and they will have to be answered—boycott or none—to the extent that local businessmen are to take full advantage of the openings that will almost inevitably result from the restrictions imposed upon the multinationals in Latin America today.

Nevertheless, for a variety of reasons, a foreign investment boycott of major proportions does not appear to be in the cards. First, the multinationals' existing investments in the region are "hostages," the safety of which rests in the continued tolerance of host governments. Few companies are in as advantageous a position as those in oil to recoup their losses. Second, unless they are really prepared to confine themselves to refining and/or marketing, the multinationals engaged in raw materials and food industries have little choice but to establish production facilities at the source of these commodities. Third, the multinationals need cheap labor to improve their global competitive positions,[56] and this, too, is a resource that Latin America has in abundance.

55. Albert O. Hirschman, "How to Divest in Latin America, and Why" in Hirschman, *A Bias for Hope: Essays on Development and Latin America* (New Haven: Yale University Press, 1971), pp. 250–51.
56. Drucker observes that "the only resource" the multinationals "cannot freely move is labor." ("Multinationals and Developing Countries," p. 128.)

Fourth, it is almost a certainty that the multinationals will go wherever money is to be made, and the rate of return on investments in Latin America is still very attractive, especially in the extractive industries (unfortunately, where the risk is greater).[57] The rate of return on investment in extractive industries is now higher in developing countries outside Latin America, and, of course, political conditions are more predictable in the United States, Europe, and Japan. Yet companies cannot escape the conclusion that "things are getting rough all over." What companies want and what they need to generate profits is a stable set of rules of the game; although political instability makes the Latin American environment particularly volatile, the rulebooks are currently being rewritten around the world. Fifth, many of the higher operating costs entailed by new host government policies can be passed on to the consumer (to the limit of consumer endurance).

Sixth, some supposedly restrictive measures may actually work to the advantage of the multinational corporation. For example, Drucker suggests that, because capital markets are rapidly becoming "polycentric" and capital is likely to be in short supply in future years, companies may find joint ventures with local capital participation increasingly attractive.[58] Moreover, devices like the joint venture lower the profile of the foreign firm and make it less of a target for nationalist resentments, thereby decreasing risks over the long haul. Already operating on this premise is a significant interstate nongovernmental actor founded in the early 1960's, the Atlantic Community Development Group for Latin America (ADELA), an association of over 200 of the largest banks and industrial companies in the United States, Europe, Japan, and Latin America (about one-third U.S. capital). ADELA has participated in more than 100 joint enterprises in Latin American countries.[59]

Seventh, many multinationals are beginning to cultivate what Luciano Martins terms a "corporate citizen" image in Latin America. In this regard Martins describes the functions of the Council of the Americas, which represents some 200 U.S. enterprises with business interests in the area as "a kind of private State Department whose main objective is to coordinate Latin American governments and individuals (business, political, intellectual, technocratic, student, and labor elites) as corporate partners in a political joint venture."[60]

Eighth and finally, as Theodore H. Moran explains, some multinationals are also lessening their risks by increasing those that host countries

57. ECLA, *Economic Survey of Latin America, 1970,* p. 272.
58. Drucker, "Multinationals and Developing Countries," p. 131.
59. Luciano Martins, "The Politics of U.S. Multinational Corporations in Latin America" in Cotler and Fagen, *Latin America and the United States,* pp. 388–89.
60. *Ibid.,* p. 396.

must face in seeking to take them over. This strategy involves seeking capital for investment from a number of countries and international lending agencies and cultivating far-flung markets, so that tremendous external pressure is brought to bear on the host government to avoid extreme actions.[61]

Hence most indications are that the multinationals, with few exceptions, in time will reach a *modus vivendi* with Latin American nation-states. This may even prove to be true for Cuba, should Cuba follow the lead of other COMECON countries in exploring new relationships with foreign firms.

We should stress in conclusion that such an accommodation would not necessarily mean the end of conflict affecting the activities of multinationals abroad. For one thing, insofar as frictions with host governments decline, they are very likely to increase with governments in countries where the headquarters of the multinationals are situated. Bergsten, for example, argues that given the tremendous impact of the multinationals on U.S. jobs and the U.S. balance of payments, it is "both undesirable and completely unrealistic . . . to anticipate continued abstention by the U.S. government."[62] Evidence for this proposition is the fact that the AFL–CIO is now urging Congress to enact legislative restrictions such as the Burke-Hartke bill on multinational investment abroad. Lastly, as recent experience in Argentina demonstrates, the multinationals' operations in Latin America (and elsewhere) will remain hostages to terrorist groups which persist in identifying them with the "reactionary" social policies of host governments and of international capitalism generally.

61. See the following by Theodore H. Moran: *Multinational Corporations and the Politics of Dependence: Copper in Chile* (Princeton, N.J.: Princeton University Press, 1974); and "Transnational Strategies of Protection and Defense by Multinational Corporations: Spreading the Risk and Raising the Cost for Nationalization in Natural Resources," *International Organization* 27:2 (Spring 1973), pp. 273–87.
62. Bergsten, "Coming Investment Wars?," p. 147.

Western Europe:
From the Cradle of the Nation-State to a Security Community and Beyond

NINE

Western Europe was the center of the global political system from the time of Imperial Rome to the present century. It was in Europe that the industrial revolution began, and it was from Europe that a "true" global political system arose, largely as a consequence of colonialism and imperialism in the period between the seventeenth and twentieth centuries. As we suggested earlier, the state-centric paradigm of global politics was "legislated into existence" in Western Europe by the Peace of Westphalia of 1648. In addition, the "nation-state" (as opposed to "state") was the result of the French Revolution and the increasing participation by citizens in the affairs of state during the Revolution and the ensuing Napoleonic Wars.

Through much of their history the six central continental states of Western Europe (Holland, Belgium, Luxembourg, France, Germany, and Italy) were the scene of almost continual warfare. Since the end of World War II, however, Western Europe has witnessed a profound experiment in increasing regional integration and cooperation. It has become—and in economic interdependence is going beyond—what Karl Deutsch calls a "security-community, . . . one in which there is real assurance that the members of that community will not fight each other physically, but will settle their disputes in some other way."[1]

The two world wars of this century ended Europe's global domination. By 1945, those nation-states that were once the most powerful in the world were exhausted and impoverished. Confronted by a threat from one superpower to the east, they were forced to rely upon another superpower an ocean away to the west for their independence. Western Europe, particularly Germany, was the arena of the first major Cold War confronta-

1. Karl Deutsch et al., *Political Community and the North Atlantic Area* (Princeton: Princeton University Press, 1957), p. 2.

tions. Later Cold War conflicts outside of Europe represented a "contagion effect" that spread outward from Europe itself.

In order to understand the complex web of interactions that constitutes the regional system of Europe of the Six, we have again divided our analysis into three time periods. The first, from 1948 to 1957, began with the Brussels Treaty that provided the initial cement for the North Atlantic alliance (NATO after 1949) and carried us through the formation of the European Common Market. The second period, from 1957 to 1967, ended with the second veto by French President Charles de Gaulle of British entry into the Common Market. The last period, from 1967 through 1972, concluded with the United Kingdom ready to enter the EEC on the following day (1 January 1973).

Nine superissues emerged from the politics of the Western European system for the twenty-five years under consideration. The first of these was *Integration,* that is, questions related to the process of ever-increasing economic and limited political cooperation among the six continental nation-states of Western Europe. *Atlantic Alliance-Strategic* involved the internal military dimension of the North Atlantic alliance. *Atlantic Alliance-Economic* included North Atlantic non-military matters such as trade and monetary standards. The *Cold War* superissue focused on the struggle of the North Atlantic group against the Soviet Union and its allies for "control" in Europe and other areas of the world. *Detente* concerned the easing of hostility and tension between these two major blocs. *Gaullism* involved the attempt by France somehow to evolve a "third path" between the two hostile camps of the Cold War and, at the same time, to engineer solutions for specific French problems. The *Colonial and Neocolonial* superissue included relations of the European nation-states with their colonies, and the relations of the colonies after independence with the former metropoles. *Extra-European Regional Crises* referred to important conflicts outside the immediate area of the European Six. Finally, *Regime Stability* concerned the political welfare, even the survival, of particular European regimes threatened from within or without.

The Apogee of the Cold War
and the Onset of Integration:
1948–1957

The key superissue in Western Europe between 1948 and 1957 was the *Cold War,* which was nearly three times as important as *Integration.* Almost as important as *Integration* were *strategic* aspects of the *Atlantic Alliance,* a superissue that represented something of an interface between the preceding superissues.

Table 62. *Ranking of Superissues by Explained Variance, 1948–1957*

1. Cold War	(4.00)
2. Integration	(1.57)
3. Atlantic Alliance-Strategic	(1.27)
4. Colonial and Neocolonial	(1.08)
5. Extra-European Regional Crises	(0.88)
6. Regime Stability	(0.64)
7. Atlantic Alliance-Economic	(0.59)
8. Detente	(0.39)
9. Gaullism	(0.27)

The pervasiveness of the Cold War during this period is shown by its appearance on ten of the eleven factors and by the fact that 36 percent of all discrete issues had some Cold War content. The most significant Cold War issues had their origins in the conclusion of World War II itself. As American and British armies swept across France, liberated Paris, and moved up through the Italian peninsula, Soviet armies advanced across Eastern Europe to a line roughly corresponding to the mouth of the Elbe River and extending south.

The points where the paths of the allied armies intersected, Berlin and Austria, developed into the leading controversies of the early Cold War. By 1948 Winston Churchill's metaphor of an "iron curtain" dividing the continent had acquired a certain reality. Both Berlin and Austria were administered by joint authorities composed of representatives of the four victorious allies (United States, Soviet Union, Great Britain, and France), an arrangement that derived from compromises reached at the Yalta Conference held prior to the end of hostilities. Berlin remained in the Soviet zone of Germany, and Western access to the city became a critical matter, particularly after the Soviet blockade of 1948.

Questions involving the status of isolated Berlin were related to Soviet efforts to secure world recognition of the sovereign independence of its zone of Germany. These efforts persisted throughout the period and were themselves inseparable from the broader problem of German reunification. The establishment of the Federal Republic of Germany (FRG) in the West in 1949 prompted the creation of the German Democratic Republic (GDR) in the East. The existence of "two Germanies" left the Western allies in a quandary; they were ostensibly committed to the principle of German reunification but not on Soviet terms.

The situation in Austria, while analogous to Germany, never provoked the same level of hostility. In fact, the resolution of the Austrian question in 1955 was one of the few permanent results of the brief detente which took place after the death of Joseph Stalin in 1953.

Another set of *Cold War* issues revolved around disarmament. Specifically it included the problems posed by the superpowers' possession of nuclear weapons and the rearming of Germany. The issue of German rearmament, which became acute after 1951, was connected both with the struggle for control of Germany and the general debate over disarmament in 1954–1955.

An additional *Cold War* issue that was resolved during the brief detente of the mid-1950's was the status of the city of Trieste, which was claimed by both Italy and Yugoslavia. The fact that one of the contestants for Trieste was communist Yugoslavia brought the controversy into the Cold War, at least until the Soviet-Yugoslav break became permanent in 1950.

Although the Cold War largely existed within a context of state-centric politics, nonstate actors were nevertheless important supporters of the principal protagonists. Communist parties—particularly in France, Italy, and the Soviet zone of Germany—were consistent allies of the Soviet Union while other groups such as West European and American Industry proved reliable supporters of the Western alliance. The alliance itself was institutionalized as a nonstate actor, NATO, in 1949, and was opposed by the Warsaw Treaty Organization, formed in 1955. Two other interstate governmental actors figured prominently in *Cold War* issues. One of these was the Southeast Asia Treaty Organization (SEATO), which was established in 1954 after the French retreat from Indochina, and the other was the United Nations. The United Nations, created at the close of the war, was, during this period, in effect, an adjunct of the Western bloc. American dominance of the organization was reflected in U.N. opposition to communist aggression in Korea between 1950 and 1953 and its legitimization of the U.S. military response there. A major step in this legitimization was passage of the "Uniting for Peace" Resolution, which transferred the issue of Korea from the Security Council, where it was subject to a Soviet veto, to the General Assembly, where support for the American position was strong. Finally, Vatican objections to the anti-Catholic measures undertaken within Soviet-dominated Eastern Europe prompted bitter anti-Soviet and strong pro-Western reactions from the Holy See.

Circumstances forced other *nostacs* into positions of relative neutrality during the Cold War. Occupation authorities were immobilized by their representative composition which included both of the major Cold War rivals. Jewish displaced persons, shunted from country to country and from camp to camp, were less concerned with the Cold War than with the easing of their own plight. During the presidential campaign of 1952 the Democratic Party in the United States found itself in the unenviable position of having to defend the foreign policy that had "lost China." Socialist Parties in Belgium, Italy, and West Germany were torn between Soviet rhetoric of a "popular front" and the reality of Stalinist pressure. The

Table 63.   *Cold War Alignments, 1948–1957: Major Coalitions*

Pro-United States	Neutral	Pro-Soviet
United States	Austria	USSR
FRG	French Industry	Czechoslovakia
France	United States Democratic	GDR
United Kingdom	Party	Communist Parties
Netherlands	West European Socialist	in East and West
Italy	Parties (FRG,	Europe (France,
Belgium	Belgium, Italy)	Italy, GDR)
NATO	Gaullists	Communist "Front"
United Nations	Italian CDU	Organizations in
European IGO's	Occupation Authorities	East and West Europe
Vatican	Jewish DP's	(Partisans of Peace,
Industry (German, Dutch,	Canada	etc.)
Italian, United States)	Egypt	
Belgium Noncentral	South Vietnam	
West Berlin	Indonesia	
Luxembourg		
Individuals		
Pakistan		
Thailand		
Australia		
New Zealand		
Philippines		

problem was particularly acute for the West German Social Democratic Party (SDP), which had as the cornerstone of its policy the reunification of Germany and which feared that Western opposition to the Soviet Union would make reunification impossible.

The second of the major superissues in this first period was *Integration*. It appeared on eight of the eleven factors and was involved in 15 percent of the total questions that arose between 1948 and 1957. The most important specific issues related to the implementation of the Schuman Plan and the impulse that the resulting "supranational" European Coal and Steel Community (ECSC) gave to greater European unity. The Schuman Plan endeavored:

> To place Franco-German production of coal and steel as a whole under a common higher authority, within the framework of an organization open to the participation of other countries of Europe. The pooling of coal and steel production should immediately provide for the setting up of common foundations for economic development as a first step in the federation of Europe, and will change the destinies of those regions which have long been devoted to the manufacture of munitions of war, of which they have been the most constant victims.[2]

2. RIIA, *Documents on International Affairs, 1948–50* (London: Oxford University Press, 1950), pp. 315–16.

The Schuman Plan had its origins in the postwar Marshall Plan and other Western efforts designed to stimulate the economic recovery of Europe, in general, and of West Germany, in particular. As with the Cold War, European cooperation evolved from a unique concatenation of events after World War II. Two specific issues that formed part of the larger superissue illustrate this point, the disposition of the areas of the Ruhr and the Saar, both important centers of German heavy industry. French policy was directed towards denying the reacquisition of industrial resources by a possibly revanchist Germany. In the case of the Ruhr, this was accomplished through internationalization; and, in the case of the Saar, it was done by forging links with France. The Soviet Union was sympathetic to French designs because it perceived a dismembered and weak Germany to be in its interests as well. Both the Saar and Ruhr issues were eventually settled by restoring the areas to the FRG. Agreement over the Ruhr came in 1948, but it took eight years longer to decide the question of the Saar. Resolution of both problems was facilitated by the hardening of the Cold War and the necessity for European unity in the face of a potential threat from the East. The creation of the ECSC had a particularly beneficial impact on the Saar issue, since it made it possible to distribute the benefits of West Germany's industry throughout Western Europe. Each step towards cooperation made it easier and, indeed, almost necessary to move on to the next step.[3]

Solutions to the Saar and Ruhr questions were also important milestones in the reconciliation of Germany and France. This reconciliation set the stage for what became a Franco-German "special relationship" within the Western community, a relationship that served to balance the special relationship between the United States and Great Britain and provided an undercurrent for the internal politics of the new European institutions themselves. At issue was the French attempt to bind West Germany to French policy positions, thereby creating a counterweight to Anglo-American influence in Europe and preventing a potential German challenge to French leadership of the continent.

Other less important *Integration* issues included the "readmission" of Italy as part of Europe between 1949 and 1951, Anglo-French joint economic measures in 1949–1950, general cooperation in sectors such as transportation that had significant integrative consequences, and the attempt to create a supranational European army linked to ECSC between 1951 and 1954.

Although few European actors were totally opposed to some form of integration, some served as leaders of the movement while others behaved as "supporters" or "neutrals." Among the most important actors on this superissue were European interstate governmental actors (European

3. See, for example, Ernst B. Haas, *The Uniting of Europe* (Stanford: Stanford University Press, 1958).

Table 64.   Integration, 1948-1957: Major Coalitions

Major Actors	Supporters	Neutrals
ECSC	United States	Trade Union Advisory
OEEC	United Kingdom	Commission of ERP
European Constitutional	Austria	Council on European
Assembly	Spain	Migration
FRG	Individuals	Council of Europe
Belgium	EEC/Euratom*	Socialist Parties
Luxembourg		(France, Belgium)
France		West Berlin
Italy		
Netherlands		

*Because they were created at the end of the period we are considering, the impact of these groups, which were designed to become, and did become, "major actors" in later periods, was not sufficiently large for them to be so classified at this point in time.

IGO's). These European institutions were established at different times and had different structures and functions. As a consequence, their ability to exercise influence varied. For instance, the Council of Europe was one of the first of Europe's postwar organizations. It was intended to function as a sort of advisory "European parliament" that would allow for the representation of diverse points of view. Debate took place, and various initiatives were passed; but the Council had no resources to implement its decisions. Therefore it remained little more than a debating society, whose continued existence was probably its greatest achievement. In this respect, the Council was quite different from the European Coal and Steel Community, which had specific responsibilities in industrial affairs and the power to make many of its decisions effective. Overall, the new European institutions served as "schools of cooperation" for many politicians and civil servants who were involved with them, and these individuals were to prove a valuable source of prointegration sentiment in the future.

In terms of *Integration* coalitions, we find that the six continental founders of ECSC were aligned as principal proponents of integration despite the existence of Franco-German tension. Among "supporters" were the United States and Great Britain. The United States advocated European integration as a means of enhancing the strength of the Western alliance and promoting European economic recovery. The role of Britain, on the other hand, remained ambiguous throughout the period. Separated from the continent geographically, Britain had traditionally been cool to permanent entanglements in the affairs of Europe. Reasons for British reluctance to embroil itself in a federalist Europe included its Commonwealth responsibilities and its unique relationship with the United States. Like many Britons, certain Socialist Parties as well as officials in West Berlin were uncertain about the eventual shape that a united Europe might take and so remained ostensibly "neutral" on *Integration* issues.

The third ranking superissue, *Atlantic Alliance-Strategic,* was closely related to the two previous superissues. It appeared on eight of the eleven factors and was involved in 13 percent of the issues. The most important subset of issues here concerned the establishment and maintenance of the North Atlantic Treaty Organization (NATO), which originated as a response to a perceived Soviet menace to Western Europe. NATO and its Council and other ancillary bodies constituted a new and important nonstate actor.

Another important strategic question that arose during this period was the extent to which the rearmament of Germany was to be encouraged and the way in which this could be brought about. Until the North Korean invasion of the South in June, 1950, this issue had remained muted. Indeed, Western rearmament in general had made little progress, and Western strategy continued to rely heavily on the American nuclear deterrent. The Korean crisis altered the situation dramatically. Korea and Germany, both divided at the end of the war into communist and noncommunist halves, appeared to be analogous. If the communists dared to attack one, why would they not attack the other which, after all, was a far more valuable prize? Hence, the belief that a Soviet attack upon Western Europe was increasingly likely reopened the issue of German rearmament. As long as West Germany possessed only a police force, it could play no part in its own defense, a situation which at face value was patently absurd.

In the context of persistent European fears of a German revival, the most logical alternative seemed to be some sort of integration of a German army into NATO and, therefore, under the control of NATO. In July, 1951 the NATO allies accepted a French proposal to establish the European Defense Community (EDC), and a treaty to this effect was signed ten months later. Under the EDC a German army would have been created as part of a West European army, and the new organization would have had many of the supranational attributes of the ECSC. The treaty was never ratified, however, and the ensuing debate became a focal point of the superissue during this period. Paradoxically, the French government, the original proponent of the scheme, now became its major opponent. There were two major reasons for this change. The first was the traditional French fear of a rearmed Germany, a fear that surfaced and increasingly divided the French electorate during the prolonged debate. The second was opposition to supranationalism itself, especially to its implications for the French Army's identity and independence. Such a possibility was anathema to the traditional forces of French nationalism, most notable among whom were the followers of Charles de Gaulle who believed that "a country without an army is no longer worthy of the name." Moreover, the Gaullists were already voicing their displeasure with the alleged Anglo-American domination of NATO.

The EDC debate dragged on indecisively for three years, impaled on the horns of the French dilemma which was, in turn, compounded by the *immobilisme* of the government structure of the Fourth Republic. Finally, following the defeat of the EDC in the French National Assembly in August, 1954, a compromise agreement to permit German rearmament emerged. Instead of the supranational EDC, Germany was admitted to the Brussels Treaty Organization, renamed the Western European Union (WEU). The WEU, an interstate governmental actor, was then effectively made part of NATO.

By this time, the sense of urgency that had given impetus to the original EDC proposal was passing, and the globalization of the Cold War was beginning to impinge on alliance defense politics. One of these issues turned upon the bloody war in Indochina and the ultimate French withdrawal from the area in 1954. Once the possibility of direct, massive American military aid to France in Indochina was rejected and the French defeat confirmed, U.S. hopes for stability in Southeast Asia were expressed in the creation of SEATO, an alliance modeled on NATO. United States sponsorship of this and similar alliances grew out of recognition of U.N. impotence and reflected the Eisenhower-Dulles strategic doctrine of "massive retaliation." In addition to *Alliance-Strategic* issues, the Indochina question also involved two other superissues—*Cold War* and *Colonialism,* and it is to *Colonialism* that we must now turn.

Colonialism was the fourth ranking superissue, appearing on seven of the factors and involved in 13 percent of the specific issues that arose during the period. The events pertaining to this superissue were exceedingly complex and conflictful, and nonstate actors were prominent as extra-regional sources of disturbance, as suggested by the superissue alignments.

At the heart of the *Colonial* superissue during this period was the agonizing dissolution of the French colonial empire, which proved a burden on the North Atlantic alliance and even created difficulties for European integration. The most dramatic of these problems was the French effort to retain control of Indochina. Unsuccessful in its attempts after World War II to link Vietnam to the French Union, France found its forces locked in a disillusioning guerrilla war with the Vietminh forces of the popular nationalist leader, Ho Chi Minh. Ho also was a communist and had support from the Soviet Union and China (after Mao took power) in his prosecution of the war. In this way the Indochina conflict acquired a *Cold War* dimension, which was heightened by the outbreak of war in Korea. The United States eventually undertook to help finance the French effort. The *Cold War* dimension helps to explain the presence in the *Colonial* alignments of many actors which, though having no direct interest in *Colonial* questions, felt compelled to back states like France, Belgium, and Holland that were their Cold War allies.

The French agony in Indochina had its parallels in North Africa and

Table 65.   Colonial and Neocolonial Alignments, 1948–1957

Pro-Colonial	Neutral	Anti-Colonial
France	Tunisia	Vietminh
Belgium	Tunisian Nationalists	FLN and Algerian
Netherlands	Ethiopia	Nationalists
United States	Yugoslavia	Moroccan Nationalists
United Kingdom	Chile	French Communists
FRG	Iceland	Belgian Workers
NATO	Portugal	USSR
Italy	Norway	French Ethnics
South Vietnam	Denmark	Other French Parties
European IGO's	Other Ethnics	(MRP, Radicals,
Governmental Noncentral	Finland	Popular Republicans,
(United States, France,	SDP	Gaullists)
West Berlin, Morocco,	Czechoslovakia	Other Parties (U.S.
Algeria, Tunisia,	Thailand	Republicans, Italian
Indochina, Vietnam)	Australia	CD's)
Sweden	New Zealand	Other Labor (United
Luxembourg	South Korea	States, Ruhr)
United Nations	Philippines	Other Belgian Parties
Canada	Iraq	(Liberals, Anti-
Cambodia	Turkey	Leopoldists)
American Cultural Groups	GATT	Egypt
(Columbia University, Joint	GDR	Poland
Distribution Committee)	Syria	India
Morocco	Spain	People's Republic of
Israel	French Labor	China
Occupation Authorities		
Interparliamentary Union		
French and Other Industry		
Indonesia		
Pakistan		
Belgian Catholic Christian		
Socialists		

Somaliland. Although a truce was achieved in Indochina as a consequence of the Geneva Conference of 1954, opposition to French rule intensified in North Africa, particularly in Algeria. The bitterness and bloodshed of the Algerian War contrasted with the granting of independence to Morocco and Tunisia in 1956. The latter events were not brought about without some nationalist agitation and violence; however, they were not characterized by the prolonged strife that accompanied Algerian independence. France was able to maintain close ties with both Tunisia and Morocco after independence, and, as the alignment table suggests, neither behaved in a consistently anticolonial or anti-French manner.

The acute difficulties inherent in the Algerian case were the consequence of four factors, all of which became apparent after the Algerian revolt began in 1954. First, Algeria did not have protectorate status and, unlike other French colonial possessions, it had been considered and governed as an integral part of France. Second, a well-organized nationalist movement, the National Liberation Front (FLN), had arisen after World War II, almost unrecognized by the French who were preoccupied with Indochina. The FLN drew its support from the Moslem community, which outnumbered French settlers by more than eight to one. Third, the French community in Algeria was large, had close ties with metropolitan France, and was represented by an effective parliamentary lobby. The fourth factor was the *immobilisme* of the Fourth Republic itself. Successive governments based on uneasy parliamentary coalitions found themselves unable to make concessions to the FLN without assuring their own demise. Indeed, chronic government instability and indecision were common to all of the country's colonial dilemmas.

Another *Colonial* issue, which was discussed earlier, was the ill-fated Anglo-French expedition against Egypt in 1956. This proved a source of dissension for the Western alliance for some time. Other *Colonial* issues included Dutch relations with Indonesia, Belgian difficulties with its colony in the Congo, the Italian-Ethiopian quarrel over Eritrea in 1950, and trusteeship questions regarding Tripolitania and Southwest Africa in 1948 and 1949 respectively. In many of these issues, the role of colonial authorities (governmental noncentral) was critically important.

Among the lesser superissues, *Extra-European Regional Crises* appeared on seven factors and was involved in 7 percent of the issues. Specific questions included Libyan independence, Suez, Vietnam, Eritrea, American airbases in Spanish Morocco, and Franco-Spanish Moroccan border disputes. The *Regime Stability* superissue appeared on six factors and was involved in 7 percent of the issues. Significant here was the behavior of the powerful French and Italian Communist Parties and the matter of the legal status of the Communist Party of West Germany. In addition, labor agitation and unrest were endemic in France in 1948, in Belgium and Italy in 1954, and in the FRG in 1957. Questions of general political instability characterized France and Italy throughout the period and reveal the importance of two types of *nostacs,* political parties and labor unions.

Superissue coappearance serves to illuminate a number of points concerning the relationship of the superissues to one another. The Cold War was closely associated with both *Integration,* to which it gave added impetus, and *Atlantic Alliance-Strategic* issues. Not surprisingly, this last superissue also often coappeared with *Integration,* and this linkage is well illustrated by recalling the implications of the EDC controversy. The high level of coappearance of *Integration* and *Extra-European Regional Crises* is further clarified when we consider the way in which the Korean and Indochinese crises acquired *Cold War* dimensions and thereby indirectly encouraged European integration. Moreover, both *Integration* and *Extra-European Regional Crises* were leading contributors to *Regime Stability.* Finally, as a result of the complexity of France's position, *Colonialism*

Table 66. Western Europe Superissue Coappearance, 1948-1957

	I	II	III	IV	V	VI	VII	VIII	IX
I. Integration	–								
II. Atlantic Alliance-Strategic	.88	–							
III. Atlantic Alliance-Economic	.71	.83	–						
IV. Cold War	.84	.82	.67	–					
V. Detente	.50	.40	.25	.45	–				
VI. Gaullism	.36	.22	.29	.33	.40	–			
VII. Colonial and Neocolonial	.75	.71	.67	.71	0	.22	–		
VIII. Extra-European Regional Crises	.88	.71	.50	.71	.60	.22	.57	–	
IX. Regime Stability	.80	.62	.55	.63	.44	.50	.62	.77	–

exhibits high coappearance scores with *Integration, Atlantic Alliance-Strategic,* and the *Cold War* superissues.

Turning from the pattern of issues to the actors themselves, we should stress the prominent role played by nonstate actors in the Western European system between 1948 and 1957. Nonstate actors initiated 31 percent of the total dyads during this period and were the targets of 33 percent of this behavior. Moreover, of the twenty-one actors occupying the first twenty activity ranks (a tie exists for the twentieth place), twelve of them were *nostacs.* Of the twenty most salient targets, one-half were nonstate actors.

Tables 67 and 68 lead us to several observations about both state and nonstate actor behavior in Western Europe during this period. France was obviously overwhelmingly significant as an actor and a target. The tables also highlight the impressive involvement of the United States and Great Britain in the affairs of Europe. Among nonstate actors, the activity level of European intergovernmental institutions (IGO's) recalls the centrality of the integration movement at the time. It should be noted in this connection that the tables underestimate the role of nonstate actors because we have *not* aggregated the various types of political parties into a single category. If they were grouped together, the aggregated category would rank ahead of Great Britain as an actor and would be almost as salient a target as Italy. A similar, though not as dramatic, change in rankings would occur if we were to aggregate Business with Multinational Corporations (MNC's).

Disruptive-supportive scores reveal the kind of impact nonstate actors had on Western Europe between 1948 and 1957. Twice as many nonstate actors are to be found in the disrupter as in the supporter column. The major disrupters were extra-regional in origin, including the category of French Ethnics, that is, the FLN, the Vietminh, and other groups opposed to French colonial policies. Indeed, this last nonstate category was responsible for more than 40 percent of the total conflict acts initiated during the period under consideration. Other Parties, Communist Parties,

*Table 67. The Most Active Initiators in
Western Europe, 1948–1957*

	France	(755)
	United States	(372)
	FRG	(370)
	United Kingdom	(234)
	USSR	(155)
	Italy	(146)
	Netherlands	(135)
(nostac)	Individuals	(114)
(nostac)	European IGO's	(99)
	Belgium	(93)
(nostac)	Other Parties	(90)
(nostac)	French Ethnics	(88)
(nostac)	Communist Parties	(87)
(nostac)	Socialist Parties	(86)
(nostac)	Labor	(86)
(nostac)	Governmental Noncentral	(85)
(nostac)	Religious	(84)
(nostac)	United Nations	(83)
(nostac)	Cultural	(79)
(nostac)	Business	(49)
	GDR	(49)

*Table 68. The Most Salient Targets in
Western Europe, 1948–1957*

	France	(573)
	FRG	(381)
	United States	(362)
	United Kingdom	(228)
(nostac)	Individuals	(207)
	Italy	(171)
(nostac)	French Ethnics	(143)
(nostac)	Governmental Noncentral	(134)
	Netherlands	(125)
	Belgium	(120)
(nostac)	United Nations	(116)
(nostac)	Business	(101)
	USSR	(100)
	Luxembourg	(84)
(nostac)	Communist Parties	(79)
(nostac)	Western Defense	(77)
(nostac)	Cultural	(76)
(nostac)	Media	(61)
	GDR	(50)
(nostac)	Labor	(48)

Labor, and Individuals were all contributors to *Regime Instability,* particularly in France and Italy.

In contrast to the disrupters, the major system supporters were nation-states, particularly those from within the region. This pattern evidences the high degree of cooperation that existed in Western Europe after World War

Table 69. Disruptive-Supportive Behavior, 1948-1957

Disrupters		Supporters	
French Ethnics	(−64)	United States	(+288)
Other Parties	(−30)	France	(+207)
Communist Parties	(−27)	FRG	(+174)
Labor	(−16)	United Kingdom	(+162)
Egypt	(−11)	Netherlands	(+105)
GDR	(−9)	European IGO's	(+89)
Other Ethnics	(−8)	Italy	(+80)
Syria	(−7)	United Nations	(+75)
Individuals	(−4)	Belgium	(+69)
South Africa	(−4)	Cultural	(+55)

II and the steps that were being taken to prevent a recurrence of the type of intra-European conflicts that gave birth to the two world wars. The appearance of the United States reflects American efforts to stimulate European recovery and to forge an alliance against the Soviet Union at a time of growing hostility between East and West. The most important nonstate supporters were the new European IGO's, themselves the institutionalization of Europe's new spirit of cooperation. Finally, the United Nations, dominated for much of the period by the United States and its European allies, was a supporter of the Western European system. United Nations' support was particularly evident at the time of the Korean War, but it became less dependable as new Afro-Asian states joined the General Assembly and that forum began to focus on questions of colonialism.

In conclusion, Western Europe between 1948 and 1957 was preoccupied with the threat from the Soviet bloc. However, the Cold War was of some benefit to the region, hastening as it did the movement towards supranational integration, the settlement of intraregional quarrels, and economic recovery. The key actor of the period was France, plagued by government instability and under increasing pressure to surrender a colonial empire that it could no longer afford to maintain. In this respect, the role of nonstate actors as sources of conflict and violence is highly visible. Yet, simultaneously, Europe witnessed the emergence of new institutions that proved to be important sources of cooperation in the system.

The Gaullist Era:
Western Europe, 1957–1967

The period between the founding of the EEC and the second veto of British entry into the Common Market by French President Charles de Gaulle was a time of transition for Europe. While many of the superissues became slightly less complex, the subtlety of the interrelationships among them increased. The beginning of the period witnessed an intensification of the *Cold War* over the divided city of Berlin. Nevertheless, the *Cold War* was no longer the overwhelming concern that it had been earlier. By the middle of the 1960's, Europe was the scene of the first tentative steps towards a detente between the major opposing blocs.

Integration continued, and its linkages to other superissues testifies to its significance in regional politics. A major change in the pattern of politics that had characterized the first period, however, began with the return to power of Charles de Gaulle in France in 1958, and this change was confirmed in the precipitous rise of *Gaullism* from last-ranking superissue in the first period to third place during the years under consideration. The circumstances surrounding the General's return from political exile were dramatic. *Colonial* problems exacerbated the *immobilisme* of the Fourth Republic and the Algerian situation degenerated into a protracted guerrilla war. With no solution in sight, the French settlers and Army in Algeria united to oppose the impotent government in Paris which threatened concessions to the FLN. An insurrection took place in Algiers. But none of the insurrectionists had sufficient prestige to take power in France, and de Gaulle was summoned after twelve years of waiting to safeguard the Republic.

De Gaulle immediately started to enact the constitutional reforms that he deemed necessary in order to rescue France from perpetual indecision and instability. The country was converted from a parliamentary to a presidential form of government, the Fifth Republic. De Gaulle believed that nationalism remained the strongest force in politics, a belief that brought him into conflict with many of France's closest allies. Yet, he had the will to solve the Algerian War, after which he turned his attention to restoring France to the position of eminence in Europe and the world that it had enjoyed before World War II.

The *Colonial* superissue remained prominent in this period, not only with regard to Algeria, but also in respect to the independence of other areas in Africa, notably the Belgian Congo. *Strategic* aspects of the *Atlantic Alliance* continued to evoke both cooperation and controversy, the latter heightened by Gaullist resistance to Anglo-American leadership. *Extra-European Regional Crises* included civil war in the Congo, tensions in the Middle East, American involvement in Indochina, and the uncertain situation on the island of Cyprus.

As in the previous period, the single most important superissue was the *Cold War,* which appeared on all ten factors but was involved in only 20 percent of the issues. With few exceptions this superissue was confined to the first five years of the period, diminishing after the successful retreat from the brink of nuclear war over the installation of Soviet missiles in Cuba in 1962. Also as in the first period, Berlin remained a major bone of contention among the Cold War protagonists, particularly in 1958. In that

Table 70. Ranking of Superissues by
Explained Variance, 1957–1967

1. Cold War	(2.78)
2. Integration	(1.80)
3. Gaullism	(1.67)
4. Colonial and Neocolonial	(1.39)
5. Atlantic Alliance-Strategic	(1.32)
6. Extra-European Regional Crises	(1.11)
7. Detente	(0.84)
8. Regime Stability	(0.64)
9. Atlantic Alliance-Economic	(0.41)

year Soviet leader Nikita Khrushchev renewed the pressure on that city in order to force Western recognition of the communist regime in East Germany (GDR). A definitive peace treaty with regard to Germany had never been signed, and the status of the two halves remained murky. Would such a treaty be signed by the FRG? The GDR? Or both? Or could the treaty only be signed by a reunited Germany? Divided Berlin symbolized the struggle for Germany as a whole, and Soviet pressure there was designed to force the West to legitimize the existence of a separate East Germany. The Western dilemma was acute. If Khrushchev were to transfer control of the access routes to Berlin to the GDR (as he threatened to do), the Western allies would have to deal directly with a regime that they claimed was illegitimate, and, perhaps, recognize it. Such recognition would imply the permanent division of Germany.

The Berlin situation dragged on through 1959, alternatively becoming tense and then relaxing on an almost day-to-day basis depending upon the extent of Eastern bloc harassment (such as the buzzing of airplanes). By the autumn of 1959, efforts to resolve the differences had proved unsuccessful, although Khrushchev's visit to the United States and the resulting "Spirit of Camp David" provided a temporary respite. Finally, an agreement was reached to convene a summit conference in May, 1960. In the meantime, continued triumphs in outer space served to bolster Soviet prestige. Then, only ten days before the conference was to take place, the Soviet Union shot down an American U-2 spy plane that had crossed deep into Russia. The ensuing controversy aborted the conference.

In June, 1961 recently-inaugurated President John F. Kennedy met with Khrushchev in Vienna. The Soviet leader, perhaps misperceiving the American commitment to an independent Berlin, continued to threaten to sign a German peace treaty. Tension heightened throughout the summer, and the flow of refugees from the GDR into the Western sectors of Berlin, long an embarrassment to the East German regime, became a flood. Finally, one morning in August the world awoke to find that the GDR had erected a wall to separate East from West Berlin. Confronted by a *fait*

Table 71.   Cold War Alignments, 1957–1967: Major Coalitions

Pro-United States	Neutral	Pro-Soviet
United States	Vatican	USSR
FRG	Indonesia	West European
France	Canada	Communist
United Kingdom	US Republican Party	Parties (France,
NATO	GDR	Italy)
Belgium	United Nations	
Netherlands	Media	
German Parties	India	
(CDU, SPD)	South Vietnam	
Cultural Groups	French Industry	
(ORTF, Hamburg	Anti-United States	
Sym., FRG Red	Demonstrators	
Cross)	(Anti-Indochina War,	
European IGO's	Disarmament Groups)	
Greece		
Turkey		
San Marino		
Individuals		
West Berlin		

accompli, the Western allies took no action, and the Berlin issue seemed to have acquired a new and uneasy *status quo.*

Alignment patterns on these *Cold War* issues reveal the changing nature of the East-West conflict. Stalinist foreign policy had largely isolated the Soviet Union. In addition, Soviet allies in the Eastern bloc had become considerably less active, in part because of acute regime instability throughout Eastern Europe. The appearance of the GDR in the "neutral" column is somewhat deceptive since it reflects a policy that alternated between hostility and conciliation.

Nonstate actors remained somewhat less important for this superissue than for others, although NATO, European IGO's, and West Berlin were active supporters of the American position. This was also true of German political parties and cultural groups that sought to maintain the favorable relationship between the United States and the FRG, especially since the German Socialists (SPD) had largely resolved their dilemma regarding reunification in their party program. Two significant nonstate actors, the Vatican and the United Nations, moved from the "pro-United States" into the "neutral" column. In the case of the former, this shift was a result of the mediatory efforts of Pope John XXIII, an increasing preoccupation with internal Church affairs (reflected by the Ecumenical Council), and a grudging acceptance of the *status quo* in Eastern Europe. In the case of the latter, changing membership patterns marked the end of Western dominance in the organization.

Integration, which appeared on eight of ten factors and was related to

19 percent of the issues, was once again the second-ranking superissue. The three most important sets of specific issues involved in *Integration* were at once logically and historically related. These were formation of the EEC itself in 1958 and ancillary organizational matters, the two abortive British applications to enter the Common Market, and the "special relationship" of Gaullist France and West Germany that dominated the regional politics of Europe and its IGO's, particularly between 1962 and 1967.

The EEC came into existence as a consequence of the Rome treaties of 1957 which also established a European Atomic Energy Community (EURATOM). Both of these bodies included a commission with the sole power of initiating proposals to implement the treaties, although such proposals had to be accepted by a Council of Ministers. In order to further supranational integration, the treaties contained provisions to increase the harmonization of socio-economic policies and to promote trade liberalization among the member states. At the outset these provisions proved a source of divisions among the six signatories. Because of its colonial empire and certain domestic considerations, France was alone in urging that these two sets of provisions be closely linked with regard to the timing of their implementation. Nevertheless, increasing cooperation characterized Europe in the years that followed, as evidenced in such areas as space (ELDO and Telstar), military logistics, cultural exchange, and civil aviation.

Meanwhile, the position of Great Britain remained ambiguous. Initially, instead of accepting the terms of the Common Market, Britain sought a looser association and promoted the idea of a free trade area within the context of the existing Organization of European Economic Cooperation (OEEC). This policy further estranged Britain from the six member states of the EEC and led to Britain's founding of the European Free Trade Area (EFTA) in 1959, the other members of which were Norway, Denmark, Sweden, Austria, Portugal, and Switzerland. This group, known as the *Outer Seven,* appeared as competitors of the *Inner Six* of the EEC. In 1960 the OEEC was renamed the Organization for European Cooperation and Development (OECD) and was joined by the United States and Japan.

In 1959 the Conservative government of Harold Macmillan was reelected, and an ensuing reevaluation of British foreign policy culminated in an announcement in July, 1961 that the United Kingdom would seek admission to the Common Market. Yet Britain's Commonwealth responsibilities and, even more, the continuing close relationship between Britain and the United States provoked doubts on the continent as to British commitment to the European ideal. De Gaulle, in particular, feared that Britain would act as a "Trojan horse" through which American influence in

Europe would be perpetuated. For his part, the French President sought to cement a Franco-German "special relationship," embodied in a treaty signed in January, 1963. Simultaneously, de Gaulle publicly rejected the British application.

As one observer comments:

> De Gaulle's veto on British entry into the common market and the Franco-German treaty had implications for the common market itself almost as important as the effect on relations with Britain. The manner in which the veto had been imposed was clearly contrary to the spirit of the Community, while the anti-Americanism which inspired it was not shared by the other members. Franco-German cooperation was indispensible to the success of the Community; but Franco-German hegemony could only be a danger to the balance of the Community as a whole. The question at issue over the next few years would therefore be whether the momentum of the Community would carry it forward to closer union, or whether the strength of Gaullism in France would prove a barrier to further progress.[4]

France's attempts to woo West Germany showed an awareness of the definitive emergence of the FRG as a leading member of the EEC and an active partner in European cooperation. The attempts recognized the FRG as a potential rival of France within the European community. Renewed German self-confidence found expression in economic cooperation with Britain in 1960–1961, frontier adjustments with Belgium in 1958, and cooperation with Portugal in 1966. Throughout the period France sought to maintain its special relationship with West Germany, even though disputes in the EEC concerning agriculture put a strain on it. One aspect of Gaullist policy with potentially important consequences for Germany was the "opening" to Eastern Europe by France in 1964, which was grounded in a desire for trade and which symbolized de Gaulle's independence of the two superpowers. Among the smaller members of the EEC, Holland, acting as a "conscience for the Common Market," opposed Gaullist positions with regard to the veto of British membership and the continuing tariff and agricultural controversies.

Some of these considerations are illustrated by the alignment patterns that existed on the *Integration* superissue during this period.

The categories of "less supportive" and "neutral" have been collapsed into a single category because a significant difference in terms of affect did not appear between the behavior of those actors such as France and the FRG which were members of the EEC but embroiled in major controversies and those which were "outsiders" such as the members of EFTA and the United States. Another interesting characteristic of the coalitions was the decline in the number of active European IGO's. There

4. Wilfrid Knapp, *A History of War and Peace 1939–1965* (New York: Oxford University Press, 1967), p. 465.

Table 72. Integration, 1957–1967: Major Coalitions

Major Supporters	Less Supportive/Neutral
EEC	France
West European Aviation Org.	United Kingdom
Netherlands	FRG
Belgium	United States
Luxembourg	Sweden
Italy	Norway
	Denmark
	Ireland
	Spain
	Greece
	Switzerland
	Austria
	Turkey
	Italian Workers
	Dutch Employers

are two explanations for this pattern. By this time the existence of many of the European organizations had become institutionalized to such an extent that the "growing pains" of the initial period were no longer in evidence. Furthermore, the existence of these institutions was no longer a principal source of controversy. Instead, *Integration* controversies were dealt with on a state-to-state basis, with certain states such as the Benelux countries acting almost as proxies for the European institutions themselves.

The third-ranking superissue was *Gaullism,* which appeared on eight factors and was involved in 16 percent of the total issues. We have already seen how de Gaulle returned during a period of domestic turmoil in which one French government after another was unable to resolve the Algerian problem. De Gaulle's first task was to find such a solution, and in doing so he was guided by his belief that nationalism was an irresistible force. Thus he sought to bring France to accept Algerian independence. In the process, he was forced to quell a revolt in Algeria by the French Army and to cope with the terrorist activities of the *Organisation de l'Armée secrète* (OAS), which was aided and abetted by both the French settlers in Algeria (known as *Pieds Noirs*) and sympathizers at home. The terrorism of the OAS, whose members felt themselves betrayed by de Gaulle's willingness to accept self-determination as the basis for a solution in Algeria (confirmed in a French referendum in 1961), extended into metropolitan France and included several attempts to assassinate the President himself. The war finally drew to an end in March, 1962, when Algeria was granted its independence.

The conclusion of the Algerian War increased de Gaulle's prestige at home and abroad. He then turned to the task of restoring France's lost influence in global affairs. His policies, as we have seen, provoked controversy in the EEC, and his vetoes of Britain's attempts to enter the Common Market placed a strain on the Atlantic Community as a whole. In addition, his opposition to America's dominance of NATO, particularly with regard to strategic issues, led to France's removal of its Mediterranean fleet from the alliance in 1959 as well as a *de facto* withdrawal from NATO in 1966. De Gaulle's suspicion of American motives was also manifested in his chagrin when the Chrysler Corporation took over Simca in 1963. Finally, as American involvement in Vietnam grew after 1963, de Gaulle publicly opposed U.S. policy there.

De Gaulle's belief in nationalism was reflected in three other important policies. One was his pursuit of the special relationship with West Germany after 1962. Another was his economic and political overtures to the Soviet Union and Eastern Europe (particularly Rumania) after 1963. The third was the rapid development by France of an independent nuclear capability, which was strongly opposed by the United States. France's testing of nuclear weapons in the Sahara between 1959 and 1961 created difficulties in French relations with Africa at a sensitive time.

Examination of the alignments with regard to *Gaullism* during this period reveals interestingly that, despite many instances of conflict, virtually every Western state remained basically friendly to France. Despite strains, the pattern of behavior among the members of the Atlantic Com-

Table 73.   Gaullism, 1957–1967: Major Alignments

Pro-French	Neutral	Anti-French
France	Noncentral Govs.	FLN and Other
FRG	(France, Morocco,	Algerian
United States	Algeria)	Nationalists
United Kingdom	Tunisia	OAS
Italy	EEC	Pieds Noirs
Belgium	GDR	French Ethnics
Poland	Other French	(Dahomey,
Individuals	Parties (Radicals,	Camerouns)
Indonesia	Socialists)	Morocco
Luxembourg	Egypt	Nigeria
USSR	Katanga	French Labor
Algeria	Ruanda	Afro-Asian Bloc
Monaco	Chile	Communist Parties
Cultural Groups	Rumania	(France, USSR,
(University of	Cambodia	GDR)
Buenos Aires,	IMF	British Media
Franco-American	United Nations	(London Times,
Society of NY,	Switzerland	London Daily
FRG Red Cross)	Spain	Herald)
Netherlands	Syria	
Argentina	Israel	
Canada	Auto Manufacturers	
NATO	(Peugeot, Simca,	
	Chrysler)	

munity remained fundamentally cooperative. It appears that the disputes took place in an environment in which cooperation had become an accepted norm. Soviet and Polish cooperative attitudes, on the other hand, reflect Gaullist initiatives to the Eastern bloc.

Among the ten actors which consistently and actively opposed de Gaulle, eight were nonstate. These included the groups involved in the Algerian question as well as Communist Parties, French Labor (a traditional electoral supporter of the communists), ethnic groups in other areas of the French Community, and British Media unhappy with France's policy towards the United Kingdom. Other important nonstate actors such as the EEC—a target of de Gaulle's attacks—the United Nations, certain industrial groups, and Other French Parties remained basically "neutral." The position of French political parties was especially difficult since they had few resources with which to counteract the popularity of de Gaulle, which was grounded in substantial accomplishment.

The *Colonial* superissue was again the fourth most important. It appeared on seven factors and was involved in 13 percent of the issues. France's difficulties with its colonial empire, particularly Algeria, continued to be prominent here. Thus, the FLN, the OAS, and French political parties were leading participants in this superissue. Another set of *Colonial* issues arose with respect to the disposition of France's colonies in Sub-Saharan Africa; there was unrest in the Camerouns in 1959 and in Mauritania in 1960.

What became the paradigmatic illustration of the range of difficulties confronting the newly-independent African states involved, not a former French colony, but a Belgian one. The Belgian Congo acquired its independence on June 30, 1960, and was immediately convulsed by civil strife, tribal warfare, and military mutiny. Belgian troops also intervened, ostensibly to prevent a massacre of Europeans and the secession of the province of Katanga, the wealthiest part of the country. The United Nations agreed to dispatch a peacekeeping force to alleviate the situation. United Nations' forces, however, quickly found themselves caught between warring factions, themselves supported by outside powers. When the Congo crisis threatened to spill over into the Cold War, the United Nations found itself faced by a truly Sisyphusian task that nearly bankrupted the organization financially and politically and cost the life of Secretary-General Dag Hammarskjold, who died in a plane crash in September, 1961, while seeking to mediate the conflict. Questions of unity versus separatism, the role of European mercenaries, and the interests of foreign corporations created an enormously complex situation, while the emergence of ideological divisions further complicated matters.

Congolese problems (the secession of Katanga, French support of the rebellious province, and various proposed solutions) accounted for much

Table 74. *Colonial and Neocolonial Alignments, 1957–1967*

Procolonial	Neutral	Anticolonial
France	French Parties	FLN and Algerian
Belgium	(Radicals,	Nationalists
Netherlands	Socialists)	OAS
United States	Iran	Pieds Noirs
United Kingdom	Canada	Belgian Labor
FRG	Ruanda	French Labor
Italy	Tunisia	Communist Parties
Luxembourg	Afro-Asian Bloc	(USSR, GDR, Belgium,
Indonesia	Cuba	France)
NATO	Egypt	Other Ethnics
EEC and European IGO	Argentina	(Cameroun rebels,
Industry (Peugeot, Chrysler,	Rumania	Dahomey demonstrators,
Simca, Banca Commerciale	GDR	Indonesian Weigo
of Milan)	Chile	Resistance)
Poland	Cambodia	Morocco
USSR		Media (Belgian, North
Congo		Sea Pirate TV)
Individuals		Nigeria
Algeria		Noncentral Governments
Belgian Ethnics (Flemish,		(France, Algeria,
Walloons)		Morocco, Ruanda-
UN		Urundi)
Financial IGO's (IMF, Inter-		
American Dev. Bank)		
Katanga		
Culture		
Norway		
Sweden		
Denmark		
IPU		
Monaco		
Switzerland		
Spain		
Israel		
Syria		
Greece		
Turkey		

of the *Colonial* superissue between 1960 and 1964. Alignments on the superissue involved a great many actors, including Third World states, when *Colonial* questions permeated the U.N. and other international forums. The alignments themselves illustrate several important patterns. The first pattern was the growing division between "have" and "have-not" actors. Most poor states were virulently "anti-colonial," and the few which appear in the "pro-colonial" column did so for reasons related to their need for economic and political support from wealthy states. Despite rhetoric to the contrary, the Soviet Union behaved as "procolonial." In part this was due to the fact by this time that it, too, had become a wealthy state and, with diminution of the Cold War, saw less need to compete with the West for the favor of the nonaligned.[5] Second, alignments on the superissue again highlight the key role of nonstate actors. On the one hand, ethnic groups and certain political parties were among those most consistently prepared to expend resources in pursuit of anticolonial objectives. On the other hand, intergovernmental institutions that were supported by the rich countries encouraged political stability and supported the colonial powers. These included NATO, European IGO's, industrial concerns, and Financial IGO's. This alignment suggests that certain types of nonstate actors are by nature conservative while others seek to overturn the global *status quo*. Finally, the existence of a large bloc of neutrals attests to the fact that many states were prepared to speak against colonialism but not to act.

Strategic issues of the Atlantic Alliance constituted the fifth ranking superissue. They appeared in nine of the factors and were involved in 14 percent of the issues. Between 1959 and 1963, tension over Berlin prompted a high level of cooperation within NATO in order to increase military preparedness in the alliance. Yet the crux of the superissue was the so-called NATO nuclear sharing controversy which became a principal source of Franco-American differences in the 1960's and led to France's effective withdrawal from NATO.

Since its founding, NATO had depended on America's possession of a nuclear deterrent, a situation which gave the United States a predominant voice in NATO strategy. In addition, the United States had favored Britain with assistance in developing its own independent deterrent, but it denied similar assistance to France. This situation had always irritated France, and the problem was exacerbated by two events. The first was de Gaulle's return to power and his pursuit of an independent foreign policy for France and Europe, a policy which required, he believed, the possession of an independent deterrent as a symbol of power and prestige. The second was the development by the Soviet Union of missiles that could strike the United States. This raised the question of whether the United States would be prepared to use its nuclear weapons to prevent a Soviet attack on Europe when such use might bring reprisals against the United States itself. Many Europeans concluded that it was necessary for them to have a finger on the "nuclear trigger" so that they could credibly deter a Soviet attack.

The Skybolt crisis of 1962 brought this issue into the open. The British nuclear strike force (based on bombers) had become obsolete, and in order to prolong its life Great Britain had begun to cooperate with the United States in developing an air-to-surface missile called Skybolt. By December, 1961, however, in view of economic constraints and its devel-

5. See Roger E. Kanet, ed., *The Soviet Union and the Developing Nations* (Baltimore: The Johns Hopkins Press, 1974).

opment of a superior missile, the Polaris, which could be fired from submerged submarines, the United States abruptly cancelled the Skybolt
program without consulting Britain. A political crisis erupted in Britain as
leading British politicians realized that their nuclear deterrent was being
sacrificed to American economic considerations. A conference was hur-
riedly convened in December, 1962 between President Kennedy and
British Prime Minister Macmillan on the island of Nassau, and an agreement was reached whereby the United States would furnish Britain with
Polaris missiles while the British would develop their own submarines and
warheads. A similar offer was made to France, but it proved unacceptable
in view of the relatively backward state of French technology.

For de Gaulle, the event epitomized Anglo-American domination of
NATO and British willingness to sacrifice European interests to the Anglo-
American special relationship. He decided that his only course was to
cultivate closer relations with Germany (a Franco-German treaty was
signed in January, 1963) and to exclude Britain from Europe. (De Gaulle
vetoed the British application to join the EEC on January 14, 1963.) In
order to assuage France, the United States revived a proposal first made in
1960 for the creation of a Multilateral Force (MLF), which would involve
a naval task force equipped with nuclear weapons and manned by crews of
mixed nationality. However, under this scheme the United States would
retain most of its own nuclear strike force as well as possess a veto over the
actions of the MLF. Hence the proposal provided little advantage to
Europe and was greeted with extreme skepticism by the French and most
other Europeans. Discussions continued until 1966, by which time the
MLF had become a "dead letter."

Gaullist leadership of a continental coalition opposed to Anglo-
American alliance hegemony is revealed by the pattern of alignments on
Atlantic Alliance-Strategic issues in this period.

A close relationship between the *Atlantic Alliance-Strategic* and *Economic* superissues derived mainly from disputes regarding the division of
costs involved in stationing American and British troops in Europe. This
issue, which remains alive today, had domestic economic implications for
several of the NATO allies, particularly with regard to American and
British balance of payments deficits. Other matters that formed part of the

Table 75. The NATO Alliance, 1957–1967

Pro-NATO	Equivocally Pro-NATO	Anti-NATO
NATO/WEU	France	USSR
United States	Belgium	Communist Parties
United Kingdom	FRG	(Belgium, CPSU)
	Canada	Dutch Labor Party
	Italy	

last-ranking superissue (appearing on only five factors and involved in 6 percent of the issues) were Franco-American socio-economic cooperation, the activities of American-based multinational corporations in Europe, Italian-American space cooperation, and EEC tariffs and trade vis-à-vis the United States.

Of the lesser superissues, *Extra-European Regional Crises* appeared on nine of the ten factors but was involved in only 10 percent of the total issues. The most critical of these was the Congo crisis between 1960 and 1964. Another important issue was European concern over the deepening American involvement in the Indochina quagmire, including the Laos crisis of 1961–1962 and the rapidly growing American commitment to South Vietnam after 1963. Other extra-regional crises that appeared were the quarrel between Indonesia and Singapore in 1957, the Cypriot crisis of 1964, the economic embargo of white-supremacist Rhodesia in 1966, and the Sino-Soviet split. Finally, heightened European attention to the Middle East was reflected in a dispute in 1964 over former Nazi scientists in Egypt and in the rapprochement between West Germany and Israel between 1963 and 1966 that prompted Germany's recognition of Israel in 1965.

As though setting the stage for the final period under consideration, *Detente* advanced a rank to seventh position, appearing on seven factors and involving 7 percent of the issues. Specific instances of lessening tension, often sandwiched between periods of Cold War stress, included FRG trade with the Soviet Union (1959) and Eastern Europe (1961), intermittent cooperation between the FRG and the GDR (1960–1964) culminating in an easing of inter-German travel restrictions, improved Italian relations with the Eastern bloc (particularly with Poland and the Soviet Union), Polish foreign policy liberalization (1967), and the Gaullist economic and political "opening to the East" (1963–1967).

The *Regime Stability* superissue appeared on six of the factors and was involved in 6 percent of the issues. It included charges of French atrocities in Algeria (1958–1959), French party conflict over Algeria (1961), French support of Katanga's secession (1960), censorship of the magazine *Der Stern* in West Germany (1959), the rise of Italian neofascism (1962), and the post-Sukarno settlement of Indonesian debts (1966).

As was the case between 1948 and 1957, the superissues once again were closely interrelated. *Integration* and *Gaullism,* which regularly coappeared with each other and were also linked to the other superissues, were the leading forces that shaped European politics in this era. In addition, the *Cold War* and *Atlantic Alliance-Strategic* superissues often coappeared, with each conditioning the other. Also of interest was the relationship between the *Cold War* and *Extra-European Regional Crises* superissues,

Table 76. Western Europe Superissue Coappearance, 1957–1967

	I	II	III	IV	V	VI	VII	VIII	IX
I. Integration	–								
II. Atlantic Alliance-Strategic	.94	–							
III. Atlantic Alliance-Economic	.77	.71	–						
IV. Cold War	.89	.95	.67	–					
V. Detente	.80	.88	.67	.82	–				
VI. Gaullism	1.00	.94	.77	.89	.80	–			
VII. Colonial and Neocolonial	.80	.75	.67	.82	.71	.80	–		
VIII. Extra-European Regional Crises	.94	.89	.71	.95	.75	.94	.88	–	
IX. Regime Stability	.71	.67	.73	.75	.62	.71	.92	.80	–

which provides further evidence of the "contagion effect" of the Cold War spreading outwards from Europe particularly into Cuba, the Congo, and Southeast Asia. Despite the altered pattern of politics in Europe, the *Cold War* and *Colonialism* continued to be prominent regional superissues. Thus, although the superissues themselves had the same relative importance between 1957 and 1967 as they had between 1948 and 1957, their content had changed and therefore the way in which they were associated with one another had altered.

Nonstate actors remained an important force in the politics of the region despite de Gaulle's belief in the power and importance of nationalism and the nation-state. While declining slightly as initiators of activity, they were still responsible for 27 percent of the dyads. Moreover, they continued to be targets in 30 percent of all dyads. Tables 77 and 78 underscore the importance of nonstate actors in the region. In the second period, nonstate actors accounted for half of the most active initiators and salient targets. Once again the role of particular political parties was critical. If all political parties were combined, they would rank just behind the Soviet Union in terms of activity and just behind the GDR in salience. If we were to aggregate Business with Multinational Corporations, they would rank ahead of Religious groups in activity.

The tables of leading actors and targets strongly resemble those of the first time period. This additional impression of continuity is confirmed by the highly significant rank-order correlations for both activity and salience between the two time periods (Spearman's rho = .84 for activity and .82 for salience). Also many of the same actors appear in both tables; they were active *and* salient. The correlation between activity and salience was statistically significant in the second period (rho = .87).

As was the case in the previous period, a look at patterns of disruptive-supportive behavior reveals the nature of the impact of *nostacs* upon the region. Again there is continuity: Many of the same actors appear as leading disrupters and supporters in both periods (rho = .64). Nonstate

Table 77. The Most Active Initiators in
Western Europe, 1957-1967

	France	(432)
	FRG	(275)
	United States	(239)
	United Kingdom	(131)
	Italy	(131)
	Belgium	(119)
	USSR	(104)
(nostac)	French Ethnic	(94)
(nostac)	Governmental Noncentral	(92)
	Netherlands	(81)
(nostac)	Religious	(58)
(nostac)	Individuals	(51)
(nostac)	Business	(49)
(nostac)	European IGO's	(48)
	GDR	(44)
(nostac)	Communist Parties	(39)
(nostac)	Western Defense	(38)
(nostac)	Cultural	(38)
(nostac)	Other Parties	(33)
	Tunisia	(32)

Table 78. The Most Salient Targets in
Western Europe, 1957-1967

	France	(371)
	FRG	(282)
	United States	(248)
(nostac)	Individuals	(125)
	USSR	(125)
	United Kingdom	(123)
	Italy	(96)
	Belgium	(94)
(nostac)	Governmental Noncentral	(80)
(nostac)	Media	(72)
(nostac)	European IGO's	(70)
(nostac)	United Nations	(67)
(nostac)	French Ethnic	(64)
(nostac)	Western Defense	(61)
(nostac)	Business	(50)
	Netherlands	(49)
	GDR	(49)
(nostac)	Cultural	(39)
	Indonesia	(38)
(nostac)	Religious	(35)

actors were once more among the principal disrupters. French Ethnics were an overwhelming source of disruption in large measure because of events attending the decline of the French colonial empire. The relevance of these events is also shown by the presence of colonial authorities (Governmental Noncentral) as the second most disruptive actor.

Table 79. *Disruptive-Supportive Behavior, 1957–1967*

Disrupters		Supporters	
French Ethnics	(−82)	France	(+164)
Governmental Noncentral	(−14)	United States	(+161)
Labor	(−13)	FRG	(+151)
Communist Parties	(−9)	Belgium	(+91)
GDR	(−8)	United Kingdom	(+87)
Media	(−8)	Italy	(+79)
Nigeria	(−6)	Religious	(+34)
Egypt	(−5)	Netherlands	(+33)
Other IGO's	(−4)	European IGO's	(+30)
Other Nostacs	(−4)	Western Defense	(+30)

Finally, it should be noted that many of the disrupters were from outside the region. Member states of the EEC were again among the system's leading supporters as were the EEC itself and other European IGO's. The appearance of NATO as a major system supporter was caused by its growing role as a forum within the Atlantic Community, and the appearance of Religious groups reflected a decline in the Vatican's anti-communist rhetoric and the conciliatory behavior of Pope John.

By the end of the period, then, certain trends were apparent. European institutions had survived the crises caused by Gaullist nationalism. Most of Europe's colonial problems had been disposed of, and many potential sources of conflict no longer directly involved the Europeans. Finally, the hostile blocs of the Cold War were showing signs of breaking up, and the tension between them was decreasing.

The Era of Detente: 1967–1972

Developments in Western Europe and in the global political system as a whole after 1967 had been foreshadowed by events in the prior period. As Europe began to confront the difficulties of the "post-industrial society," it became less a source of global tensions. Instead, it was the scene of the first tentative steps towards East-West detente at the same time as attention was focused on potentially explosive situations in the Middle East, Indochina, and the Sino-Soviet frontier. This new focus accounted for the emergence of *Extra-European Regional Crises* as the leading superissue of the final period. Regional politics was more dependent upon events originating outside of Western Europe, but an increasingly prosperous and independent Western Europe was no longer merely a pawn in the rivalry between the two superpowers.

Detente became the second leading superissue, and *Gaullism* remained the third most important, although much of the content of *Gaul-*

lism had changed. *Gaullism* had less impact within Europe after the General was swept from power in 1969. This event was part of a larger wave of unrest, mainly among youth, that crested throughout the West at this time and was partly responsible for the increasing salience of *Regime Stability*. Indeed, this new spirit of resistance to authority was a reflection of the West's inability to cope with "post-industrial" problems such as pollution, inflation, and swollen bureaucracy. As French leadership in Europe ebbed, the center of activity shifted to West Germany where Willy Brandt led his socialist followers to power. Brandt embarked on the policy of *Ostpolitik,* thereby setting the scene for further steps towards detente.

During the third period, *Integration* was only the fifth-ranking super-issue since, with the passing of de Gaulle, many of its issues ceased to be major sources of controversy. On January 22, 1972, Great Britain, along with Ireland, Norway, and Denmark, was finally admitted to the EEC, and all but Norway became full members in January, 1973. (British membership in the EEC was confirmed by an overwhelmingly pro-Market vote in a referendum that took place in June, 1975.) Yet much of the momentum towards further integration seemed to come to a halt, at least temporarily. Both *Strategic* and *Economic* questions of the *Atlantic Alliance* remained sources of division, particularly those involving international monetary problems. Finally, the *Cold War* and *Colonialism* superissues all but disappeared as focal points of European attention and concern. Thus, between 1967 and 1972, Western Europe gave every indication of having become a "security community," a type of community that it would have been difficult to envision a mere twenty-five years earlier.

The leading superissue of the period, *Extra-European Regional Crises,* appeared on six factors and included 21 percent of the issues. One of the leading questions here concerned American involvement in Indochina, including the invasion of Cambodia in 1970, and Gaullist criticisms of U.S. behavior. In addition to criticism of the United States, there were various European attempts, in particular by de Gaulle, to mediate the hostilities. A second set of issues concerned continued antagonisms in the

Table 80. Ranking of Superissues by Explained Variance, 1967-1972

1. Extra-European Regional Crises	(1.94)
2. Detente	(1.77)
3. Gaullism	(1.64)
4. Regime Stability	(1.10)
5. Integration	(1.05)
6. Atlantic Alliance-Strategic	(0.96)
7. Atlantic Alliance-Economic	(0.84)
8. Cold War	(0.26)
9. Colonial and Neocolonial	(0.21)

Middle East. Specific events included French participation in Four-Power discussions intended to resolve the problem and the French sale of arms to certain Arab states, notably the controversial sale of jet aircraft to Libya in 1970. This last action represented a change in the policy of France, the previous supplier of arms to Israel. (Despite French assurances that the aircraft would not be used against Israel, some were, in fact, turned over to Egypt by Libya and employed in the Yom Kippur War.) Preoccupation with petroleum formed another dimension of Europe's involvement in the Middle East. An Italian-Iraqi oil agreement in 1972 inaugurated a pattern in which the industrial economies of Western Europe would seek independently of other consumers to ensure a sufficient flow of petroleum, a pattern that had been foreshadowed by Italian-Tanzanian cooperation in 1970. Increasing Arab militancy in oil matters was heralded by Iraq's nationalization of its oil resources in 1972. Another Middle Eastern issue that involved Europe was civil strife in the Sudan, especially in 1972.

Alignment patterns on Middle East issues reveal that Israel was effectively isolated and that European concern about oil had produced a "pro-Arab" bias where once there had been a "pro-Israel" bias. Moreover, the activities of certain nonstate actors forcibly brought the Middle East dilemma to Europe's attention, in particular the attack by Arab commandos on the Israeli compound at the Munich Olympics in 1972 and the bargaining of OPEC (Organization of Petroleum Exporting Countries) over petroleum prices. Other important issues that arose in the context of *Extra-European Regional Crises* included the Sino-Soviet split and the U.N.-sponsored embargo of Rhodesia.

Detente appeared on only three factors but was involved in 16 per-

Table 81. European Perspectives on the Middle East, 1967–1972: Major Alignments

Pro-Israel	Neutral	Pro-Arab
Israel	FRG	Egypt
Jews in Europe	Belgium	"Black September"
and the World	Spain	Organization of the
	Portugal	Arab Boycott
		Algeria
		Tunisia
		Libya
		Iraq
		French Industry (CFP,
		Société Nationale
		d'Études et de Con-
		struction de Moteurs
		d'Aviation)
		France
		Vatican
		Italy

cent of the issues. We noted that the origins of *Detente* appeared in the second period, with principal reference to de Gaulle's "opening to the East." French overtures were also in evidence in 1968 and 1969. Other precursors of *Detente* early in the final period were discussions of East-West trade and cooperation between the Benelux Union and the Soviet Union. The major movement towards *Detente,* however, stemmed from the *Ostpolitik* activities of Chancellor Willy Brandt between 1968 and 1972.

As West German Foreign Minister, Brandt had taken the first step in his *Ostpolitik* by recognizing Rumania in January, 1967. The policy suffered a temporary setback with the Soviet occupation of Czechoslovakia in 1968, but it gained new momentum after Brandt became Chancellor in October, 1969. Within a week of taking office, Brandt indicated that he recognized that two German states existed. This was a momentous shift for a government which had previously threatened to sever relations with any government that recognized the East German regime or provided it with a semblance of legitimacy. By the end of the year discussions had been initiated between the Soviet Union and the FRG that were capped with success on August 12, 1970 by the signature of a West German-Soviet treaty of friendship and cooperation. Under the terms of the treaty, the FRG recognized the inviolability of Europe's postwar boundaries including the Oder-Neisse line as the western boundary of Poland; the Soviet Union promised not to oppose the peaceful reunification of Germany. A similar treaty was signed between West Germany and Poland in December. Further progress, however, was to depend on improvement of the status of West Berlin. Brandt took part in a series of unprecedented meetings with his East German counterpart, Willy Stoph, in 1970, and a treaty concerning the basis of their relations was signed between the two Germanys on December 21, 1972. Thus, agreement was reached on many of the very issues which had been at the heart of the early Cold War in Europe. *Ostpolitik* also involved closer trade and diplomatic relations between the FRG and the countries of Eastern Europe and became linked to broader issues of East-West relations. Among these issues were arms control and European security. For his efforts, Brandt received a Nobel Peace Prize.

The domestic politics of the Federal Republic during this period illustrates the role that nonstate actors, as political parties, can play in world affairs. Brandt governed as the leader of a coalition of his Social Democratic Party and the smaller Free Democratic Party. He realized that the Soviet Union and its Eastern European allies for their own reasons were prepared to normalize relations with West Germany, but he was faced with the Herculean task of convincing the German electorate that a revision of foreign policy was timely and prudent. He was strongly opposed by the Christian Democratic Union, the party which had governed the FRG from its creation until 1969, and by the ultra-conservative National Democratic

Party of Adolf von Thadden. Thus, Brandt pursued *Ostpolitik* with one hand, while staving off domestic opposition with the other. As *Detente* replaced the *Cold War,* the latter became the last-ranking superissue, appearing on only two factors and involving only 2 percent of the issues.

The third most important superissue continued to be *Gaullism,* which appeared on six factors and was associated with 20 percent of the issues. Its most significant aspect was France's opposition to an expansion of the functions or powers of the EEC. But, by the end of the period, even this had largely disappeared as had France's opposition to British entry into the Common Market. It was during this period that France underscored its attitude towards NATO by withdrawing from the Western European Union (1969).

Gaullist involvement in the Middle East has already been discussed briefly. At the outset of the period and following the June War of 1967, de Gaulle outraged world Jewish opinion by making what were interpreted as anti-Semitic remarks in public. These gave rise to anti-French gestures by Jewish groups throughout the world, including some in the United States. During this period French ties to the Arab world became more intimate, as was reflected in the sale of arms to Libya and the endorsement of certain Arab policy positions (1972).

A final Gaullist policy that provoked controversy was the continuation of nuclear testing in the atmosphere (1970, 1972). The French had refused to sign the treaty banning such tests in 1963 in order to perfect an

Table 82. Gaullism, 1967–1972: Major Coalitions

Pro-French	Neutral	Anti-French
France	Italy	United Nations
United States	Turkey	Other IGO's (Stockholm
United Kingdom	Spain	Conference on Envir-
USSR	Finland	onmental Pollution,
Netherlands	Norway	South Pacific Con-
FRG	Denmark	ference)
Belgium	GDR	French Ethnics (Chad
PRC	Laos	Rebels, Celtic League)
Libya	Ivory Coast	Israel
	Uganda	Jews
	Japan	Individuals
	Sweden	EEC
	Poland	Luxembourg
	Canada	South Vietnam
	U.S. Industry	Algeria
	(Ford, Westinghouse)	
	European Molecular	
	Biology Lab	
	NATO/WEU	
	French Media	
	(Le Monde, Le Figaro)	

independent deterrent. The shift in test site from the Sahara to the South Pacific did not reduce the outcry against France's flouting of world public opinion.

Once again *Gaullism* evoked a lively response on the part of both states and nonstate actors. The success of de Gaulle's independent policies is to some extent illustrated by the presence of both superpowers, as well as China, Britain, and West Germany, in the "pro-French" column. Yet the "special relationship" between France and the FRG, which was so important in the previous period, was coming to an end. The success of *Ostpolitik* and continuing German economic prosperity catapulted the FRG into a position of co-leader of Western Europe. French resistance to integration and NATO military cooperation was partly responsible for swelling the "neutral" column with several of the smaller European states such as Italy, Norway, and Denmark. Moreover, as before, nonstate actors were leading opponents of *Gaullism*. Although much of French Ethnic opposition had dissipated as a result of the solution of colonial difficulties, a rebellion in Chad against the French-supported regime and the appearance of separatist sympathies at home, in Brittany, were troublesome. French behavior also led to strong responses from the United Nations (payment of assessments), the EEC (British entry), and the South Pacific Conference (nuclear testing).

The fourth most important superissue was *Regime Stability,* which appeared on eight of the nine factors and involved 18 percent of the issues. Various nonstate actors such as political parties, labor unions, and groups of organized and unorganized demostrators were major participants in the superissue. Threats to the stability of particular regimes arose from both the political left and the political right. Thus, the leftist French revolutionary, Régis Debray, was active in Latin America, while leftist-led labor unions were partly responsible for unrest in France and in Italy. However, the activities of various right-wing groups proved to be an even greater threat to stability. Widespread right-wing opposition to detente surfaced throughout Europe in 1970, and the excesses of the Greek military junta elicited comment from many parts of the political spectrum in the same year. In addition, the specter of fascism in the form of the National Democratic Party in West Germany and the Italian Social Movement was disquieting. Other questions of *Regime Stability* arose in relation to Christian Democratic opposition to Brandt, Breton separatism, and unrest in the former Belgian trust territory of Ruanda.

In the third and final period, *Integration* dropped to fifth among the superissues, appearing on five factors and involved in 14 percent of the issues. The most important specific question was that of the expansion of the Common Market itself, especially in respect to Britain's proposed entry. The EEC was also divided over several economic issues in 1968, but

Table 83.   Integration, 1967–1972: Major Coalitions

Major Supporters	Somewhat Supportive	Neutral
EEC	Canada	France
FRG	Ireland	Individuals
Italy	Norway	
USSR	Sweden	
Netherlands	Denmark	
United Kingdom	Australia	
Belgium		
Luxembourg		
Benelux Union		
European Molecular Biology Lab		
European Inter-Parliamentary Conference on Water Pollution		
United States		
French Industry		
Lichtenstein		

many of these were resolved the following year. Finally, Europe witnessed the establishment of several new institutions to enhance cooperation in a variety of problem-oriented areas such as water pollution (1971), aircraft construction (1972), oceanic pollution (1972), and television technology (1972). The alignment table reflects the degree to which France became increasingly isolated in resisting Common Market expansion both in membership and in function.

The *Atlantic Alliance-Strategic* and *Economic* superissues ranked sixth and seventh respectively. The *Strategic* superissue appeared on four factors and involved 9 percent of the issues. It included general questions of NATO organization (1967), reaction to French withdrawal, proposals for arms control and a European Security Conference (1969), and questions of American troop levels in Europe (1970). The *Economic* superissue appeared on six factors and in 10 percent of the issues. Questions related to international monetary stability and adjustments between 1968 and 1971 were particularly important. They, in turn, held implications for EEC-U.S. trade relations, which were discussed in 1968 and again in 1970–1971. Lastly, the *Colonial* superissue, just as the *Cold War,* all but disappeared; it appeared on only two factors and included a mere 3 percent of the issues. For the most part it was related to civil strife in Ruanda in 1967 and the boycott of Rhodesia in 1972.

The pattern of superissue coappearance for the third period reflects the sharp changes brought about by the lessening of the *Cold War,* the emergence of *Detente,* and the end of traditional *Colonialism.* The relationships involving the *Cold War* and *Colonial* superissues, many of which were critical in earlier periods, "washed out."

Table 84.   Western Europe Superissue Coappearance, 1967–1972

	I	II	III	IV	V	VI	VII	VIII	IX
I. Integration	–								
II. Atlantic Alliance-Strategic	.89	–							
III. Atlantic Alliance-Economic	.91	.80	–						
IV. Cold War	.29	.33	.50	–					
V. Detente	.75	.86	.67	.40	–				
VI. Gaullism	.91	.80	.83	.25	.67	–			
VII. Colonial and Neocolonial	.57	.33	.50	0	.40	.50	–		
VIII. Extra-European Regional Crises	.73	.60	.67	.25	.67	.83	.50	–	
IX. Regime Stability	.62	.50	.71	.20	.36	.71	.40	.71	–

When we turn to the coappearance scores themselves, it is clear that the *Gaullist-Integration* link remains the closest. *Integration* also coappears regularly with *Atlantic Alliance-Strategic* and *Economic* issues, and *Detente* is closely linked to *Strategic* questions. The most important superissue of the period, *Extra-European Regional Crises,* is most closely associated with *Gaullism,* largely because of France's intrusion into non-European issues. Yet it shows few important links with other superissues. Finally, *Regime Stability* exhibits a somewhat idiosyncratic pattern of coappearance because of the particularistic nature of the issues of which it was composed.

The extent of the changes which took place in European politics between the second and third periods is revealed in the weak correlation between superissue coappearance for the two periods (rho = .08). The coappearance correlation between the first and third periods is, in fact, negative (rho = −.13), thereby suggesting the cumulative change in specific issues over the entire period of the study.

The years between 1967 and 1972 marked something of an eclipse in the role of nonstate actors in Europe. There were a number of reasons for this. In the first place, *Detente* occurred largely within a state-to-state context even though nonstate actors such as NATO were often indirect targets. In addition, the demise of *Colonialism* deprived the region of many of its major nonstate disrupters such as the FLN and OAS. Consequently, the period was largely peaceful, and cooperative dyads outnumbered conflictful ones on the order of three-and-one-half to one; organized violence was virtually non-existent.

Of the most active initiators, only five were nonstate, and the French Ethnic, Governmental Noncentral, Individuals, Business, Communist Parties and Other Parties categories disappeared; salience showed a similar trend away from nonstate groups.

Despite their reduced activity in this period, nonstate actors were

Table 85. *The Most Active Initiators in Western Europe, 1967–1972*

	France	(255)
	FRG	(161)
	United Kingdom	(114)
	United States	(104)
	Netherlands	(64)
	USSR	(63)
	Belgium	(58)
(nostac)	Religious	(56)
(nostac)	European IGO's	(52)
	Sweden	(52)
	Italy	(49)
	GDR	(44)
(nostac)	Cultural	(42)
(nostac)	Western Defense	(36)
(nostac)	Labor	(35)
	Norway	(35)
	Spain	(33)
	Portugal	(33)
	Finland	(33)
	Denmark	(33)
	Iceland	(33)

Table 86. *The Most Salient Targets in Western Europe, 1967–1972*

	France	(190)
	FRG	(155)
	United Kingdom	(131)
	United States	(128)
	Netherlands	(73)
	USSR	(70)
(nostac)	Individuals	(66)
(nostac)	Cultural	(56)
	Italy	(54)
	Belgium	(52)
	Sweden	(47)
(nostac)	Business	(45)
	Spain	(41)
	Denmark	(41)
(nostac)	European IGO's	(37)
(nostac)	Media	(36)
	Portugal	(35)
	Norway	(35)
(nostac)	Religious	(34)
	Finland	(33)
	Iceland	(33)

Table 87.   Disruptive-Supportive Behavior, 1967–1972

Disrupters		Supporters	
Labor	(−23)	France	(+135)
Media	(−14)	United Kingdom	(+114)
Other Ethnics	(−11)	FRG	(+99)
Israel	(−8)	United States	(+90)
Zaïre	(−6)	Netherlands	(+60)
Other Parties	(−5)	Sweden	(+52)
Greece	(−4)	USSR	(+49)
Cambodia	(−3)	Norway	(+35)
(Four actors tied with −2)		Religious	(+34)
		(Five actors tied with +33)	

again among the system's major disrupters. With the disappearance of the French Ethnic category, the major sources of disruption were regional in origin. Labor groups and Media played important roles in the resurgence of the *Regime Stability* superissue, especially in France, Italy, and West Germany. The presence of Other Ethnics reflects the disturbances in Chad and Ruanda, while that of Other Parties represents the right-wing revival that we have mentioned. Finally, all of the disruptive nation-states took part in *Extra-European Regional Crises,* the dominant superissue of the period. Among supporters, the most interesting addition was the Soviet Union, a fact which reflected the progress of detente in Europe.

Western Europe as a Complex Conglomerate

The behavior of nonstate actors as they shifted sides on various issues and superissues over time reveals that the complex conglomerate model is as suitable for a politically and economically developed region like Western Europe as for less developed regions like Latin America and the Middle East.

Table 88.   Western European Superissue Coappearance, 1948–1972

	I	II	III	IV	V	VI	VII	VIII	IX
I. Integration	−								
II. Atlantic Alliance-Strategic	.90	−							
III. Atlantic Alliance-Economic	.79	.78	−						
IV. Cold War	.77	.81	.63	−					
V. Detente	.69	.73	.55	.63	−				
VI. Gaullism	.79	.72	.69	.59	.69	−			
VII. Colonial and Neocolonial	.74	.67	.63	.68	.41	.56	−		
VIII. Extra-European Regional Crises	.86	.76	.63	.73	.69	.74	.68	−	
IX. Regime Stability	.71	.60	.67	.57	.48	.67	.67	.76	−

Table 89. *The Most Active Initiators in Western Europe, 1948-1972*

	France	(1442)
	FRG	(806)
	United States	(715)
	United Kingdom	(479)
	Italy	(326)
	USSR	(322)
	Netherlands	(280)
	Belgium	(270)
(nostac)	Governmental Noncentral	(206)
(nostac)	European IGO's	(199)
(nostac)	Religious	(198)
(nostac)	Individuals	(192)
(nostac)	French Ethnics	(182)
(nostac)	Cultural	(159)
(nostac)	Other Parties	(154)
(nostac)	Labor	(150)
	GDR	(137)
(nostac)	Communist Parties	(133)
(nostac)	United Nations	(125)
(nostac)	Business	(121)

Table 90. *The Most Salient Targets in Western Europe, 1948-1972*

	France	(1134)
	FRG	(818)
	United States	(738)
	United Kingdom	(482)
(nostac)	Individuals	(398)
	Italy	(321)
	USSR	(295)
	Belgium	(266)
	Netherlands	(247)
(nostac)	Governmental Noncentral	(230)
(nostac)	French Ethnic	(213)
(nostac)	United Nations	(204)
(nostac)	Business	(196)
(nostac)	Cultural	(171)
(nostac)	Media	(169)
(nostac)	Western Defense	(149)
(nostac)	European IGO's	(146)
	GDR	(129)
(nostac)	Religious	(116)
	Luxembourg	(115)

By examining shifting loyalties, we have observed the forging of linkages and the exertion of influence on the political processes of the region. In this way it was possible to assess the changing role that nonstate actors have played. They have clearly had more direct influence in the context of certain superissues such as *Colonialism* than in others such as *Detente*. However, the fact that in Europe the superissues were highly interrelated (as shown by coappearance scores) suggests that nonstate actors have had an indirect impact even on questions in which they did not often directly participate.

The pattern of superissue coappearance for the entire period underscored the centrality of *Integration* and hence the growth of European institutions for the European region. *Integration, more than any other superissue, was closely associated with the other superissues. Strategic* issues of the Atlantic Alliance also regularly coappeared with other superissues, particularly with *Integration*. The dominant superissue of the 1967– 1972 period, *Extra-European Regional Crises,* showed a strong overall pattern of coappearance, while *Gaullism* and the *Cold War* were somewhat less strongly associated with the other superissues. Finally, *Detente* and *Regime Stability* coappeared the least with other superissues and therefore involved more idiosyncratic behavior than did the others.

Activity and salience levels also demonstrated the significance of nonstate actors for the Western European region over the entire period. At least half the members in each category were nonstate. The disruptive-supportive scores are even more eloquent indicators of *nostac* behavior. French Ethnics were overwhelmingly the most consistent source of disruption in the system, and seven of the ten leading disrupters were *nostac*. The nation-states of the region were generally supporters, and the three national disrupters (Egypt, Zaïre, and Syria) were extraregional. Thus, throughout the period as a whole, disruption in Western Europe originated in large measure from outside the system itself. Indeed, five of the seven leading supporters of the system were members of the European Common Market,

Table 91. Disruptive-Supportive Behavior, 1948-1972

Disrupters		Supporters	
French Ethnic	(−146)	United States	(+539)
Labor	(−52)	France	(+506)
Other Parties	(−38)	FRG	(+424)
Communist Parties	(−33)	United Kingdom	(+363)
Other Ethnics	(−21)	Netherlands	(+198)
Media	(−15)	Belgium	(+190)
Egypt	(−13)	Italy	(+186)
Governmental Noncentral	(−9)	European IGO's	(+147)
Zaïre	(−8)	Religious	(+114)
Syria	(−7)	Cultural	(+107)

and a sixth (Great Britain) joined later. The leading supporter of the system was the United States, a fact which reflected the massive aid and involvement of the United States in speeding European recovery during the initial period and maintaining it thereafter. The leading nonstate supporter was the group of European IGO's that included the following institutions:

Table 92. Western European Intergovernmental Organizations, 1948-1972

European Coal and Steel Community
European Economic Community (Common Market)
European Atomic Energy Community (EURATOM)
Organization for European Economic Cooperation
Organization for Economic Cooperation and Development
European Payments Union
European Cooperation Administration
Marshall Plan Council
European Constitutional Assembly
Western European Aviation Organization
European Interparliamentary Conference on Water Pollution
Council of Europe
Intergovernmental Committee for European Migration
Benelux Union
Trade Union Advisory Commission of the European Recovery Program

In sum, our analysis has indicated the key role played by nonstate actors from within the region as well as those which penetrated it from without. The gradual disappearance of these external sources of disruption permitted the region to make even greater progress towards resolving controversial problems. European institutions that were created as part of the postwar process of integration also were important contributors to regional stability. It is, in part, for this reason that other regions have sought to emulate Western Europe in creating similar institutions, although up until now, they have not enjoyed the same degree of success.

The Halfway House
of Europe:
A Perspective

TEN

Europe, we have seen, is an exceedingly complex regional system. It has a much greater number and variety of internal pressure groups and political parties than the Middle East or Latin America, and many of these are highly institutionalized. The same holds true for governmental and nongovernmental entities that overarch and cross the nation-states.

Traditional distinctions between "domestic" and "international," especially as far as Europe is concerned, obscure more than they reveal. The proliferation of actors in all of our categories and the multiplicity of links among them have reached a point where it might be said that the European system is like a "halfway house" and that Europeans are like wayfarers upon an uncharted road. To illustrate the growth of these links consider that between 1960 and 1972 Brussels, the headquarters of the Common Market, has been the site of an over 200 percent increase in the number of headquarters and secondary offices of interstate groups (both governmental and nongovernmental). This is almost twice the increase experienced by any other major world city.[1]

Thus answering a general question like "what is foreign policy?" in the European context becomes an extremely difficult task. European Economic Community institutions have decision-making authority over matters such as antitrust and agricultural prices that previously have been under the exclusive jurisdiction of national governments. Other sectors, such as education, social welfare, and public safety, remain under the primary control of nation-states. France has maintained jealous guard over its own national defense policies—including an independent nuclear deterrent—which has had a profoundly retarding effect on regional efforts to achieve greater coordination in this area. (Such an attitude toward the core are of defense is, however, not characteristic of France alone.) To com-

1. E. Tew, *Yearbook of International Organizations, 1972–1973*, p. 886.

plicate the situation still further, the label *foreign policy* is often used for *joint* European positions on tariffs, monetary reforms, and so forth, vis-à-vis the outside world. In effect, then, there are at least three manifestations of "foreign policy": one is the policies of "Europe" toward the outside world; another is the policies of the various actors toward one another as well as toward "outsiders"; and the third involves the relations of states with nonstate actors including the EEC itself. (A similar difficulty in identifying "foreign policy" has existed, for example, in the British Empire and the Soviet bloc.)

Charles de Gaulle was a defender of the traditional nation-state system, specifically of the national integrity and "destiny" of France. Moreover, the French President's balkiness in this regard was a major source of *intra-* as well as *interstate* conflict during the early years of the Common Market experiment. De Gaulle was suspicious of *all* nonstate actors including alliances and corporations that, he believed, diminished his state's "sovereignty" or freedom of decision and action. Nevertheless, even de Gaulle saw "Europe" as a great deal more than a hodgepodge of nation-states, that is, as more than the simple sum of its parts. This is a view shared by those, like Henry Kissinger, who conceive of a global trend toward multipolarity, a new "pentagonal" relationship among the United States, the Soviet Union, Europe, Japan, and China. It is significant that "Europe" is the only unit in the relationship that is not a nation-state.

In Chapters 6 and 8, we focused on a specific nonstate actor prominent in the region under consideration: guerrilla groups in the Middle East and multinational corporations in Latin America. We are continuing this practice for Europe, in that our emphasis will be on the EEC "family." We will not be providing a comprehensive discussion of the past evolution, present status, and possible future of the EEC. There are already a plethora of such studies in the literature.[2] Rather, we will be looking at the EEC in the light of neo-functionalist theories of regional "integration," which over the years have derived much of their inspiration from the European experience. Neo-functionalist theorists have themselves engaged in a continuing critique of their own propositions, taking into account ongoing events in Europe and elsewhere, and this body of theory is considerably more sophisticated than it was at the outset.[3] It is our contention,

2. The reader might want to begin with Leon N. Lindberg and Stuart A. Scheingold, *Europe's Would-Be Polity* (Englewood Cliffs, N.J.: Prentice-Hall, 1970); W. Hartley Clark, *The Politics of the Common Market* (Englewood Cliffs, N.J.: Prentice-Hall, 1967); and A. E. Walsh and John Paxton, *The Structure and Development of the Common Market* (London: Hutchinson & Co., 1968).

3. We have drawn the basic organization of this chapter and numerous insights from Roger D. Hansen's review-essay, "European Integration: Forward March, Parade Rest, or Dismissed?" *International Organization* 27:2 (Spring 1973), pp. 225–54.

and the main purpose of the present chapter is to demonstrate, that refinements in neo-functionalist theories point in the direction of the complex conglomerate model. Put another way, the complex conglomerate model may offer a more productive way—or at least a complementary way—of analyzing the phenomena with which neo-functionalists are concerned.

Toward a More Precise Definition of "Integration"

Neo-functionalist theorists, indeed all integration theorists, have gradually recognized the need for a more precise definition of the central concept (the "dependent variable") of "integration." The concept has often been used almost interchangeably with words like "cooperation" and "community"[4] and, as this might suggest, has seemed to involve both "process" and "outcome."[5] Moreover, there has been a good deal of uncertainty as to exactly which "outcome" should be emphasized in theory-building. Joseph S. Nye argues that the most "fruitful approach is to break apart the concept of integration, develop concrete measurements for its component parts, and leave the relationship between them open for empirical verification."[6] He has urged the breaking down of the central concept into three basic types: "economic integration (formation of a transnational economy), social integration (formation of a transnational society), and political integration (formation of a transnational political system)." He then subdivides the three basic types into "more specific and useful sub-types."[7] For instance, he distinguishes several subtypes under the heading of political integration: "institutional integration," "policy integration" ("the extent to which a group of countries acts as a group in making domestic or foreign policy decisions," regardless of institutional integration), "attitudinal integration" ("the extent to which a group of people develop a sense of common identity and mutual obligation"), and "security community" (the emergence of "reliable expectations of nonviolent relations" among particular states).[8]

It is especially the subtype of policy integration that appears to be a natural bridge to the "issues" and "actors" emphases of the complex con-

4. J. S. Nye, *Peace in Parts* (Boston: Little, Brown and Co., 1971), p. 24.
5. Ernst B. Haas, "The Study of Regional Integration: Reflections on the Joy and Anguish of Pretheorizing," in Leon N. Lindberg and Stuart A. Scheingold, eds., "Regional Integration: Theory and Research," special edition of *International Organization* 24:4 (Autumn 1970), p. 622. This issue later appeared as *Regional Integration: Theory and Research* (Cambridge: Harvard University Press, 1971).
6. Nye, *Peace in Parts*, p. 26.
7. *Ibid*, pp. 26–27.
8. *Ibid*, pp. 27–28, *passim*.

glomerate model. "Issues" may be conceived so as to delineate the principal areas of policy-making, including those like welfare, trade, and
education that are usually regarded as basically economic and social.
Furthermore, the "actors" dimension of the model suggests that the notion
of "policy-making" should be expanded to embrace other entities than
"groups of countries." For that matter, a firm measurement of "the extent
to which a group of countries acts as a group in making domestic or foreign
policy decisions" would seem to imply that it is important to determine
what other actors are, in fact, influential in the decision-making process.
The distinction between "domestic" and "foreign" policies might be abandoned altogether. In sum, why not ask simply what actors actually influence what kinds of policy in the region?[9] How they influence it is an
additional question, which concerns the processes (as distinct from outcomes) that are of interest to the neo-functionalist.

The Relevance of Transaction Data
and "Public Opinion"

Neo-functionalists have also been reassessing the usefulness to the study of
regional integration of transaction data about the flows of such things as
goods, mail, and persons across national boundaries. In general, they seem
to agree that data of this type are reasonably "objective" indicators of
increasing interdependence, that is, of the emergence of various forms of
"community." Although it appears probable that some degree of objective
interdependence is a precondition for successful political integration, the
precise relationship between the two is as yet poorly understood.[10] In
addition, it remains to be determined whether a certain level of transactions is a *precondition* for the process of integration, whether it is the *result*
of such a process, or whether it is no more than an *indicator* or "symptom"
of the process. Once again, the complex conglomerate model offers a promising framework for future research. If policy-making with respect to particular issues is to be a principal concern, then correlations between
transactions and prevailing patterns of decision-making can be explored in

9. This seems parallel to those decision-making models which focus on issues,
interests, and values as central concepts. See, for example, Graham T. Allison,
Essence of Decision (Boston: Little, Brown and Co., 1971); and Theodore
J. Lowi, "Making Democracy Safe for the World: National Politics and
Foreign Policy," in James N. Rosenau, ed., *Domestic Sources of Foreign
Policy* (New York: The Free Press, 1967), pp. 295–331.
10. See, for example, Donald J. Puchala, "International Transactions and
Regional Integration," in Lindberg and Scheingold, eds., "Theory and Re-
search," pp. 732–63. See also, Richard Rosecrance and Arthur Stein, "Inter-
dependence: Myth or Reality?" *World Politics* 26:1 (October 1973), pp. 1–27.

a much more specific context. For example, trade flows are likely to be related to trade policies, though possibly not to questions of defense.

Nye's category of "attitudinal integration" leads us to another issue, the relevance of "public opinion" to regional integration. Ronald Inglehart concludes that the public's influence "can vary widely,"[11] depending on three main factors. The first is the structure of national decision-making institutions; that is, the degree to which they are pluralistic or monolithic, including the extent of ideological unity among decision-making elites both as to policy *per se* and as to the legitimacy of public input. The second is the distribution of political skills within a society, which involves a distinction between an "attentive public" and the rest of the citizenry with little interest in, or knowledge about, public affairs. And the third is "the degree to which the given decision relates to deep-seated values among the public or evokes only relatively superficial feelings."[12]

Inglehart points out that European countries have democratic political institutions and modern, pluralistic societies. The expansion of higher education also has made for a relatively broad distribution of political skills. Public opinion polls, he demonstrates, consistently indicate that European publics (with the possible exception of British citizens) are basically favorably disposed to regional integration and that members of the younger generation are even more supportive of integration than their elders.[13] According to Inglehart, over the years public awareness and influence have actually been increasing to such an extent that what was once regarded as the public's "permissive consensus" allowing elites to pursue integration at their own speed now has become a definite force pushing elites into making ever-greater concessions to European supranationalism. In a case study, Inglehart maintains that pro-integration sentiment on the part of the French people contributed greatly to a decline in de Gaulle's electoral majority and forced his successor, Georges Pompidou, to adopt a much more positive stance toward the EEC.

Inglehart's analysis centers on public opinion *in general* as expressed in opinion polls and at the ballot box. Yet it should be stressed that in Europe, public opinion is aggregated and articulated, led and manipulated, and even occasionally flagrantly misrepresented by many varied and highly institutionalized subnational groups. Periodic national elections account for the important role of political parties in this regard. When the EEC ceased to be a matter of interest solely to "technocrats" and broke through the threshold of public consciousness, it was almost inevitable that rival parties

11. Ronald Inglehart, "Public Opinion and Regional Integration," in Lindberg and Scheingold, *Theory and Research,* p. 764.
12. *Ibid,* pp. 765–68.
13. National identity is less of a deep-seated value for the younger generation.

would use it as a political "football." One may perhaps view in this light the British Labour Party's attempt to renegotiate the terms accepted by the previous Conservative government for entry into the EEC.[14]

Pressure groups are also of major significance in the European context. Even prior to the 1965 presidential elections and contributing to the erosion of his electoral support, de Gaulle's boycott of the EEC in that year met determined opposition from a host of internal groups, most notably farmers' organizations and agricultural workers' trade unions. The reasons for the 1965 crisis, ostensibly disagreements over the Common Agricultural Policy (CAP), were actually much more complicated.[15] De Gaulle objected to the proposed transfer of budgetary authority over the CAP to the European Parliament and to a related proposal that would have given the EEC Commission independent sources of financial support from industrial tariffs and agricultural levies. Moreover, he used the occasion to make a more fundamental protest against both the federalist philosophy of the Commission and the qualified majority voting in the Council of Ministers provided for in the Treaty of Rome that had established the EEC. In addition, he indirectly lashed out at his European allies for their continued preference for leadership in matters of defense by the United States, rather than by France. Nevertheless, the breakdown of the CAP was of the most immediate consequence to French agriculture, and the "attentive"·*and organized* public in that sector responded accordingly. De Gaulle's popularity in opinion polls declined sharply with the rise of interest group opposition to official policy,[16] and there were massive defections from the Gaullist camp in certain rural regions on election day.[17]

The role of internal pressure groups has been greatly in evidence, as well, in the continuing debate over the United Kingdom's association with the EEC.[18] Major groups that owe their very existence to the debate included, on the side of the supporters, the Common Market Campaign and the U.K. Council of the European Movement, and on the side of the opposition, the Anti-Common Market League and the Keep Britain Out Campaign (subsumed under the Common Market Safeguards Campaign after 1969). Other groups also participated in the controversy, although

14. See Uwe Kitzinger, *Diplomacy and Persuasion: How Britain Joined the Common Market* (London: Thames and Hudson, 1973), Chap. 10.
15. See Leon N. Lindberg, "Integration as a Source of Stress on the European Community System," in Joseph S. Nye, Jr., ed., *International Regionalism* (Boston: Little Brown and Co., 1968), pp. 231–68; and John Newhouse, *Collision In Brussels* (New York: W. W. Norton, 1967).
16. Hanns Peter Muth, *French Agriculture and the Political Integration of Western Europe* (Leyden, Holland: A. W. Sijthoff, 1970), p. 236.
17. *Ibid*, p. 244.
18. See Kitzinger, *Diplomacy and Persuasion;* and Robert J. Lieber, *British Politics and European Unity* (Berkeley: University of California Press, 1970).

their primary interests always lay elsewhere. Church leaders, the Council of British Industries, and the British media were all supportive of British membership in the EEC; indeed, in the case of the first two, more supportive than their rank and file generally. The National Farmers Union gradually moved from opposition to U.K.–EEC ties to a position of public neutrality with behind-the-scenes negotiations both with the British Government and with the NFU's interest group counterparts in the Common Market. On the other hand, with its leadership badly divided, the powerful Trades Union Congress from the start adopted a rather ambivalent stance.

Several additional observations amplifying Inglehart's analysis are in order at this juncture. Inglehart recognizes that whatever overall patterns of institutional structures, skills, and values may be, the influence of public opinion varies as well with "the given decision"—elite competition may offer the public a wider range of policy choices on some occasions than others, and different decisions may touch different values. We have already implied that it is also important to emphasize the roles of parties and pressure groups that presume to speak for the public, that shape public attitudes, and that have more consistent influence over national decision-makers than the public-at-large (even an "attentive public") could ever hope to have as an unorganized mass. Moreover, the complex conglomerate model suggests that a key variable here is the nature and content of specific issues, not particular decisions.[19] Specific issues tend to involve certain national decision-makers (and not others), certain political parties (and not others) or no political parties at all, certain pressure groups (and not others), and certain members of the attentive public whether organized or not (and not others). The issue of industrial complementarity, for example, over a period of time will likely involve government ministries that are responsible for national policies of concern to their business clientele, various business pressure groups, and possibly labor and consumer groups to the extent that jobs or consumer interests may be affected. But political parties, the Church, farm groups, the media, the vast majority of unorganized citizens, and so forth *may* ignore the issue entirely.

Thus far, following Inglehart's lead, we have confined our attention to public opinion as it influences policy-making at the national level. However, Inglehart's analysis can be faulted precisely because it is too anchored in a state-centric view of European affairs. Policy-making with respect to many central issues now involves not only government officials and subnational groups but Community institutions and regional parties and pressure groups as well.

19. For a suggestive list of "issue areas" drawn up for the rather different purpose of assessing the "scope of collective decision-making," see Leon N. Lindberg, "Political Integration as a Multidimensional Phenomenon Requiring Multivariate Measurement," in Lindberg and Scheingold, eds., "Theory and Research," p. 664.

The Commission, made up of individuals appointed by, but not directly accountable to, national governments has the *sole* formal power of policy initiative within the EEC. Its work is supported by several thousand highly-skilled civil servants who have acquired a stake in the survival and prosperity of the Common Market. Final decisions as to EEC policies rest with the Council of Ministers, although on the basis of an "understanding" that resulted from the 1965 crisis which gives an informal "veto" over all "important" matters to member governments. Leon N. Lindberg and Stuart A. Scheingold observe:

> If we define power traditionally, that is, in terms of formal authority or the ability to impose sanctions or the possession of a monopoly of legitimate force, then it is clear that the Council is all-powerful and the Commission is powerless. But political scientists have tended to move away from such formal and "negative" definitions of power. In this revised view, power can be defined "positively," that is, as *participation* in decision making, as *objective success* in getting one's preferences or goals accepted by others. By such a standard the Commission has wielded and continues to wield substantial decision-making power in the Community process.[20]

The European Parliament is a lesser "advisory" body, composed of "parliamentarians" elected by national legislatures. A protocol concluded by member-states in April, 1970 envisaged an expansion in the European Parliament's budgetary powers, which was a direct reversal of yet another outcome of the 1965 crisis. In addition, the Parliament by a two-thirds majority can dismiss the Commission. The Court of Justice hears suits by Community institutions, governments, private groups, and even individuals concerning actions or inaction by the EEC or other interested parties. Requests for interpretation of Community law by national courts are wholly voluntary, but the Court nevertheless has had a full case load.

The European Parliament is organized along national party lines, and most of the major pressure groups organized in national societies have their regional counterparts. W. Hartley Clark comments:

> By 1964, a total of some 233 different organizations concerned with numerous special aspects of private and economic life had been established to deal with the Common Market, and about half of them had set up offices near the Common Market headquarters in Brussels, at their own expense and on their own initiative. The list of their names reads like the roster of lobbying organizations published in the American *Congressional Record*—The Association for the Coffee Trade and Industry in the EEC, The Banking Federation of the EEC, the Common Market Opticians Group, to name but a few. Even Italy's Communist-led labor union, the C.G.I.L. opened a Brussels office in 1963 as a revisionist gesture. . . .[21]

20. Lindberg and Scheingold, *Europe's Would-Be Polity*, p. 92.
21. Clark, *Politics of the Common Market*, p. 103.

Consider also examples of Community-wide interest groups, mentioned by Lindberg,[22] which issued formal statements condemning President de Gaulle's threat to the EEC in the 1965 crisis: the Committee of EEC Farmers' Organization, the EEC Farm Cooperative Community, the Conference of EEC Agricultural Workers Trade Unions, the Executive Committee of the EEC Free Trade Unions, the Federation of EEC Industries, and the Permanent Conference of EEC Chambers of Commerce. Many groups are directly represented in the EEC's Economic and Social Committee, which advises both the Commission and the Council of Ministers. The Committee represents employers, trade unions, consumers, and so forth. Clark explains the affinity between such groups and the EEC Commission: "Since it is the sectors of European life represented by these groups that the Common Market will be serving or regulating, effective lines of communication have to be developed with them so that policies can be formed in the context of all relevant facts and interests."[23] In addition, the Commission welcomes these groups as exponents of "European thinking" both at the Community level and, especially, through their local affiliates within member states.[24]

The Dynamics of the Integration Process and Probable Outcomes

Initially, neo-functionalist thinkers explicitly or implicitly posited an almost inexorable trend toward greater regional integration, beginning with joint exercise of less controversial economic tasks, moving to more "political" sectors, and possibly culminating in full fledged political unification. In their view, there would be a virtually *automatic* "spillover" of tasks. Joint tasks were presumed to have an inherent "expansive logic," which would be revealed to decision-makers through experience ("feedback"). The competent performance of initial tasks would necessitate the assumption of ever-wider tasks. Hence greater regional integration would emerge as an "unintended consequence" of previous decisions.[25] Insofar as the process was not entirely automatic, it was expected that the actors involved would be inclined to opt for more integration whenever the opportunity presented itself. As Roger D. Hansen comments, "The national decision-

22. Lindberg, "Integration as a Source of Stress," pp. 243–44.
23. Clark, *Politics of the Common Market*, p. 105.
24. *Ibid*, pp. 105–6.
25. See, for example, Ernst B. Haas, *Beyond the Nation-State* (Stanford: Stanford University Press, 1964); and Haas and Philippe C. Schmitter, "Economics and Differential Patterns of Political Integration: Projections about Unity in Latin America," in *International Political Communities: An Anthology* (Garden City, N.Y.: Doubleday & Company, 1966), pp. 259–99.

makers in the early models were almost exclusively assumed to be what [Ernst] Haas originally called economic incrementalists, actors who would be most responsive to the demands of spillover."[26] Moreover, the neo-functionalists placed considerable faith in the policy leadership of "technocrats" residing in regional institutions like the EEC Commission.

Without question, there has been an impressive amount of spillover in Europe's progress over the years from the European Coal and Steel Community, to the Treaty of Rome, to the 1969 Hague Summit protocols, to the admission of the United Kingdom and other new members in 1973. Successive crises have been resolved and, however serious many of these were at the time, in retrospect most appear to have been more in the nature of "creative dissonance" rather than insurmountable obstacles to forward momentum. Quite in accord with the complex conglomerate model, spillover has been achieved in large part by shifting coalitions among different actors, with considerable use being made of mechanisms normally associated with coalitions such as "side payments" and "log-rolling."[27] Spillover still seems to be at work in current attempts to create a monetary union in Europe, which is a "logical" step in the light of the difficulties previously encountered in financing the CAP without a common currency. Furthermore, some observers believe that there may yet be additional spillover inherent in the CAP,[28] for example, in the area of transport or perhaps even the full economic union forseen by the Hague Summit.

Nevertheless, neo-functionalists have concluded from experience in the European setting and elsewhere that spillover is much less automatic than they had originally expected. Paralleling the complex conglomerate model's stress on the need to differentiate among issues, they have recognized a much wider range of possible interim and final outcomes within particular policy sectors. Philippe C. Schmitter, for instance, has outlined several "strategic options" available to actors in specific contexts. These options include "spillover," "spill-around," "build-up," "retrench," "muddle-about," "spill-back," and "encapsulate."[29] We shall not dwell on Schmitter's definition of each of these options, but it is notable that several of them involve an actual *decrease* in the "scope" of *existing* joint tasks and/or of the actual authority granted to community institutions. Schmitter maintains that "encapsulation"—the "marginal modification" of a single sector without significant spillover—will be the one likely to prevail most frequently.[30]

26. Hansen, "European Integration," p. 232.
27. Lindberg and Scheingold, *Europe's Would-Be Polity,* Chap. 4.
28. See, for instance, James A. Caporaso, "Encapsulated Integrative Patterns vs. Spillover: The Cases of Transport Integration in the European Economic Community," *International Studies Quarterly* 14:4 (December 1970), p. 385.
29. Philippe C. Schmitter, "A Revised Theory of Regional Integration," in Lindberg and Scheingold, eds., "Theory and Research," p. 846.
30. *Ibid,* p. 867.

An early criticism by Stanley Hoffmann of the virtually-automatic-spillover thesis was that it failed to distinguish between sectors of "high politics" and those of "low politics." According to Hoffmann, spillover and further integration were much more likely to occur in the latter, mainly consisting of economic sectors that could be handled on a technical basis, than in the former, consisting of sensitive sectors such as national defense.[31] Nye added that "high politics" sectors are rather different in the Third World, where development issues are matters of foremost concern.[32] In any event, the unqualified inclusion of economic sectors in the "low politics" category early-on seemed questionable even in Europe, since issues like agriculture generated tremendous controversy. Lawrence Scheinman examined the effort to integrate nuclear research and development under Euratom and found that this sector, though technical on the surface, in practice proved to be extremely "political" and crisis-ridden. Crises, at least in this sector, were disintegrative in their consequences.[33] Certainly, recent European difficulties in formulating a joint energy and petroleum policy confirm the potential explosiveness of apparently economic questions.

On the other hand, James D. Caporaso suggests that the most useful distinction to be made is between "functionally diffuse" and "functionally specific" sectors such as agriculture and transport, respectively. Although agriculture has been a "highly dynamic" sector, characterized by "periods of enormous success . . . followed by periods of disappointment and crisis," its functionally diffuse nature has made "package deals" and "attendant intra-sector trade-offs" possible.[34] Also, the very diffuseness of the agricultural issue, coupled with crises like the one in 1965, has forced decision-makers to reexamine the entire structure of the Community—thus enhancing spillover.[35] In contrast, the transport sector has bogged down and has become controversial precisely because it is "technical." "The very concreteness of transport's tasks," Caporaso contends, "prevented elites from entering into compromises based on 'splitting the difference'."[36]

The thrust of the foregoing critiques of the spillover thesis has been that different patterns are likely to characterize different policy sectors. Still another line of response to the thesis has emphasized "the range of relevant actors and actor motivations."[37] Karl Kaiser has argued that the distinc-

31. Stanley Hoffmann, "Obstinate or Obsolete? The Fate of the Nation State and the Case of Western Europe" in Nye, ed., *International Regionalism*, pp. 377–429.
32. Joseph S. Nye, Jr., "Central American Regional Integration," in Nye, ed., *International Regionalism*, pp. 377–429.
33. Lawrence Scheinman, "Euratom: Nuclear Integration in Europe," in J. S. Nye, ed., *International Regionalism*, pp. 269–83.
34. Caporaso, "Integrative Patterns," p. 393.
35. *Ibid*, p. 385.
36. *Ibid*, p. 394.
37. Hansen, "European Integration," p. 232.

tion between high and low politics exists solely in the minds of actors and may shift on occasion even within particular sectors.[38] Indeed, our own research into the relationship between issues, alignments, and behavior over a period of time in Europe appears to support Kaiser's hypothesis. Haas himself has conceded that "dramatic-political" actors such as de Gaulle may step forward from time to time and temporarily arrest the integration process.[39] In general, as Hansen expresses it (himself quoting Nye):

> The idea that supranational technocrats and economic-incrementalist politicians "could bypass the electoral or support politicians and forge links to the ever stronger regional organization until *engrenage* had proceeded so far that it was too late for anyone to change the pattern" has been set aside. In its place one finds a broad spectrum of actors, subnational to supranational, economic-incremental to dramatic-political, with all the combinations in between.[40]

Whatever their attitudes toward integration in principle or with regard to certain sectors, national decision-makers, subnational groups, and the citizenry-at-large constantly have other preoccupations as well. Edward L. Morse remarks:

> In any one year the probability is high that one of the major European states is preparing for or in the process of an electoral campaign. Each time, it is obliged to suspend its own momentum in the organization of Europe—or it may attempt to manipulate the EC for electoral ends.[41]

National elections *may* (à la Inglehart) give the citizenry an opportunity to express their views on integration, but often elections also turn on local issues with little relevance to the region as a whole. At any rate, elections are powerful "distractions" for national leaders and subnational groups alike. The same might be said for a host of internal problems that persist between elections (not to mention continuing problems of relationships external to the region, to which we shall turn shortly). Italy offers an example of a country that has been almost paralyzed by successive governmental shifts and endemic economic ills. In this way what we have called *Regime Stability* may become deeply enmeshed in the integration process.

The multitude of policy preoccupations of national leaders especially has been a factor contributing to what Lindberg and Scheingold call "the

38. Karl Kaiser, "The U.S. and the EEC in the Atlantic System: The Problem of Theory," *Journal of Common Market Studies* 5 (June 1967), pp. 401–2.
39. Ernst B. Haas, "The 'Uniting of Europe' and the Uniting of Latin America," *Journal of Common Market Studies* 5 (June 1967), pp. 315–43.
40. Hansen, "European Integration," p. 232.
41. Edward L. Morse, "Why the Malaise?" *Foreign Affairs* 51:2 (January 1973), p. 373.

conservative dynamics set in motion by the integration process itself."[42] As a rule, political leadership launches joint efforts in a particular sector and then (as Hansen puts it) "turns its attention elsewhere, leaving the sector in the care of technicians and sub-national interest group actors."[43] These caretaker actors concentrate on "adjustive bargaining within the established rules" rather than coalition-building that might lead to additional progress in the sector or to spillover. Therefore, unless the politicians renew the impetus to integration, the sector tends to become in Schmitter's term, encapsulated. Drawing on the responses of various interest groups to de Gaulle's position in the 1965 crisis, Lindberg and Scheingold conclude that such actors are primarily intent on *"conserving* the level of integration already achieved" and protecting their interests "from the unpredictability that attends reopening the political bargaining process."[44]

Many observers have noted that since the confrontation with de Gaulle, a certain conservatism has permeated the EEC and regional relationships as a whole. This may reflect an effort on the part of the European institutions to preserve their legitimacy in the eyes of national politicians and to preserve for themselves as much as possible of the roles which had previously been set aside for them. (After the conflict engendered by its forceful participation in the Congo question of 1960–1964, the U.N. Secretariat went through a similar period of passivity and consolidation.) The Commission has been much more cautious in making proposals to the Council, although the Commission did play a significant bargaining role in the 1966 agricultural negotiations, the Kennedy Round trade negotiations that ended in 1967, and the 1971 monetary crisis. As for governments: "the intra-EC bargaining process has toughened, and the willingness of any member-state to make short term sacrifices for the prospect of longer term benefits has been constricted."[45] The situation during the energy crisis of 1973–1974, when governments could not agree on a joint policy to counteract the Arab petroleum boycott of the Netherlands, was a glaring example of this trend. On numerous other occasions, when some cooperation has obviously been needed, governments have opted for informal policy coordination as opposed to institutionalized measures. Moreover, even insofar as EEC initiatives have been concerned, there has been a preference for the mechanism of periodic summit meetings rather than the regular procedures involving the Commission and Council.

Considering intra-regional trends alone, then, it is painfully clear that much of the unilinear development originally foreseen for Europe by the neo-functionalists is unlikely to materialize. Lindberg and Scheingold's

---

42. Lindberg and Scheingold, *Europe's Would-Be Polity,* especially Chaps. 6 and 9.
43. Hansen, "European Integration," p. 239.
44. Lindberg and Scheingold, *Europe's Would-Be Polity,* p. 191.
45. Hansen, "European Integration," p. 238.

rather pessimistic forecast, which is echoed by many neo-functionalists today, seems entirely justified:

> . . . although we cannot with certainty specify the level of scope and capacity at which the [EEC] system will stop growing, we see that occurring well short of the point where we can talk of federal or pseudo-federal structures . . . At the projected level of growth the Community will be an unprecedented, but curiously ambiguous "pluralistic" system—in its economic, social, and political aspects alike.[46]

This "new" pluralism, we should reemphasize, contributes to the halfway-house character of present-day Europe, and can perhaps best be understood by reference to the complex comglomerate model.

Europe and the World

Though Europe is difficult enough to comprehend as a region unto itself, it still cannot be considered in isolation from the complex conglomerate of the global system.

To some extent neo-functionalists have responded to this intellectual challenge. Nye criticized early neo-functionalist theories for paying scant attention to the external dimension of integration experiments, especially to the role of outside powers such as the United States acting as "catalysts" for such schemes.[47] Schmitter hypothesized (his "externalization" thesis) that regional integration would be enhanced by the need for participants to adopt common policies vis-à-vis nonparticipants.[48] Nevertheless, other scholars warn, the likelihood remains that participants would have somewhat different "images of the world" and views about the future of the region in that world, as well as varying bilateral ties to the external universe—with the result that yet another set of controversial issues could be injected to impede the integration process.[49]

The European experience provides evidence for all of these propositions. Beginning with the Marshall Plan and at least until recently, the United States has given full encouragement to intra-European cooperation. At the same time, regional integration unquestionably has been spurred by the need to hammer out joint policies vis-à-vis the outside world, particularly in regard to the perceived threat of Soviet aggression. A common external tariff has also been achieved, and, although the receptivity to

46. Lindberg and Scheingold, *Europe's Would-Be Polity*, pp. 305–6.
47. Joseph S. Nye, Jr., "Patterns and Catalysts in Regional Integration," *International Organization* 19:4 (Autumn 1965), pp. 870–84.
48. Philippe C. Schmitter, "Three Neo-Functional Hypotheses About International Integration," *International Organization* 23:1 (Winter 1969), p. 165.
49. On this point, see Hansen, "European Integration," p. 238.

foreign multinational investment varies from country to country, EEC rules do ensure that such investment will not threaten monopoly in particular market sectors. Despite the French government's sensitivity about matters of defense, the Euro-Group has been reasonably successful in developing a set of European positions for consideration at the East-West European Security Conference. Kissinger's proposed "Year of Europe" was, however, a dismal failure largely because the Europeans could not agree among themselves soon enough to negotiate effectively with Washington on key issues such as monetary reform and sharing the burdens inherent in the NATO alliance.[50] And, of course, European unity collapsed almost entirely in the face of the Arab oil boycott.[51]

Consistent with theory, opposing world-views and different national patterns of engagement in the external world have divided Europe. The Gaullist perspective of an "independent" Europe united under French leadership has clashed with the desires of much of the rest of Western Europe for trans-Atlantic "partnership"; it was, as we have seen, especially incompatible with the United Kingdom's "special relationship" with the United States. Moreover, France in its own interest has deviated from European inclinations to join the United States in backing Israel and instead has courted the Arabs. Brandt's *Ostpolitik* has also been a source of some division, insofar as it has given the Germans a special stake in detente not shared by other Europeans.

One may perhaps view the recent addition of the United Kingdom (along with Denmark and Ireland) as the "internalization" of part of the external system that was previously troublesome for the Six. But as yet it is too early to determine whether the geographical expansion of the EEC will help or hinder integration over the long haul. On the positive side of the ledger, Britain has now definitely indicated its intention to give priority to Europe over the "special relationship" with the United States, and that issue seems to be more or less resolved. On the negative side, there are now more actors with divergent views that must be reconciled within the EEC. Geographical expansion, with new possibilities for coalition-building, could signal the start of a new era of innovation in the Common Market, or it could reveal that the integrative experiment is already overextended and so bring about a retreat in or at least a grinding halt to forward advance.

However imaginative Europeans are in their attempts to avoid stalemate, the external world will continue to create many of the issues with which they must deal. Of particular relevance to the European system are several other major relationships or systems in the global complex conglomerate, in shorthand form: United States-Europe, United States-Soviet

50. See Z, "The Year of Europe," *Foreign Affairs* 52:2 (January 1974) pp. 237–48.
51. See Walter Laqueur, "The Idea of Europe Runs Out of Gas," *The New York Times Magazine*, 20 January 1974.

Union, United States-Europe-Japan, and North-South (DC-LDC). These systems are themselves clusters of what might be termed *minisystems,* the boundaries of which are defined by specific issues and which evidence characteristic patterns of actor involvement and behavior. For example, the United States-Europe system includes the functional system of agriculture, which involves not only a wide range of actors in the EEC but also the United States' departments of State and Agriculture, certain Congressional committees, American farm and consumer groups, and so forth. As the example of agriculture suggests, systems overlap, and the links among them contribute greatly to the general complexity of global politics. For instance, U.S. restrictions on soybean exports to Japan add to the legitimacy of neo-mercantilist policies in Europe, and the United States-Soviet Union wheat sale bolsters Congressional insistence on further protectionist measures and a harder line on detente. Finally, the salience and outputs of each system tend to be discontinuous; particular issues come to the fore at different times, and progress toward a resolution of them is often uneven.

What, then, are the principal problems originating in the external environment that currently confront Europe? A perennial issue is, of course, the role of the United States in Europe's defense, which is now all the more uncertain because of detente and the SALT talks—the Europeans have not been fully privy to Kissinger's promises to the Russians—the ongoing European Security Conference, and pressures in the U.S. Congress for a reduction in America's troop commitment to Europe. There has been some speculation about the possible "Finlandization" of Europe under the Soviet shadow if the United States opts for isolationism.[52] Europeans worry, as well, about the presence of many U.S.-based multinationals in their economies, about the future of international monetary reform (Secretary of the Treasury John Connally's "Texas poker" came as a rude shock), and about U.S. desires for a revamping of the CAP and a lowering of other EEC barriers to trade. Some analysts have predicted a U.S.-Japanese alliance against Europe on trade and monetary matters. Other issues are how to cope with Third World commodity cartels and the inflation generated in part by increasing fuel prices. Finally, Europe must continue to respond convincingly to Third World demands for additional aid and access to EEC markets.

Against this background, what is often seen as a "malaise" in present-day Europe[53] has anything but a simple explanation—or cure. For, as Morse perceives:

52. For a contrary view, see George F. Kennan, "Europe's Problems, Europe's Choices," *Foreign Policy,* no. 14 (Spring 1974), pp. 3–16.
53. See, for example, Alfred Grosser, "Europe: Community of Malaise," *Foreign Policy,* no. 15 (Summer 1974), pp. 169–79; John Newhouse, "Stuck Fast," *Foreign Affairs* 51:2 (January 1973), pp. 353–66; and Morse, "Why the Malaise?"

. . . (T)he trap that Europeans are in . . ., transcends Europe and characterizes the other states of the industrialized world. These industrialized states find themselves in an unprecedented web of interdependence whose unscrambling now seems inconceivable. . . . It is clear that activities in almost any field affect those in others. . . . It is also clear that domestic politics and foreign policies have become more and more dependent upon one another in ways that are often surprising. No one knows how stable these interdependent relationships are. No one has any idea what sort of institutionalized arrangements are proper for handling them.[54]

These are some of the implications of the complex conglomerate, which makes the road beyond the halfway house of Europe so difficult to discern.

54. Morse, *ibid.,* p. 377.

The Complex Conglomerate Model and Contemporary Global Politics

PART III

Nonstate Actors
in Global Politics:
Conclusions

ELEVEN

At the outset we suggested that the state-centric model of the global political system that focuses exclusively upon the interaction of nation-states has become, at least for the purposes of theory-building, obsolete. Our review of the politics of three regions confirms that the model is inadequate for the analysis of any of them. Far from facilitating an accurate and systematic mapping of political behavior, the model precludes an analysis of actors and activities that have profound consequences for statesmen and citizens everywhere. This generalization holds especially (though not exclusively) for the study of conflict and violence, which has long been a preoccupation of political scientists.

Although they have failed to grasp the full significance of their observations, several prominent scholars have appeared to sense the shortcomings of the state-centric model in this regard. Hans Mongenthau, for instance, notes that some 28 percent of the wars that took place between the years 1480 and 1941 were civil in nature, that is, wars that occurred within rather than among nation-states.[1] In another study Samuel Huntington shows that between the years 1958 and 1968 no less than 93 percent of all "military conflicts" were something other than conventional interstate wars.[2] In the words of Quincy Wright: "Civil wars such as the French Huguenot wars of the sixteenth century, the British War of the Roses of the fifteenth century and the Civil War of the seventeenth century, the Thirty Years' War from the standpoint of Germany, the Peninsula War from the standpoint of Spain, the American Civil War, the Chinese Taiping Rebel-

1. Hans J. Morgenthau, *Politics Among Nations,* 5th ed. (New York: Alfred A. Knopf, 1973), p. 488.
2. Samuel P. Huntington, *Political Order in Changing Societies* (New Haven: Yale University Press, 1968), p. 4.

lion were costly both in lives and in economic losses far in excess of contemporary international wars."[3] These historical "civil" wars have contemporary parallels in others that have occurred in places like Pakistan, Nigeria, Angola, Cyprus, Ireland, and Jordan. The endemic nature of civil strife both in the past and present refutes any attempt to erect artificial analytic barriers between the study of "domestic tranquillity" and "international anarchy."

Consistent with our objections to the state-centric model, we have assiduously avoided making the traditional distinction between "domestic" and "international" politics. Instead, we have sought to identify and analyze events that have direct or indirect consequences for global or regional outcomes regardless of whether they took place within or across national frontiers.[4]

In this concluding chapter, we shall address two major questions. First, is a state-centric framework more applicable to certain regions and/or to particular kinds of behavior than it is to others? Second, is there a relationship between the behavior of nonstate actors and the characteristics of the regional systems in which they are found?

Nonstate Actors:
Their Unique Contribution
to Political Conflict and Violence

The concept of sovereignty on which the state-centric model rests actually has two dimensions. We have already stressed the first of these: the notion that global politics encompasses exclusively the interaction of "sovereign" nation-state actors. However, the other side of the sovereignty coin is that nation-states are preponderant over all those nonstate actors lying within their boundaries. This is, as Martin Wight expresses it, "the principle that every individual requires the protection of a state, which represents him in the international community."[5] The relative autonomy of nonstate actors in each of our categories severely undermines any such propositions.[6]

3. Quincy Wright, *A Study of War,* vol. 1 (Chicago: University of Chicago Press, 1942), p. 247.
4. The state-centric model disregards such interactions, and, as a consequence, most analyses of international relations ignore intrastate behavior. Such behavior is therefore largely left to students of foreign policy and comparative politics, who, in turn, often assume that it has at most *indirect* consequences for interstate politics.
5. Martin Wight, "Why Is There No International Theory?" in Herbert Butterfield and Martin Wight, eds., *Diplomatic Investigations* (Cambridge: Harvard University Press, 1968), p. 21.
6. We have assessed autonomy in terms of whether an actor initiated more behavior than would have been expected based upon the amount of behavior it received. See Appendix, p. 313.

Intrastate nongovernmental actors, we found, were just as autonomous as nation-states for all of the time periods across all of the regions. While variations in the autonomy scores across all three time periods were not statistically significant, it is nonetheless noteworthy that in the last two time periods *both* intrastate nongovernmental actors and governmental noncentral actors were relatively more autonomous than nation-states.[7]

An analysis of dyads that took place in the three regions for the entire twenty-five year period testifies to the deficiencies of the other dimension of the sovereignty concept, the supposed nation-state monopoly of global politics. The state-centric model implies that nation-states are the *sole* actors and targets. *Yet, of all the dyadic interactions in the three regions for twenty-five years, under half involved nation-states simultaneously as actors and targets, and over 11 percent involved nonstate actors exclusively!* Under half of the dyads which took place in Western Europe, Latin America, and the Middle East could have been accounted for by the state-centric model.[8] Other major dyadic combinations included intrastate non-

Table 93. Dyadic Combinations of Actor Types for all Regions, 1948-1972
(*N* of dyads in cell)
(Cell as percentage of total dyads)

Target	I	II	III	IV	V	VI	Row Total
Actor							
I. Individuals	2	31	7	155	15	7	217
	0	0.4	0.1	2.0	0.2	0.1	2.7
II. Intrastate	52	243	35	736	97	41	1204
Nongovernmental	0.7	3.1	0.4	9.3	1.2	0.5	15.2
III. Governmental	30	48	20	72	12	8	190
Noncentral	0.4	0.6	0.3	0.9	0.2	0.1	2.4
IV. Nation-States	254	661	123	3506	371	623	5538
	3.2	8.3	1.5	44.2	4.7	7.9	69.8
V. Interstate	26	43	3	175	54	9	310
Nongovernmental	0.3	0.5	0	2.2	0.7	0.1	3.9
VI. Interstate	14	17	6	375	20	45	477
Governmental	0.2	0.2	0.1	4.7	0.3	0.6	6.0
Column Total	378	1043	194	5019	569	733	7936
	4.8	13.1	2.4	63.2	7.2	9.2	100.0*

*Variation from 100.0% for cell, row or column totals due to rounding errors.

7. Overall, four of the six types of actors received more behavior than they initiated. The exceptions were states and intrastate nongovernmental actors. In contrast, interstate governmental actors typically were targets far more often than they were initiators.
8. It should be noted that many analysts have broadened the model to include intergovernmental organizations like the United Nations, thereby increasing its power.

governmental actors-to-states, states-to-intrastate nongovernmental actors, and states-to-intergovernmental actors.

The phenomenon in evidence here might be called the "democratization of global politics."[9] Global politics, in theory, and, to a considerable extent in practice, was once the exclusive preserve of a nation-state "aristocracy." However, as national societies grew more complex, as the world became increasingly interdependent, and as nation-states consequently became less "sovereign" and "impermeable," other types of actors have come to play an ever-more prominent and autonomous role. While differential possession of the resources needed to undertake global political behavior continues to influence the relative participation of various actors, the fact remains that they all actually do participate and that their roles must be comprehended if global and regional systems are to be accurately mapped.

Without doubt, nation-states through their governments are still the primary actors involved in global politics if we take "involvement" to mean the appearance of a given actor as *either* the actor or target in a dyad. Nation-states appeared in almost 89 percent of all dyads. Yet nonstate groups appeared in about two-thirds as many, or 56 percent.[10] Among the various types of nonstate actors, intrastate nongovernmental groups were the most involved, appearing in over one-quarter of all dyads. Interstate actors were also involved in one-quarter of all dyads: Interstate governmental organizations appeared in almost 15 percent, and interstate nongovernmental groups, in over 10 percent. Individuals were involved in almost 8 percent of the dyads. Finally, governmental noncentral actors were the least involved of actor types, appearing in fewer than 5 percent of all dyads.

The relative impact of nonstate actors and the actual complexity of global politics become clearer when we examine the dyadic combinations found in the different regions. In Latin America, for example, while states were involved in over 84 percent of all dyads, nonstate groups taken together were involved virtually to the same extent. *In Latin America 83.5 percent of the interactions involved some kind of nonstate actor.* Intrastate nongovernmental actors such as political parties, labor unions, and guerrillas were involved in over 40 percent of the total regional interactions. Thus, in Latin America the relationship between states and intrastate groups accounted for more behavior than the relationship among states alone. Indeed, if we paid attention only to relations among states in this region, there would be precious little to study! The most important dyadic combinations of actor types for Latin America between 1948 and 1972 are

9. This concept is related to Huntington's notion of "international pluralism." See Samuel P. Huntington, "Transnational Organizations in World Politics," *World Politics* 25:3 (April 1973), pp. 333–68.
10. Involvement figures can exceed 100 percent owing to the fact that they combine both initiation and reception in dyads.

listed below. The percentage of total behavior for which each combination accounted is given in parenthesis:

1. State-to-state (24.8 percent)
2. State-to-intrastate nongovernmental (15.0 percent)
3. Intrastate nongovernmental-to-state (14.0 percent)
4. State-to-interstate governmental (8.8 percent)
5. State-to-interstate nongovernmental (7.6 percent)
6. Intrastate nongovernmental-to-intrastate nongovernmental (4.8 percent)

In Western Europe, over half of the dyads involved states alone. Intrastate nongovernmental groups were also prominent in the politics of this region. Political parties were, on the whole, more institutionalized than in Latin America. Labor unions and other interest groups, the significance of which is emphasized in pluralistic theories of politics, were important as well.[11] Needless to say perhaps, there were no Western European counterparts of Latin American guerrillas with the possible exception of North African nationalists. Interstate governmental organizations, including the EEC and NATO, were additional key actors. The most important dyadic combinations in Western Europe were as follows:

1. State-to-state (51.6 percent)
2. Intrastate nongovernmental-to-state (8.5 percent)
3. State-to-interstate governmental (6.2 percent)
4. State-to-intrastate nongovernmental (5.4 percent)
5. Interstate governmental-to-state (5.4 percent)
6. State-to-interstate nongovernmental (3.3 percent)

While nonstate actors were highly involved in Latin America and somewhat involved in Western Europe, they were least involved in the Middle East! This is a somewhat surprising finding in view of the headline attention received by Palestinian terrorist groups and multinational petroleum corporations in that region. While in Western Europe the integrating effect of interstate governmental organizations has been apparent, in the Middle East it has been the penetrative behavior of the United Nations which has been characteristic. This penetrative behavior has taken a number of forms, including the creation of multinational peace forces to separate belligerent parties and the provision of refugee relief as well as a forum for charges and countercharges among the parties. The most important dyadic combinations in the Middle East between 1948 and 1972 were as follows:

11. See, for example, David B. Truman, *The Governmental Process* (New York: Alfred A. Knopf, 1951); and Robert A. Dahl, *Who Governs?* (New Haven: Yale University Press, 1961).

1. State-to-state (52.1 percent)
2. State-to-interstate governmental (9.9 percent)
3. State-to-intrastate nongovernmental (6.3 percent)
4. Interstate governmental-to-state (5.4 percent)
5. Intrastate nongovernmental-to-state (5.3 percent)
6. Interstate nongovernmental-to-state (4.3 percent)

The relative involvement of nonstate groups in the different regions is shown in Table 94. The data given in this table once again reflect overall involvement as both initiators and targets.

Having compared nonstate actor involvement in the three regions, we now turn to the question of what *nostacs* did. Another way of posing this question is to ask whether the state-centric model is more suitable for explaining certain behavior patterns than it is for others. The answer is at once clear: *The more conflictful the behavior, the less the state-centric model can explain; the more cooperative the behavior, the more the state-centric model can explain!* State-to-state interactions accounted for 59.6 percent of all cooperative deeds in the data set and 52.5 percent of all verbal cooperation. In contrast, they accounted for only 39.5 percent of verbal conflict, a mere 19.9 percent of conflict deeds, and 18 percent of the violence. Apparently, nonstate actors are prepared to invest a higher level of their resources in conflict and to take greater risks than states. Much of their conflict behavior took the form of deeds not words. States, on the other hand, indulged in considerable verbal and rhetorical conflict and tended to eschew conflict deeds.

When we combine verbal and deed behavior, the overall importance of nonstate actors for the affective dimension of conflict is even more striking. As Table 95 suggests the state-centric model suits cooperative behavior rather well. State-to-state interactions accounted for over 55 percent of cooperation. The only significant nonstate actor in this context was intergovernmental organizations.

This pattern, however, was *not* characteristic of overall conflict.

Table 94. Overall Involvement of Actor Types in Three Regions, 1948-1972
(in percentages of total dyads as both actor and target)

	Middle East	Western Europe	Latin America
Individuals	6.5	7.0	9.4
Intrastate Nongovernmental	15.2	21.5	40.3
Governmental Noncentral	3.5	4.9	5.5
Nation-States	93.8	88.6	84.3
Interstate Nongovernmental	10.3	8.1	13.8
Interstate Governmental	17.4	13.6	14.5
Total Nonstate Actor Involvement	52.9	55.1	83.5

Table 95. *Overall Cooperative Dyads for all Regions, 1948–1972*

(N of dyads in cell)
(Cell as percentage of total dyads)

Target	I	II	III	IV	V	VI	Row Total
Actor							
I. Individuals	1	8	1	61	4	1	76
	0	0.2	0	1.6	0.1	0	2.0
II. Intrastate	26	115	20	195	22	11	389
Nongovernmental	0.7	3.0	0.5	5.1	0.6	0.3	10.1
III. Governmental	6	10	11	29	2	2	60
Noncentral	0.2	0.3	0.3	0.8	0.1	0.1	1.6
IV. Nation-States	87	164	65	2138	71	350	2894
	2.3	4.3	1.7	55.5	1.8	9.1	75.1
V. Interstate	17	24	2	81	27	4	155
Nongovernmental	0.4	0.6	0.1	2.1	0.7	0.1	4.0
VI. Interstate	8	7	3	233	5	25	281
Governmental	0.2	0.2	0.1	6.0	0.1	0.6	7.3
Column Total	145	328	102	2737	150	393	3855
	3.8	8.5	2.6	71.0	3.9	10.2	100.0*

*Variation from 100.0% for cell, row, or column totals due to rounding errors.

Table 96 reveals that the state-centric model accounted for less than one-third of the conflict interactions. As for violence, the state-to-state dyad was no longer even the most important! The finding concerning *nostac* involvement in conflict and violence

Table 96. *Overall Conflict Dyads for all Regions, 1948–1972*

(N of dyads in cell)
(Cell as percentage of total dyads)

Target	I	II	III	IV	V	VI	Row Total
Actor							
I. Individuals	1	14	6	70	4	5	100
	0	0.5	0.2	2.6	0.2	0.2	3.8
II. Intrastate	19	102	10	464	13	16	624
Nongovernmental	0.7	3.8	0.4	17.4	0.5	0.6	23.4
III. Governmental	22	34	7	25	4	1	93
Noncentral	0.8	1.3	0.3	0.9	0.2	0	3.5
IV. Nation-States	148	405	36	833	89	152	1663
	5.6	15.2	1.4	31.3	3.3	5.7	62.5
V. Interstate	5	8	0	73	9	2	97
Nongovernmental	0.2	0.3	0	2.7	0.3	0.1	3.6
VI. Interstate	4	6	1	66	2	6	85
Governmental	0.2	0.2	0	2.5	0.1	0.2	3.2
Column Total	199	569	60	1531	121	182	2662
	7.5	21.4	2.3	57.5	4.5	6.8	100.0*

*Variation from 100.0% for cell, row, or column totals due to rounding errors.

Table 97. Overall Violence Dyads for all Regions, 1948–1972
(N of dyads in cell)
(Cell as percentage of total dyads)

Target	I	II	III	IV	V	VI	Row Total
Actor							
I. Individuals	0	6	3	19	0	1	29
	0	1.3	0.6	4.0	0	0.2	6.1
II. Intrastate	5	20	6	106	2	0	139
Nongovernmental	1.1	4.2	1.3	22.3	0.4	0	29.3
III. Governmental	2	10	1	0	2	0	15
Noncentral	0.4	2.1	0.2	0	0.4	0	3.2
IV. Nation-States	35	119	6	85	18	3	266
	7.4	25.1	1.3	17.9	3.8	0.6	56.0
V. Interstate	1	1	0	17	1	0	20
Nongovernmental	0.2	0.2	0	3.6	0.2	0	4.2
VI. Interstate	0	1	0	5	0	0	6
Governmental	0	0.2	0	1.1	0	0	1.3
Column Total	43	157	16	232	23	4	475
	9.1	33.1	3.4	48.8	4.8	0.8	100.0*

*Variation from 100.0% for cell, row, or column totals due to rounding errors.

has enormous implications since, if the scholar of global politics is interested in discovering answers to anything at all, it is to the causes and dynamics of conflict. One need only look at the first sentence in virtually all international relations texts to draw this conclusion. To wit: "After the armies of Imperial Germany invaded Belgium in August, 1914, launching one of the most destructive and futile conflicts in history, the German Foreign Minister . . . asked his Chancellor why all the diplomatic steps to avoid the war had failed."[12] "The crucial fact about the human situation in the mid-twentieth century may be simply and starkly expressed: Mankind stands in grave danger of irreparable self-mutilation, or substantial self-destruction."[13] "No one aware of the unending disaster of Vietnam, the extended torment of the Middle East, the tragedy of Czechoslovakia, and the catastrophes of Biafra, Bangladesh, and so many other states needs to be reminded of the continuing unsatisfactory state of international relations. . . ."[14] "In the autumn of 1962 the United States and the Soviet Union confronted each other in an interaction that brought the world to the brink of war."[15]

The role of nonstate actors in conflict and violence is further estab-

12. K. J. Holsti, *International Politics* (Englewood Cliffs, N.J.: Prentice-Hall, Inc., 1967), p. 1.
13. Inis L. Claude, Jr., *Power and International Relations* (New York: Random House, 1962), p. 3.
14. David V. Edwards, *Creating A New World Politics* (New York: David McKay, 1973), p. 3.
15. Raymond F. Hopkins and Richard W. Mansbach, *Structure and Process in International Politics* (New York: Harper & Row, Inc., 1973), p. 3.

Table 98. Actor Involvement in Different Behaviors, 1948–1972
(in percentage of total dyads as both actor and target)

	Cooperation	Conflict	Violence
Individuals	5.7	11.2	15.2
Intrastate Nongovernmental	15.8	40.9	58.2
Governmental Noncentral	4.2	5.5	6.3
Nation-States	90.3	88.6	87.1
Interstate Nongovernmental	6.7	7.9	8.8
Interstate Governmental	16.8	9.8	2.1
Total Nonstate Actor Involvement	49.2	75.3	90.6

lished by analyzing their involvement in different types of behavior. Overall, nonstate actors of one kind or another were involved in over three-fourths of all conflict dyads and in over 90 percent of all violent dyads! In contrast, they appeared in under 50 percent of all cooperative interactions. Indeed, nonstate actors accounted for almost 40 percent of the disruption in the three regions but only one-quarter of the supportive behavior.[16]

Similar findings emerge from analyzing these data in two other ways, both of which are centered on the *initiation of behavior rather than overall dyadic involvement*. When initiation is considered alone, we find what should be by now an expected pattern about the contribution of the various actor types to disruptive-supportive behavior. Nation-states accounted for about three-quarters of the overall system support, but almost 12 percent less of the total disruption. On the other hand, intrastate nongovernmental actors alone accounted for almost one-quarter of the system disruption but only slightly more than 10 percent of the system support. The contributions of the other actor types were somewhat mixed, but interstate governmental actors, as might be expected, were more than twice as important to system support than they were to disruption.

A similar conclusion emerges when we scrutinize each actor type separately and the way in which it distributes its behavior. We then obtain a behavior "profile" for each actor and can compare these "profiles." Among actor types, intrastate nongovernmental groups initiated conflict most consistently, while intergovernmental organizations were the least likely to initiate such behavior. Nation-states were relatively cooperative. These findings are summarized in Table 99. Individuals and intrastate nongovernmental groups were the most prone to violence, while nation-states and intergovernmental organizations were the least likely to initiate violence. *Thus, we may conclude that nation-states or groups composed of nation-states are less likely to initiate conflict or resort to violence than individuals or nongovernmental groups.* Table 100 suggests the relative likelihood of different actors resorting to violence.

16. Recall that disruption and support are based on "weighted" dyads and that support includes cooperation and participation.

Table 99.   Distribution of Actor Initiations in All Regions, 1948–1972
(Percentages are in terms of the total behavior of a given actor type)

	Cooperation	Participation	Conflict
Individuals	35.1	18.9	46.1
Intrastate Nongovernmental	32.1	15.9	50.5
Governmental Noncentral	31.6	19.5	49.0
Nation-States	52.3	17.7	29.9
Interstate Nongovernmental	50.0	18.7	31.3
Interstate Governmental	58.9	23.3	17.9

These findings indicate that interstate governmental actors especially and nation-states secondarily are more prepared than other actors to follow the advice attributed to Winston Churchill that "to jaw, jaw, jaw is better than to war, war, war." There are at least two possible explanations for this. In the first place, nation-states typically have access to a greater variety of resources than do other kinds of actors. Consequently, in seeking to influence other actors, they can reward as well as coerce them. In contrast, urban guerrillas, ethnic minorities, and individuals, for example, often find that recourse to violence is necessary in order to bring their grievances to public consciousness. Such actors rarely possess the means to engage in public debate or to offer rewards to exert influence.[17]

Second, as we have suggested, national governments have constituted something of an "aristocracy" in global politics, a position they generally try to retain. In seeking to dampen the "participation explosion" in order to maintain their preeminence in decision-making and to control those issues which "enter the public arena," the use of rewards, promises, and symbols is often more effective than the use of coercion and threats. Moreover, governments are prepared to protect their status by responding conservatively to many potentially destabilizing issues. The creation of intergovernmental organizations often represents efforts to oppose change and eliminate unpredictability by the formation of exclusive "gentlemen's

Table 100.   Violence as a Percentage of Total Actor Initiations

Individuals	13.4
Intrastate Nongovernmental	11.5
Governmental Noncentral	7.9
Interstate Nongovernmental	6.8
Nation-States	4.8
Interstate Governmental	1.3

17. See Harold D. Lasswell and Abraham Kaplan, *Power and Society* (New Haven: Yale University Press, 1950), pp. 92–94.

clubs." On the other hand, actors that wish to alter the *status quo* or to seek drastic remedies for pressing problems find theirs to be a much more difficult position.[18] Fewer means are appropriate to changing a *status quo* than to maintaining it. Thus, nonstate actors, which are regularly associated with efforts to achieve rapid change, find recourse to conflict and violence essential in order to create the climate of urgency that is required before governments will deal seriously with their concerns.[19] At the same time, governments by and large attempt to prevent those issues that are likely to engender violence and conflict from arising. (Obviously, this is not true of all governments. Certain "revisionist" governments will behave in much the same way as the bulk of nonstate actors that we have described.)

The overall tendency of nonstate actors (except intergovernmental organizations) to behave conflictfully and violently more often than states is mirrored in each of the regions. Thus, individuals were involved in 16 percent of the violent interactions in the Middle East, 15 percent in Latin America, and 14 percent in Western Europe. In contrast, they were involved in only 4.8 percent of the cooperative dyads in Western Europe and the Middle East.

Intrastate nongovernmental actors were, as we have pointed out, deeply enmeshed in regional conflicts, particularly in Latin America where they were involved in 81.6 percent of the violent and 55.1 percent of the conflict dyads. Indeed, looking at violence in Latin America, we discover that the two leading dyadic combinations were state-to-intrastate nongovernmental (34.0 percent) and intrastate nongovernmental-to-state (33.3 percent). In contrast, state-to-state interactions accounted for only 2 percent of the violence and 19 percent of the conflict in that region. As a rule, Latin American governments appeared to be in constant conflict with "domestic" groups rather than with one another. Such groups also engaged in conflict with governments in Western Europe and the Middle East, though to a somewhat lesser extent. In Western Europe they were involved in 74.3 percent of the violent interactions and 41.3 percent of the conflict

18. William A. Gamson, *Power and Discontent* (Homewood, Ill.: The Dorsey Press, 1968), p. 63.
19. This interpretation is similar to certain "elite theory" treatments of American politics. On control of "issues which enter the public arena" see Peter Bachrach and Morton S. Baratz, *Power and Poverty* (New York: Oxford University Press, 1970), pp. 3–63. The employment of "symbols" and the ways in which they are related to system outcomes is discussed in Murray Edelman, *The Symbolic Uses of Politics* (Chicago: University of Illinois Press, 1967). A classic treatment of elite theory in the American context is C. Wright Mills, *The Power Elite* (New York: Oxford University Press, 1956). An excellent synthesis of this perspective may be found in Thomas R. Dye and L. Harmon Zeigler, *The Irony of Democracy,* 2nd ed. (Belmont Cal.: Duxbury, 1972), Chaps. iii–v.

interactions; in the Middle East the figures were 30.5 percent and 19.5 percent respectively.

Governmental noncentral actors such as colonial authorities or provincial and city officials accounted for the least overall behavior of the actor types. Nevertheless, they were critical factors in certain conflict situations. They were highly involved in Western European violence (though there was little of this), especially as French colonial authorities. They were also involved in Latin American conflict and violence, often as provincial officials acting in defiance of central regimes or quelling local demonstrators and terrorist groups.

Nation-states, as we have noted, were the most involved in cooperative interactions in all regions. The state-to-state combination was most significant in Western European and Middle Eastern cooperation, where it accounted for 62.9 percent and 57.5 percent of the interactions respectively. Overall, nation-states were most significant in the Middle East where they were involved in 94.1 percent of all cooperative interactions as well as most of the conflict and violence dyads. The findings regarding nation-state involvement in conflict and violence in the Middle East are, in part, explained by the focal position of Israel (a nation-state) in that region either as initiator or target.

Interstate nongovernmental actors (transnational groups) were most highly involved in the politics of the Middle East. There they appeared in 16.5 percent, 12.8 percent, and 9 percent of the violent, conflict, and cooperative interactions respectively. This was largely the consequence of the activities of the Palestinian organizations, particularly in the later years. A striking discovery was that the interstate nongovernmental groups were involved more deeply in conflict and violence than in cooperation *only* in the Middle East. In Western Europe and Latin America, where they often appeared as multinational corporations, they generally tended to cooperate with local regimes. Like states, such corporations possess resources that make it easier for them to exert influence by means of cooperation and reward than by resort to conflict or violence.

The final category of actor, interstate governmental organizations (IGO's), were, as we have noted, the most conspicuously and consistently cooperative of all actor types. This was particularly true in Latin America, where organizations such as the Organization of American States were involved in 20.7 percent of the cooperative interactions but only 6.6 percent of the conflict and 0.7 percent of the violent dyads. In all three regions, they appeared to cooperate willingly with national regimes, a finding that is not surprising in view of the fact that, unlike many other non-state actors, they are the creations of states. However, such organizations did participate in over 13 percent of the conflict that took place in the

Middle East. This reflects the controversial roles of the United Nations and the Arab League in the Arab-Israeli dispute.

Once again, the behavior of the different types of actors illustrate how global politics can be viewed as analogous to local politics. The behavior of many nonstate actors, "lower class" actors, resembles the behavior of minority groups and poorer citizens who resort to "street crime" against which local authorities inveigh. Elite crime rarely involves violence since the elite need not engender conflict in public to exert influence. "Upper class criminals" such as the Watergate conspirators only come to our attention when they are "caught in the act."

Nonstate Actors:
Their Impact on Political Issues
and System Change

We now know, among other things, that regardless of region nonstate actors are more prone to conflict and violence than nation-states. We also know that such actors are of particular significance in Latin America and Western Europe. As key components of systems, however, actors are intimately linked to other system attributes such as interaction-behavior and issues. In effect, these variables form a "package," and it is difficult to explore or analyze any one of them in isolation. Thus, in this section, we shall explore the ways in which the different actors and their behaviors relate to particular issues and the effects of all of these on system change through time.[20]

Of the twenty-five years we have reviewed for the three regions, the first time period manifested the highest level of cooperation. Over half of the events between 1948 and 1956–1958 were cooperative, while less than a third were conflictful.[21] East-West conflict was more than offset by the high degree of cooperation in the noncommunist world. The second period, which lasted from 1956–1958 until 1967, brought an upsurge in conflict and a decline in cooperation. Indeed, the easing of East-West hostility and the loosening of bipolarity appeared to permit increasing regional and local bickering. To some extent allies turned against one another, and the

20. For the method used to calculate system change longitudinally and the contribution of different actors to such change, see Appendix, pp. 315–17.
21. The ensuing discussion distinguishes between cooperative and conflictful behavior. These are separable dimensions, and one is not a function of the other in part because of differing levels of overall activity in different periods and in part because of changes in levels of participative behavior. Thus it is possible that cooperation and conflict can increase or decrease simultaneously.

struggle against European colonialism entered a final and decisive phase. Cooperative events between the first and second periods declined by nearly 8 percent. Nation-states were largely responsible for this decline, although intergovernmental and interstate nongovernmental actors also contributed to it. Meanwhile, conflict increased by almost 20 percent over its "expected value," an upsurge accounted for mainly by state and intrastate nongovernmental groups.[22]

The third period, from 1967 through 1972, saw a moderate increase in cooperation and a somewhat larger decrease in conflict. *At the same time, violence increased over 25 percent above the level we would have expected on the basis of the second time period!* The major source of this new violence was interstate nongovernmental actors, notably Palestinian terrorist groups. Nation-states also contributed to this trend toward greater violence, as did individuals, though to a much lesser degree than nation-state or interstate nongovernmental actors. As might have been expected, much of this violence was centered in the Middle East, extending to Europe and beyond in the Munich Massacre at the 1972 Olympics and various airline hijackings.[23]

The third period witnessed the virtual disappearance of many of the controversial superissues that previously had dominated the regional systems and had generated much of the conflict. *Colonialism* was no longer a factor, and *Castroism,* while still a force in Latin American regional politics, no longer invoked the passions of an earlier era. Lately, the *Cold War* was replaced by a somewhat uneasy but nonetheless significant *Detente* between the two superpowers. Nation-states greatly contributed to the slight increase in global cooperation. Surprisingly enough, interstate nongovernmental actors, although in this case multinational corporations rather than terrorists, also increased their cooperation; but they were only about one-third as responsible as nation-states for the cooperative direction of system change.

We can understand overall patterns of change better by examining simultaneously the issues, actors, and behaviors that characterized each of the three regions. The Middle East was the only region in which there was a consistent trend throughout the entire twenty-five years toward decreasing cooperation and increasing conflict. Furthermore, the magnitude of

22. We calculate an "expected value" for cooperation, conflict, and violence for the system as a whole and for each of the different types of actors based upon levels in the prior period. In effect, expected value constitutes a projection of what these levels would be in the later period if activity remained constant. See Appendix, p. 316.
23. Interstate nongovernmental was the only actor type other than individuals which did not decrease its level of conflict in relation to the previous period, and its behavior was in marked contrast to the overall trend in the three regions.

these changes from period to period was larger in the Middle East than in the other regions. The pattern for Latin America was variable. Cooperation declined slightly throughout, while conflict peaked in the second period and then fell back to just below its beginning level in the third period. Finally, the trend for the twenty-five year period in Western Europe was the opposite of that for the Middle East. Conflict steadily declined while cooperation climbed.

These patterns of behavior can be attributed in part to certain characteristics of each region that brought particular types of actors to the fore. In the Middle East the "traditional" simplicity of most societies, except Israel and later Egypt, meant that, although interstate relations were very important to the politics of the region, there was comparatively little "domestic" (intrastate) politics. In Latin America there were some interstate relations but also considerable "domestic" activity. Western Europe was characterized by high levels of both inter- and intrastate politics as well as a "new" regional politics that centered around integration.

The Middle East: "An Embattled Region"

The second period in the Middle East, that is, the period between the invasion of Suez in 1956 and the June War of 1967, involved an almost 15 percent reduction in cooperation and a 25 percent increase in conflict compared with the first period. Both of these trends largely owed to the activities of nation-states. While overall violence declined during the second period, this was much more attributable to less frequent resort to violence on the part of intrastate nongovernmental actors. As a matter of fact, nation-states ran strongly counter to this trend of reduced violence. Individuals, intrastate nongovernmental groups, and noncentral governments (largely local colonial administrators) also played substantial roles in decreasing cooperation. On the other hand, intergovernmental organizations and interstate nongovernmental groups contributed to increasing conflict, while intrastate nongovernmental groups, noncentral governments, and intergovernmental organizations gravitated toward cooperation. The behavior of this last group reflected the reduction of the United Nations' presence as a source of conflict and the increased activities of groups like the Arab League that had previously been dormant.

Changing actor behavior was strongly influenced by the changing nature of regional superissues. During the first period two superissues, *Arab-Israeli* and *Colonialism,* predominated. In the second period, however, five of the six regional superissues (*Palestine* being the exception) were of almost equal importance. Recall that the Middle East was the most state-centric of our regions and especially so during the second period. The nation-state role in conflict derived from the penetration of the great powers and the spectrum of rivalries among Arab regimes. These issues, along with *Regime Stability,* involved relatively little violence but considerable conflict. For example, the *Arab-Israeli* issue at times assumed an almost purely verbal form as the various Arab regimes assailed one another with charges and countercharges as to which was actually contributing the most to the effort to "push Israel into the sea." Israel served to mask many of the critical divisions among the Arab regimes themselves. Superissue coappearance showed how *Superpower* penetration became linked to the basic *Arab-Israeli* division and to *Inter-Arab* rivalry during the second period.

Compared with the second period, the Middle East between 1967 and 1972 showed a slight increase in conflict and a large decline in cooperation (almost 30 percent). *At the same time, there was the greatest single jump (almost a two-thirds increase) in violence for any of the regions in any of the periods.* Violent actions accounted for over 13 percent of all behavior. The decrease in cooperation was largely caused by nation-states, although intergovernmental organizations also contributed to this trend. The United Nations was attempting to hasten an Israeli withdrawal from territories occupied in the 1967 war and was serving as a forum for the expression of this view by many governments. Although nation-states were less cooperative, they were actually greatly reducing their involvement in conflict, while other kinds of actors were increasing conflict. This was particularly the case for interstate nongovernmental guerrilla groups, which exhibited more than three times as many conflict actions as might have been expected on the basis of their behavior in the second period.

It was not so much shifts in the changing rank of the superissues as it was their changing content that influenced these behavior patterns. With the virtual disappearance of the *Colonial* superissue after 1967, two clusters of interrelated superissues remained: *Arab-Israeli* and *Superpower* and, secondarily, *Inter-Arab* and *Regime Stability.* The cause of this bifurcation was largely the *Palestinian* superissue which, although the fifth ranking superissue, rose in importance. The role of the *Palestinian* superissue after 1967 can be likened to that of the intrusion of Zionism before 1948. Both galvanized regional politics; both provided a set of controversial symbols around which other issues tended to be focused. Both tended to hide the complexity of regional politics by highlighting the presence of an alleged "European intruder."

In fact, during the twenty-five years, issues in the Middle East became more complexly related to one another. This trend has persisted since 1972 with the injection of the issue of oil and the energy crisis. The Middle East has combined traditional questions generally associated with a politically less developed region, such as ethnic separatism and nationalism, with "supermodern" ones posed by the Israeli model, oil, and superpower penetration. This fundamentally backward region has thus not been permitted to enter gradually into the modern world.

Latin America: "A Stable Pattern of Instability"[24]

In the second period in Latin America, between the Castro revolution in Cuba and the death of Ché Guevara in Bolivia in 1967, there was a moderate decrease in cooperation and an increase in conflict. Nation-states accounted for much of the reduction in cooperation, although intrastate nongovernmental actors and also individuals and interstate nongovernmental actors were almost as important in this regard. Intergovernmental organizations, notably the OAS, increased their cooperative activities in the second period, thus running counter to the overall regional trend. At the same time, however, these groups were contributing greatly to increased conflict within the region, albeit not as significantly as intrastate nongovernmental actors. Nation-states made only a minor contribution to increased conflict, and interstate nongovernmental actors inclined away from conflict.

The major superissue accounting for these changing behavior patterns was *Castroism*. It was the last ranking superissue in the first period, but it climbed markedly in the second. The increase in intrastate nongovernmental conflict linked to *Castroism* was not so much a result of the export of the Cuban Revolution after 1958 as it was of the emulation of Castro by indigenous groups in several Latin American countries. What we see here is a phenomenon characteristic of an interdependent world known as the "demonstration effect," that is, the adoption by others of a set of symbols, goals, and tactics from a group that has enjoyed success. Furthermore, the decrease in cooperation on the part of nation-states appears also to have been a result of the rise of *Castroism*. The divisive Dominican intervention of 1965, for example, was initiated by the United States because of its fear of "another Cuba." *Regime Stability, Castroism,* and *Security* superissues exhibited perfect coappearance scores. *Democracy-Dictatorship* and *External Assistance* were also closely associated with the nexus of *Castroism, Security,* and *Regime Stability.* In brief, the second period in Latin America was characterized by a syndrome in which five superissues produced less cooperation and more conflict on the part of both intrastate nongovernmental actors and nation-states. The period, in addition, saw the OAS intergovernmental organization drawn irrevocably into the *Castroism* superissue, with a disastrous impact on the organization's legitimacy.

There was a slight increase in violence in Latin America during the

24. Several students of Latin American politics have pointed to this characteristic. See, for example, Charles W. Anderson, *Politics and Economic Change in Latin America* (New York: D. Van Nostrand, 1967), Chap. 4.

second period. Nation-states were the most massive contributors to violence in the system, while every kind of nonstate actor (with the exception of intergovernmental organizations) decreased its initiation of violence. The causes of this nation-state violence were twofold: primarily, purges of supporters of the old regime in Cuba after Castro came to power and, secondarily, "peacekeeping" efforts in the Dominican Crisis of 1965. Although their initiation of violent acts declined from the first to the second period, intrastate nongovernmental actors remained the second leading source of regional violence.

Turning from the second to the third period, the major development in the region was a lessening of the polarization that had been caused by Cuba after 1958. Conflict declined slightly, while regional levels of cooperation remained about the same. The marginal decrease in cooperation (from 39.3 percent to 39.0 percent of the total dyads) was most apparent in the behavior of interstate nongovernmental actors such as multinational corporations. Yet these actors also went against the trend of decreasing conflict, slightly increasing their contribution to regional conflict. Nation-states and individuals were the other actors that reflected the system pattern of decreased cooperation. Nevertheless, nation-states were the principal contributors to the decrease in conflict, with intergovernmental organizations as secondary contributors. The relatively high level of IGO participation in conflict in the second period was a result of the fact that the Castro issue was fundamentally perceived as a state issue, and the OAS was a useful tool of those nation-states that opposed Cuba. In addition, the United Nations became involved with two major conflict-producing issues of regional politics during the second period, the Cuban Missile Crisis and the Dominican problem of 1965. While patterns of behavior between the second and third periods did not change greatly, they became somewhat less related to region-wide issues and more to local and parochial concerns. Many Latin American states sought to cope with guerrilla groups, but these groups were less likely to be perceived as part of the threat of Communist penetration of the Western hemisphere and as supported in a major way by Cuba. In part this perceptual change was the consequence of a broadening detente in Soviet-American relations.

Regime Stability remained the dominant superissue in the third period. *Castroism,* however, declined to third place, and *Security* returned to the second rank that it had occupied between 1948 and 1958. The links between *Security* and declining conflict were not only the eclipse of *Castroism* but also the effective end of the exile invasion phenomenon in the Caribbean. The strong coappearance of *Regime Stability* with *Security* continued from the second to the third periods and partly reflected increased involvement by the military of various Latin American countries in political affairs. Indeed, one of the major reasons that *Democracy-Dictatorship* was eliminated as a superissue in this period was that the ranks of the Latin American "democratic left" had been decimated by a series of military coups. In addition, new civilian politicians emerged who were not explicitly associated with the "democratic left" of the heyday of the Alliance for Progress and the "twilight of the tyrants." Most notable among these civilian leaders was Salvador Allende, the popularly-elected Marxist president of Chile, who was overthrown in a coup and died violently in 1973. In an atmosphere of military intervention and increasing urban terrorism, violence rose in the third period by 22 percent. This increase was confined to intrastate nongovernmental actors and individuals. Thus, an increase in anomic violence took place within the context of domestic repression in many Latin American states by the military and the fading of Castro's Cuba as a "revolution for export."

Latin American politics during the twenty-five years evidenced what has been termed a stable pattern of instability. Between 1948 and 1958 a democratic left emerged and began to do battle with long-established dictators like Trujillo and Batista. The second period brought the Cuban revolution, attempts to export Cuba's revolutionary experience to other Latin American countries, and a higher level of Soviet involvement in the Western hemisphere. By the third period, Castroism was no longer seen as a viable option for most Latin countries; the democratic left—except in Colombia, Venezuela, and Costa Rica—was in disarray; and political intervention by "technocratic" military groups was something that few civilian regimes could prevent and some elites desired. The military in Peru was an anomaly in its dedication to rapid social change. In Chile the rightist military ultimately crushed an experiment in gradual transformation to socialism within a legitimate democratic context. In Argentina, however, the military finally stepped aside and allowed Juan Perón to return from exile in an unsuccessful attempt to bring unity to the fragmented politics of that country.

The future prospects for Latin American politics are somewhat obscure. In terms of security, with the Castro regime no longer perceived to be the threat to security that many once thought it was, this region has now returned to the periphery of the global political system. Nevertheless, the energy crisis has underscored Latin America's importance as a source of raw materials and, in this regard, has given new significance to the region's linkages with the rest of the developing world.

Western Europe: "Beyond the Nation-State"[25]

Western Europe in the period between the founding of the European Economic Community and the second de Gaulle veto of British entry into the EEC witnessed a slight increase in both cooperation and conflict. The frequency of violence, however, did decrease some 20 percent as the region enjoyed a period of relative social peace and government stability. Nation-states largely accounted for the moderate total increase in cooperation,

25. Ernst B. Haas, *Beyond the Nation-State* (Stanford: Stanford University Press, 1964).

which to some extent compensated for a dramatic decline in cooperation by all nonstate actors. Interstate nongovernmental groups and intergovernmental organizations in particular played distinctive parts in altering the nature of regional conflict from the first to the second period.

Patterns of nonstate and state behavior were associated with the rise of *Gaullism* from the last-ranking superissue of the first period to the third-ranking superissue in the second period. The first two ranking superissues, *Cold War* and *Integration,* remained in the same ranks in both periods, as did the fourth ranking superissue, *Colonialism.* The leading conflict-producing superissues of the first period, *Cold War* and *Colonialism,* represented Europe's transition from the center of world politics before 1939 to a secondary status. At the moment when the European colonial empires began to crumble, Europe itself became the major stake and prize in the East-West confrontation. In part *Integration* was a response to this external challenge. However, the easing of *Cold War* tensions at the midpoint of the second period, following the Cuban Missile Crisis in 1962, permitted the rise of more parochial conflicts. Many of these conflicts revolved around *Gaullism* and de Gaulle's attempt to revive the independence of the separate European nation-states. The rise of *Gaullism* in France and the conflicts it generated with other governments and with the EEC, NATO, and multinational corporations delayed the trend toward decreasing regional conflict and increasing regional cooperation that emerged after 1967.

The dilemma posed by the Gaullist assertion of nation-state supremacy pervaded the entire second period. It was reflected, for example, in the role played by the Federal Republic of Germany. During the first period the FRG was essentially the "state between" the two superpowers penetrating European politics. Regional integration and military planning were the Western response to this situation. By the second period the FRG had become a full-fledged "state within" Western Europe, prepared to balance de Gaulle and many of his objectives with a thrust toward a "new" Europe. For West Germany the question was whether the nation-state could best be reasserted in isolation or through the regional IGO. Similarly, the smaller Western European nation-states were satisfied to voice their differences with Gaullist France and their other concerns from within intergovernmental organizations such as the EEC and NATO.

Compared with the second period, the third period showed very dramatic shifts in the direction of increasing cooperation (up 27 percent), decreasing conflict (down over 31 percent), and the virtual elimination of violence (down almost 70 percent). *Gaullism* ceased to be a major generator of regional friction. *Integration* processes were again under way, although this superissue was not as salient as before. Moreover, East-West tensions were on the wane, with the progress of *Detente.* Nation-states and, secondarily, transnational groups were the major source of increasing cooperation.

Intrastate nongovernmental actors also reduced their conflict as *Gaullism* faded and, more importantly, as *Colonial* issues practically disappeared. Even though intrastate nongovernmental actors remained major sources of conflict, they were associated more directly with questions like *Regime Stability*. In effect, the extra-regional actors that had contributed so much to conflict within the region during previous periods were replaced by groups, such as the neofascists in Germany and Italy, that were located in the region. The major conflict-producing superissues, with the exception of *Regime Stability,* no longer involved the region as a stake or prize but were rooted in disputes originating outside of Western Europe. Thus, Europe became a worried observer of crises in Vietnam and the Middle East in which its own involvement was peripheral.

Changing issues, actors, and behavior in Western Europe have, of course, had important consequences for world politics as a whole. Between 1948 and 1957 Europe was the scene of the major East-West clashes. Indeed, unless one rates the 1954 Guatemalan episode in this category, such clashes rarely disturbed the politics of Latin America or the Middle East at this time. But, as the 1950's drew to a close, the Cold War left Europe behind in certain respects, and the major confrontation of the early 1960's took place in Latin America (the Cuban Missile Crisis). After 1967 the Cold War itself all but vanished in Western Europe, and the Middle East became the scene of what are potentially the world's most explosive issues.

Interestingly, we see in Europe omens of what many analysts believe is an emerging worldwide emphasis on economic and resource interdependencies rather than on more traditional military security issues. Since 1967 Europe has been troubled by problems concerning monetary stability, resource accessibility, trade balances, social progress, and environmental pollution. The vast majority of nation-states in the world will remain largely unable to cope with such new global issues as oil and energy, technology, and food supplies. Although predictions are always hazardous, the nation-states of Western Europe *may* be in a superior position to deal with these issues because, having created strong regional intergovernmental organizations, they have begun the complicated processes of social learning that new forms of multilateral cooperation will require. Then again, these very issues may reveal additional discontinuities in Western Europe's commitment to regional cooperation and make for new conflicts.

Reflections on Three Regions

There are certain characteristics of the three regional systems that seem to bear importantly on emerging patterns of global politics.

In many respects the Middle East is the least advanced of the three regions politically and economically. Yet the region involved the highest degree of nation-state dominance throughout the twenty-five-year period. One reason for this association between backwardness and nation-state dominance is to be found in the nature of the nation-states themselves. Many of these are monarchical and feudal in character; they lack complex social structures and interest groups and are governed by dynastic rulers and ideological regimes.

Because of their general lack of institutional and social complexity, the continued dominance of nation-states in this region may actually retard modernization processes. (Several of the states in the region have begun to modernize during the period we have analyzed.) At least when viewed from a Western perspective, much of the politics of the Middle East appears to be characteristic of an early stage of historical development. States are only now becoming linked to nations, and many still bear the imprint of their colonial past. The issue of a "stateless" Palestinian nation today bears a striking surface resemblance to the earlier creation of Israel for the "stateless" Jewish nation.

The relative inactivity of intrastate nongovernmental groups reflects the fact that many Middle Eastern societies lack the pluralistic groups common in the West. With the exception of groups in Israel and Egypt, the main autonomous intrastate groups in the region have been ethnic minorities such as the Kurds in Iraq and the Blacks in the Sudan, independence movements such as the FLN in Algeria, and ideological movements such as the Baathists in Syria and Iraq. In contrast, there is little activity on the part of modern political, economic, or technical organizations and groups.

Latin America, in contrast, is characterized by a rich constellation of intrastate groups and by the degree to which it has been penetrated from without, primarily by the United States. (One might compare the Jordanian civil war of 1970 and the politics of Chile during the Allende period in order to appreciate the apparent simplicity of the former and the extraordinary complexity of the latter.) In Latin America, unlike the Middle East, ethnicity has been largely submerged as a source of conflict. In most of this region, with the exception of some isolated Indian minorities, the nation and the state have been linked for more than a century. Yet the region is only now going through the sort of social chaos associated with an earlier period of economic and political development in Western Europe. Economic development began relatively early in Latin America, which produced the social complexity of a new industrial-commercial-financial elite, the middle classes, an urban working class, and an urban marginal population in city slums. The *Democracy-Dictatorship* superissue in the first two periods and the rise of *Castroism* marked a symbolic end to many of the patterns associated with traditional agricultural societies characterizing much of Latin America well into the twentieth century. The growth in intrastate nongovernmental participation in politics, in some instances first galvanized by the *Democracy-Dictatorship* superissue, suggests that Latin America in the final decades of this century is going through a process that (though vastly accelerated) is similar to that experienced in Western Europe a century before.

In Latin America, however, increased participation in political life is more likely than not to take the form of conflict than cooperation. Many of the fundamental political questions revolve in Latin America around the phenomenon of increasing political participation linked to increasing social and economic interdependence that transcends nation-state frontiers. In effect demands for reform and change are outstripping the capacity of older institutions, like national governments, to cope with them. This is a formula for endemic political instability.

Western Europe stands in stark contrast to Latin America. Here, an increasingly cooperative pattern has dominated the twenty-five years we have analyzed. Western European nation-states have an even longer history than those in Latin America. Partly for this reason, many of the problems associated with the participation explosion have been, to a considerable extent, solved. Western Europe already has institutionalized political parties, conjoint economic groupings, and huge indigenous corporate enterprises, which make coping with citizens' demands considerably easier (although generating new and different ones). Moreover, unlike Latin America, the existence of divisive issues has not led in Western Europe to a challenge to the basic fabric of society. In a word, Western Europe has begun to adapt to the challenges of the present, whereas Latin America has only begun to define them. Of course, as the British coal miners' strike of 1973 suggests, Europe may not be able to cope with the coming problems of post-industrial society.

The fact that Latin America and the Middle East are undergoing developments that Western Europe has already experienced does not necessarily mean that the outcomes of these processes will be the same. The impact of a "future shocked" global political system characterized by rapid communication and transportation, as well as complex interdependencies, means that developmental processes will speed up tremendously. In Latin America, the social groups created by relatively early economic development have become monsters in states that cannot keep pace with rising demands. Indeed, the economic "pie" itself is not sufficiently large to meet demands even if it were to be more equitably divided.

In the Middle East, the existence of ethnic, religious, and national divisions also portends conflict. Even more ominous is the fact that in a world of such accelerated change the Middle East may be confronted by economic and ethnic challenges at the same time. In both Latin America and the Middle East, the actors around whom the keenest controversies have swirled, Cuba and Israel, form part of the region. Both regions have been catalyzed, and the Middle East remains so, by the presence of a regional "adversary" of the older regimes. The Middle East and Latin America both have regional interstate governmental actors—the Arab League and the OAS—which have played principal antagonistic roles with regard to these "adversaries." In contrast, in Western Europe the major "adversary" was the Soviet Union, an extraregional actor. Instead of dividing the region, the "adversary" fostered its unity.

Conclusions:
Political Change and the Future of the State

We have argued that the nation-state has never been the sole actor in global politics. Although it remains the principal actor, it is no more than *primus inter pares;* it interacts and shares influence with an array of other types of organizations and groups. But in addition to asking to what degree power is shared in contemporary politics, we must also ask whether such a world is preferable to one in which states were omnipotent or, for that matter, one in which they did not exist at all.

One school of thought has held that the creation of territorial states was ultimately destructive since these institutions permitted the waging of organized violence on a scale previously unknown. (Although their reasoning differed markedly, this view was shared by Rousseau, Marx, and the Anarchists.) A more common strand of thought has been that the development of states has benefited global society by permitting men to organize in rational fashion toward the attainment of economic and social objectives; the state, it has been argued, encourages a division of labor among men and peaceful social change. This last point was emphasized by philosophers such as Thomas Hobbes who saw the state as an instrument for maintaining domestic tranquility. The state, in their view, was a decisive step towards organizing large numbers of people while protecting them from external predators. These ideas were expressed in the two main assumptions of state sovereignty. As we have seen, however, modern nation-states are neither fully independent, nor do they exercise supreme power internally; they cannot guarantee peaceful change and adjustment either within or without. Indeed, it is possible that, to the degree that states exercise total power within, they may perpetuate old injustices or give rise to new ones. Terms such as "totalitarianism" and "authoritarianism" embody this suspicion.

One obvious reason for this disagreement and confusion is that, other than in their common possession of sovereignty, states differ markedly from one another. Some are linked to nations; others are multinational. Some are powerful and effective regulators of their foreign affairs and have strong governments; others are deeply penetrated from without or are mere geographic receptacles of "civil" strife. Some states have globe-girdling influence; others are virtual satellites of more powerful entities. The point is that, while certain nation-states appear to further the consummatory ends of man such as security and peace, others are poorly suited to these tasks. Some nation-states and their governments have become so large and powerful that they seem insensitive to the needs and demands of citizens at home and people abroad. Where this is the case, cries for decentralization of authority and administration tend to arise. Still other nation-states are so weak and fragmented that they seem totally incapable of fulfilling the aspirations of their own inhabitants. In such cases, increased centralization or the formation of even larger political units may be demanded.

The German philosopher Hegel saw the modern nation-state as the final and supreme stage of political organization. In this respect, he was implicitly discussing one conception of what scholars have more recently termed *political development*. Since change is a multidimensional process, it is not at all surprising that there exist many definitions of political development, only one of which is explicitly related to the creation of nation-states. Of this school of thought Lucian Pye writes:

> Political development . . . becomes the process by which communities that are nation-states only in form and by international courtesy become nation-states in reality. Specifically, this involves the development of a capacity to maintain a certain level of public order, to mobilize resources for a specific range of collective enterprises, and to make and effectively uphold types of international commitments.[26]

But any and all of the above functions can and have been performed by entities other than nation-states. In addition, many contemporary nation-states do not meet these stringent criteria. There are instances, as in the Congo in 1960 and Cyprus in 1964, when "public order" could only be imposed by external actors. Moreover, actors such as multinational corporations and international organizations are often more capable of mobilizing resources for "collective enterprises" than many nation-states. Finally, many nonstate actors, as we have shown, are fully able to uphold "international commitments."

Historically, the creation of modern nation-states where none existed before has even retarded the developmental processes as a whole. After World War I, the multinational Austro-Hungarian Empire was dissolved

26. Lucian W. Pye, *Aspects of Political Development* (Boston: Little Brown and Co., Inc., 1966), p. 37.

into a number of small, quarrelsome, and economically unviable nation-states such as Yugoslavia, Austria, and Hungary. Many of the successor states, though moving closer towards the ideal of national self-determination in Central and Eastern Europe than ever before, quickly succumbed to local despots and later proved unable to resist Nazi economic penetration or military aggression. In contrast, the Empire had been a center of art and science as well as a relatively prosperous economic unity. More recently, many of the successor states of the former British and French Empires have suffered similar fates.

Pye identifies other definitions of political development, none of which *necessarily require* the existence of nation-states.[27] The processes which they involve are not linked to any particular institutions. One definition of political development, for example, sees it as related to the growth of industrial societies. Such societies are presumed to be governed by orderly bureaucratic procedures. Yet such procedures and the economic and social development which they presumably foster can as easily be associated with political parties, corporations, and intergovernmental organizations as with nation-states. Indeed, one of the outstanding characteristics of industrial societies is the existence of a rich array of functionally specific and interest-oriented groups and institutions. Paradoxically, the greater the number of and the more autonomous these groups, the less omnipotent states are likely to be internally and the greater the probability that transnational associations will arise and that transnational links will be forged.[28]

Still another definition maintains that political development is related to mass mobilization of people and their participation in politics. Once again there is no logical necessity that such a process be associated exclusively with nation-states. Nationalist and ethnic movements, ideologically-inclined parties, and labor unions may encourage mass mobilization and participation in collaboration with or, as is often the case, in opposition to national governments.

As our brief discussion of political development suggests, there is no necessity to associate the existence or dominance of nation-states or national governments with global change from a less desirable to a more desirable state of affairs. In fact, to the degree that present-day nation-states are unable to cope with the challenges of ecological disasters, demands for personal freedom and self-fulfillment, and large-scale violence, they may be inimical to political development. As "aristocratic" institutions, they may continue to go on using "the same old ways" while confronting challenges that are novel. Among those who have sought to

27. *Ibid.*, pp. 33–45.
28. Referring to the American political system, Theodore J. Lowi makes a similar point in *The End of Liberalism* (New York: W. W. Norton, 1969).

perpetuate the dominance of the nation-state are "nationalists" who are unaware of, or resistant to, the impact of global interdependence. Finally, regardless of one's normative predispositions, it is impossible to ignore the presence of nonstate actors that have played such a central role in many of the conflicts that have arisen in world politics during the last thirty years. As we enter the last quarter of the twentieth century, we must ask whether the state-centric model is either normatively or empirically desirable. To those who would ignore nonstate actors, we offer Samuel Johnson's observation:

> If the changes that we fear be thus irresistible, what remains but to acquiesce with silence, as in the other insurmountable distresses of humanity? It remains that we retard what we cannot repel, that we palliate what we cannot cure.[29]

29. Cited in E. L. McAdam, Jr. and George Milne, eds., *Johnson's Dictionary: A Modern Selection* (New York: Pantheon Books, 1963), p. 27.

Methodological Appendix

This section is intended for the advanced reader who may be interested in the methodology and the data used in this book.

The Nostac Event Data and Their Coding

In seeking to answer the key question of "who does what to whom" in global politics, we have examined behavior as manifested in discrete "events." As Harold D. Lasswell and Abraham Kaplan once observed:

> (T)he subject matter of political science [may be expressed] in terms of a certain class of *events* (including "subjective" events), rather than time-less institutions or political patterns . . . The developmental standpoint is concerned, not with systems in equilibrium, but with patterns of succession of events . . . (Italics in original.)[1]

The systematic assessment of behavior by analyzing event data has been undertaken in the *World Event/Interaction Survey* (*WEIS*) and the *Comparative Research on the Events of Nations* (*CREON*) among other projects. The use of events as comparable units provides for the kinds of operational definitions that are necessary to build and test empirical theories about the political universe. They permit us to discern the objectively demonstrable attributes or consequences of abstract concepts such as hostility and cooperation which formerly were thought to be untestable.

Event data have certain limitations. For instance, it is difficult to

1. Harold D. Lasswell and Abraham Kaplan, *Power and Society* (New Haven: Yale University Press, 1950), pp. xiv–xv.

distinguish purposive from nonpurposive behavior, and the data do not permit direct inquiry into the motivations that lie behind behavior. Thus, while event data allow for the analysis of inputs and outputs, they do not easily permit analysis of the process by which the one is translated into the other.

While the definition of what constitutes an event has been a subject of controversy, most analysts concur that it must include an "actor" or "initiator" which undertakes an "action" or "behavior" toward some "target" or "object." In the *Nonstate Actor (NOSTAC) Project,* the coding rules require that each event have only one actor and at least one target. Either the actor or the target must be an organized unit having a membership of more than one person. The behavior must be an observable phenomenon, reported in the coding source.

NOSTAC coding rules also specify that an action may have one or more "indirect targets" if a target which does not receive the actual behavior of the event is explicitly mentioned by name in the coding source. (This also allows us to consider the special case we term "reflexive action." For instance, legislatures vote, cabinets meet, and other organizations and groups undertake observable behavior directed toward the group itself.) The numbers of events and dyads in the NOSTAC data set are shown in Table 101.

Analysis of "events" permits accumulation of data, but it remains to classify events into behavior categories. The classification that we employed was translated into the NOSTAC framework from the work of Stephen Salmore in conjunction with Charles Hermann and others in the CREON Project. (They, in turn, had adapted this five-fold classification from the original WEIS analysis that provided for twenty-two categories and a number of subcategories.) The relationship of the categories we employed to the original twenty-two WEIS categories is shown in Table 102.

A number of further comments about the NOSTAC coding are in order. First, what is "political" is determined by the situation in which an event occurs. We have coded all of the events conforming to the rules summarized above because any event *can be* political. Second, events were coded even though they took place within the borders of individual nation-

Table 101. The Nostac Data Set

Time Period	Middle East Events	Dyads	Western Europe Events	Dyads	Latin America Events	Dyads		
I	578	819	1376	1839	555	624		
II	469	561	897	1154	1053	1135		
III	522	598	422	729	450	477		
Total	1569	1978	2695	3722	2058	2236	6322	7936

Table 102.   The Nostac Classification and the WEIS Behavior Categories

Nostac	Weis
Cooperative Deeds	yield, grant, reward
Word Cooperation	approve, promise, agree, request, propose
Participation	comment, consult
Word Conflict	reject, protest, deny, accuse, demand, warn, threaten
Conflictful Deeds	demonstrate, reduce relationship, expel, seize, force

states. Although traditionally not considered a part of "international" politics, such events nevertheless have important direct and indirect consequences.[2] Moreover, as recent essays on "transnationalism" suggest, the national frontier does *not* pose an obstacle to many global processes. Thus, *any unit* which was within the region or was involved in action according to the coding rules was considered part of the regional system.

We employed a geographically-based classification of regional systems, coding any event that involved a unit within them. Events involving units that were organized within the region but that took place outside of it were also coded, such as a meeting between an Ecuadorian chief of state and a French President at the United Nations. The regions are depicted in Table 103.

Finally, the basic units of much of the NOSTAC analysis were dyadic combinations defined by the events. Thus, a single event involving three direct targets was considered as three separate dyads (one for the actor with each target). There were a number of advantages in the use of dyads, including a more precise evaluation of the scale and magnitude (or scope and domain) of particular events. Assuming that "more important" events would involve greater numbers of targets, we provided an additional means of compensating for the relative insensitivity of event data to the importance of a given action. Another advantage in the use of dyads was that they enabled us to consider simultaneously patterns of initiation and reception by the same analytic techniques.

2. This accords with Rosenau's conception of "national-international linkages." James N. Rosenau, "Introduction: Political Science in a Shrinking World," in Rosenau, ed., *Linkage Politics* (New York: Free Press, 1969), pp. 1–17. Considerable research has been undertaken to investigate the hypothesized relationship between "domestic" stability and "external" conflict. See R. J. Rummel, "Dimensions of Conflict Behavior Within and Between Nations," *General Systems Yearbook* 8 (1963), pp. 1–50; Jonathan Wilkenfeld, "Domestic and Foreign Conflict Behavior of Nations," in William D. Coplin and Charles W. Kegley, Jr., eds., *A Multi-method Introduction to International Politics* (Chicago: Markham Press, 1971), pp. 189–204.

Table 103. *The Nostac Regions*

Middle East	Latin America	Western Europe*
Aden	Argentina	Belgium
Algeria	Bahamas	France
Bahrain	Bolivia	Federal Republic of Germany
Egypt	Brazil	(including West Berlin)
Ifni	British Honduras (Belize)	Italy (including Vatican)
Iraq	Chile	Luxembourg
Israel	Colombia	Netherlands
Jordan	Costa Rica	
Kuwait	Cuba	
Lebanon	Dominican Republic	
Libya	Ecuador	
Morocco	El Salvador	
Muscat and Oman	Federation of the West Indies	
Qatar	French Guiana	
Saudi Arabia	Guatemala	
South Aden	Guyana (British Guiana)	
Spanish Morocco	Haiti	
Sudan	Honduras	
Syria	Jamaica	
Trucial Oman States	Mexico	
Tunisia	Nicaragua	
Yemen	Panama	
	Paraguay	
	Peru	
	Puerto Rico	
	Surinam (Dutch Guiana)	
	Trinidad and Tobago	
	Uruguay	
	Venezuela	

*Including colonies of the above.

Validity and Reliability

Two key questions must be addressed in considering any measurement procedure(s). These are validity and reliability. Validity means that what the investigators *believe is being measured* is that which *is being measured*. Reliability demands that such measurement be consistent and hence implies criteria of scientific replicability.[3]

Many of the criticisms of event data *per se* have centered around questions concerning the validity of coding sources. The *New York Times* is the sole source for the NOSTAC event data. Although arguments about foreign language coders, regional sources, and reporting biases may never

3. A more detailed discussion of many of the methodological points raised in this and the ensuing sections may be found in Donald E. Lampert, "The Developmental Bases of Nonstate Behavior: Nonstate Actors and Regional Political Development in Western Europe and Latin America," Unpublished Ph.D. Dissertation, Rutgers University, 1975.

be resolved to everyone's satisfaction, adherence to a single source of high quality appears to remain the best way of assuming either consistency of bias or randomness of error no matter what the idiosyncrasies of reportage or editorial position might be. As Charles McClelland argues:

> The question of whose coding system matches correctly to reality is virtually unanswerable. When everybody has a bias, what test could there be for objectivity? . . . The solution that is available is to set aside the problem of unbiased truth and to analyze over time the reports that pass through *one* bias-filter of a national press. The best choice that can be made of a single source is the *New York Times*. This paper must be assumed to filter the news with an American bias but it is an exceptionally rich source of reports of international political events.[4]

In assessing the validity of the *New York Times,* Stephen Salmore noted three criticisms against which the *Times* should be defended to be considered a valid source.[5] The first involved the quality of the source itself. As Ithiel Pool argues:

> (D)espite local and individual variations, the prestige paper has come to be an important and respected institution. Governments, politicians, and businessmen depend upon it. One might ask what would happen in Washington if the *New York Times* stopped publication . . .[6]

The second criticism, that of consistency of reportage across geographic regions, is somewhat more troublesome. Several responses are in order. *Times* coverage is as satisfactory, and often better, than that of other "elite" newspapers here and abroad. Moreover, use of the *Times* alone avoids the problems of comparability inherent in regional sources. In addition, if the *New York Times* represents the outlook of an American "foreign policy establishment," we believe that this would be apparent in a bias *against* reportage of nonstate activity in various regions. Finally, the United States has not been included as a "core actor" in any of the regional systems. This partly controls for the overreportage of American activities. American events were not coded unless the interaction involved an actor in one of the regional systems that we have defined. A final criticism concerns whether the *New York Times* is more sensitive to certain kinds of events, particularly those involving conflict. On the one hand, the important variable here may not be conflict, but rather the extent to which a given event is precedent-breaking or unexpected. If so, then the criticism is trivial

4. Charles A. McClelland, "International Interaction Analysis: Basic Research and Some Practical Applications," Technical Report no. 2 (Department of International Relations, University of Southern California, 1968), pp. 46–48.
5. Stephen A. Salmore, "National Attributes and Foreign Policy: A Multivariate Analysis," Unpublished Ph.D. Dissertation, Princeton University, 1972, Chap. 3.
6. Ithiel de Sola Pool, *The "Prestige Papers"* (Stanford: Stanford University Press, 1952), p. 8.

because such events may equally involve conflict or cooperation. On the other hand, it appears that many nonstate actors play political roles that are similar to those of small states which lack resources. Thus, if the criticism were important, we would expect *Times* reporting to demonstrate a bias towards conflict involving such states. The *New York Times* has been shown not to be overly sensitive in the reportage of conflict events for this variety of state actor, and thus logically one would not expect a bias toward conflict involving nonstate actors.[7]

In considering the NOSTAC event data, "intercoder reliability" is particularly important. Intercoder reliability involves the extent to which the coders of the events agree upon what constitutes "reality." We tested intercoder reliability twice for each regional data set, between the first and second, and the second and third time periods. A news item was selected at random to be coded by all of the coders. Intercoder reliability can be calculated in a number of ways. We chose Scott's *Pi,* appropriately adjusted, because it "corrects for the number of categories in the code, and the frequency with which each was used."[8] *Pi* is designed to be applicable to the kinds of noninterval data the NOSTAC categories represent. "In the practical coding situation it varies from 0.00 to 1.00, regardless of the number of categories in the dimension, and is thus comparable with the 'percentage agreement' figure:"[9]

$$\pi = \frac{P_0 - P_e}{1 - P_e}$$

P_0 (observed percent agreement) represents the percentage of judgments on which any two coders agree when coding the same data independently, and P_e is the percent agreement to be expected on the basis of chance. *Pi* is the ratio of the actual difference between obtained and chance agreement to the maximum difference between obtained and chance agreement. It can be roughly interpreted as the extent to which coding reliability exceeds chance.

By treating the set of coders pairwise across a given category, we approximated the most important considerations raised by Krippendorf's technique, although his "tree model" itself was deemed overly complex for what we felt to be a relatively simple set of categories.[10] We adjusted our use of the Scott model to allow for the extent to which the coders and authors were in agreement. This was done by having the authors determine separately how they thought the article should be coded. If more than two-thirds of the coders considered a given action to have taken place where

7. Salmore, "National Attributes," Chap. 3.
8. William A. Scott, "Reliability of Content Analysis: The Case for Nominal Scale Coding," *Public Opinion Quarterly* 19 (Fall 1955), p. 323.
9. *Ibid.*
10. See Klaus Krippendorf, "Reliability of Recording Instructions: Multivariate Agreement for Nominal Data," *Behavioral Science* 16 (May 1971), pp. 228–35.

Table 104. Average Inter-Coder/Coder-Investigator Agreement

	Middle East*		Latin America		Western Europe	
	I	II	I	II	I	II
Event/Actor Type	.86	.91	.88	.86	.84	.84
Action Area	.73	.77	.88	.83	.88	.86
Violence	.83	.87	.94*	.96*	.95*	1.00*
Action Type	.75	.87	.74	.83	.75	.87
Direct Target	.80	.85	.74	.86	.76	.79
Indirect Target	.76	.84	.60	.76	.67	.70

*Observed percent agreement only.

the investigators disagreed, this was included in the calculation of reliability figures for the coders themselves. Therefore, we have accounted for coder/investigator agreement as well.

The coders were also required to describe *qualitatively* each action they coded. This provided additional information about the context in which events occurred and the issue(s) that they involved. This further allowed the authors to change apparent "errors" in the data when they were collated.[11] Given the "fail-safe" procedures with regard to the data, the reliability figures are satisfactory and, in some cases, high.[12]

The Flow of the NOSTAC Analyses

We shall now consider the ways in which the NOSTAC data were analyzed prior to the derivation of the results which are found in the chapters. Let us reconstruct the steps of the analysis.

Inductive Categorization

As the data were collated, intrastate and interstate actors were inductively reclassified. The inductive categories, with illustrations, are shown in Table 105. The categories were derived through visual inspection of a cross-tabulation matrix.

11. Also, since none of a coder's responses could be considered correct if the action were not properly identified, it was possible to adjust for coding errors in those cases in which the action was properly identified but in which the "actor type" had been miscoded.

12. Thirty coders were used in the Middle East, twelve in Latin America, and twenty-two in Western Europe. If one generalizes the equation by which P_e is derived, one finds that the probability of chance agreement between any pair of coders is virtually 0 under all situations, except where a particular category is chosen over 85 percent of the time by all coders. None of the categories were employed over 76 percent of the time in the Middle Eastern intercoder reliability tests so that all of these figures are P_o. The selection procedure for the inter-coder reliability tests in both Latin America and Western Europe resulted in only nonviolent events. Since the violence category was a binary code (i.e., "violent" or "nonviolent"), this meant that there could be no distribution across the categories, so the figures reported are also P_o.

Table 105.   *Inductive Classifications of Nonstate Actors*

Category	Example
Middle East	
Finance and Industrial	Bank of America, Shell Oil
Intrastate Jews	American Jewish Congress, Hadassah (U.S.)
Interstate Jews	World Zionist Congress, Jewish Agency
Intrastate Arabs	FLN, Saiqa
Interstate Arabs	Al Fatah, Palestinian Liberation Organization
Political Parties	Mapam (Israel), Radicals (France)
United Nations	Security Council, Jarring Mission
Media	*Jerusalem Post, London Times*
Other Nonstate Actors	American Black Panthers, Harvard University
Arab IGO's	Arab League, OPEC
Other IGO's	NATO, OAS
Religious	Coptic Church, Vatican
Latin America	
Communists	Chilean Communist Party, Continental Peace Conference
Castroites	National Army of Liberation, 26th of July
Anti-Castroites	Alpha 66, Brigade 2506
Other Parties	Institutional Revolutionary (Mexico), APRA (Peru), Democratic Action (Venezuela)
Multinational Corporations	United Fruit, Texaco, ITT
Extraregional Business	Mercedes-Benz, BOAC
Latin Business	Varig, Argentine carpet syndicate
Labor	Drivers Union (Bolivia), ILGWU (U.S.)
Demonstrators, Rebels, and Terrorists	Tacuara (Argentina), Boschists (D.R.), Young Patriots (Nicaragua)
Military	Venezuelan Army dissidents Couping Military (Brazil)
Students and Universities	Mexican students, Columbia University
Cultural, Service, and Professional	International Lawn Tennis Federation, Ford Foundation, N.Y. World's Fair
Media	*New York Times, La Prensa* (Argentina)
Catholic	Vatican, Cuban Catholic Church
Other Religious	Jewish School in Caracas, Baptists
Other Nonstate Actors	Lithuanian Government-in-Exile (Arg.)
United Nations and Other IGO's	General Assembly, IMF, EEC
Organization of American States	Secretary General, Pan-American Union
Regional IGO's	LAFTA, US-Mexican Cattle Disease Laboratory
Western Europe	
Communists	French Communist Party, Italian Communist Party
Socialists	SPD (FRG), Nenni Socialists (Italy)
Other Parties	Gaullists (France), Free Democrats (FRG)
Media	*Le Monde, Der Speigel,* WNET (N.Y.)
Business	KLM, Simca, Lufthansa, Hilton Hotels
Multinational Corporations	Bank of America, Volkswagen, ARBED Steel
Labor	National Union of Uniformed Police (France)
Religious	Vatican, American Jewish Congress
French Ethnic	Viet Minh, Tunisian nationalists
Other Ethnic	Walloons, Ustasha, Celtic League
Cultural and Service	Mount Holyoke College, ORTF (France)
Other Nonstate Actors	House of Savoy (Italy)
United Nations	UNESCO, ILO, Trusteeship Council
Occupation	Allied High Commission, Commandants (Berlin)
Western Defense	NATO, SEATO, WEU
European IGO's	ECSC, EEC, ELDO, EURATOM
Other IGO's	Arab League, Afro-Asian Bloc

The NOSTAC Factor Analyses[13]

We employed R-factor analysis (in which the variables as opposed to cases are factored) to discover the underlying dimensions of behavior in each regional system during each time period. Factor analysis requires interval data that possess linear independence. This requirement entailed a number of research decisions.

The basic information in the factor analyses consisted of behavior directed toward the eight most salient direct targets for the twenty-five-year period and whatever additional behavior was undertaken toward these eight as indirect targets.[14] (In this case, salience was determined by raw numbers of acts.) These eight and the percentages of dyads in which they were direct targets are shown in Table 106. The inductive categories of nonstate actors and the individual nation-states were employed for both actors and targets. Each actor/case was characterized by thirty-two variables. These variables were the percentages of cooperative and conflictful dyads undertaken toward the eight both as direct and indirect targets. The percentages were derived from the ratio of either type of behavior to the total behavior (including participation) that an actor undertook toward each of the eight first as direct and then as indirect targets.[15]

Two additional points should be made with regard to the factor analyses. First, we adhered to the "rule of thumb" criterion for the number of

Table 106. *The Eight Most Salient Direct Targets, 1948-1972*
(as percentage of total dyads)

Middle East		Latin America		Western Europe	
Israel	(13.0)	United States	(10.2)	France	(13.9)
Egypt	(11.2)	Media	(8.3)	F R of Germany	(10.5)
United Nations	(9.8)	Cuba	(6.8)	United States	(9.6)
United States	(7.7)	Individuals	(6.4)	United Kingdom	(6.2)
France	(4.8)	OAS	(5.9)	Individuals	(4.3)
Jordan	(4.7)	Argentina	(4.1)	USSR	(4.0)
Individuals	(3.8)	Other Parties	(4.1)	Italy	(3.7)
Intrastate Arabs	(3.1)	Labor	(3.6)	Media	(3.6)
Total	(58.1)	*Total*	(49.4)	*Total*	(55.8)

13. For a detailed description of factor analysis as a research technique, see R. J. Rummel, *Applied Factor Analysis* (Evanston, Ill.: Northwestern University Press, 1970).
14. Only eight targets were used to avoid there being more variables than cases. In addition, word and deed behavior were collapsed, yielding the categories of cooperation and conflict.
15. Percentages were employed because initial factor analyses that used raw numbers of acts yielded factor structures that were overly sensitive to the mere quantity of activity.

factors throughout the analysis (eigenvalues greater than unity). Second, orthogonal (varimax) rotation was used. This ensured that each factor delineated a statistically independent pattern of variation, produced factor scores for each case that were linearly independent and uncorrelated, and increased the likelihood that the factors would be substantively interesting.

Factor Scores, Issues, and Superissues

At this point the patterns of interrelationship among conflictful and cooperative acts were known. Stated in terms of the metaphor with which this Appendix began: We knew "who did what to whom" and how the set of "whats" and "whoms" fit together. However, we did not yet know what lay behind such patterns. To address this, we examined the set of normalized factor scores for all of the actors on each of the factors. A factor score for a given actor reveals the extent to which its behavior reflects the pattern of behavior described by a factor. Those actors most representative of the patterns of behavior described by a factor, we assume, outlie in the positive and negative 50 percent of the distribution of the factor scores for that factor. In terms of the normal distribution, this means a normalized factor score larger than $\pm$ 0.68. If the principal loadings (greater than $\pm$ 0.40) were all positive, we examined only those actors with factor scores greater than $+$ 0.68; if they were all negative, we examined only those actors with factor scores less than $-$ 0.68; if the pattern of principal loadings was mixed, we examined both.

We then set out to discover the specific actions responsible for each factor. This was done by examining the raw events undertaken by the outlying actors that conformed to the type of behavior represented by the principal loadings. The qualitative descriptions of the events allowed us to determine the specific issues associated with the behavior.

These issues were inductively aggregated into clusters which we termed *superissues*. In effect, a superissue is a cluster of specific issues that are related primarily on the basis of "the kinds of values or interests over which controversy ensues."[16] The superissues, some of which were regional in scope and others of which transcended the boundaries of a region, encompassed virtually all of the behavior in the NOSTAC data set. Certain events involved more than one superissue.

"Result-Oriented" Factors: A Conceptual Summary

Having described the logic of the factor analysis, let us pause and examine the question of what this represents in a methodological sense. The factors,

16. This is akin to what Rosenau terms a "value typology." James N. Rosenau, "Foreign Policy as an Issue-Area," in Rosenau, ed., *The Scientific Study of Foreign Policy* (New York: Free Press, 1971), p. 406.

which we have termed "result-oriented," are both *"theoretical"* and *"empirical"* as these terms are used by Rummel.[17] The empirical inputs were the cooperative and conflictful patterns of behavior toward the eight most salient targets. These patterns were interrelated through the factor analysis so that the interrelationships (factors) that emerged constituted a classification of the original phenomena.

There appear to be theoretical reasons behind the classification. Specific issues, it was assumed, were related to the actor's behavior. As the factor analysis revealed interrelationships among behavior, it should also have revealed interrelationships among the issues themselves.

In sum, the factors are the *results* of the events and the issues related to them; they are the consequences of the political interaction in the regions.

The Data in Chapters 5, 7, and 9

Ranking of Superissues by Explained Variance

(Chapter 5, Tables 1, 10, 19; Chapter 7, Tables 33, 42, 51; Chapter 9, Tables 62, 70, 80.) The *scores* with which each section of these chapters are introduced represent an attempt to assess the relative importance of each of the superissues for the patterns of regional politics during that period. The factors derived from the factor analysis are listed in approximately descending order in terms of the amount of variance that a given pattern of interrelationship can explain. In this case *explained variance* means the amount of the original behavior on which a factor matrix is based that is accounted for by the rotated matrix. It is used here to assess the relative importance of superissues. Each superissue received the *score* of the amount of variance explained by a factor each time a given specific issue that was subsumed by it appeared. The scores for each superissue were then summed. On the whole, these scores represent ordinal data, a "level of measurement (which) does not supply any information about the *magnitude* of the difference between elements." (Italics in original.)[18] Thus, in examining these tables the reader should remember that the magnitude of the actual scores are dependent upon the factor structure. Within a given factor analysis we can compare the *intervals*. Yet in comparing one factor analysis to another the rankings have meaning only as ordinal data.

We also refer to *percentage of total issues*. This was derived by summing the total number of specific issues and dividing it into the total

17. Rummel, *Applied Factor Analysis*, p. 19.
18. Hubert M. Blalock, Jr., *Social Statistics* (New York: McGraw-Hill, 1960), p. 14.

number of times a given superissue appeared.[19] This method of addressing the relative importance of superissues did *not* control for the amount of variance explained by the factors.

Alignments and Coalitions

(Chapter 5, Tables 3–5, 11–14, 20–22; Chapter 7, Tables 34–37, 43–46, 52, 53; Chapter 9, Tables 63–65 71–75, 81–83.) Examination of the factor structure suggested that actions undertaken toward certain targets were associated with selected superissues. This allowed us to determine the "pivots" around which the superissue revolved. Alignments and coalitions were determined by examining *all* the behavior of *all* actors towards the "pivots" as well as the behavior of the "pivots" towards their targets.

A coalition or alignment indirectly reflected postures toward the superissues, and not necessarily towards another coalition. For this reason, not all coalitions were labeled "pro" or "anti." Often, they reflected intermediate positions.

Superissue Coappearances

(Chapter 5, Tabes 6, 15, 23, 17; Chapter 7, Tables 38, 47, 54, 58; Chapter 9, Tables 66, 76, 84, 88.) Superissue coappearance scores reflect the degree to which the various superissues were related to each other. To the extent that superissues appeared on the same "result-oriented" factors, thereby reflecting similar patterns of behavior, they were the consequence of similar events which gave rise to the patterns in the first place. Thus, if two superissues were perfectly related, we would expect them to be present together on the same factors. The formula for calculating the coappearance between any two given superissues reflects the possible number of times that the two superissues *could have appeared* together,[20] which is divided into the number of times two superissues *did appear* on the same factors. (The appearance of each superissue on the same factor is counted once so a coappearance means that a "2" is scored.) The higher the average level of superissue coappearance for a given system in a particular time period, the more interdependent were the politics of the system.

Activity and Salience

(Chapter 5, Tables 7, 8, 16, 17, 24, 25, 28, 29; Chapter 7, Tables 39, 40, 48, 49, 55, 56, 59, 60; Chapter 9, Tables 67, 68, 77, 78, 85, 86, 89, 90.)

19. Summing percentages of total issues resulted in totals greater than 100 percent because specific issues could involve more than a single superissue.
20. *"Could have appeared* together" meant that each time either superissue appeared on a given factor it was scored. Therefore, it could not exceed the total number of factors $\times$ 2.

Activity and salience were determined by weighting action initiated and received. In part, the purpose of weighting was to account for different levels of commitment. Thus, we multiplied the number of deed actions initiated or received by a factor of three, the number of word actions initiated or received by a factor of two, and added participative actions to this total. (Theoretically, participative actions were multiplied by one because they represented the lowest commitment level.) The weighted scoring system provided a means of combining the actions of various types of behavior instead of treating each separately. While the weighted scoring had little overall effect in terms of the rank-orders of actors, occasionally it did increase the precision of this ranking. For instance, by using only raw scores the United Nations would have ranked as the second most salient target in the Middle East between 1948 and 1972. This would have obscured the fact that the United Nations was largely the target of verbal activity whereas Egypt (which ranked second in the weighted system) was the target of events that involved a relatively higher level of commitment on the part of initiators.

Disruptive-Supportive Behavior

(Chapter 5, Tables 9, 18, 26, 31; Chapter 7, Tables 41, 50, 57, 61; Chapter 9, Tables 69, 79, 87, 91.) The distinction between disruptive and supportive behavior is particularly important in determining the role of different types of actors and their impact on the regions.[21] Various system-level theorists have put forward conceptions of "balance," "regulation and stress," and a ratio of system "loads to capabilities."[22] Their work suggests that a distinction be made between behavior that "disrupts" a system, thereby placing strains upon it, and behavior that "supports" a system, thereby enhancing its adaptive or survival capacity.

Conflictful actions, we assume, are fundamentally disruptive, placing a strain on a system's capacity to adjust or even to survive. In contrast, cooperative behavior is supportive.[23] To determine levels of disruption or

21. For a discussion of roles in global politics see K. J. Holsti, "National Role Conceptions in the Study of Foreign Policy," *International Studies Quarterly* 14:3 (September 1970), pp. 233–309.
22. See, for example, Karl W. Deutsch, "Social Mobilization and Political Development," *American Political Science Review* 55:3 (September 1961), pp. 493–514; Samuel P. Huntington, *Political Order in Changing Societies* (New Haven: Yale University Press, 1968); Raymond F. Hopkins and Richard W. Mansbach, *Structure and Process in International Politics* (New York: Harper and Row, 1973); Richard N. Rosecrance, *Action and Reaction in World Politics* (Boston: Little, Brown and Co., 1963), *International Relations: Peace or War?* (New York: McGraw-Hill, 1973).
23. For an alternative view of the role of conflict see Robert C. North, H. E. Koch and Dina A. Zinnes, "The Integrative Functions of Conflict," *Journal of Conflict Resolution* 4:3 (September 1960) pp. 355–74.

support, behavior is weighted to account for affect and commitment. The scores also permit us to look at the *overall direction* of an actor's behavior. In weighting, we considered participative acts as the weakest form of system support (theoretically multiplied by +1).

The Data in Chapter 11

Autonomy

The basic model employed in the calculation of our autonomy measure was that of the *relative acceptance* index.[24] This is a "null model" that evaluates the actual value of a given variable in terms of its expected value in the system as a whole. In other words, actual–expected/expected. We employed salience as the expected value and activity as the actual value. Thus,

$$\text{Autonomy} = \frac{\text{Activity} - \text{Salience}}{\text{Salience}}$$

In order to determine whether the variations among autonomy scores for actor types 'were significantly different, analysis of variance (F-test) was used. All intrastate actors (individuals, intrastate nongovernmental actors, and governmental noncentral actors) were grouped together as were interstate governmental and interstate nongovernmental actors. States were treated separately. We then calculated autonomy scores for each of these grouped categories across all regions for each of the periods. Analysis of variance showed that the differences in autonomy scores were significant at the .05 level, but were not significant at the .01 level. For the test of such an important proposition, we thought that the .01 level should be required; and, consequently, we accepted the null hypothesis. If the state-centric model accurately reflected reality, significant variation should exist in autonomy scores for actor types. In other words, we would have expected states to be more "sovereign."

Crosstabulations

(Tables 93, 95, 96, 97.) Crosstabulation is merely a tabular display of the relationship between two variables. We present four such tables and a number of findings based on various others in the text. In each, dyadic combinations were used. Dyads initiated appear along the rows, and dyads

---

24. I. Richard Savage and Karl W. Deutsch, "A Statistical Model of the Gross Analysis of Transaction Flows," *Econometrica* 28:3 (July 1960), pp. 551–72.

received along the columns. Separate crosstabulations were derived for each regional system. The data in the overall table represents a summing of the various cells in each regional matrix and does *not* attempt to control for the relative number of events and dyads in the different regions. Cell percentages which are presented in the text were determined by taking the number of dyads in a given cell of a matrix and dividing it by the total number of dyads in the matrix.

Involvement

(Tables 94, 98.) Involvement figures were derived by summing the cell percentages in which a given actor type was either the actor or the target. If one sums the total given in Table 94, one finds that involvement totals more than 100.0 percent. This is so because various cells in the matrix are counted more than once depending on both the type of actor and target represented by a given cell. A second set of involvement figures are presented in Table 98 for cooperation, conflict, and violence. These figures were calculated in the same fashion as overall involvement for the respective types of behavior.

Disruption and Support

These figures were calculated by separately determining the amount of disruptive and supportive behavior in the system as a whole. The percentage contributions of each actor type were then calculated by dividing this disruptive or supportive total into the actor type's total of either disruption or support.

Initiations

(Tables 99, 100.) Initiations, in essence, reflect the "profile" of a given actor type. They reveal the distribution of an actor's total behavior among cooperation, participation, conflict, and violence.

System Change

We sought a simple method for the analysis of the relative amount of change between two given periods and the relative contribution of each actor type to that change. Consider the data in Table 107.

We have already noted that *cooperation* and *conflict* can be considered as separate analytic dimensions. The same is true also of violence. Thus, the first step was to consider whether these dimensions increased or decreased relative to the prior period as a percentage of the total number of

Table 107. *Comparison of Periods I and II for all Regions*

Type of Behavior (as percentage of total dyads)	Period I	Period II	Change Factor
Cooperation	50.3	46.5	
Conflict	31.1	37.0	
Violence	5.9	5.5	
Total N *of Dyads*	3279	2847	86.8% (Total N of Period II:I)

	Number of Dyads in Period I	Expected Number of Dyads in Period II (based on Period I)	Number of Dyads in Period II	Expected Value, Period II – Actual Number of Dyads	Percentage of Overall Change in Behavior
Cooperation					
Individuals	36	31.2	23	8.2	7.5%
Intra. Nongov.	162	140.6	145	−4.4	−4.0%
Gov. Noncentral	21	18.2	26	−7.8	−7.1%
State	1235	1072.0	995	77.0	70.5%
Inter. Nongov.	69	59.9	44	15.9	14.6%
Inter. Gov.	127	110.2	90	20.2	18.5%
TOTAL	1650	1432.2	1323	109.2	92.4%
Conflict					
Individuals	42	36.5	33	3.5	−2.1%
Intra. Nongov.	255	221.3	248	−26.7	15.8%
Gov. Noncentral	38	33.0	42	−9.0	5.3%
State	631	547.7	671	−123.3	73.1%
Inter. Nongov.	24	20.8	25	−4.2	2.5%
Inter. Gov.	30	26.0	35	−9.0	5.3%
TOTAL	1020	885.4	1054	−168.6	119.0%
Violence					
Individuals	12	10.4	8	2.4	22.9%
Intra. Nongov.	64	55.6	51	4.5	42.9%
Gov. Noncentral	8	6.9	5	1.9	18.1%
State	102	88.5	92	−3.5	−33.3%
Inter. Nongov.	3	2.6	0	2.6	24.8%
Inter. Gov.	4	3.5	1	2.5	23.8%
TOTAL	193	167.5	157	10.5	93.7%

dyads. We then examined the *total number of dyads* in the later period and divided it by the total number of dyads in the earlier period. This constituted our *change factor*.

The number of dyads initiated in a prior period by each type of actor for the different behavior dimensions was used to calculate *expected value*. This was done by multiplying these prior-period figures by the overall change factor. This is not dissimilar to the way in which, for instance, indices of economic inflation are converted to a "real value" in terms of 1950 dollars. In other words, the expected value represents the contribution that each actor type would have made to the total system behavior along a given behavioral dimension if *both* activity levels and the actor's contribution remained constant in the later period.

The actual number of dyads initiated by each actor type in a later period were then subtracted from the expected number of dyads. This was also done for the totals of the expected values and actual values in the later period for the given behavioral dimension. This determined the total *behavioral change* for a given dimension, the underlined figures in the table. If the behavioral change figure was *positive,* this meant that there was *less* of this kind of behavior than expected on the basis of prior-period levels. It meant the expected value for the behavior type was greater than the actual value and that this kind of behavior declined in the system as a whole. If the behavioral change figure was *negative,* this meant there was *more* of this kind of behavior in the later period than expected.

The final column in the table, *percentage of overall change in behavior,* was calculated by dividing the expected value based on the prior period minus the actual value in the later period by the overall behavioral change for that dimension. Thus:

$$\begin{array}{l} \% \text{ of Overall Change} \\ \text{in Behavior}_i \end{array} = \frac{\text{Expected Value}_i - \text{Actual } N \text{ of Dyads, Later Period}_i}{\text{Expected Dyads}_T - \text{Actual } N \text{ of Dyads, Later Period}_T}$$

where i is a given deductive actor type and T indicates the total for all actor types. We kept the plus and minus signs for these various percentages of overall change in behavior. A minus sign in the final column meant that a given actor type's behavioral change was in the *opposite* direction from the change in the system as a whole. Such figures were analyzed with, but were distinct from, the total percent of overall behavioral change. This total figure was calculated by dividing the actual total number of dyads in the later period by the expected total number of dyads based on the prior period. This total percent figure was always positive. Total percents *smaller* than 100.0 percent meant that there was *less* of the particular kind of behavior relative to the prior period. Total percents *greater* than 100.0 percent meant that there was *more* of the particular kind of behavior.

Finally, we should note that it is possible for the various figures for the actor types to be more than 100.0 percent in either a positive or negative direction in the final column. For instance, in regards to Middle East conflict for the second and third periods, states reduced their conflict dyads by a total (+19.0) that was greater than the overall change in conflict dyads for the system as a whole (−11.4, indicating a slight rise in conflict). Thus, states were −174.6 percent in the final column. This indicated that the change in their conflict behavior was greater than that of the system as a whole and was in the opposite direction. At the same time, interstate nongovernmental actors increased their conflict by a factor of more than twice the change, but in the same direction (-24.3) as the system as a whole. Hence, this actor type had a change score of $+213.2$ percent which indicated a massive shift in the direction of the system as a whole.

We were thus able to identify those actors whose behavior was responsible for overall shifts in regional behavior as well as those actors whose behavior limited the extent of overall change.

Index